Franz Michael Fischer

The Application of the Controllability Principle and Managers' Responses

GABLER RESEARCH

Research in Management Accounting & Control

Herausgegeben von Professor Dr. Utz Schäffer,
WHU – Otto Beisheim School of Management, Vallendar.

Die Schriftenreihe präsentiert Ergebnisse betriebswirtschaftlicher Forschung im Bereich Controlling. Sie basiert auf einer akteursorientierten Sicht des Controlling, in der die Rationalitätssicherung der Führung einen für die Theorie und Praxis zentralen Stellenwert einnimmt.

The series presents research results in the field of management accounting and control. It is based on a behavioral view of management accounting where the assurance of management rationality is of central importance for both theory and practice.

Franz Michael Fischer

The Application of the Controllability Principle and Managers' Responses

A Role Theory Perspective

With a foreword by Prof. Dr. Utz Schäffer

GABLER

RESEARCH

Bibliographic information published by the Deutsche Nationalbibliothek
The Deutsche Nationalbibliothek lists this publication in the Deutsche Nationalbibliografie; detailed bibliographic data are available in the Internet at http://dnb.d-nb.de.

Dissertation European Business School Oestrich-Winkel, 2009

D 1540

The author of the dissertation „The application of the controllability principle and managers' responses: A role theory perspective" thanks the Hanns-Seidel-Stiftung (HSS) for financing this research with funds from the Bundesministerium für Bildung und Forschung (BMBF).

1st Edition 2010

Editorial Office: Ute Wrasmann | Anita Wilke

Gabler Verlag ist eine Marke von Springer Fachmedien.
Springer Fachmedien ist Teil der Fachverlagsgruppe Springer Science+Business Media.
www.gabler.de

Cover design: KünkelLopka Medienentwicklung, Heidelberg
Printed on acid-free paper
Printed in Germany

ISBN 978-3-8349-2267-0

Foreword

The starting point of Franz Fischer's dissertation thesis is the long-established claim to hold people accountable only for what they can control. Whereas early publications take the application of the so-called controllability principle as a matter of course, subsequent works justify the principle's application with the help of psychological or social psychological findings: The violation of the controllability principle is supposed to have negative motivational effects and thus decreases managers' effort on the job. Recently, however, doubts have been raised about the principle's meaningfulness. Also, empirical studies show that the principle is frequently not applied in corporate practice. In short: We do not have satisfactory knowledge about the effects of the principle's application or nonapplication on managers' mental models and their behavior. At the same time, we recognize that the question of whether or not to apply the principle is a major issue for management control in organizations of all sizes.

In view of this, Franz Fischer's dissertation thesis contributes to existing literature in at least three ways: First, Franz Fischer successfully adopts a role theory perspective in the investigation of cognitive, affective, and behavioral consequences of (not) applying the controllability principle in managers' performance evaluation. Thus, he demonstrates that role theory enriches a stream of literature that has so far been dominated by motivational theories. Second, he introduces a new conceptualization and operationalization of the application of the controllability principle which depict this latent variable as a second-order construct. Third, Franz Fischer does not restrict his empirical study to the investigation of mechanistic relationships between the (non)application of the controllability principle in managers' performance evaluation on the one hand and their perceptions and work behavior on the other. He rather draws a more sophisticated conclusion: Franz Fischer reveals that the relationships between the (non)application of the controllability principle and its affective and behavioral implications are mediated by managers' role perceptions. He also shows that the relationships between the (non)application of the controllability principle and these mediating variables are additionally moderated by organizational factors and personality factors, i.e. managers' hierarchical level and their self-efficacy.

Together with further findings delineated in this work, Franz Fischer's dissertation thesis is highly conducive to academic research in the field of management accounting and control. It also contains several practical implications and suggestions. For these reasons, I hope that the dissertation thesis will be well received by a large circle of readers and that it stimulates further research on this topic. If this did not happen, it would be a pity.

Utz Schäffer

Preface

The politician Woodrow T. Wilson is known to have said: "I not only use all the brains that I have, but all that I can borrow". It is my firm conviction that such an approach is not only beneficial to the work of great political minds but, more generally, adds value to any intellectual endeavor. In fact, I rather intensively borrowed the brains of others while writing my dissertation thesis "The Application of the Controllability Principle and Managers' Responses: A Role Theory Perspective". And I did not only borrow the brains of others, but also their commitment, devotion, patience, and encouragement. For this, I would like to give credit to all of them.

First and foremost, I would like to thank my doctoral supervisor and academic mentor Prof. Dr. Utz Schäffer. At many stages in the course of my dissertation project I benefited from the resources he made available to me and, more importantly, from his advice and guidance, particularly so when developing my research questions and hypotheses. His positive attitude, open-mindedness towards new ideas, and clear trains of thought inspired me and made the dissertation project a rewarding experience. At the same time, I would like to thank Prof. Dr. Andreas Hackethal who was kind enough to undertake the secondary review of my dissertation thesis demonstrating an unusually high level of involvement and interest.

Several others have contributed to my dissertation thesis in one way or another. To name only a few, I would like to thank Dr. Michael Burkert, Dr. Augustin Kelava, Prof. Dr. Pascal Langevin, Dr. Martin Messner, Dr. Clemens Pelster, Prof. Dr. Bob Scapens, Prof. Dr. Karin Schermelleh-Engel, and Prof. Dr. Dr. h.c. Jürgen Weber for their ideas, suggestions for improvement, discussions at doctoral workshops and conferences, feedback to my working papers, and their general interest in my topic. I also owe thanks to Sebastian Becker, Danijela Fischer, Gerhard Fischer, Maria Fischer, and Rüdiger Schmidt who all read this dissertation and contributed much helpful advice concerning its linguistic quality, layout, and style. Furthermore, I would like to thank the office managers Angela Molinari and Sabine Petrakakis as well as the research fellow Stevan Lutz who numerously assisted the administrative side of my work in a very professional and friendly manner.

I further want to express my gratitude to several colleagues at the European Business School (EBS). Sebastian Becker, Marc Ehrenberg, Kerim Galal, Dr. Christian Gessner, Dr. Philipp Götting, Yvonne Kiefer, Dr. Carsten Kruchen, Dr. Rainer Lueg, Dr. Marius Mann, Dr. Philip Matlachowsky, Eike Perrey, Nico Rose, Christian Schürmann, Dr. Joachim Vogt, and Elmar Wyszomirski created an enjoyable and, at the same time, stimulating working environment with many of them having become true friends. Their helpfulness, sense of humor, and honesty have a large share in making my dissertation project an unforgettable experience.

Apart from great friends and colleagues, my utmost thanks go to my family. My wife Danijela Fischer was at any moment willing to grant me the necessary freedom to finish my dissertation thesis and supported me in such an amicable way for which I will always admire and love her. My parents Gerhard and Maria Fischer, my sister Luisa Fischer, and my uncle Dr. Helmut Steinsdorfer always had a sympathetic ear for my everyday research problems, helped me to stay focused, and constantly supported me throughout my academic career without asking for anything in return. This dissertation thesis is, therefore, dedicated to my family.

Franz Michael Fischer

Table of Contents

List of Tables

List of Figures

List of Abbreviations

AGFI	Adjusted goodness-of-fit index
AVE	Average variance explained
BBE	Brutto-Betriebsergebnis
CEO	Chief executive officer
CFA	Confirmatory factor analysis
CFI	Comparative fit index
CTT	Classical test theory
EBIT	Earnings before interest and tax
EFA	Exploratory factor analysis
EVA	Economic value added
FR	Factor reliability
df	Degrees of freedom
GFI	Goodness-of-fit index
GLS	Generalized least squares
HR	Human resources
IR	Indicator reliability
IT	Information technology
JIT	Just in time
LISREL	Linear structural relationship
MA	Management accounting
MAS	Management accounting system
MBA	Master of business administration
MbO	Management by objectives
MCS	Management control system
MIMIC	Multiple indicators and multiple causes
ML	Maximum likelihood

NPM	New public management
PEP	Performance excellence process
PLS	Partial least squares
PM	Performance measure
RAPM	Reliance on accounting performance measures
RMSEA	Root mean square error of approximation
RPE	Relative performance evaluation
RQ	Research question
R&D	Research and development
SEM	Structural equation modeling
S-O-R	Stimulus-organism-response
SPMS	Strategic performance measurement system
Std. dev.	Standard deviation
Std. er.	Standard error
TQM	Total quality management
VHB	Verband der Hochschullehrer für Betriebswirtschaft e.V.
VIF	Variance inflation factor
yrs.	Years

A Introduction

"The effectiveness of performance measurement systems will depend on how they affect individuals' behavior" (Chenhall & Langfield-Smith, 2007, p. 277)

1. Motivation and Objective

The controllability principle stipulates that managers should be held accountable only for what they can control (Atkinson, Kaplan, Matsumura, & Young, 2007, p. 588; Bhimani, Horngren, Datar, & Foster, 2008, p. 488). Mostly regarded as a normative principle (Bourguignon & Chiapello, 2005, p. 686), it is intuitive and well-accepted throughout management accounting literature (Merchant & Otley, 2006, p. 793). Due to its importance in the design of management control systems (MCSs) the controllability principle has even been termed one of the strongest maxims in management accounting (Merchant & Van der Stede, 2007, p. 33; Simons, 2007, p. 1).

At first glance, the application of the controllability principle seems to be in the interests of both the organization and the managers evaluated (Giraud, Langevin, & Mendoza, 2008, p. 32). From a corporate perspective, the adherence to the controllability principle is supposed to circumvent dysfunctional managerial behavior (Dent, 1987, p. 135; Magee, 1986, p. 337; Marginson & McAulay, 2001, pp. 2-3; Merchant, 1989, p. 130) and to facilitate reliable assessment of managerial performance (Choudhury, 1986, pp. 189-190; Merchant, 1989, p. 87). Similarly, the striving for fairness in their performance evaluation should lead managers themselves to desire the controllability principle to be applied (Atkinson et al., 1997, p. 84; Hartmann & Slapničar, 2007, pp. 7-8).

Notwithstanding, several empirical studies find that the controllability principle is rarely applied in practice (Bushman, Indjejikian, & Smith, 1995; Dent, 1987; Drury & El-Shishini, 2005; Giraud et al., 2008; Merchant, 1987; 1989; Otley, 1990; Ugras, 1994; Vancil, 1979). Managers are rather often confronted with performance evaluation practices that are based on a mismatch of responsibility and authority. In the light of these findings, doubts on the appropriateness of the controllability principle arise (Choudhury, 1986, pp. 196-197; Giraud, Langevin, & Mendoza, 2004, p. 33; Simons, 2007, p. 3). However, management accounting researchers have just begun to investigate the rationale and the effect of holding managers accountable for more than they can control. There is growing evidence that organizational interests often lead superiors and designers of performance evaluation systems to intentionally include uncontrollable factors in appraisals (Drury & El-Shishini, 2005, pp. 22, 35-37; Fremgen & Liao, 1981, pp. 7, 21-23; Merchant, 1989, pp. 105-107; Simons, 2005, pp. 94-153; Skinner, 1990, pp. 136-140). Apart from organizational interests, high degrees of complexity and uncertainty in modern business contexts represent practical constraints that often render it impossible to separate controllable from uncontrollable factors (Hartmann, 2000, p. 472; Merchant & Manzoni, 1989, p. 541). Marginson and Ogden (2005b, p. 49) therefore conclude that "the principle of controllability is more honoured in the breach than its observance".

Notably, the behavioral responses of managers confronted with breaches of the controllability principle are apart from initial case study insights still barely explored (Drury & El-Shishini, 2005, pp. 45-46; Giraud et al., 2008, p. 34; Shields, Deng, & Kato, 2000, p. 198). As it is their responses that eventually determine the principle's importance for the effective design of MCSs, further research is warranted here (Marginson & Ogden, 2005b, p. 49). The lack of empirical research in this area was already highlighted by McNally (1980, p. 165) three decades ago: "The 'principle of controllability' has attracted widespread support in accounting, however examinations of its desirability or necessity . . . have been limited. Consequences of not observing [the principle] . . . are related topics which have been rather neglected". Since then management accounting research on the controllability principle has made only little progress (Drury & El-Shishini, 2005, p. 3; Simons, 2007, p. 3) and, accordingly, we do not have satisfactory insights into the drawbacks or merits of holding managers accountable for more than they can control. Addressing this research gap, this study aims in the first place to investigate the effects of the principle's application (and therewith also its nonapplication) on behavioral outcomes. Correspondingly, the first research question is:

Research question 1: Does the application of the controllability principle have an effect on managers' behavior?

Apart from behavioral responses, this study intends to investigate managers' affective responses (i.e. the experience of feeling and emotion) to the inclusion of uncontrollable factors in their performance appraisals. Despite the voluminous research on accountability in general (Lerner & Tetlock, 1999, p. 255; Merchant & Otley, 2006, p. 792) and performance evaluation in particular (Hartmann, 2000, p. 451; Neely, Gregory, & Platts, 2005, p. 1228), there is surprisingly little and inconclusive research on managers' psychological well-being when faced with the nonapplication of the controllability principle in performance evaluation.

Again, one finds some empirical evidence from case study research which indicates that breaches of the controllability principle seem to induce discomfort and tension (Dent, 1987, pp. 133-135; Merchant, 1989, pp. 103-104; Simons, 2005, p. 94). The intuitive assumption that managers would always desire to have the controllability principle applied, however, is questionable. On the contrary, managers are sometimes even reported to find a lack of controllability positively challenging and a source of motivation (Budding, 2004, p. 301; Frow, Marginson, & Ogden, 2005, pp. 288-289; Giraud et al., 2008, pp. 40-41). For this reason, the second research question extends the scope of this study by an affective dimension:

Research question 2: Does the application of the controllability principle have an effect on managers' psychological well-being?

In an effort not only to identify but also to explain the relationships between the application of the controllability principle and the above outcomes, this work proposes managers' role perceptions as potential mediators (Kahn, Wolfe, Quinn, & Snoeck, 1964, pp. 55-96; Parker, Wall, & Jackson, 1997, pp. 900-901; Rizzo, House, & Lirtzman, 1970, pp. 155-162). It is suggested that the application of the controllability principle does not directly affect behavioral and affective responses. This study rather adopts the view that the effects are indirect in nature and operate through cognitive constructs. Individuals are thought to process and to reflect on environmental stimuli before they respond to them (Robbins, 2003, pp. 145-146). Such a view is in agreement with other contemporary management accounting studies investigating related effects of MCSs on behavioral and affective outcomes (Burney, Henle, & Widener, 2009; Burney & Widener, 2007; Hall, 2008; Marginson & Bui, 2009; Nouri & Kyj, 2008). The inclusion of mediators which transmit the influence of an antecedent to a consequence has a long tradition in behavioral research (Ajzen, 1991, p. 179; James & Brett, 1984, p. 307; Tetlock, 1985, pp. 300-301) as it serves a better understanding of the underlying mental mechanisms (Baron & Kenny, 1986, p. 1176). In detail, this work integrates the classical constructs of role conflict and role ambiguity (Rizzo et al., 1970, pp. 155-162) as well as the recently developed construct of role orientation (Parker, 2007, pp. 404-407). The third research question addresses the potential relevance of these mediating variables:

Research question 3: Do managers' role perceptions mediate the proposed relationships between the application of the controllability principle and managers' behavior and psychological well-being?

Additionally, this work examines the existence of moderating effects in order to assess the strength of the above relationships across different contexts and types of managerial personality. As indicated in prior studies on performance evaluation (Giraud et al., 2008;

Marginson & McAulay, 2001; Ross, 1994) and role stress (Gilboa, Shirom, Fried, & Cooper, 2008; Jackson & Schuler, 1985; Schuler, 1977; Viswesvaran, Sanchez, & Fisher, 1999), organizational factors, personality factors, and interpersonal relations are likely to have an influence on the relationships under investigation. Generally, many scholars in the field of organizational behavior call for an increased attention to potential moderators when conducting research that incorporates role perceptions (Elovainio & Kivimäki, 2001, p. 366; Ilgen & Hollenbeck, 1991, p. 199; Örtqvist & Wincent, 2006, p. 416). The intended investigation of such moderating effects is reflected in the fourth research question:

Research question 4: Do organizational factors, personality factors, and interpersonal relations moderate the proposed relationships between the application of the controllability principle and managers' role perceptions?

From a theoretical perspective, the outlined research is embedded in a role theory framework (Kahn et al., 1964; Kahn, Wolfe, Quinn, & Snoeck, 1966; Katz & Kahn, 1966; 1978). Role theory states that the building blocks of any organization are the roles assigned to its members. For every role in the organization there are expectations which the incumbents of those roles are confronted with and which influence their perceptions, affectivity, and behavior. In the context of this study, it is argued that the design of performance evaluation systems and in particular the application or nonapplication of the controllability principle can be interpreted as such role expectations. These expectations come from the representatives of organizational interests (i.e. superiors and designers of performance evaluation systems) and translate into role forces which act upon the role incumbents (i.e. managers whose performance is being evaluated). Role theory predicts that role incumbents will respond to the role forces imposed on them and engage in various coping efforts which can imply both affective and behavioral symptom formation. Due to its focus on the subjective perception of organizational realities and its emphasis on the causal interplay of cognition, affectivity, and behavior (Ilgen & Hollenbeck, 1991, p. 203), role theory represents a meaningful framework for studying managers' responses to the application of the controllability principle (Collins, 1982, p. 119; Frink & Klimoski, 1998, p. 21).

To summarize, this work intends to shed empirical light on the relationship between the application of the controllability principle and several individual outcomes. The underlying motivation is a lack of empirical research in this field: "Managers' position regarding the controllability principle is not as clear as it seems and needs further investigation" (Giraud et al., 2008, p. 33). This study contributes to existing literature on the controllability principle in three ways. First and foremost, it pioneers in the utilization of role theory to investigate the cognitive, affective, and behavioral consequences of applying the controllability principle in managers' performance evaluation. Second, the impact of several contextual variables on the basic relationships is investigated, which results in the development of moderated mediation models. Third, from a methodological point of view, this work introduces a new measurement scale for the application of the controllability principle that operationalizes this variable as a second-order construct (Bisbe, Batista-Foguet, & Chenhall, 2007, p. 805) and integrates the construct in its nomological net. The resulting causal frame of reference for this work and the corresponding research questions are summarized in Figure 1:

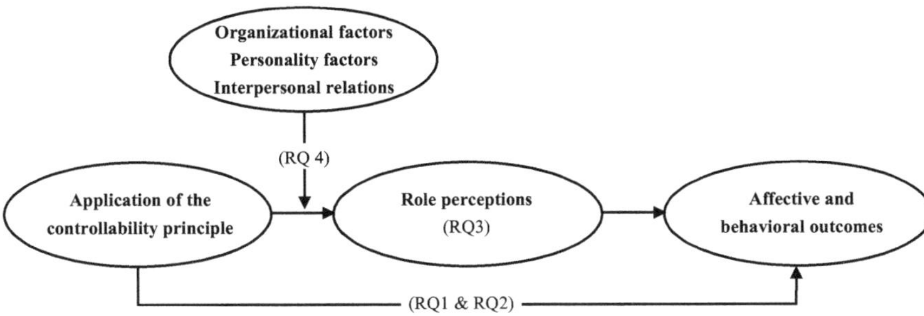

Figure 1: Causal Frame of Reference

2. Course of Analysis

This work is split into three consecutive sections (see Figure 2). The first section (parts B, C, and D) includes the theoretical basis of this work. It reviews existing literature on the controllability principle, introduces role theory and, on this basis, develops testable hypotheses. The second section (parts E and F) refers to the empirical research which has been conducted to test the proposed hypotheses. It presents the methodological conception of this work as well as the corresponding empirical results. The third and final section (parts G and H) contains a discussion of the empirical results and some concluding remarks.

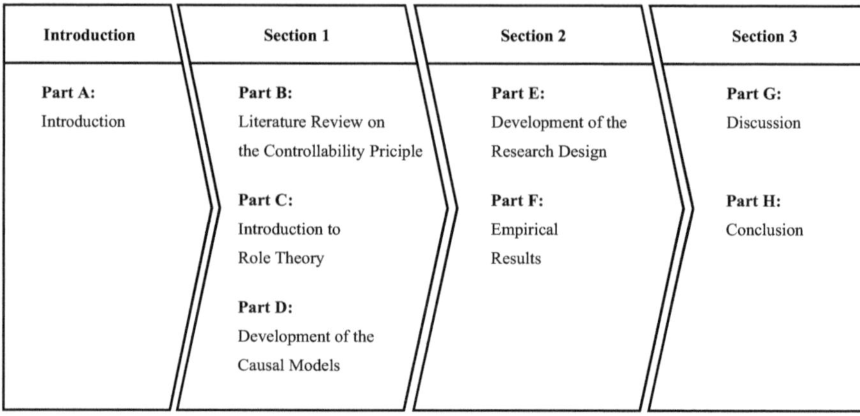

Figure 2: Course of Analysis

The controllability principle is the central theme of this work. It represents the starting point for the reasoning in the following chapters which is why part B provides an in-depth elaboration of the principle and its research tradition. In particular, part B contrasts the principle's rationale with its application in practice.

Since this work relies on role theory for developing hypotheses, part C gives an overview of the theory, its key concepts, and the basic causal relationships predicted by the theory. As can be learned in this part, formulations of role theory vary across the several social sciences which have employed the theory. For the purpose of this study, the role theory framework developed by Kahn et al. (1964; 1966) and Katz and Kahn (1966; 1978) is used since it is this version of role theory that has had a profound influence on behavioral management accounting research during the last decades.

The insights from parts B and C are vital for the development of this study's hypotheses in part D. Several direct and indirect relationships between the application of the controllability principle and managers' cognitive, affective, and behavioral responses are proposed. Also, an exploratory set of research questions is generated in order to allow the testing of potential moderating effects.

Part E details the research design chosen to test the proposed hypotheses. It outlines this study's mixed-methods approach which combines semi-structured interviews with 12 managers and a questionnaire survey among 432 managers. Such an approach focuses on method triangulation, for which a number of calls have been made in recent management accounting literature (Hopper & Hoque, 2006, p. 482; Modell, 2005, p. 232; Shields, 1997, p. 10). In addition, part E highlights this study's contribution in terms of the successful development of a new survey instrument to measure the application of the controllability principle.

The empirical results of this study are presented in part F. It commences with the descriptive statistics for all variables used in later analyses. Subsequently, the hypotheses advanced in part D are tested. For this purpose, structural equation modeling (SEM) employing a linear structural relationships (LISREL) approach is used (Jöreskog & Sörbom, 2001).

Parts G and H discuss the empirical results and summarize the study's main contributions to management accounting theory and practice. This also encompasses a critical evaluation of the controllability principle's relevance for the design of performance evaluation systems. Suggestions for a more expedient application of the principle are also made. Finally, part H presents some notes on this study's limitations and gives an outlook on promising directions for future research addressing these very limitations.

B Literature Review on the Controllability Principle

Today, the controllability principle appears throughout the management accounting literature (Merchant, 1985, p. 21). Historians trace the origin of the principle back to the founding of American railroads. Charles Perkins, who was president of the Chicago, Burlington, and Quincy Railroad in 1885, is quoted with the following statement: "It is obvious that to hold a manager responsible for results it is necessary to give him pretty full power over the property which he must use to produce those results" (Chandler, McCraw, & Tedlow, 1996, p. 26). At that time, companies were confronted for the first time with the problem of managing people who worked at considerable distance from central executive offices (Simons, 2007, p. 2). With companies being structured into decentralized and autonomous divisions, questions arose as to the best way to control such organizations (Sloan, 1963, p. 46). Results control instead of direct supervision of behaviors and the corresponding management by objectives (MbO) school of thought (Odiorne, 1965) gained in importance (Giraud et al., 2004, p. 3). It is Solomons (1965, p. 83) who closely relates the controllability principle to the decentralization of business operations. In the course of the devolution of authority to make decisions, he recommends that "in appraising the performance of divisional management, no account should be taken of matters outside the division's control". It appears that the application of the controllability principle is particularly relevant when organizational decision-making becomes decentralized (Chenhall & Langfield-Smith, 2007, p. 267; Modell & Lee, 2001, pp. 191-192). More generally, Merchant and Van der Stede (2007, p. 33) argue that any indirect form of control requires that "the employees whose behaviors are being controlled must be able to affect the results in a material way in a given time period". This leads to the core of the controllability principle which is often depicted to play a decisive role in the struggle for organizational effectiveness and managerial motivation (Kennedy & Schleifer, 2006, p. 126; Merchant, 1998, p. 583; Otley, 2006, pp. 299-300).

Having briefly highlighted the history of the controllability principle, the following chapters of part B provide an overview of extant literature on the principle. First, the research streams that deal with aspects of controllability are introduced in chapter B1. Chapter B1 also outlines a variety of definitions of the controllability principle originating from the different research streams as to demonstrate that notions of controllability may vary and depend on the respective school of thought. In the following, chapters B2 and B3 review the key findings from prior research. While chapter B2 describes the theoretical rationale of the controllability principle, chapter B3 contrasts the principle's rationale with its application in practice. Chapter B3 concludes with some remarks on the seeming contradiction between the principle's theoretical rationale and its observed relevance for company practice.

1. The Conceptual Scope of the Controllability Principle

1.1 The Controllability Principle in Different Research Streams

To foster a comprehensive understanding of the controllability principle, it is first advisable to acquaint oneself with the main research streams that either implicitly or explicitly deal with aspects of controllability. For this purpose, the current chapter introduces three relevant research streams (management accounting, administrative science, and psychology) and briefly refers to the different disciplines and schools of thought from which they originate.

1.1.1 Management Accounting

Certainly, the field of management accounting represents the primary source of insight when addressing the controllability principle. The principle was first mentioned in management accounting literature by Solomons (1965) in his work on the divisionalization of US companies. Meanwhile the controllability principle is an integral part of virtually all management accounting textbooks (e.g. Atkinson et al. (2007, p. 581), Bhimani et al. (2008, p. 488), or Merchant and Van der Stede (2007, p. 32))[1]. As such, it is usually addressed as being vital for systems of responsibility accounting (see also chapter B2.1) which refers to the various concepts and tools used to measure the performance of people and work units in order to foster goal congruence in organizations (Hilton, 2008, p. 502). Within the field of management accounting, there is both an analytical and an empirical research stream focusing on the controllability principle (Giraud et al., 2008, pp. 33-34). Both start from a traditional normative formulation of the principle and attempt to either (a) gather evidence that (at least partially) supports the principle (e.g. Hopwood (1972), Lawler and Rhode (1976), Ronen and Livingstone (1975), or Merchant (1989)), (b) refine the principle (e.g. Merchant (1987), Antle and Demski (1988), or Banker and Datar (1989)), or (c) test its practical application (e.g. Bushman et al. (1995) or Giraud et al. (2008)).

1.1.1.1 Analytical Management Accounting

This stream of literature employs analytical modeling to conduct research on the controllability principle. Its proponents draw predominantly on agency theory (Jensen & Meckling, 1976; Levinthal, 1988; Pratt & Zeckhauser, 1985). Broadly speaking, agency

1 Similarly, the controllability principle is also covered in most German management accounting textbooks, see e.g. Ewert and Wagenhofer (2005, p. 380), Küpper (2005, p. 246), or Weber and Schäffer (2008, p. 248). Though a single, generally accepted translation for the term controllability principle has not been established in the German literature. Instead, the terms "Beeinflussbarkeitsprinzip", "Verantwortlichkeitsprinzip", "Kongruenzprinzip", and "Prinzip der sachlichen Entscheidungsverbundenheit" are used (Pelster, 2007, p. 16).

theory is directed at the ubiquitous agency relationship in which one party delegates work to another who performs that work (Eisenhardt, 1989a, p. 58). Typically the owners of a company are called principals in agency models. The term agents refers to the managers who are engaged to perform work on behalf of the principals and who receive compensation in return. Hence, corporate management can be considered to be the agents of the company's shareholders, and, throughout the organizational hierarchy, subordinate managers can be seen as the agents of their respective superiors (Jensen & Meckling, 1976, p. 308; Merchant & Simons, 1986, p. 188; Milgrom & Roberts, 1992, p. 214).

In order to solve incentive problems in the design of MCSs, agency theory relies on the application of economic principles and tools of organizational control (Lambert, 2001, p. 4). Deliberations based on the agency theory paradigm thereby generally strive for "maximizing behavior on the part of all individuals" (Jensen & Meckling, 1976, p. 307). The agency problem can thus be thought of as maximizing a weighted combination of the expected utilities of the principals and the agents (for a mathematical formulation see e.g. Lambert (2001, p. 12)). According to Jensen and Meckling (1976, p. 308), the agency costs related to incentive problems are the sum of (a) the monitoring expenditures by the principals, (b) the bonding expenditures by the agents, and (c) the residual loss which refers to the monetary reduction in welfare experienced by the principals due to the divergence between the agents' decisions and those decisions which would maximize the principals' welfare, given the optimal monitoring and bonding activities by the principals and the agents. These costs occur at every level of the company and are generally non-zero (Jensen & Meckling, 1976, p. 328).

As agency costs most notably depend on contracts, agency theory considers organizations as "legal fictions which serve as a nexus for a set of contracting relationships among individuals" (Jensen & Meckling, 1976, p. 310). Against this background, agency theory often claims to address the generality of the incentive problem: How can the contracts within a company induce agents to behave as if they were maximizing the principals' welfare? This motivation arises from the theory's underlying assumption that the motives and the behavior of individuals operating in a company differ. It is most likely that agents choose actions and decisions which are not in accordance with the principals' objectives. This is due to the characteristics and utility functions of agents which are specified as follows: agents are risk- and effort-averse, their utility functions are additively separable in utility from compensation and disutility from effort, and they select effort levels that maximize their expected utility (Frederickson, 1992, p. 651). The principals, on the contrary, are commonly assumed to be risk-neutral and their expected utilities are simply the expected net profits of the company (Lambert, 2001, p. 9).

Within agency models, a small set of variables is typically used to explore the conditions that maximize the expected utilities of the principals and the agents and to describe the characteristics of principal-agent relationships and the environments in which they function (Merchant & Simons, 1986, p. 188). To assess the quality of particular contract designs, agency theory refers to the so-called first-best solution where actions are chosen cooperatively with all individuals' interests in mind and all reports issued truthfully (Lambert, 2001, pp. 11-12). The agents' opportunism and the asymmetry of information thereby pose two of the main challenges in agency models. As the agents' actions cannot always be observed by the principals, incentive problems which are referred to as moral hazard or hidden actions (Macintosh, 1994, pp. 32-33; Milgrom & Roberts, 1992, pp. 166-196) preclude first-best solutions and necessitate second-best solutions where only the outcome of the agents' actions is observable to the principals. Agency models strive to identify contracts which come as close to first-best solutions as possible (Holmström, 1979, pp. 76-80).

Facing the two central challenges of agents' opportunism and asymmetry of information, the agency models employed in management accounting research traditionally focus on the latter challenge: "Principal-agent modeling emphasizes information asymmetries in understanding responsibility accounting" (Demski & Sappington, 1989, p. 40). Among the agency-inspired management accounting publications on the controllability principle, the work of Antle and Demski (1988) represents the most frequently cited article (Pelster, 2007, p. 33). Offering a "refined version of the controllability principle", Antle and Demski (1988, p. 715) develop an information content perspective which is supposed to allow for a more precise notion of controllability (see chapter B1.2.2).

Even though agency research (for reviews see e.g. Baiman (1982; 1990), Prendergast (1999), and Lambert (2001)) represents one of the "most important theoretical paradigms in accounting during the last 20 years" (Lambert, 2001, pp. 3-4), the use of analytical models in management accounting research has met with mixed reception from academics. They often tend to dismiss such analytical models as irrelevant to the real concerns of managers in highly complex environments (Anthony, 1989, pp. 15-16; Baiman, 1990, pp. 344-345; Kaplan, 1984, pp. 404-405; Merchant & Otley, 2006, p. 787). The "simplifying assumptions" (Merchant, 1987, p. 318) of agency models cannot fully take the context of organizational settings into consideration. For example informal arrangements and understandings which are involved in many employer-employee relationships have been hardly addressed. It is also questionable if risk aversion is as important as classical agency models commonly suggest (Indjejikian, 1999, pp. 152-153). Similarly, labeling all motivation as self-serving does not adequately explain employee actions (Davis, Schoorman, & Donaldson, 1997, p. 24; Jensen & Meckling, 1994, p. 10). Next, especially early work inspired by agency theory focuses on only one control mechanism (e.g. incentive payments or supervisor monitoring) and tradeoffs or interactions among the types of control mechanisms are neglected (Merchant & Simons, 1986, p. 188). A lack of empirical tests of agency models is a further point of criticism (Baiman, 1990, pp.

345-346). Nevertheless, analytical modeling with its roots in agency theory is frequently applied in management accounting research on the controllability principle (Lambert, 2001, p. 23; Pelster, 2007, p. 36).

1.1.1.2 Empirical Management Accounting

As fieldwork is essential to the progress of management accounting research (Kaplan, 1986, p. 429; Modell, 2005, p. 231), scholars have also carried out empirical studies on the controllability principle. While analytical studies have predominantly focused on the refinement and redefinition of the principle, most empirical work attempts to provide evidence on the degree of the principle's application in practice and, based on these findings, searches for justifications why (or why not) the principle is applied. Apart from rare exceptions (Bushman et al., 1995; Merchant, 1987), empirical and analytical research approaches however hardly "talk to each other" – whether this is because their ontological stances are too different or because of other reasons is not clear (Baiman, 1990, p. 367).

Also, as Merchant (1987, p. 319) states when discussing early works by Hofstede (1967) and Vancil (1979), empirical researchers have not always discussed the controllability principle by name. Instead, many empirical insights into the application of the controllability principle stem from research which has originally been devoted to related topics such as decentralization or budgeting. Given the large body of analytical work on the controllability principle, Simons (2007, p. 3) criticizes what he considers a lack of empirical research that has been undertaken in direct relation to the principle during the last years. In a similar vein, Drury and El-Shishini (2005, p. 3) recommend further empirical research as most previous studies were undertaken more than 20 years ago when the business environment and management practices differed from those existing today.

In terms of the methods used to collect data, previous empirical studies on the controllability principle have relied on a diverse repertoire: the case study approach (e.g. Merchant (1989)) is employed most frequently, but surveys (e.g. Giraud et al. (2008)) and, to a minor degree, experiments (e.g. Shields and Waller (1988)) as well as archival research (e.g. Bushman et al. (1995)) also contribute to knowledge gathering (Pelster, 2007, pp. 155-158). Unfortunately, most empirical research on the controllability principle has adopted a very specific viewpoint, namely that of superiors and designers of performance evaluation systems (Giraud et al., 2008, p. 34). As a consequence, a major drawback of previous empirical research lies in the scarce evidence on how managers who are themselves confronted with a certain degree of controllability respond in terms of their cognition, affectivity, and behavior. Another caveat against previous empirical research on the controllability principle refers to the descriptive nature of most prior studies. Commonly, research has merely investigated the factual degree of the principle's application in the design of performance evaluation systems (Pelster, 2007, p. 74). It has hardly focused on the functional and dysfunctional effects resulting from different levels of application. Marginson and Ogden (2005b, p. 49) therefore argue that

> the real import of the limited feasibility of applying the controllability principle . . . is not so much a question of whether the principle is compromised or not, but how much does it matter when it is. This depends largely on the reactions of the . . . managers affected by breaches of the controllability principle.

1.1.2 Administrative Science

Management accounting is not the only academic discipline that has addressed aspects of controllability. Scholars in the field of administrative science have also given attention to the controllability principle, however labeling it as "classical principle of administration" (Filley & House, 1969, p. 72), "principle of correspondence" (Urwick, 1943, p. 45), "structural principle of organization" (Mooney, 1998, p. 538), or "law of responsibility and authority" (Alford, 1928 quoted according to: McNair, 1994, p. 87). They argue that for the smooth operation of business processes "authority and responsibility should be coterminous and coequal" (Urwick, 1943, p. 46) at all levels. On this basis, the universal need for organizations to delegate authority and to match authority with responsibility is identified (Lussier, 2000, pp. 186-187).

Even though management accounting researchers often seem to claim that the controllability principle has its academic origin in early accounting works, it is surprising to date the first mentioning of the principle back to the work of Taylor (1911). In his classical book on scientific management, the author advises managers of "always bearing in mind that responsibility should invariably be accompanied by its corresponding measure of authority" (Taylor, 1911, p. 136). Taylor (1911, p. 1) relates the controllability principle to what he calls "principles of scientific management". The ultimate objective of these principles is to optimize the way in which tasks are performed and consequently to secure maximum efficiency in organizations.

The classical principles of administration (and the controllability principle being one of them) were advanced by various writers in this field partly on the basis of deductive reasoning and partly as a result of the uncontrolled observations of practitioners of management. However, these principles became the subject of heated controversy. The attacks came principally from behavioral scientists, or from those who considered administrative science in the light of behavioral findings (Filley & House, 1969, p. 73). Common points of criticism are that the principles are limited in their applicability in practice, that they often foster dependency on superiors, stifle individual growth, and prevent individual identification with organizational goals (Filley & House, 1969, pp. 72-77).

Nevertheless, the classical principles of administration have influenced management accounting literature on the controllability principle (Hirst, 1983a, p. 29; McNally, 1980, p. 166). Caplan (1966, p. 496) is one of the first authors who explicitly based his "assumptions of management accounting" upon ideas from the fields of administration science and organization theory. Calling it a "principle of management", the author writes that "there must be a balance between the authority a person has and his responsibility for performance" (Caplan, 1966, p. 497). Similarly, Simons (2007, p. 2) admits that what management accounting academics refer to as the controllability principle has its roots in general management theory.

1.1.3 Psychology

Without doubt, knowledge from cognitive, motivation and social psychology has influenced management accounting research during the last decades (Birnberg, Luft, & Shields, 2006, p. 113; Merchant & Simons, 1986, pp. 189-190). And, with the concept of controllability playing an important part in these fields of psychology (Büssing, Bissels, Fuchs, & Perrar, 1999, p. 1005), management accounting scholars here find a broad array of psychological studies that are helpful in the investigation of cognitive, affective, and behavioral phenomena related to the application of the controllability principle.

However, the term controllability has a different connotation in psychology (McNally, 1980, p. 165). Whereas the controllability principle as defined in management accounting literature is a relative concept tying together responsibility and authority (Bourguignon & Chiapello, 2005, p. 688), psychology uses the term controllability variously: It may refer to instrumental control (i.e. the individual is able to make responses that modify events), self-administration (i.e. the individual delivers events to him- or herself), or potential control (i.e. the individual believes that some response to events is available to him or her but refrains from using it) (Miller, 1979, pp. 287-289).

Notwithstanding these different interpretations of the term controllability, scholars from psychology have produced several research streams which provide insightful points of reference for the work of management accounting scholars. For exemplification, two of these research streams are briefly introduced in the following. The first research stream is based on the person-environment fit model developed by French, Caplan, and Van Harrison (1982). The second research stream originated from the demand-control model developed by Karasek (1979) and elaborated further by Karasek and Theorell (1990). Both research streams are concerned with a relative view on job control and investigate the effects of confronting employees with situations of imbalance or incongruence at work (Siegrist, 1996, p. 28).

Based on the notion that human behavior is a function of both the individual and external conditions, the person-environment fit model describes the degree of similarity or convergence between a particular set of person-related attributes (e.g. resources, skills, or aspirations) and a set of environment-related attributes (e.g. organizational values or objectives). The model predicts feelings of misfit within the individual when he or she perceives an imbalance between what he or she aims to achieve and what the job supplies to him or her (French et al., 1982, pp. 27-32). According to the model, particular types of misfit perceptions arouse different levels of occupational strain and behavioral reply mechanisms (James & Mazerolle, 2002, pp. 55-60; Kristof, 1996, pp. 19-30).

Similarly, Karasek's model (1979) provides a basis for studies on job attributes and their consequences for the individual (Fox, Dwyer, & Ganster, 1993, p. 290). The model posits an interaction between job demands and job control which together represent the two central attributes in work settings as modeled by Karasek (1979, p. 288). Depending on the actual job design, the individual is confronted with either a balance or an imbalance between demands (e.g. workload) and control (e.g. decision-making latitude or autonomy). In jobs where demands are high but control is low (referred to as a high strain job), negative outcomes for the individual's well-being are predicted because the individual cannot respond optimally to the situation (Parker & Sprigg, 1999, pp. 925-926; Van der Doef & Maes, 1999, pp. 88-89). Thus, in order to minimize the detrimental effects on the individual's well-being and to increase learning and motivation, demands should be matched to control such that when demands are high, control should correspondingly be high (referred to as an active job).

The above research streams from psychological literature bear considerable relevance for management accounting research on the controllability principle. In its core, the application of the controllability principle is concerned with an occupational imbalance as well – namely an imbalance between responsibility and authority. Just like the work from administrative science scholars and their influence on prior management accounting studies, insights from psychology also lend themselves to research endeavors on the controllability principle. Accordingly, as depicted in chapter B2.3, management accounting scholars have variously consulted psychological theories and elaborations from administrative science in their work on the controllability principle.

1.2 Definitions of the Controllability Principle

For further clarification of the scope of the controllability principle, an overview of definitions from prior literature is provided in the following chapter. Originating from distinct schools of thought, these definitions vary in their wording and highlight different facets of controllability. Moreover, the definitions tend to differ in terms of the organizational unit they focus on. Most definitions are aimed at the individual manager. However, some definitions also adapt the principle in a way that it applies to corporate units such as groups of personnel or departments (Llewellyn, 1998, p. 295; Pelster, 2007, pp. 16-18). Consequently, it is difficult to identify one single, generally accepted definition of the controllability principle. Rather it is important to recognize that authors often have diverging conceptions in mind which evokes a somewhat nebulous character of the principle (Choudhury, 1986, p. 197). Basically, three perspectives can be distinguished when definitions of the controllability principle are classified: traditional definitions of the principle which are normative in nature, and two sets of redefinitions – one emphasizing informativeness and one emphasizing influenceability.

1.2.1 Traditional Definition of the Controllability Principle

The wording of most traditional definitions of the controllability principle closely adheres to the congruence of the parameters responsibility[2] and authority. Starting with Drucker (1962, p. 118) who states that a manager's job "has its own necessity; it must therefore have its own authority and its own responsibility", these two parameters represent the common theme of a multitude of definitions. Table 1 depicts some exemplary definitions of the traditional controllability principle.

[2] Even though business ethics and related disciplines differentiate between the terms responsibility and accountability (Jackson, 2009, p. 66; Kaler, 2002, pp. 327-329), management accounting literature (and, as such, most publications on the controllability principle) tend to use the terms interchangeably (Lindkvist & Llewellyn, 2003, p. 252). Searching for German translations, Pelster (2007, p. 106) also disbelieves that there is a clear difference in meaning for the terms responsibility and accountability. In this work, the two terms are therefore taken as synonyms.

Source	Definition
Dalton (1971, p. 27)	A man should be held accountable for only that which he alone can control.
Ugras (1994, p. 256)	Managers should be evaluated only on the basis of the factors within their control. Therefore, costs should not be allocated to responsibility centers if these costs are beyond their control.
Atkinson et al. (2007, p. 588)	The controllability principle states that the manager of a responsibility center should be assigned responsibility only for the revenues, costs, or investment controlled by responsibility center personnel. Revenues, costs, or investments that people outside the responsibility center control should be excluded from the accounting assessment of that center's performance.
Merchant and Van der Stede (2007, p. 533)	The controllability principle . . . states that people should be held accountable only for what they control.

Table 1: Exemplary Definitions of the Traditional Controllability Principle

The unifying element of the traditional definitions is their normative nature. They postulate the way in which managers *should* be evaluated (Drury & El-Shishini, 2005, p. 5) without providing a rationale for the principle and without elaborating on the precise scope of its parameters responsibility and authority. Rhetorically declaring the controllability principle to be "self-evident" (Solomons, 1965, p. 83), "obvious" (Merchant & Van der Stede, 2007, p. 533) and a "general rule-of-thumb" (Gibbons & Murphy, 1990, p. 33), management accounting literature has long and somewhat uncritically acknowledged the importance of the principle (Giraud et al., 2004, p. 1). Many management accounting researchers therefore agree that the principle is "one of the few accepted tenets in managerial accounting" (Demski, 1976, p. 230) and offer the principle as an imperative in most management accounting textbooks (Modell, 1997, p. 314).

For the implementation of the controllability principle two approaches are frequently proposed which can be used alone or in combination: ex ante and ex post adjustments for the effects of uncontrollable factors (Drury, 2005, pp. 316-318; Giraud et al., 2004, p. 4; Merchant, 1998, p. 575; Modell & Lee, 2001, p. 195). Ex ante adjustments typically comprise the beforehand design of MCSs in a way that performance measures only include controllable items, budgetary allowances for unforeseen influence, and the purchases of insurance before the measurement period begins (Merchant, 1998, pp. 575-577). After the measurement period, ex post adjustments may be used to remove the distorting effects of uncontrollable factors from those results that are used for performance evaluation. This removal can be done using variance analyses, flexible performance standards, relative performance evaluations or simply through the exercise of subjective judgment (Merchant, 1998, pp. 577-582). Both types of adjustment help to decrease the risk of uncontrollable influence that managers must bear and hence safeguard them against violations of the controllability principle (Merchant & Manzoni, 1989, p. 549).

1.2.2 Redefinition of the Controllability Principle Emphasizing Informativeness

Some accounting researchers criticized traditional formulations of the controllability principle as being "casual" (Antle & Demski, 1988, p. 701), lacking "a precise definition of controllability" (Lambert, 2001, p. 23), suffering from "some ambiguity" (Budde, 2009, p. 169), and precluding "desirable risk-sharing opportunities and risk-taking incentives" (Demski, 1976, p. 230). Amey (1979, p. 256) even claims that the "conventional accounting notion of controllability is rather meaningless".

Subsequent deliberations based on agency theory have shown that under certain conditions the application of the traditional controllability principle is to the disadvantage of the principals and that it may hence be in the principals' interest to use performance measures beyond the agents' control to assess their efforts. This led to the formulation of the conditional controllability principle which is based on Holmström's (1979, pp. 83-86) concept of informativeness. It states that agents should be evaluated on the basis of all information that provides insights into their actions (Antle & Demski, 1988, p. 716). Proponents of the conditional controllability principle such as Lambert (2001, p. 20) insist on the information content of performance measures when deciding on which measures should be used for evaluation: "Additional performance measures can potentially increase the expected utilities of the principal and the agent if they can be used to increase the incentives or improve the risk sharing of the contract". Following this perspective, the desirability of using particular performance measures depends on whether they carry information content over and above alternative measures, which represents an important precondition for the aspired increase in expected utilities (Bushman, Indjejikian, & Smith, 1996, p. 162). The conditional controllability principle thereby leaves the normative grounds on which the traditional controllability principle is built and provides the following rationale: Performance evaluation applying the conditional controllability principle helps to resolve the control problem in organizations.

The very idea of the conditional controllability principle implies that it is not important whether agents can literally control a particular performance measure, but whether the performance measure carries information content (Ittner & Larcker, 2002, p. S59; Milgrom & Roberts, 1992, p. 219). It is suggested that this perspective may be thought of as offering a more precise definition of the term controllability (Antle & Demski, 1988, p. 700). In cases where principals cannot observe their agents' decisions and efforts (hidden action) and are thus exposed to potential opportunistic behaviors, they are advised to fall back on alternative measures when evaluating agents' performance – but only as long as the agents can affect the statistical pattern of these alternative measures (Antle & Demski, 1988, p. 715; Budde, 2009, pp. 169-170; Holmström, 1979, pp. 83-88; Shavell, 1979, pp. 54-57). Controllability as interpreted by the conditional controllability principle therefore means that the agents' "input influences the distribution of the variable" (Arya, Glover, & Radhakrishnan, 2007, p. 184). This interpretation stands in contrast to the notion of the traditional controllability principle which stipulates that managers should be able to literally control a measure instead of merely influencing its statistical distribution.

Source	**Definition**
Holmström (1979, p. 89)	By using other available information about the agent's action or about the state of nature, contracts can generally be improved . . . Additional information is of value because it allows a more accurate judgment of the performance of the agent.
Antle and Demski (1988, pp. 714-716)	The key . . . is to define controllability in terms of the conditional probability of the output statistic, thereby taking account of the available information . . . If the manager can affect the statistical pattern of some particular variable, the manager controls that variable. If the manager can affect the statistical pattern conditioned on whatever else we know, the variable carries information content about the manager's behavior.
Feltham and Xie (1994, p. 441)	It is not always optimal to merely eliminate the uncontrollable events from the performance measure, since the identified events may provide information about the unidentified events.
Reichelstein (2002, p. 1705)	Modern agency theory has refined the traditional controllability principle by moving away from the criterion of 'control' to the criterion of 'informativeness' . . . A particular variable should be included in a manager's performance measure only if it provides incremental information about the manager's decisions.

Table 2: Exemplary Definitions of the Conditional Controllability Principle

As can be seen from the definitions in Table 2 the traditional controllability principle and the conditional controllability principle are not the same. Consequently, they can also lead to different choices in the design of MCSs (Baiman, 1990, pp. 352-353). Examples can be found in Baiman and Demski (1980), Baiman and Noel (1985), Demski (1976), Demski (1981), Rajan (1992), and Zimmerman (1979). These publications use the conditional controllability perspective for the investigation of the utility of indirect cost allocations. Such allocations – which would violate the traditional controllability principle because indirect costs are not under the exclusive control of the manager who is subject to the allocation – are here found to be beneficial from the principals' point of view. They provide additional information that can be contracted upon (Demski, 1981, pp. 156-158), influence the principals' capacity decisions (Baiman & Noel, 1985, p. 487), or control the agents' overconsumption of perquisites

(Zimmerman, 1979, p. 519). Generally speaking, the conditional controllability perspective depicts indirect cost allocations as a means to induce agents to act in the manner desired by their principals (Rajan, 1992, p. 528).

The notion that performance measures should be used for evaluation purposes if they carry additional information content – which represents the key finding from the work of Holmström (1979), Shavell (1979), and Antle and Demski (1988) – has been heavily used in later management accounting research and produced additional insights into the choice of performance measures. Banker and Datar (1989) follow Holmström's (1979) concept of informativeness and suggest that measures should be included in compensation contracts when they are in some way sensitive to the agents' actions. Additionally, they recommend a linear aggregation of measures while the weight of each measure in the consolidated performance measure should correspond to the measure's degree of precision. If a measure is noisy, i.e. if it lacks precision, its weight in the linear aggregate should be small (Banker & Datar, 1989, pp. 22-23). Similarly, Holmström and Milgrom (1987, pp. 325-326) argue for the aggregation of measures using linear functions.

Analytical research on the aggregation of performance measures further shows that the use of aggregate measures such as team performance measures (instead of individual measures for each agent) can contribute to the resolution of the control problem in organizations. Arya, Fellingham, and Glover (1997, p. 20) reveal that interdependency among team members can be desirable from the principals' perspective because "introducing such an interdependency provides the managers with incentives to monitor each other and a (self-enforcing) means of disciplining each other". One of the few studies into aggregated performance measures that combines a simple agency model with empirical data to test the model's predictions is provided by Bushman et al. (1995). Again, the concept of informativeness represents the starting point for hypothesis development. The authors hypothesize and empirically confirm that managers' annual bonus that is based on performance above the individual managers' own organizational level (which is used as a proxy for aggregate performance measures in this study) is significantly associated with intrafirm interdependencies (Bushman et al., 1995, pp. 120-123). Due to their information content, these aggregated performance measures are used in conjunction with more localized performance measures (Bushman et al., 1995, p. 124).

Further analytical research by Holmström (1982) shows that, when keeping the concept of informativeness in mind, even information on the performance of an agent's peer group should be used for evaluation purposes. In case of common underlying uncertainty, Holmström (1982) points out that valuable information about agents' efforts can be derived from comparing their individual outputs. This finding represents a plausible explanation for the corporate practice of relative performance evaluation (RPE) that is often reported in empirical research (Antle & Smith, 1986; Gibbons & Murphy, 1990; Janakiraman, Lambert, & Larcker, 1992). Holmström (1982, pp. 334-339) demonstrates that sometimes also an aggregate measure like the weighted average of peer performance is likely to capture all the relevant information about the common uncertainty to which agents are exposed.

The utility of additional performance measures is also of central concern to the work of Feltham and Xie (1994). They regard congruity and precision as the key characteristics of performance measures (Feltham & Xie, 1994, p. 430). The former refers to the degree of congruence between the impact of agents' actions on their performance measures and on the principals' expected gross payoff, while the latter implies the degree of noise in the performance measures. Feltham and Xie (1994) arrive at the conclusion that if the basic measure for evaluating agents' performance is perfectly congruent, then the primary role for additional measures is to reduce noise, i.e. to minimize the risk that is imposed on the agents (Feltham & Xie, 1994, p. 447). However, in the work of Feltham and Xie (1994), the formula of incongruity is given only for a single performance measure. Datar, Kulp, and Lambert (2001, pp. 80-81) therefore extend the formula to the multiple measures situation in a later work on the balancing of performance measures.

In a related analytical study on the use of additional measures for performance evaluation, Arya et al. (2007) argue that some measures may be informative, but are, for this reason, not necessarily valuable. Within a specific setting of multiple acts and interdependencies, they show that the inclusion of team performance measures as additional measures is not always optimal (Arya et al., 2007, pp. 190-195). Another annotation to the informativeness literature is provided by Yim (2001). The author demonstrates that when the possibility of renegotiating contracts is incorporated into agency models, performance measures' usefulness in incentive contracting depends on their information quality, not simply on whether the performance measures are informative (Yim, 2001, pp. 91-92).

In the light of the numerous studies based on information content, the formulation of the conditional controllability principle may, at least at first glance, appear like an elegant advancement of the traditional controllability principle. However, there are "practical difficulties of assessing the content of all information used for performance evaluation" (Modell, 1997, p. 315). Antle and Demski (1988) also note that the application of the conditional controllability implies severe challenges. Not only that the task of performance evaluation becomes more demanding, but also – from a research perspective – the field investigator's task is likewise "dramatically complicated by the importance of identifying the conditioning information" (Antle & Demski, 1988, p. 716).

1.2.3 Redefinition of the Controllability Principle Emphasizing Influenceability

Building on the agency-inspired notion of conditional controllability (Spicer, 1992, p. 8), some management accounting scholars have developed a further redefinition of the traditional controllability principle which again comes up with a new interpretation of the term controllability. As these scholars perceive the conditional controllability principle to be "at best incomplete" (Merchant, 1987, p. 336), they suggest that the principle should instead be called influenceability principle (Merchant & Otley, 2006, p. 794). The rationale behind this redefinition says that while some factors may be uncontrollable, organizations still want their managers to respond to changes in those factors and therefore should not eliminate the uncontrollable factors in the evaluation of managerial performance.

There is a subtle but important difference between the conditional controllability principle and the influenceability principle. According to the conditional controllability principle, the use of all available performance measures which add information content is prescribed. In the extreme, imperfect measures and measures totally uncontrollable by managers can be included in appraisals for reasons of informativeness (Holmström, 1979, p. 89). A frequently cited example of this phenomenon is the use of RPE with the performance of their peers being a variable that cannot at all be controlled or influenced by managers (Antle & Demski, 1988, p. 715; Baiman & Noel, 1985, p. 487; Holmström, 1982, pp. 334-339). The influenceability principle, however, requires that managers still have a certain degree of influence on the measures which are used to assess their performance (Skinner, 1990, pp. 139-140). Merchant and Otley (2006) mention the example of oil price rises. Obviously, managers cannot control changes in oil prices, but they can take steps to reduce their organizations' consumption of oil. And if managers can influence the impact of a seemingly uncontrollable factor, organizations are advised to hold them accountable for the effects of that factor (Merchant & Otley, 2006, p. 794).

Source	Definition
Dearden (1987, p. 86)	Very few items are entirely controllable by managers, but very few items cannot be influenced by managers. It is important to remember that the distinction is not controllability but the ability to influence.
Manzoni (2002, p. 33)	One's evaluation should take into account all the elements on which one has influence.
Merchant and Otley (2006, p. 794)	The controllability principle should probably be called the "influenceability principle". If managers can materially influence the effects of a factor on performance, they should be held accountable for the effects of that factor, whether or not the factor itself is controllable.
Giraud et al. (2008, p. 41)	The literature indicates that companies tend to hold managers responsible for factors that they can influence more than for factors that they can totally control . . . Managers adhere to this 'influenceability' principle.

Table 3: Exemplary Definitions of the Influenceability Principle

The focus of the definitions from Table 3 is on managers' ability to influence rather than to control. With this word choice, management accounting literature emphatically refers to differences in the degree of impact that managers theoretically have on the measures which are used for performance evaluation. As the ability to influence has a weaker connotation than the ability to control (Pelster, 2007, p. 29), it is suggested that the influenceability principle provides a better description of the practical circumstances managers are facing in organizational realities (Drury & Tayles, 1995, p. 276; Frow et al., 2005, p. 280; Merchant, 1987, pp. 336-337). The semantic use of influence seems advantageous not only because it cannot be misinterpreted as an absolute state of total control (Merchant, 1989, p. 87), but also because it entails a meaning of managers' informal impact across departmental boundaries (McNally, 1980, p. 170). A related differentiation between control and influence can be found in the work of Simons (2005). On the one hand, the author refers to "span of control" as a hard lever of organizational resources for which managers are (formally) given decision rights (Simons, 2005, p. 39). "Span of influence", on the other hand, represents a soft lever which conceptualizes a rather informal net that managers cast in collecting data, probing for new information, and attempting to influence the work of others (Simons, 2005, p. 119). The formulation of the influenceability principle can hence be seen as a means to revise the use of control – a word that "does not have a universally accepted definition" (Merchant, 1998, p. 2) in management accounting literature – and instead to apply influence as a substitute.

The foregoing discussion led management accounting scholars to reach the conclusion that the controllability principle is a gradual concept and that managers' controllability of their performance measures should accordingly be framed along a continuum (Krishnan, Luft, &

Shields, 2005, p. 52; Merchant, 1998, p. 571; Modell, 1997, p. 314). Even though some older publications recognize only a binary decision of either establishing full control or no control (e.g. Tannenbaum (1968) or Inkson, Pugh, and Hickson (1970)), it is apparent that such a twofold classification of performance measures being controllable or uncontrollable is too simplistic (McNally, 1980, p. 170).

At the one extreme, there may be a complete disregard for the controllability principle, with organizations holding managers accountable for all uncontrollable factors. At the other extreme, there may be a strict application of the controllability principle, where organizations hold their managers accountable only for controllable factors and attempt to (ex ante or ex post) eliminate any uncontrollable influence. In between these extremes, managers are confronted with at least some uncontrollable factors with the reality of organizational endeavor being one of partial controllability (Drury & El-Shishini, 2005, p. 3). In most cases, managers can exert some influence on the measures which are used in the evaluation of their performance. However, they are likely to be still dependent upon some external factors such as the decisions and actions of others if they are to achieve their own objectives (Frow et al., 2005, p. 271).

This state of only partial controllability which is supposed to be normality in complex business settings (Merchant & Van der Stede, 2007, p. 33; Simons, 1995, p. 72) can be best illustrated by examples found in organizational interdependency. In situations where outcomes associated with tasks performed in some organizational unit might be affected by individuals located outside this unit, only some degree of control over the outcomes is likely (Hirst, 1983a, p. 29). Several authors therefore refer to an almost tautological relationship between the existence of shared responsibilities and partial controllability. Interdependencies in the form of delegated tasks or combined objectives cause managers not to be able to exert anything other than partial control over the results for which formal responsibilities have been established (Collier & Agyei-Ampomah, 2006, p. 76; Frow et al., 2005, p. 277; Simons, 2005, p. 166).

1.3 The Importance of Subjectivity for the Controllability Principle

Having acknowledged that the controllability principle is a gradual concept, management accounting literature also emphasizes that a high degree of subjectivity underlies the concept of controllability. Management accounting literature in general and publications on the controllability principle in particular have meanwhile departed from strictly positivist assumptions of all reality being objective and existing independently of human beings (Armstrong, 2008, p. 871; Birnberg & Shields, 1989, p. 56; Tinker, Merino, & Neimark, 1982, p. 168). Controllability cannot be a solely objective design characteristic of performance evaluation systems. Instead, it is "the manager's *perception* [emphasis in original] of control that is the motive force" (Choudhury, 1986, p. 190).

Social scientists have since long done research under the assumption that humans act according to their subjective perceptions of reality rather than to any reality per se (see e.g. the work of Lewin (1936)). Following the assumption that "perception is reality", researchers have been advised to consider individuals' perceptions of their work, rather than the seemingly objective context (Hall & Lord, 1998a, p. 160; 1998b, p. 209). Today, there is consensus among researchers from many disciplines that control has primarily a perceptual and hence subjective dimension (Ajzen, 1991, pp. 181-184; Greenberger, Strasser, Cummings, & Dunham, 1989, p. 31; Parkes, 1989, pp. 22-23). In this context, Öhman and Bohlin (1989) point to the findings from experimental investigations: Even if a particular situation in experiments can be objectively defined as uncontrollable, one cannot unequivocally infer that it will be so perceived by the participants in the experiments (Öhman & Bohlin, 1989, p. 260). Spector (1986, p. 1005) and Fox et al. (1993, p. 291) further underline that perceived control is the variable that plays an important part for individuals' behavior and attitude. The extent to which individuals perceive their environment to be controllable has considerable impact on their reactions toward the environment. The focus clearly is on perceived control rather than objective control: "Quite simply, it is unlikely that control can have an effect unless it is perceived" (Parker, 1993, p. 950).

Again, organizational interdependency as one type of uncontrollable factor (see chapter B3.2) can be picked up for exemplification. Various studies have shown that individuals experience varying levels of interdependency due to their varying perception (see e.g. Shea and Guzzo (1987), Tjosvold (1986), or Wageman (1995)). Reasons such as bounded rationality or uncertainty have been suggested as explanations (McCann & Ferry, 1979, pp. 115-116). As a consequence, perceived interdependency is posited to be distinct from objective interdependency (Tjosvold, 1986, pp. 526-527). Recent research on the consequences of organizational interdependency therefore focuses on the perceived amount of interdependency (as opposed to any objective measure of interdependency) as it is this variable that most likely affects individuals' behavior and attitudes (Wong, DeSanctis, & Staudenmayer, 2007, p. 287).

Choudhury (1986) suggests that the subjective nature of perception is due to a broad array of potential referents: personality (e.g. need for autonomy), past experiences (e.g. personal history of control), as well as organizational factors (e.g. corporate delegation practices) in combination evoke individualized expectations regarding the aspired level of control (Choudhury, 1986, pp. 190-191). Consistent with this view, Parkes (1989, p. 22) depicts control as a subjective variable which reflects situational characteristics as appraised in the light of individuals' beliefs, attitudes, expectations, and experiences. As a result, managers' perceptions of their controllability are deemed to be highly specific and cannot be generalized on the basis of seemingly objective situational characteristics (Bourguignon & Chiapello, 2005, p. 688; Hirst, 1983a, p. 32; Pelster, 2007, p. 90; Ronen & Livingstone, 1975, pp. 680-681).

The preceding paragraphs demonstrate that subjectivity is a central aspect in research on the controllability principle because managers' intrapersonal perception is the decisive criterion. And it is worth noting that the concept of subjectivity becomes even more relevant due to its importance in interpersonal performance appraisals between managers and their superiors. When superiors evaluate subordinate managers' performance, they typically rely on a certain degree of subjectivity (Ittner, Larcker, & Meyer, 2003, p. 726; Moers, 2005, p. 79). Especially adjustments for uncontrollable factors are a much disputed issue in performance appraisals: If superiors "want to remove the effects of the uncontrollables, they must generally do so subjectively" (Merchant, 1989, p. 131). Hence, it is not only managers' own subjectivity that determines their perceived degree of controllability, but also their superiors' subjectivity in protecting them from uncontrollable factors or exposing them to these factors.

Subjective performance evaluation has undeniable advantages. With objective performance measures often varying in terms of their ability to provide accurate, informative, and timely indications of managers' contribution to organizational goals, subjective evaluators can take this imperfectness of formal MCSs into consideration. Subjective judgments, which commonly form implicit parts of employment contracts (Merchant, 1989, p. 132), can be used to fill in these gaps and enable evaluation flexibility so as to make the contracts nearly perfect (Baker, Jensen, & Murphy, 1988, pp. 597-598; Gibbs, Merchant, Van der Stede, & Vargus, 2004, p. 412). According to Lawler (1990, p. 90), subjective judgments often turn out to be inevitable because, in many cases, there are simply no measures at all that would allow the appraisal to be based on objective data. Recent research by Nisar (2006) reveals further evidence on the advantages of subjectivity: Subjective performance evaluation can be usefully employed when companies are seeking to promote long-term managerial behavior and to reward human capital investment (Nisar, 2006, pp. 37-39). Furthermore, subjectivity may be helpful to reduce complexity in performance evaluation and to reflect corporate emphasis on fairness and trust (Merchant, 1989, pp. 132-133). Last but not least, subjective performance evaluation is frequently popular with superiors because it provides a significant source of power over subordinate managers (Merchant, 1998, pp. 580-581). In brief, subjectivity allows the recalibration of performance evaluation whereby superiors can use subjective assessments to mitigate problems arising from unobservability, unverifiability, dysfunctional incentives, and related challenges in performance evaluation.

Despite these advantages, opponents of subjective performance evaluation have noted that there can be major difficulties associated with the use of subjectivity in appraisals. Because superiors' discretion is involved in making subjective assessments of managerial performance, it is necessary that unbiased judgments are made if subjectivity can work in the interest of both the organization and the managers. However, managers seem to have strong feelings against subjective performance evaluation for this reason (Baker et al., 1988, p. 598; Giraud et al., 2004, pp. 17-18; Manzoni, 2002, p. 29; Milgrom & Roberts, 1992, p. 215). Subjectivity raises their concerns about uncertainty in the standards used for evaluation, possible favoritism, and hence unfairness. Probably, the use of subjective performance measures is only effective when managers have a high trust in their superiors: "The more subjective the measure, the higher the degree of trust needed, because without high trust there is little chance that the subordinate will believe that his pay is really fairly based on performance" (Lawler, 1971, p. 171). Otherwise, Merchant (1989) argues that subjectivity in performance evaluation may lead to dysfunctional effects. In the case of subjective ex post adjustments for uncontrollable factors – i.e. adjustments which are intended to lower the risk managers have to bear – the author finds that the managers' perceived risk actually often increases. They now face higher uncertainty about how their performance will be evaluated and therefore fear that the evaluation will be distorted and biased against them (Merchant, 1989, p. 135).

Empirical research provides evidence that subjective performance evaluation is indeed likely to incorporate biases. Based on an experimental investigation by Mitchell and Kalb (1981), it is shown that superiors' judgments about subordinates' performance are affected by knowledge of the outcome of behavior and by the valence of the outcome (Mitchell & Kalb, 1981, pp. 609-610). This phenomenon is called the outcome effect. Later experiments by Baron and Hershey (1988), Brown and Solomon (1987; 1993), Fisher and Selling (1993), Ghosh (2005), Lipe (1993), Lipshitz (1989), and Tan and Lipe (1997) as well as a field study by Ghosh and Lusch (2000) support the existence of the outcome effect. Managers who achieve good financial results are therefore likely to be given better performance evaluation ratings than managers who achieve poor financial results, even when the reasons for their performance are uncontrollable.

A related bias is known as the hindsight bias. Initial work by Fischhoff and Beyth (1975) and Fischhoff (1975) indicates that evaluators with knowledge of results tend to assume that evaluatees had information about the pre-result circumstances, while in reality it was not available to them. This means that superiors with such knowledge may falsely believe that they would have predicted the reported outcome of an event (Hawkins & Hastie, 1990, p. 311). Again, the hindsight bias has been investigated empirically using primarily laboratory experiments: Bukszar and Connolly (1988), El-Sehity, Haumer, Helmenstein, Kirchler, and Maciejovsky (2002), Hölzl, Kirchler, and Rodler (2002), and Lowe and Reckers (1994; 2000) find at least partial evidence for the hindsight bias.

Moers (2005) reports that subjectivity may lead to a further bias in performance evaluation. He finds that if more subjectivity is used in evaluating and rewarding employees, superiors give higher performance ratings and compress these ratings. As a result, a company may become unable to separate the highly skilled employees from the less skilled employees when deciding on pay and promotions (Moers, 2005, p. 79).

Apart from the biases described above, subjectivity in performance evaluation may pose additional problems. In case studies conducted by Merchant (1989, p. 135) and Modell and Lee (2001, p. 202), subjective appraisals result in the emergence of an "excuse culture". The possibility of subjective adjustments for uncontrollable factors seems to encourage managers to make excuses for poor performance. Researchers often refer to attribution theory (Heider, 1958; Kelley, 1971; Weiner et al., 1971) to explain this psychological phenomenon. This theory describes attributions as the result of fundamental cognitive processes by which people ascertain cause and effect so that they can solve problems and become more efficacious in their interactions with their environment (Heider, 1958, pp. 15-17; Kelley, 1973, pp. 107-108). Specifically, individuals tend to attribute their success to their own efforts, abilities, skills, knowledge, or competence, whereas they attribute their failures to factors which are at least partially out of their control, such as bad luck or task difficulty (Merchant, 1998, p. 581; Shields, Birnberg, & Frieze, 1981, p. 88).

1.4 Controllability of Performance Measures as Conceptual Specification

The preceding chapters reveal that the controllability principle is a relative, gradual, and subjective concept. It is relative because it relates responsibility to authority, it is gradual because it reflects a continuum of different degrees of controllability, and it is subjective because managerial perception is its decisive criterion. For further specification of the controllability principle, this work has to take these three aspects into consideration. And further specification is necessary because management accounting scholars frequently describe the principle and its underlying concept to be vague and imprecise (Antle & Demski, 1988, pp. 700-701; Budde, 2009, p. 169; Choudhury, 1986, p. 197; Pelster, 2007, pp. 32-33).

The specification adopted in this work follows Ghosh (2005), Gibbs et al. (2009), Hartmann and Slapničar (2007), Merchant (2006), and Moers (2000) who depict controllability as a property (or design characteristic) of performance measures. The controllability of performance measures therefore represents the conceptual specification of the controllability principle: If performance measures are designed to be controllable (uncontrollable), this means that the controllability principle is applied (not applied) in the evaluation of managerial performance. This conceptual specification rests upon the notion that managers' responsibility in their organization generally becomes manifest in the measures which are used to assess their performance (Hatry & Wholey, 1999, pp. 157-158).[3]

It is accepted in management accounting literature that managers' controllability over alternative performance measures varies (Ghosh, 2005, p. 56). First, nonfinancial measures are argued to be more controllable than financial measures (Ghosh, 2005, p. 58; Giraud et al., 2004, p. 8). This is because financial measures are often too aggregated and may not provide detailed information about the performance of individual managers (Baker, Gibbons, & Murphy, 1994, p. 1126; Chow & Van der Stede, 2006, p. 7; Ittner & Larcker, 2002, p. S60). Second, accounting measures are often regarded to be more controllable than market-based measures (Feltham & Xie, 1994, p. 437). Third, and not unexpectedly (see chapter B1.3 on the importance of subjectivity), there is empirical evidence that subjective performance measures seem to be associated with a higher degree of controllability than objective performance measures (Chow & Van der Stede, 2006, p. 6; Ittner, Larcker, & Rajan, 1997, p. 252).

Having recognized that different types of performance measures (nonfinancial versus financial, accounting-based versus market-based, subjective versus objective) are associated with varying degrees of controllability, management accounting scholars have sought to identify the determinants of perceived controllability of performance measures. Hence, their question is: What is it that makes performance measures appear to be controllable (or uncontrollable) to managers? In an answer to this question, Bisbe et al. (2007) stipulate that the controllability of performance measures depends on two separate dimensions: the sensitivity of the measures and their precision. Referring to sensitivity, the authors mean that changes in the performance measures are due to managers' actions, while precision implies a lack of noise or variability in the measures (Bisbe et al., 2007, p. 805). Managers can therefore only be confident in the controllability of their performance measures when their efforts and decisions have an influence on the measures (Merchant, 1989, p. 87; Simons, 2005, p. 79) and when the measures are simultaneously not distorted by uncertain, uncontrollable events (Merchant, 1985, p. 25; Merchant & Van der Stede, 2007, p. 34). This

3 In accordance with Neely, Gregory, and Platts (2005, p. 1229), this work defines a performance measurement and evaluation system as "the set of metrics used to quantify both the efficiency and effectiveness of action". A performance measure then refers to one quantitative or qualitative metric which is part of a such a system (Armstrong & Baron, 2005, pp. 27-30). To distinguish between a performance measurement and evaluation system and a management control system (MCS), this work adopts the view of Henri (2006, p. 529) who considers the former as one component of the latter. Since there appears to be some confusion in the literature about the terms management accounting (MA), management accounting system (MAS), and MCS, which are sometimes used interchangeably, this work defines the terms as follows: MA refers to a collection of practices (such as budgeting, transfer pricing, or product costing), while MAS refers to the systematic use of MA to achieve organizational goals. MCS is a broader term that encompasses MAS, but also includes other forms of control (Chenhall, 2003, p. 129). Throughout this work, the broader term MCS will therefore be used instead of MAS. It refers to all "formal, information-based routines and procedures managers use to maintain or alter patterns in organizational activities" (Simons, 1995, p. 5).

specification is also reflected in agency research on the controllability principle. Reviewing key findings from the works of Holmström (1979) and Banker and Datar (1989), Gibbs et al. (2004) state that "the relative importance (weight) of performance metrics should be a decreasing function of their noise and an increasing function of their sensitivity to employee effort or decisions" (p. 412). Similarly, Feltham and Xie (1994, pp. 430-434), Demski (1994, pp. 499-500), Lambert (2001, p. 8), and Milgrom and Roberts (1992, p. 221) agree that the controllability of performance measures depends on these two dimensions.

Controllability is – despite its importance for the design of performance measures – only one of many performance measure properties. There is a long research tradition in management accounting that is concerned with the properties of performance measures and their effects on various outcomes, in particular managers' behavior and performance (Chenhall & Langfield-Smith, 2007, pp. 275-278; Ittner & Larcker, 1998, pp. 205-238). Even though critics like Henri (2006, p. 538) note that empirical results concerning the exact relationship between the use of performance measures and actual performance are somewhat ambiguous, previous literature has unanimously highlighted the importance of performance measure properties for the effective design of incentive systems and, hence, managerial motivation (Bouwens & Van Lent, 2006, p. 57; Gibbs et al., 2009, p. 240).

The properties which have been researched so far are manifold (for overviews see Burkert (2008, pp. 65-71), Merchant (2006, pp. 894-897), or Sandt (2004, pp. 125-145)). Above all, the diversity of performance measures defined as the use of multiple measures for incentive purposes (Moers, 2005, pp. 67-68) has attracted considerable attention by management accounting scholars. The discussion about the incompleteness and inadequacies of traditional performance measures led to the call for such multiple performance measures (Eccles, 1991, p. 132) which then motivated a variety of innovations in performance measurement such as Kaplan and Norton's (1992; 1996) balanced scorecard (Ittner & Larcker, 1998, p. 205). Closely related to the use of multiple measures is the integration of subjective measures in performance evaluation. Subjective performance measures are defined as superiors' subjective judgments about managerial performance (Moers, 2005, p. 68). As shown in chapter B1.3, subjectivity is argued to bring about several advantages as well as disadvantages in performance evaluation (Gibbs et al., 2004, p. 410; Moers, 2006, p. 897). More recently, the alignment with strategy has been proposed as a further important property of performance measures. Based on contingency theory which argues that performance measures should be aligned with organizational strategy and value drivers (Fisher, 1998, p. 48; Langfield-Smith, 1997, p. 207), performance is theoretically enhanced when measurement gaps between strategic priorities and measurement practices are minimized (Chenhall, 2005, pp. 397-398; Ittner, Larcker, & Randall, 2003, p. 716).

Diversity, subjectivity, and alignment with strategy represent some of the most heavily researched performance measure properties. Several other design characteristics such as aggregation (Nikias, Schwartz, & Young, 2005), comprehensiveness (Hall, 2008), integration (Chenhall & Morris, 1986), or timeliness (Chia, 1995) have been addressed in related management accounting studies. However, literature has not yet achieved consensus with respect to what constitutes the ideal nature of properties (Berry, Coad, Harris, Otley, & Stringer, 2009, p. 5; Bouwens & Van Lent, 2006, p. 57). Ittner et al. (2003, p. 739) therefore call for the investigation of a broader set of properties which potentially increase the perceived usefulness of MCSs. In order to contribute to existing literature, this work suggests the controllability of performance measures (which includes the subdimensions precision of performance measures and sensitivity of performance measures) as an important property.

2. The Rationale of the Controllability Principle

2.1 Responsibility in Organizations

Responsibility – which is together with authority the central parameter of the controllability principle – can be broadly defined as the extent to which actions are evaluated by an external constituency who is believed to have reward and sanction powers that are contingent on this constituency's view of actions (Ferris et al., 1997, p. 163). It generally forms a key element for organizational stability (Frink & Klimoski, 1998, p. 2; Tetlock, 1985, p. 307; Yakel, 2001, p. 234). Accordingly, every "setting organizes its activities to make its properties as an organized environment of practical activities detectable, countable, recordable, reportable, tell-a-story-about-able, analyzable – in short *accountable* [emphasis in original]" (Garfinkel, 1967, p. 33). Following Roberts and Scapens (1985, p. 448), MCSs are thereby paramount in shaping and maintaining particular patterns of responsibility within organizations. Accounting information and performance measures in particular play an important role since they act as a mirror through which their producers and their activity are made visible (Roberts, 1991, p. 363).

Today, responsibility-oriented MCSs predominate at managerial levels of most organizations. In some organizations they are even in use at the lowest levels, as in piece rate systems used with production line employees (Merchant & Otley, 2006, p. 792; Merchant & Van der Stede, 2007, p. 271; Simons, 2005, pp. 9-10). From an organizational perspective, several advantages result from holding employees accountable for their actions. Reitzug (1987) finds in his review of studies on the practice of MbO that accountability generally has a positive effect on employee productivity and attitudes (Reitzug, 1987, p. 21). Research by Fandt (1991, pp. 306-309) likewise indicates that individuals who feel to be accountable to their superiors for their performance are more likely to be high performers, develop greater accuracy in their work, and are more attentive to the needs of others. Positive effects on performance are also reported in a study by Yarnold, Mueser, and Lyons (1988, p. 358). Similarly, establishing responsibility arrangements is found to have a strong effect on managers' cost consciousness in the work of Abernethy and Vagnoni (2004, pp. 219-220). Even in a public management setting, Budding (2004, p. 298) observes that when managers are held accountable for their doings, their incentive to improve efficiency is greater. Related studies provide evidence that holding employees accountable essentially has a desirable attention-directing effect. Felt responsibility is reported to be an important variable when encouraging employees to perform activities which might otherwise be discretionary (Frese, Kring, Soose, & Zempel, 1996, p. 49; Morrison & Phelps, 1999, p. 414; Pearce & Gregersen, 1991, pp. 842-843). Drucker (1993, p. 71) therefore concludes that, without structures of responsibility, organizations "degenerate into mediocrity and malperformance".

Establishing structures of responsibility is not only desirable from an organizational perspective. Also from the perspective of the individual employee, responsibility plays a vital role in terms of finding a place and an identity in the organization (Messner, 2009, p. 928; Shearer, 2002, pp. 543-544). Roberts (1991) claims that there is an intimate relationship between responsibility and the constitution of an individual's self. Being held accountable for one's actions is assumed to sharpen the individual's sense of self and has the potential to introduce a clarifying focus into the lived reality of everyday organizational life. Conversely, the absence of being held accountable is supposed to weaken and blur one's sense of self and situation (Roberts, 1991, p. 356). Such a positive effect of responsibility is also reflected in the work of Burns (1997). The author describes responsibility as a basic need of employees that organizations need to fulfill. Thoms, Dose, and Scott (2002) provide empirical evidence on this issue. In their large-scale study, a significant correlation is found between job satisfaction and employees' perceived responsibility to their superiors. Thoms et al. (2002) additionally find that responsibility is positively related to employees' trust in their superiors (Thoms et al., 2002, p. 318). In sum, many scholars dealing with the concept of responsibility have predicted that more responsibility is better because it produces individually and organizationally desired outcomes (Frink & Klimoski, 1998, p. 34).

The idea of holding employees accountable for their actions is also the basis of what is regarded to be "one of the most important developments in management accounting" (Anthony, 1989, p. 10), namely responsibility accounting. Responsibility accounting means the creation of responsibility centers which are defined as organization units or parts of business for whose performance managers are held accountable. It implies the implementation of reporting systems which enable responsibility to be allocated throughout the organization. Responsibility can thereby be expressed in terms of quantities of inputs consumed, physical units of output, particular characteristics of the production or service process, or financial indicators of performance in these areas. In the process of responsibility accounting, deviations from performance targets (e.g. the budget) are to be identified and attributed to the individual managers who are accountable for the responsibility centers (Bamber, Braun, & Harrison, 2008, p. 584; Bhimani et al., 2008, p. 487; Drury, 2007, p. 38; Hilton, 2008, pp. 502-505; Lucey, 2003, pp. 189-190; Merchant & Van der Stede, 2007, pp. 270-271). According to Anthony (1989, p. 10), the term responsibility accounting was first used and defined in an early article by Higgins (1952). In this original definition, responsibility accounting is described as a system for attributing only controllable costs to managers (Davidson & Weil, 1978, pp. 2-10). In most modern management accounting textbooks, the term responsibility center is not restricted to costs only, but encompasses cost centers, revenue centers, profit centers, and investment centers.

In cost (or expense) centers, managers are held accountable for costs only (Drury, 2007, p. 395). With managers being instructed to control costs, the focus in such responsibility centers is primarily on efficiency (Bamber et al., 2008, p. 585; Jun Lin & Yu, 2002, p. 460). Commonly, the costs incurred in cost centers are gathered together according to their incidence (Drury, 2007, p. 48; Lucey, 2003, p. 13). Merchant and Van der Stede (2007, pp. 273-274) differentiate between standard cost centers and discretionary cost centers. In standard cost centers, outputs are relatively easy to measure and the causal relationship between inputs and outputs is direct and stable. Drury (2007, p. 395) recommends that standard cost centers are particularly suited in operation units of manufacturing companies. In discretionary cost centers, such as research and development units or administrative units, the outputs are more difficult to value in monetary terms and the relationship between inputs and outputs is not well known. Evaluations of discretionary cost center managers' performance are therefore more complicated and often require a subjective component.

Revenue centers are responsibility centers where managers are held accountable for generating revenues (Hilton, 2008, p. 502). They provide a simple and effective way to encourage managers to attract and retain customers. However, the design of revenue centers often creates undesirable consequences (Atkinson et al., 2007, p. 586). A revenue center design can distract managers from focusing on the most profitable customers and instead tempt them to "make easy sales" (Merchant & Van der Stede, 2007, p. 273). Common examples of revenue centers are regional sales units or fund raising departments. Revenue center managers may sometimes be held accountable for particular selling expenses, such as salesperson salaries. However, they are usually not made accountable for the costs of the goods or services that they sell (Drury, 2007, p. 396).

In order to put emphasis on profits instead of revenues or costs only, profit centers are an important control element (Drury, 2007, p. 478). In practice, there are many different forms of profit centers, some of which are more limited in scope of operations than others (Merchant &

Van der Stede, 2007, p. 272). However, profit centers generally imply a higher degree of autonomy for their managers than cost centers or revenue centers do (Drury, 2007, p. 396; Milgrom & Roberts, 1992, pp. 229-230). Managers of such responsibility centers are normally free to set selling prices, choose which markets to sell in, make output decisions, and select suppliers. Often profit center managers may generate revenues not only via external sales, but also via internal sales (Merchant & Van der Stede, 2007, p. 273). They derive revenues from selling their products or services to other entities within the same organization, which necessitates transfer pricing policies to coordinate these internal transactions (for literature reviews on this topic see Emmanuel and Mehafdi (1994) and McAulay and Tomkins (1992)).

The fourth type of responsibility centers is called investment center. Whereas profit centers hold their managers accountable for profits, investment centers additionally consider the investments which were made to generate these profits (Bhimani et al., 2008, p. 487). However, as Lucey (2003, p. 517) and Drury (2007, p. 396) note, many investment centers are in practice often referred to as profit centers. The term profit center is used whether the respective business unit is responsible for just profit or profit in relation to the capital invested in the unit. Additionally, it is worth mentioning that the term investment center does not necessarily mean that managers are responsible for all investment decisions in these units. Above a fairly low limit, investment decisions are often the prerogative of central management (Lucey, 2003, p. 517). For true investment centers, there are different labels to be put on the investment centers' bottom line, such as return on investment, return on equity, return on capital employed, or return on net assets (Merchant & Van der Stede, 2007, p. 271). According to Bamber et al. (2008, p. 586), mainly large divisions of corporations are true investment centers.

Integrating the concept of the controllability principle with the idea of responsibility accounting, Lucey (2003, p. 190) comments: "The terms, controllable and uncontrollable, only have meaning related to a particular responsibility center". Baiman and Noel (1985, p. 486), Ferrara (1967, p. 43), Frow et al. (2005, p. 271), Modell (2001, p. 191), and Ugras (1994, p. 256) agree that responsibility accounting and the controllability principle are inherently related to one another and "may be viewed as being inseparable" (Choudhury, 1986, p. 189). Following Demski and Sappington (1989, p. 40), the controllability principle can hence be regarded as the key imperative underlying the idea of responsibility accounting.

2.2 Authority in Organizations

As Merchant (2006, p. 896) writes in a recent publication, "controllability depends on the authority given to the individual". Authority adds to responsibility as the second parameter of the controllability principle. According to Simon (1951, p. 294), authority can be defined as the right to select actions and decisions affecting parts or the whole of an organization. In management accounting literature on the controllability principle, authors often seem to use the terms authority and control interchangeably. Basically, the two terms do have a very similar connotation because both refer to the decision-making powers and resources on which managers can rely in their jobs. Still, there is some difference in meaning: Authority is often interpreted as the organizational force that legitimizes control (Barker, 2008, p. 981). Or, as Parsons (1958, p. 210) puts it, authority involves "the complex of institutional rights to control the activities of members of a society, with reference to their bearing on the attainment of collective goals".

Scholars in the field of administrative science have long since agreed that authority in organizations can generally take one of two forms: formal or informal (Filley & House, 1969, pp. 55-65; Greenwald, 1972, pp. 207-208; Zeitz, 1980, pp. 280-282)[4]. Filley and House (1969) differentiate between these two complementary but distinct approaches to authority as follows: The first encompasses planned or spontaneous schemes of ranking on a superordination-subordination basis. The second refers to the means whereby one individual affects the perceptions, attitudes, or behaviors of another on an influence-submission basis (Filley & House, 1969, p. 55). The two forms of authority may coexist in the same social system, and even in the same authoritative action (Greenwald, 1972, p. 208). Many management accounting scholars follow this distinction between formal and informal authority. Abernethy and Vagnoni (2004) rely on the distinction in their investigation of the impact of authority structures on the use of MCSs for decision control and decision management. Similarly, Frow et al. (2005) differentiate between formally directed structures and procedures, on the one hand, and informal channels of social influence, on the other hand, when investigating how managers exert different types of control in the pursuit of their personal objectives.

Formal authority can be viewed as the classical view of organization (Filley & House, 1969, p. 56). It implies that authority first and foremost results from an explicit or implicit contract allocating the right to decide on specified matters to a member or a group of members of the organization (Aghion & Tirole, 1997, p. 2). Formal authority is thereby put into effect through hierarchy and structural arrangements (Baker, Gibbons, & Murphy, 1999, p. 56; Nirel et al., 1994, p. 39). In other words, formal authority and its delegation of decision rights are related

4 In related contexts, scholars often refer to the term of power. Here, the focus is usually on interpersonal relationships with power being defined as "the extent that A can get B to do something that B would not otherwise do" (Dahl, 1957, pp. 202-203). The concept of power can be seen as an umbrella term that describes the maximum ability of a person to formally or informally influence individuals or groups (Filley & House, 1969, p. 55). In order to clearly distinguish between authority and power, Nirel, Schmid, and Stern (1994, p. 39) suggest that while authority is the right to seek compliance, power is the demonstrated ability to achieve it.

to individuals' position in a ranked hierarchical structure (Barnard, 1968, pp. 172-173; Pfeffer, 1992, pp. 128-133). The idea that individuals' formal authority is derived from the position they hold in the hierarchy dates back to the Weberian view of bureaucracy (for a collection of Weber's classical essays, see Weber, Gerth, and Mills (1946)). In Weber's (1946, pp. 78-80) work, a typology of authority is developed that comprises charismatic, traditional, and legal (or rational) authority. In legal (or rational) authority, legitimacy resides in the hierarchical structure and rational rule system of organizations. Hence, Weber's (1946) legal (or rational) authority type largely captures what many scholars today define as formal authority. According to Abernethy and Vagnoni (2004, p. 210), this formal type of authority constitutes "the official system of . . . control". As such, it has immediate relevance for this study's discussion on the controllability principle: Since formal authority is the key indicator of how decision rights are officially allocated and organizationally enforced, the managers' perception of their controllability is likely to be primarily shaped by formal authority arrangements.

As opposed to formal authority, informal authority refers to individuals' ability to influence organizational decisions and activities in ways that are not prescribed by the formal authority system (Abernethy & Vagnoni, 2004, p. 210). Behavioral theories of organizations (Cyert & March, 1963; Simon, 1951) have emphasized the importance of informal authority for decades. It may also be interpreted as the allocation of decision rights. However, these decision rights are quite distinct from the decision rights that are formally assigned from superiors to subordinates. Informal decision rights are rather captured by virtue of persuasion, informal power bases such as expertise or referent power, or the ability to control the critical resources of an organization (Nirel et al., 1994, p. 39; Pfeffer, 1992, pp. 69-186). Informal authority is mainly prevalent in small social systems (Filley & House, 1969, p. 57; Greenwald, 1972, p. 208). On this microcosmic level, close personal and emotional ties between individuals are facilitated and informal influence is supposed to be most effective. The idea of informal authority and the recognition that managerial influence can go beyond the levels of control stated in formal organizational plans and charts is also reflected in the influenceability principle (see chapter B1.2.3): Remember that this redefinition of the controllability principle allows for a broader definition of the term control and explicitly takes aspects of (informal) influence into consideration.

2.3 Justifications for the Application of the Controllability Principle

On the basis of the foregoing chapters which introduced responsibility and authority as the two parameters of the controllability principle, the following provides an overview of the central arguments which are typically mentioned in literature to justify the principle's application. According to Merchant (1998, p. 572), several related arguments explain why superiors should not urge their subordinate managers to bear the influence of uncontrollable factors. In an earlier publication, the same author even writes about the "universality of benefits of eliminating the effects of uncontrollable influences" (Merchant, 1989, p. 130). Since "there is support in the accounting, administrative science and social psychology literatures for the claim that subordinates should be evaluated on the basis of performance measures which capture controllable outcomes" (Hirst, 1983a, p. 29), the following chapters rely on theories and insights from these three disciplines.

2.3.1 Justifications Based on Agency Theory

The starting point for many agency-inspired studies on the controllability principle is risk aversion. In agency theory, agents are generally modeled to avoid risk (Eisenhardt, 1989a, p. 58; Frederickson, 1992, p. 651). It is assumed that agents are hired to apply their performance capability in a productive task rather than to share risk with their principals (Shields & Waller, 1988, p. 584). Business risks should therefore be left with the principals since they are expected to be better able to bear these risks. Principals are risk-neutral because, unlike agents, they can diversify their portfolios through elaborate financial markets set up for exactly that purpose. Actually, the principals' rewards stem directly from the risk-bearing function they perform (Merchant, 1998, p. 573). When principals hold risk-averse agents accountable for the effects of factors that they cannot control, principals have to carry some costs for doing so. Facing uncontrollable influence on their measured performance represents an extra risk to agents. And agents must be compensated for bearing this extra risk (Bloom & Milkovich, 1998, p. 286; Feltham & Xie, 1994, p. 447; Manzoni, 2002, p. 33; Milgrom & Roberts, 1992, p. 207). The company's compensation costs will hence increase due to the use of uncontrollable performance measures which is why principals should generally be interested in not holding agents accountable for uncontrollable factors. Following this reasoning, Bouwens and Van Lent (2006) generalize findings from Banker and Datar (1989), Gibbons (1998), and Indjejikian (1999) and conclude that uncontrollable "measures impose undesired risk on agents and reduce the efficacy of incentives" (Bouwens & Van Lent, 2006, p. 57).

In accordance with such agency predictions on the effective design of incentive systems, Moers (2006) argues that the more controllable – which in his work means precise and sensitive – a performance measure, the greater the returns from using this measure in incentive systems. Moers (2006) provides empirical evidence on this conjecture. Analyzing survey questionnaire data, he finds that when measures are high in precision and sensitivity, their utility to solve the incentive problem rises and, thus, they are increasingly used for delegation purposes (Moers, 2006, pp. 918-919). Further empirical evidence on the desirability of using controllable performance measures comes from Abernethy, Bouwens, and Van Lent (2004). Their empirical findings indicate that, when divisional performance measures become uncontrollable due to noise inherent to them, the measures are less effective in evaluating division managers' performance. The use of such measures by central management is accordingly decreased (Abernethy et al., 2004, p. 562).

Apart from risk-related aspects, agency theorists often suggest selection and effort effects as arguments for the application of the controllability principle. Selection effects refer to contracts offered in a labor market that can affect performance by attracting those agents to the company who have certain personal attributes (Demski & Feltham, 1978, p. 341; Milgrom & Roberts, 1992, pp. 341-343; Shields & Waller, 1988, pp. 583-584; Waller & Chow, 1985, p. 458). According to the "general pattern of self-selection" (Waller & Chow, 1985, p. 471), agents choose among alternative employment contracts based on their performance capability. Agents with higher (lower) performance capability levels are assumed to select contracts with higher (lower) performance incentives. Contracts can hence be structured so that more productive agents self-select into the company. The application of the controllability principle is thereby supposed to have selection effects because agents generally care about the way their performance is measured. Prospective agents form expectations about how well their effort levels are reflected in measured performance and base their decision whether to join the company on these expectations. With other things being equal, more skilled agents, who believe they can earn high performance-dependent pay, are more likely to join an incentive-intensive company than low-skilled agents are, especially if they believe that the performance measures in use are controllable and capture their contributions to the company accurately (Bouwens & Van Lent, 2006, pp. 57-58).

Effort effects mean that incentive contracts potentially induce agents to increase or to better allocate their effort. This notion is rooted in the prediction from agency theory that performance-based contracts motivate agents to learn more productive ways to perform their tasks (Banker, Seok-Young, Potter, & Srinivasan, 2001, p. 316; Bouwens & Van Lent, 2006, p. 56). If agents recognize that their effort levels have an effect on their measured performance, this is supposed to positively influence their effort in the job, which thus advocates the application of the controllability principle. Effort effects in particular increase long-term performance because, after accounting for the selection effect, the remaining agents in the company are motivated to continually improve their productivity (Banker et al., 2001, p. 347).

There is empirical evidence for the selection and effort effects of applying the controllability principle in performance evaluation. Waller and Chow (1985) show experimentally that more skilled employees prefer to work under more incentive-intensive contracts. The correlation between performance capability and performance incentives in the contracts is found to be higher in the presence of controllability filters, i.e. when there are adjustments for the influence of uncontrollable factors (Waller & Chow, 1985, p. 471). In a more recent study investigating the compensation practices in a large sample of Dutch companies, Bouwens and Van Lent (2006) likewise report that performance measure properties are associated with the selection and effort effects of incentive contracts. More precise and undistorted, and hence more controllable, performance measures are associated with more intense incentives. Higher incentive intensity then increases the selection of better employees and employees' effort levels (Bouwens & Van Lent, 2006, p. 71).

2.3.2 Justifications Based on Administrative Science

Calling for an "efficiency-seeking organizational design" (Freeman, 1999, p. 165) scholars from the field of administrative science provide further reasons for the application of the controllability principle. In order to increase efficiency, i.e. to establish smooth processes, set up reliable structures, and ultimately save costs, the application of the controllability principle is postulated (Mooney, 1998, p. 543). Costs arising from the principle's nonapplication include (a) managers' game-playing behaviors, (b) development of an "excuse culture", and (c) staff turnover.

Game-playing behaviors include various actions which managers undertake to lower their exposure to uncontrollable factors. Among these actions are earnings management or the creation of budgetary slack (Collins, 1978, pp. 329-331; Dent, 1987, pp. 138-139; Merchant, 1998, p. 573). Especially the creation of slack as the difference between the total resources available to the organization and the total necessary to maintain the organization (Cyert & March, 1963, pp. 36-38) is critical. From an organizational perspective, slack is commonly assumed to hinder coordination of activities and to be detrimental to overall performance (Davis, DeZoort, & Kopp, 2006, p. 21; Douglas, HassabElnaby, Norman, & Wier, 2007, p. 93; Kren, 2003, p. 144; Van der Stede, 2000, p. 619). When MCSs do not capture the impact of uncontrollable factors, further dysfunctional effects may be managers' reluctance to use the systems' accounting data and the development of local record-keeping systems to verify or dispute the accuracy of the data (Hopwood, 1973, p. 123; McNally, 1980, p. 168). In extreme cases, managers may even be tempted to manipulate the data they report with the extent and severity of such game-playing behaviors being hard to detect by superiors (Eccles, 1991, p. 132). Modell and Lee (2001, p. 194) suggest that the nonapplication of the controllability principle is also likely to be detrimental to managers' acceptance of and commitment to budgetary responsibility. Llewellyn (1998, p. 305) empirically confirms that the failure to match budgetary responsibility and decision-making authority leads managers to abdicate their individualized responsibility.

Dysfunctional behaviors which result in inefficiencies and costs may also come from the development of an "excuse culture" (Giraud et al., 2008, p. 34). Managers are reported to waste considerable time and effort trying to convince superiors that their poor performance is due to factors beyond their control (see also chapter B1.3). They spend time arguing about the extent of the distortions and developing alternative explanations for their results, at the expense of doing their job (Merchant, 1989, pp. 104, 135-137). Unnecessary investigations on the part of superiors as well as defending and blame shifting on the part of the managers whose performance is affected by the uncontrollable factors can hence be avoided when applying the controllability principle (Ansari, 1979, p. 154).

The application of the controllability principle can additionally serve to prevent staff turnover. If companies do not adjust for the effects of uncontrollable factors, they potentially bear the consequences of managers leaving the company and, as a result, higher recruiting costs (Merchant, 1998, p. 572; Modell & Lee, 2001, p. 192). Investigating the performance evaluation systems of 12 US corporations, Merchant (1989, p. 116) finds that all companies in this sample seem to follow the controllability principle for job retention purposes.

2.3.3 Justifications Based on Theory of Learned Helplessness

Psychological theories provide further arguments for the application of the controllability principle. Among these theories, some management accounting scholars (Choudhury, 1986, pp. 191-192; Giraud et al., 2004, p. 4) refer to the theory of learned helplessness (Maier & Seligman, 1976; Seligman, 1975). In its core, this theory outlines the "generalization of no-control beliefs" (Kofta, 1993, p. 122) and predicts that, during contact with uncontrollable situations, individuals learn that there is no contingency between their behavior and the outcomes obtained. This learning gives rise to the expectation of a sustained lack of control in the future, which leads to the emergence of a learned helplessness syndrome. Such a learned helplessness syndrome emerges because individuals assume that there is no response in their repertoire that might alter the probability of outcomes. The consequences of the syndrome may include cognitive deficits (e.g. impaired detection of new contingencies), motivational deficits (e.g. decreased tendency to initiate behavior), and affective deficits (e.g. decreased satisfaction) (Kofta, 1993, pp. 122-125; Maier & Seligman, 1976, p. 3; Seligman, 1975, pp. 45-56).

The original theory of learned helplessness has been modified in a later publication by Abramson, Seligman, and Teasdale (1978). In this work, the authors suggest that the range and the permanence of helplessness deficits in new situations depend on the attribution of the control loss to causes varying in stability, internality, and globality. Causes can be stable or unstable, internal or external, and global or specific. Different types of attribution influence individuals' expectations of future helplessness and the possible development of a learned helplessness syndrome (Abramson et al., 1978, p. 49).

Following the theory of learned helplessness, the enduring nonapplication of the controllability principle potentially directs managers into a state of passiveness (Hayes, 1992, p. 159; Hiroto, 1974, p. 192). Such a state of passiveness is the result of managers' belief that there is no connection between their actions and their measured performance. As a consequence, not only managers' ability to learn nonelementary cause-effect relationships deteriorates, but also their use of initiative is likely to decrease (Choudhury, 1986, p. 192).

In literature on the theory of learned helplessness, psychologists often make reference to a related theory, namely reactance theory (Brehm, 1966; Brehm & Brehm, 1981). This theory postulates that psychological reactance as a motivational state of arousal occurs when individuals perceive some personal freedom being eliminated or threatened with elimination. The fear of losing further freedoms sparks this arousal and motivates efforts to reestablish the threatened freedom. What makes reactance theory worth mentioning in the context of this study is its referral to a lack of controllability as a "theoretically equivalent to eliminations of freedom" (Brehm & Brehm, 1981, p. 61). Unlike the theory of learned helplessness, reactance theory predicts active and sometimes even aggressive efforts to regain control rather than passive states of helplessness. In the light of these supposedly opposing predictions, the Wortman and Brehm (1975) model attempts to integrate reactance and helplessness. It suggests that reactance should only appear under a specific set of conditions and, in the course of time, will cease once the opportunity to control is unequivocally eliminated (Wortman & Brehm, 1975, pp. 306-317).

2.3.4 Justifications Based on Expectancy Theory

Apart from learned helplessness, management accounting scholars often call for the application of the controllability principle based on motivational grounds (Frow et al., 2005, p. 289; Hirst, 1983a; Merchant, 1998, p. 572; Modell & Lee, 2001, p. 192). Above all, expectancy theory (Vroom, 1964) is cited when arguing that managers might lose their motivation if they are confronted with uncontrollable factors in their performance evaluation. This theory, which is sometimes also referred to as valence-instrumentality-expectancy theory, is based on three variables: (a) expectancy – the perceived probability that exerting a given amount of effort leads to performance, (b) instrumentality – the belief that one outcome (first level outcome, e.g. a high performance level) leads to another outcome (second level outcome, e.g. a reward), and (c) valence – the degree to which a particular outcome is attractive or unattractive to individuals (Vroom, 1964, pp. 14-45).

Vroom (1964) suggests that individuals' beliefs about expectancy, instrumentality, and valence interact psychologically to create a motivational force. According to Vroom (1964, pp. 27-28), the product of the three variables represents individuals' motivation. Individuals hence elect to pursue effort levels that they believe will maximize the subjectively expected utility (Muchinsky, 2006, pp. 394-395).

In a later publication, Vroom (1970, p. 213) relates his basic ideas to control beliefs:

> The effectiveness of any system in which rewards and punishments are contingent on specified performance outcomes appears to be dependent on the degree of control which the individual has over these performance outcomes. The increment in performance to be expected from an increase in the extent to which the individual is rewarded for favorable results and/or punished for unfavorable results is directly related to the extent to which the individual can control the results of his performance.

Combining Vroom's (1964) expectancy theory and his elaboration on control beliefs (1970), Ronen and Livingstone (1975) explain why the controllability principle should constitute the basis for performance evaluation. First, they argue that only managerial tasks which are perceived as controllable are likely to be associated with a high expectancy of goal-directed behavior to accomplish the managers' objectives. The same reasoning can be found in the work of McNally (1980, p. 166) and Huffman and Cain (2000, p. 822) who agree that confronting managers with controllable tasks should result in a higher expectancy of obtaining attractive outcomes. Second, performing tasks that are perceived as controllable is also thought to be associated with a high intrinsic valence (Ronen & Livingstone, 1975, p. 681). Under both conditions, managers' motivation to exert effort in their job will tend to increase because they perceive the controllability principle to be applied.

Similar effects are proposed by related theories of motivation. The Porter-Lawler (1968) model of work motivation represents an extension of Vroom's (1964) expectancy theory. It provides a more complex explanation of the relationship between effort, performance, and satisfaction since it integrates additional variables which are supposed to contribute to an understanding of individuals' motivation (Kesselman, Hagen, & Wherry, 1974, p. 570). The model recognizes that individuals may possess varying abilities, traits, and perceptions hindering them from achieving high levels of performance (Porter & Lawler, 1968, pp. 22-25). In their model, Porter and Lawler integrate a variable called "perceived effort-reward probability" (Porter & Lawler, 1968, p. 19) which refers to individuals' judgment of the probability that differential rewards depend upon differential effort levels. If individuals are facing uncontrollable influence on their measured performance, their perceived effort-reward probability and consequently their motivation are expected to decline (Frow et al., 2005, p. 289; Lawler & Rhode, 1976, p. 97).

2.3.5 Justifications Based on Justice Theory

Justice theory, which is also subsumed under motivational theory[5], represents the type of theory which management accounting scholars most typically refer to when arguing for the application of the controllability principle (Atkinson et al., 1997, p. 84; Hartmann, 2000, p. 475; Merchant, 1989, p. 87; Shields & Waller, 1988, p. 583). This goes back to the seminal work of Hopwood (1972, p. 158) who writes that "for a fair evaluation, the controllable component of the reports should be isolated". It seems to be generally acknowledged that the degree of applying the controllability principle is an important determinant of managers' perceived fairness (Giraud et al., 2004, p. 3).

Justice theory explores individuals' perceptions of several justice (or fairness) dimensions whereby the terms justice and fairness are often used interchangeably in literature (Cohen-Charash & Spector, 2001, p. 279; Giraud et al., 2008, p. 34; Horvath & Andrews, 2007, p. 204). According to the theory, there is not one single source of justice. Scholars in the field of organizational justice rather differentiate between (a) distributive, (b) procedural, and (c) interactional justice (Cohen-Charash & Spector, 2001, pp. 280-282; Colquitt, 2001, p. 386; Greenberg, Colquitt, & Zapata-Phelan, 2005, pp. 3-11). It is assumed that individuals' motivation and effort levels depend on their perceptions regarding the protection of these different justice dimensions (Kaplan & Atkinson, 1998, p. 682; Stewart & Brown, 2009, p. 412).

Distributive justice which is grounded in equity theory (Adams, 1963; 1965) deals with the "discrepancies between a man's job inputs and job outcomes" (Adams, 1963, p. 435). Accordingly, its focus is on individuals' judgment of the fairness of outcomes and their subsequent reactions to these outcomes (Cohen-Charash & Spector, 2001, p. 280). MCSs are commonly assumed to be a major determinant of organizational outcomes (e.g. the allocation of resources) and are hence likely to influence managers' perceptions of distributive justice in the organization (Huffman & Cain, 2001, p. 592; Lindquist, 1995, p. 124; Milkovich, Newman, & Milkovich, 2008, p. 72). Distributive justice is judged by comparing outcomes to some referents. Referents may be either interpersonal or intrapersonal. When interpersonal referents are used, the ratio of individuals' inputs and outcomes is compared to the same ratio for others, e.g. colleagues. Alternatively, referents can be intrapersonal which implies the application of a ratio obtained by individuals in an alternative situation (Goodman & Friedman, 1975, p. 155; Mowday, 1991, pp. 124-125; Summers & DeNisi, 1990, p. 498).

---

5 Strictly speaking, agency theory (see chapters B1.1.1.1 and B2.3.1) is a motivational theory as well because it prescribes the motivation of agents with the help of contractual arrangements (Stewart & Brown, 2009, pp. 415-416).

Unlike distributive justice, procedural justice (Leventhal, 1980; Thibaut & Walker, 1975) does not refer to the fairness of outcomes, but to the fairness of the formal procedures by which outcomes are determined (Thibaut & Walker, 1975, p. 3). Again, MCSs play an important part because they embody organizational procedures for participation in decision-making, resource allocation, or calculation of financial results and thus affect managers' perceptions of procedural justice (Lau & Tan, 2006, p. 174; Lau, Wong, & Eggleton, 2008, pp. 130-133; Lind & Tyler, 1988, pp. 129, 212-213). Such perceptions then lead to reactions toward the organization. When the process leading to a certain outcome is perceived to be unfair, individuals' reactions are supposed to be directed at the entire organization rather than at merely the outcome. This differs from the predictions made for distributive justice which emphasize outcome-focused rather than organization-focused consequences (Cohen-Charash & Spector, 2001, p. 281).

Interactional justice (Bies & Moag, 1986; Bies & Shapiro, 1987; Tyler & Bies, 1990), an extension of procedural justice and sometimes regarded as the social side of justice, represents the third dimension of justice (Ambrose, 2002, p. 804; Greenberg et al., 2005, p. 29). It pertains to interpersonal aspects of fairness and, more specifically, to individuals' perceptions of whether they are treated with dignity, honesty, and respect during organizational processes (Tyler & Bies, 1990, pp. 88-94). One of the processes which are critical from an interactional justice perspective is the process of performance evaluation between individuals and their superiors (Cropanzano, Prehar, & Chen, 2002, p. 328; Masterson, Lewis, Goldman, & Taylor, 2000, p. 746). Because perceptions of interactional justice are determined by the interpersonal behavior of superiors, interactional justice is first and foremost concerned with individuals' reactions toward these persons (Cohen-Charash & Spector, 2001, p. 282).

Altogether, individuals' reactions and behavior at work are predicted to be strongly influenced by assessments of distributive, procedural, and interactional justice (Greenberg, 1990, pp. 403-412). Following Giraud et al. (2008, p. 35), the typology of distributive, procedural, and interactional justice also provides the "basis for a deeper discussion of the relationship between the controllability principle and managerial motivation". The application of the controllability principle is supposed to be related to all three dimensions of justice. First, eliminating the influence of uncontrollable factors may increase input-outcome ratios and hence managers' perceived distributive fairness. Second, the controllability principle is commonly implemented through the use of procedures which aim to neutralize the effects of uncontrollable factors on managers' performance. A pronounced emphasis on fair organizational procedures is therefore inherent to the application of the controllability principle. Third, performance evaluation takes place within the frame of relationships between the managers assessed and their superiors. The superiors' attitude toward the controllability principle and their willingness to eliminate uncontrollable factors hence influence interactional fairness as perceived by the managers (Giraud et al., 2008, pp. 35-36). In short, the principle's application is likely to have positive effects on managers' fairness perceptions with perceived fairness regulating their motivation and behavior.

3. The Application of the Controllability Principle

Even though the preceding chapters document that there are strong theoretical arguments for the application of the controllability principle in the design of MCSs, empirical research reveals that the principle is not always implemented in a strict manner. The following chapters B3.1 to B3.3 review existing studies which examine the principle's application in company practice. Chapter B3.4 summarizes the key findings and attempts to detect underlying patterns which explain the limited application of the principle in practice.

3.1 General Remarks on the Applicability of the Controllability Principle

As Scapens (1985, p. 3) notes, there are often differences between the conventional wisdom of management accounting as portrayed in textbooks and management accounting practice. Many scholars in the field agree that the same goes for to the application of the controllability principle (Drury & El-Shishini, 2005, p. 20; Frow et al., 2005, p. 272; Hartmann, 2000, p. 472; Modell, 1997, p. 314; Otley, 1994, p. 290; Schäffer & Pelster, 2007, p. 430). There is a "paradox" (Hirst, 1983a, p. 36) or an "apparent contradiction" (McNally, 1980, p. 167) between the importance of the controllability principle in theory and its application in practice. It seems as if breaches of the principle do not represent rare exceptions in company practice; it is rather "common, even typical, for managers to be held accountable for areas over which they have little, or even no, control" (Merchant, 1987, p. 316).

The equivocal relevance of the controllability principle for the design of MCSs is often related to high levels of uncertainty and complexity in modern business environments (Atkinson et al., 2007, p. 588; Choudhury, 1986, pp. 196-197; Hartmann, 2000, p. 473; Merchant & Manzoni, 1989, p. 541). Giraud et al. (2004, p. 7) suggest that noncompliance with conditions of low uncertainty and complexity are important explanations for the nonapplication of the principle in many organizations. Complexity implies that revenue and cost items are most often jointly earned or incurred. Only very few items are under the sole influence of one manager. Rather they are subject to various interdependencies. Costs of direct materials, for example, can be influenced by a purchasing manager, but such costs are also dependent on market conditions which are beyond the manager's control. The quantities used may be determined by a production manager, but the quantities used also depend on the quality of materials purchased (Atkinson et al., 2007, pp. 588-589; Bhimani et al., 2008, pp. 488-489). Obviously, complexity hinders the application of the controllability principle because the possibility of singling out individual controllability becomes severely limited (Marginson & Ogden, 2005b, p. 49).

Next to complexity, it is argued that uncertainty causes difficulties in the application of the controllability principle (Besson, Löning, & Mendoza, 2008, pp. 4-5; Marginson & McAulay, 2001, p. 13; Modell, 1997, p. 324). Thompson (1967, p. 159) even claims that uncertainty is the "fundamental problem" of organizations. Uncertainty not only makes it difficult to ex ante formalize work using job descriptions, standards, and fixed procedures (Griffin, Neal, & Parker, 2007, p. 329), it also hampers superiors' ability to judge ex post whether good (bad) performance is the result of managerial effort or simply of (un)lucky circumstances. According to Hartmann (2000, pp. 471-473), especially business settings which are characterized by high uncertainty pose challenges to the application of the controllability principle because here the risk of being held accountable for uncontrollable factors is particularly high. Seen from this angle, the application of the principle may seem particularly desirable in uncertain situations. However, at the same time, the strict application of the principle appears not to be possible since especially in uncertain situations pinpointing individual controllability is difficult. The apparently limited feasibility of applying the controllability principle in cases where it may be most needed (Hartmann, 2000, p. 473) adds up to the contradictory nature of the principle as mentioned in the beginning of this chapter.

Increases in complexity and uncertainty are often attributed to changes in competition, market conditions, technology, and economy (Scott & Tiessen, 1999, p. 263). Several authors believe that continuous and turbulent changes are one of the main characteristics of modern business contexts (Beer, Voelpel, Leibold, & Tekie, 2005, p. 446; Dutton, Ashford, O'Neill, Hayes, & Wierba, 1997, p. 407; Eisenhardt, Kahwajy, & Bourgeois, 1997, pp. 77-78). These changes have resulted in many pressures on the management of organizations and the design of MCSs (Spicer, 1992, p. 1). They have led to diverse organizational developments such as front line empowerment, greater interdependence of units, more frequent mixings of both centralized and decentralized approaches to management, greater use of multi-functional management teams, or more process-oriented organizational structures (Hopwood & Young, 1998, p. 357; Østergren & Stensaker, 2008, p. 8). Some of these developments also affect organizational arrangements of accountability. In this respect, Frese and Fay (2001, p. 139), along with Holmström and Milgrom (1994, p. 989), suggest that there is a general trend in modern workplaces towards greater individual accountability. Messner (2009, p. 918) also observes that "calls for greater accountability from managers . . . are regularly voiced these days". Frow et al. (2005, p. 272) go one step further and predict that "managers are more rather than less likely to have accountability without controllability" due to contemporary changes in organizational realities.

3.2 A Classification of Uncontrollable Factors

Increases in complexity and uncertainty make the controllability principle more difficult to apply (Giraud et al., 2004, p. 8; Hartmann, 2007, p. 160). Uncontrollable influence on managers' performance appears to mainly stem from these two phenomena, which is why complexity and uncertainty represent the starting point for the following, more profound discussion of uncontrollable factors. In previous literature on the controllability principle, several authors (Choudhury, 1986; Demski, 1976; Drury, 2005; Drury & El-Shishini, 2005; Giraud et al., 2008; Merchant, 1989; 1998) have suggested classifications of uncontrollable factors.

<table>
<tr><th>Source</th><th colspan="6">Classification</th></tr>
<tr><td>Demski (1976)</td><td colspan="2">Actions of other managers</td><td colspan="2">Random factors</td><td colspan="2">Future-period consequences</td></tr>
<tr><td>Choudhury (1986)</td><td colspan="2">Actions of other managers</td><td colspan="2">Uncontrollable events</td><td colspan="2">Effects from past decisions</td></tr>
<tr><td>Merchant (1989)</td><td>Decisions made by personnel at higher organizational levels</td><td colspan="2">Unexpected, non recurring events</td><td colspan="2">Economic factors</td><td>Competitive factors</td></tr>
<tr><td>Merchant (1998), Drury (2005)</td><td colspan="2">Interdependence</td><td colspan="2">Acts of nature</td><td colspan="2">Economic and competitive factors</td></tr>
<tr><td>Drury and El-Shishini (2005)</td><td>Interdependence</td><td colspan="2">Uncontrollable costs of common resources</td><td colspan="2">General and administrative costs</td><td>Environmental factors</td></tr>
<tr><td>Giraud et al. (2008)</td><td colspan="2">Horizontal inter-dependencies</td><td colspan="2">Vertical inter-dependencies</td><td colspan="2">External factors</td></tr>
</table>

Table 4: Classifications of Uncontrollable Factors in Prior Literature

Demski (1976) provides an early approach to the differentiation between uncontrollable factors. He divides such factors into three basic categories. The first category refers to the influence from actions of other managers. The second category covers random factors that are essentially beyond managers' control. The third category is applicable to multi-period settings where current-period assessments of future effects may have an influence on the evaluation of managerial performance (Demski, 1976, pp. 231-232). Depending on the type of uncontrollable factors, Demski (1976) comes to different conclusions whether to make adjustments for these factors or not. Based on analytical models that focus on the distribution of risk between managers and their superiors, it is stated that the elimination of intermanager effects may preclude desirable risk-sharing arrangements whereas the inclusion of future effects in the multi-period setting is not necessary to support desirable risk-sharing arrangements (Demski, 1976, p. 242).

Choudhury (1986) builds on Demski's (1976) classification and argues that each type of uncontrollable factors entails a different sort of controllability filter. Uncontrollable influence from other managers' actions necessitates manager separation filters. According to Choudhury (1986), such manager separation filters should be designed not only to isolate one manager's performance from one another's but also to exclude the effects of decisions made by the manager's superior. Next, the author proposes the application of event separation filters when uncontrollable events come up. Finally, uncontrollable influence from past decisions not made by the manager him- or herself calls for the use of period separation filters (Choudhury, 1986, pp. 192-194).

In his often-cited work on the controllability principle, Merchant (1989) develops a further classification of uncontrollable factors. He distinguishes between four basic types of such factors: (a) decisions made (or approved) by personnel at higher organizational levels, (b) unexpected, non recurring events, (c) economic factors, and (d) competitive factors. According to the author's empirical investigation, company practice in adjusting for uncontrollable influence varies depending on the type of uncontrollable factors. Whereas a few companies in Merchant's (1989) sample adjust for the effects of decisions made at higher organizational levels, adjustments for the effects of economic factors are very rare (Merchant, 1989, pp. 119-126).

Merchant's (1989) classification has served as a basis for subsequent approaches to distinguish between uncontrollable factors. A later work of Merchant (1998) himself and the work of Drury (2005) both rely on a typology of uncontrollable factors which resembles Merchant's (1989) original classification. It categorizes uncontrollable factors into three types. The first type of uncontrollable influence is caused by interdependence. The authors thereby divide interdependencies into different subcategories. Pooled interdependencies exist where a company's departments use common resources or resource pools. Sequential interdependencies arise when the outputs of one department are the inputs of another department. Reciprocal interdependencies are bi-directional sequential interdependencies. Additionally, interventions from higher-level management are mentioned as another type of interdependencies. The second type of uncontrollable factors includes acts of nature such as accidents or thefts. The third type of uncontrollable factors in Merchant's (1998) and Drury's (2005) classification refers to economic and competitive factors which are external to the company (Drury, 2005, pp. 313-316; Merchant, 1998, pp. 573-575).

A further classification of uncontrollable factors can be found in the work of Drury and El-Shishini (2005). The authors distinguish between (a) effects of divisional interdependencies, (b) uncontrollable costs of common resources, (c) general and administrative costs, and (d) uncontrollable environmental factors such as changing economic conditions, competitors' actions, or business climates (Drury & El-Shishini, 2005, p. 6). The empirical results of Drury and El-Shishini's (2005) study suggest that companies apply the controllability principle for some factors but not for others (Drury & El-Shishini, 2005, p. 44) – an insight which is shared by Merchant (1987; 1989) and which is difficult to explain (Merchant, 1987, p. 335).

In the light of similar, however distinct previous approaches to classify uncontrollable factors, Giraud et al. (2008, p. 36) attempt to integrate these typologies into one framework. They propose to differentiate between three types of uncontrollable factors: horizontal interdependencies (i.e. decisions made by other managers in the company), vertical or hierarchical interdependencies (i.e. decisions made by superiors), and external factors (i.e. unforeseen changes in the economic and competitive environment, natural catastrophes, etc.). Since Giraud et al.'s (2008) integration appears to provide the most recent and comprehensive classification of uncontrollable factors, this work applies their approach in the organization of the following chapters.

3.3 Empirical Evidence on the Application of the Controllability Principle

Using Giraud et al.'s (2008) classification of uncontrollable factors, the following provides an overview of prior empirical research on the application of the controllability principle. Chapter B3.3.1 covers those studies that relate the principle's application to horizontal and vertical interdependencies. Chapter B3.3.2 outlines prior research on uncontrollable external factors. A chronological list[6] of all empirical studies examining the application of the controllability principle in company practice can be found in Table 5.

6 The empirical studies in this list have been identified with the help of a database search (in EBSCO and Sciencedirect) for "controllability" in either title, abstract, key words, or full text. All search results in management, organizational behavior, (applied) psychology, and accounting journals have been scanned whether they report findings of empirical research related to the application of the controllability principle. Additionally, all monographs, (edited) books, working papers, etc. which are referred to in these journal publications have been investigated in terms of their relevance for this work.

Study and year of origin	Sample	Application of the controllability principle is complicated due to...		
		...horizontal interdependencies	**...vertical interdependencies**	**...external uncontrollable factors**
Vancil (1979)	Profit center managers from 291 manufacturing companies in the US	✓	✓	
Fremgen and Liao (1981)	123 financial and accounting executives from divisionalized companies in the US		✓	
Hirst (1983a; 1983b)	111 Australian managers participating in tertiary education classes		✓	
Eccles (1986)	144 managers from 13 large companies in the US	✓	✓	
Waller and Chow (1985)	61 students of an upper-level cost accounting course in the US		✓	
Antle and Smith (1986)	117 top managers from 39 companies in the US	✓		
Dent (1987)	Functional managers from a large IT company in the US	✓		
Maher (1987)	Managers from five large, manufacturing-dominated companies in the US	✓		
Merchant (1987)	General managers from three divisionalized corporations in the US		✓	✓
Shields and Waller (1988)	110 students enrolled in accounting courses in the US		✓	
Merchant (1989) / Merchant and Manzoni (1989)	Managers of 54 profit centers in 12 corporations in the US		✓	✓
Ramadan (1989)	120 executives, controllers, and accountants from divisionalized companies in the UK		✓	
Shields, Chow, and Whittington (1989)	121 students enrolled in finance courses in the US		✓	
Gibbons and Murphy (1990)	1,668 CEOs from 1,049 publicly listed corporations in the US	✓		

Study and year of origin *(cont.)*	Sample	Application of the controllability principle is complicated due to... …horizontal interdependencies	…vertical interdependencies	…external uncontrollable factors
Otley (1990)	Managers from the British Coal Corporation		✓	✓
Skinner (1990)	114 controllers and accountants from diversified companies in Australia and New Zealand		✓	
Frederickson (1992)	36 first-year MBA students from a US university		✓	
Ueno and Wu (1993)	70 (US) and 149 (Japanese) corporate controllers and managers from large manufacturing companies		✓	
McNair and Carr (1994)	Managers from nine companies which have recently introduced a new manufacturing technique	✓		
Ugras (1994)	159 controllers from manufacturing and service companies in the US		✓	
Bushman et al. (1995)	Top managers from 246 large companies in the US		✓	
Merchant, Chow, and Wu (1995)	Profit center managers from two US and two Taiwanese companies		✓	
Bushman et al. (1996)	Top managers from 396 large companies in the US		✓	
Moon and Fitzgerald (1996)	Head office and depot managers from TNT in the UK	✓	✓	
Ittner et al. (1997)	317 top managers from US companies		✓	
Keating (1997)	78 division managers from US corporations		✓	
Modell (1997)	Employees of a dental practice under county council governance in Sweden	✓		✓
Ghosh and Lusch (2000)	204 store managers from a retail company in the US		✓	✓

Study and year of origin *(cont.)*	Sample	Application of the controllability principle is complicated due to… ...horizontal interdependencies	...vertical interdependencies	...external uncontrollable factors
Huffman and Cain (2000)	92 sales force executives (survey 1) and 117 salespeople (survey 2) from US companies			✓
Huffman and Cain (2001)	156 undergraduate students from a US university			✓
Marginson and McAulay (2001)	125 executive managers from a large UK communications company		✓	
Modell and Lee (2001)	57 department heads from one of the largest hospitals in Norway		✓	✓
Abernethy et al. (2004)	78 divisional managers from publicly listed companies in the Netherlands	✓	✓	
Budding (2004)	19 managers from Dutch municipalities	✓		✓
Malina and Selto (2004)	Employees from a large equipment manufacturing company in the US	✓		
Bourguignon and Chiapello (2005)	Managers from the retail division of a French textile group	✓		✓
Drury and El-Shishini (2005)	124 finance directors, controllers, and accountants from divisionalized companies in the UK		✓	
Frow et al. (2005)	26 managers from a US-based multinational corporation operating in the technology sector	✓		
Toms (2005)	Managers from companies in the British cotton textile industry			✓
Bento and White (2006)	64 responsibility center managers from different companies and industries		✓	
Bouwens and Van Lent (2006)	CEOs and chief human resources officers from 151 Dutch companies		✓	
Bouwens and Van Lent (2007)	140 business unit managers from 125 Dutch companies	✓	✓	

Study and year of origin *(cont.)*	Sample	Application of the controllability principle is complicated due to... ...horizontal interdependencies	...vertical interdependencies	...external uncontrollable factors
Larmande and Ponssard (2007)	Managers from a multinational corporation operating in the construction industry			✓
Pelster (2007)	71 managers (survey participants) and 16 managers (interview participants) from three companies in Germany	✓	✓	✓
Simons (2007)	Senior managers from 102 US companies		✓	
Giraud et al. (2004; 2008)	265 business unit and functional managers (alumni from a French business school)	✓	✓	✓
Van Veen-Dirks (in press)	84 production managers from industrial companies in the Netherlands		✓	

Table 5: Empirical Studies Investigating the Application of the Controllability Principle

3.3.1 Organizational Interdependencies

In accordance with Van de Ven, Delbecq, and Koenig (1976, p. 325), this work defines interdependence broadly as "the extent to which . . . personnel are dependent upon one another to perform their individual jobs" (for more recent however almost identical definitions of interdependence, see Griffin et al. (2007, pp. 329-330) or Dierdorff and Morgeson (2007, p. 1230)). It is claimed that most "modern organizations . . . are characterized by a high degree of interdependence" (Graen, 1976, p. 1214) and the interdependent nature of work is assumed to further increase in the future (Griffin et al., 2007, pp. 327-328; Wong et al., 2007, p. 285). Managing these interdependencies represents a central component of managerial work (Wong et al., 2007, p. 287), as evidenced by the significant portion of time managers spend in communicating and coordinating information to other managers (Ancona & Caldwell, 1992, p. 634; Kellogg, Orlikowski, & Yates, 2006, p. 42; Perlow, 1999, p. 57). However, organizational interdependencies have a detrimental impact on the effectiveness of MCSs (Choudhury, 1986, p. 191; Merchant, 1982, pp. 54-55). Interdependencies – irrespective of whether they are horizontal or vertical – represent a barrier to individual controllability because they make it difficult to assess managers' contribution to overall results (Ronen & Livingstone, 1975, p. 681) or, put more generally, because they add noise to performance measurement (Abernethy et al., 2004, p. 549).

3.3.1.1 Horizontal Interdependencies

Horizontal interdependencies complicate the application of the controllability principle because they imply that certain parameters which may be important for managers to achieve their targets are under the control of others in the organization (Gist & Mitchell, 1992, p. 196). Vancil (1979) provides an early study which portrays horizontal interdependencies as uncontrollable factors that managers are frequently confronted with. In his investigation of decentralization among US manufacturing companies, he explores the degree of interdependencies between profit center managers of different organizational units. According to Vancil's (1979) empirical results, such interdependencies have a considerable impact on profit center managers' performance, which tempts the author to state that "the notion of truly independent profit centers is rare if not absent in the US manufacturing firms" (Vancil, 1979, p. 169). In particular, Vancil (1979) reports that profit center managers only have physical custody of some of the resources needed to manufacture or sell their products. They must also use resources that are physically located either in other profit centers or in corporate headquarter units which makes them dependent on these entities. For example when profit center managers want to implement changes that will improve the quality of their products, they must persuade other managers (those who have functional authority over the resources that will be affected) to modify their operating routines in order to accommodate to the proposed changes.

Horizontal interdependencies between buying and selling profit centers are also discussed in Eccles's (1986) work. Based on intensive field investigation, the author develops a typology of basic organizational types. One type of organization, which Eccles (1986, p. 277) refers to as the collaborative organization, is characterized by a high degree of interdependencies between the organization's subunits. According to Eccles (1986, p. 278), such a high degree of interdependencies is accompanied by an "excess of responsibility over authority" for the subunit managers. With regard to the nature of these interdependencies, Eccles (1986) finds that interdependencies are often symbiotic, which means that gains or losses in the outcomes of one profit center result in gains or losses for the other. Eccles (1986) mentions the example of internal transactions where standard cost transfers are used and volume variances are not allocated. In this case, when the buying profit center experiences reduced demand for the final product, it uses less of the intermediate product which directly affects the performance of the selling profit center (Eccles, 1986, pp. 205-206). Since such interdependencies have strong effects on profit center managers' financial performance, Eccles (1986, p. 206) claims that the degree of interdependencies is directly related to the amount of conflict between the units.

However, simultaneous emphasis on interdependence and responsibility for subunit outcomes is reported to not necessarily produce dysfunctional disputes. Rather, Eccles (1986, p. 282) finds that conflict is often regarded as something positive. In many places, corporate management seems to have realized that there are several advantages of confronting profit center managers with horizontal interdependencies. First, it is found that conflicts between the units can lead to improved performance by making one profit center more responsive to the needs of others (Eccles, 1986, pp. 81, 204). Within structural interdependencies, there is pressure on the profit center managers who must resolve their multiple perspectives on the efficient use of resources. Second, top management may benefit from conflicts between the profit centers because they provide a useful and cheap source of information. Eccles (1986) exemplifies that if a selling profit center claims that the price for an internal transaction is too low, it may supply corporate management with information about its contracts with potential external customers or about the prices its competitors are obtaining. Third, Eccles (1986) reports that conflicts enable corporate management to use each involved profit center to discipline and exercise some control over other centers. Rather than intervening directly to ensure that profit centers are taking steps to achieve agreed-upon objectives, corporate management may rely on interdependencies to provide an incentive for the profit centers to do so (Eccles, 1986, p. 215).

Further empirical evidence on the uncontrollable influence that originates from horizontal interdependencies comes from case studies conducted by Dent (1987), Bourguignon and Chiapello (2005), and Frow et al. (2005). In Eurocorp, the company under Dent's (1987) investigation, the author finds that manufacturing, development, and sales units are profoundly dependent on each other. All three types of units are not treated as profit centers in the conventional sense of buying and selling to each other. Rather they are jointly held accountable for total corporate profit. According to Dent (1987), such overlapping accountabilities are pervasive at Eurocorp in that the performance of development unit managers also reflects the performance of manufacturing and selling units. Vice versa, sales unit managers' results include the performance of development and manufacturing units. This is due to Eurocorp's cost sharing system. Sales and support costs incurred in the company's sales regions are apportioned to development unit managers in the measurement of product profit. Likewise, product development costs are apportioned to sales managers in the regions when measuring their territory profit (Dent, 1987, pp. 131-135). Although Dent (1987) admits that the design of such a MCS produces irritation and ambiguity among the managers involved, he argues that there is a specific rationale behind the implementation of such a system: Senior management wants to activate managers' informal interactions in the company and lateral flows of information. Dent (1987, p. 137) summarizes managers' situation at Eurocorp as follows:

> Responsibility exceeds authority; managers depend on others to achieve performance objectives, and spend much of their time coaxing other units to act on their behalf. This creates tensions in the organization, encouraging managers to think beyond their functional tasks and to manage laterally. The atmosphere is competitive, but the structure of accountability fosters an interest in bringing diverse activities into alignment.

Bourguignon and Chiapello (2005) report about horizontal interdependencies which resemble those in Dent's (1987) study. In the retail division of a French textile group, production managers' performance is constrained by the activities of sales managers. Bourguignon and Chiapello (2005) find that when the company's overall business activity goes down, the production managers' bottom line is a loss which has a direct impact on the amount of their variable pay, even though the drop in activity is attributable to the sales managers, not to the production managers (Bourguignon & Chiapello, 2005, p. 680).

A case study by Frow et al. (2005) provides further insights into horizontal interdependencies and suggests organizational arrangements for the management of such interdependencies. At Astoria, a US-based multinational corporation which is Frow et al.'s (2005) research site, the tensions between the need to make people accountable and the simultaneous lack of individual controllability are resolved through the use of "a broadly based approach to control" (Frow et al., 2005, p. 280). The approach chosen includes the implementation of a performance excellence process (PEP) which is aimed at directing and coordinating managers' decisions and behaviors in line with overall corporate objectives (Frow et al., 2005, p. 277). Even though the PEP formally enforces individual responsibilities at Astoria, it allows and supports at the same time the identification of interdependencies and their informal management. That way, the confrontation of managers with uncontrollable interdependencies does not detract from individual responsibilities, but signals the importance of exerting influence over other managers so that individuals achieve their targets. The majority of the managers interviewed by Frow et al. (2005) indicate that relatively few, if any, of their responsibilities can truly be regarded as individual. It is rather perceived to be an integral managerial task to determine where influence over others is required and to negotiate how it should be exerted. Influencing the behavior of others appears as part of the challenge of managing (Frow et al., 2005, pp. 280-283). Frow et al. (2005) provide several examples of the successful management of horizontal interdependencies at Astoria. One product manager who is involved in the development of new products is reported to be heavily dependent on a variety of related business units in terms of their deliverables. However, these uncontrollable interdependencies do not lead to negative feelings with the manager, he rather feels that it is his job to "guide desired behaviour, particularly with respect to managing the co-operation and co-ordination required to complete tasks or individual projects" (Frow et al., 2005, p. 281).

Frow et al.'s (2005) indications on the successful management of horizontal inter-dependencies stem from a single research site. They are not reflected in later cross-sectional studies. Whereas Frow et al. (2005) suggest that managers accept uncontrollable interdependencies and are thereby encouraged to cooperate with others, the work of Pelster (2007) provides divergent results from a survey on the application of the controllability principle. Pelster (2007, pp. 256-257) finds that the managers in his sample predominantly tend to see horizontal interdependencies as violations of the controllability principle, which makes them reduce their effort in the job. Additionally, a large-scale study conducted by Giraud et al. (2008, p. 38) reveals a positive relationship between the impact of horizontal interdependencies and the degree to which managers want this impact to be neutralized. Pelster's (2007) and Giraud et al.'s (2008) studies demonstrate that, from the managers' perspective, horizontal interdependencies seem to be associated with unfavorable consequences which is why managers generally prefer their elimination in performance appraisals.

Empirical insights into horizontal interdependencies can also be found in research on teams and team-based work structures. Team-based work structures are inherently related to horizontal interdependencies (Dierdorff & Morgeson, 2007, p. 1230; Scott & Tiessen, 1999, pp. 266-267) and, according to Frink and Klimoski (1998, p. 4), the popularity of these structures poses challenges to traditional systems of accountability. A study by McNair and Carr (1994) indicates that horizontal interdependencies and the reliance on teams may impede the application of the controllability principle. McNair and Carr (1994) investigate the implementation of new manufacturing techniques (i.e. just in time (JIT) and total quality management (TQM) approaches) at nine companies and their effect on the design of MCSs. It is found that the use of these new techniques often requires the introduction of team-based work structures. This introduction is in some places paralleled by the recognition that individualized responsibilities do not appear to be a viable basis for management control any longer. McNair and Carr (1994) refer to problems of controllability at the level of the individual managers. Not only that managers' contributions to team-based outcomes are unclear, even more importantly managers do no longer have control over key aspects of their job, such as the pace and the structure of work. According to the authors' observations, responsibility is therefore redefined from the individual level to the team level at several companies (McNair & Carr, 1994, pp. 88-103).

Moon and Fitzgerald (1996) provide a related study on horizontal interdependencies. In their case study with depot managers from TNT (which is the UK market leader in the distribution of parcels), they find that the network nature of TNT's business operations implies high interdependencies between the depots. The depot which collects a particular parcel is not necessarily the depot which subsequently delivers the parcel. Business is hence generated through the collection of parcels for which the collecting depot receives the revenue, but which may in fact be difficult to deliver and the costs of which have to born by the delivering depot. Such business processes impact the profit statements of both depots, with the company's MCS not formally adjusting for these horizontal interdependencies. As a consequence, informal discussions between depot managers are used to manage these issues. Organizational arrangements are in place which facilitate such an informal management at the depot level (Moon & Fitzgerald, 1996, p. 454).

Relying on empirical observations in the public sector, Modell (1997) reports about the uncontrollable impact of horizontal interdependencies. In his case study with a dental practice in Sweden, he finds that several of its clinics are far from being independent responsibility centers, but have to rely on the decisions and processes in other clinics. For example the clinic for prosthetics is mentioned as being dependent on the clinic for specialist dentistry and its administrative routines (e.g. planning activities). According to Modell (1997), it is above all specialization that gives rise to the complex interdependencies between the clinics. However, even though the management of these interdependencies may seem inefficient, the author warns against integration of the clinics into larger units since this might result in even more time-consuming administration for the clinic managers (Modell, 1997, pp. 325-326).

A second case study in the public sector which is concerned with horizontal interdependencies is conducted by Budding (2004). The author provides insights from interviews with municipality managers on how they cope with new public management (NPM) concepts being introduced to Dutch governmental organizations. According to Budding (2004, pp. 286-288), Dutch municipalities have changed their management and internal organization since the mid-1980s, which has placed more emphasis on measuring the output of subunits and holding their managers accountable. Such an increase in individual responsibilities is problematic because, for the achievement of their performance objectives, managers depend upon the acceptance of their position and responsibilities by other people in the organization (Budding, 2004, p. 294). This complicates the application of the controllability principle, which appears to be mainly relevant in public sector settings where individual responsibilities have often not been part of concepts for organizational control before.

Horizontal interdependencies are also discussed in management accounting research on RPE. Companies often tend to have a competitive element in that managers' performance is not viewed in isolation but in relation to their peers. According to Choudhury (1986, p. 195), this is a "violation of the controllability principle although it is rarely noted as such in the literature"[7]. The empirical works of Antle and Smith (1986), Maher (1987), Gibbons and Murphy (1990), and Malina and Selto (2004) all provide at least partial support that, in company practice, managers are evaluated and compensated relatively to their peers. Evidence from an experimental study by Frederickson (1992) reveals that the use of RPE is particularly advantageous in situations of high common uncertainty. Being confronted with RPE contracts (as opposed to non-RPE contracts) individuals' effort levels increase as the degree of common uncertainty increases (Frederickson, 1992, p. 648). Consistent with agency theory, Maher (1987, p. 307) adds that the use of RPE increases when corporate management's knowledge about the activities of managers' business units is limited.

3.3.1.2 Vertical Interdependencies

Vertical interdependencies refer to decisions made by managers' superiors (Giraud et al., 2008, p. 36). In literature on the controllability principle, cost allocation schemes are mentioned as such vertical interdependencies (Choudhury, 1986, p. 193). Vancil (1979) is among the first researchers to provide empirical evidence on the uncontrollable influence stemming from allocation practices. He finds that corporate managers in US manufacturing companies frequently assign corporate-level costs to decentralized profit center managers. Even though profit center managers do not have authority over the costs, Vancil's (1979) results show that 72% of the companies in his sample assign research and development costs to them, 73% assign finance and accounting costs, 62% assign interest expenses, and 44% assign income taxes (Vancil, 1979, pp. 102-103). Vancil (1979) explains that such allocations of uncontrollable corporate costs are meant to influence profit center managers' behavior. The message corporate managers send to decentralized profit center managers in deciding to assign these costs is that the scope of profit center managers' initiative should not be restricted solely to the resources over which they have direct functional authority. On the contrary, profit center managers are expected to try to influence the management of corporate-level resources and costs (Vancil, 1979, p. 105). Vancil (1979) hence suggests that the allocation of uncontrollable costs by corporate management has an attention-directing effect. Managers who have to bear such cost assignments are thereby informed about what aspects of their job they are expected to pay attention to (Vancil, 1979, p. 21).

---

7 Note that the interpretation of whether RPE represents a violation of the controllability principle or not is dependent on one's underlying definition of the principle. The traditional definition of the controllability principle would clearly advise to exclude peer performance in managers' appraisals because managers do not have control over their peers' performance. The conditional controllability principle, however, argues on grounds of informativeness that data about peers' performance should still be included because it "tells us something about that environment and, thus, indirectly something about the performance of the agent in question" (Antle & Demski, 1988, p. 715). Since the performance of the agent and the performance of his peers are often affected by common random factors, data on peer performance permits conclusions to be drawn concerning the agent's own performance (Banker & Datar, 1989, p. 32; Holmström, 1982, pp. 334-337; Lambert, 2001, p. 25; Milgrom & Roberts, 1992, p. 404).

This proposition by Vancil (1979) is also reflected in the work of Merchant (1987). Merchant (1987) reports that two out of three companies in his sample intensively assign uncontrollable costs to their managers. Examples of these allocations are taxes, interest expenses, exchange losses, or the costs of centralized administrative functions (Merchant, 1987, p. 331). Again, the reason for these allocations is to make managers pay attention to the cost items. Merchant (1987) finds empirical support that, due to such allocation practices, managers indeed take the allocated costs into consideration in their everyday decision-making (Merchant, 1987, pp. 332-333).

In a later study conducted by Merchant (1989) with large US corporations, it is also found that corporate managers often intentionally avoid adjusting for the distorting effects of vertical interdependencies. Vertical interdependencies result from taxes and general and administrative expenses being assigned to decentralized profit center managers in several companies of Merchant's (1989) sample. Both, taxes as well as general and administrative expenses, represent uncontrollable cost items to the individual managers (Merchant, 1989, p. 98). Out of the 12 companies in Merchant's (1989) sample, two decide to allocate federal income taxes. This means that after-tax figures are calculated and used for the evaluation of managers' performance. Another seven companies hold their profit center managers accountable for assigned corporate general and administrative expenses (Merchant, 1989, pp. 98-104). As suggested by Merchant (1989), there are basically three explanations for such a nonapplication of the controllability principle. First, corporate managers opt to assign uncontrollable tax items because they feel that the decisions of profit center managers should reflect tax expenses and corresponding savings potential. Second, corporate managers realize that general and administrative expenses can be somewhat influenced by the profit center managers and charging them is likely to increase the communication between profit center managers and corporate staff. It is hoped that the allocations can generate constructive conflict between the two sides so that corporate costs are kept in line. Third, corporate managers allocate general and administrative expenses because if these allocations are made on some reasonable basis, meaning that they are associated with the actual factors causing the costs to be incurred, the evaluation of profit center managers' performance is based on a closer approximation of the full costs of their actions than they would be if these costs were not allocated (Merchant, 1989, pp. 100-101).

The allocation of uncontrollable costs by corporate management is also the central theme of Ugras's (1994) study on the application of the controllability principle among US manufacturing and service companies. The author reports that out of the 159 companies participating in his survey only 46 companies do not allocate or only allocate a small amount (< 10%) of uncontrollable costs to their responsibility centers. He further indicates that 58 companies allocate some (10-80%) of the uncontrollable costs and 54 companies even allocate high amounts (> 80%) of these costs. Building on agency theory and previous studies on cost allocations, Ugras (1994) investigates the relationship between several structural characteristics of the companies in his sample and the extent to which corporate management decides to allocate uncontrollable costs. It is found that unobservability of performance, sequential hierarchy, size, divisional diversity, and the need for coordination are all significantly related to uncontrollable cost allocation (Ugras, 1994, pp. 270-274).

Further empirical support for Vancil's (1979), Merchant's (1987; 1989) and Ugras's (1994) findings comes from several related management accounting studies. Fremgen and Liao (1981), Ramadan (1989), Otley (1990), Skinner (1990), Moon and Fitzgerald (1996), Modell and Lee (2001), Drury and El-Shishini (2005), and Pelster (2007) all report similar results as to the allocation of uncontrollable costs to responsibility center managers. Also the reasons for the observed allocation practices are often alike across the studies.

In their work on the allocation of corporate indirect costs, Fremgen and Liao (1981) find that 84% of the companies in their sample allocate these costs to their profit center managers even though the choice of the allocation base is often regarded to be arbitrary, which makes the allocated costs uncontrollable by the profit center managers (Fremgen & Liao, 1981, p. 33). The authors describe such an allocation practice to be advantageous from a control perspective since "it is better to make cost allocations based on partial responsibility or on overlapping responsibilities than to leave these costs unallocated at their source" (Fremgen & Liao, 1981, p. 21). They identify several reasons for the allocation of uncontrollable costs most of which are primarily behavioral. Among the top reasons for uncontrollable cost allocations provided in Fremgen and Liao's (1981) questionnaire are corporate managers' intentions to "remind profit center managers that indirect costs exist and that profit center earnings must be adequate to cover some share of those costs" and to "stimulate profit center managers to put pressure on central managers to control service costs" (Fremgen & Liao, 1981, p. 61). Noteworthily, it is these two behavioral reasons which again rank among the most frequently mentioned explanations for uncontrollable cost allocations in later surveys by Ramadan (1989, p. 34) and Skinner (1990, pp. 139-140).

Otley's (1990) case study with the British Coal Corporation provides another example of the uncontrollable influence associated with cost allocations. The MCS implemented at the British Coal Corporation generally puts extensive emphasis on the financial results of the company's collieries. The most important measure for colliery managers as prescribed by the MCS is the bottom-line figure of profit after capital charges. However, according to Otley (1990), the calculation of this figure incorporates the allocation of several cost items over which colliery managers have little or no control. Examples of these items are normal wages costs (which are a consequence of operating plans imposed on the colliery manager) or interest and depreciation charges. Otley (1990) assumes that the reason for the flawed application of the controllability principle at the British Coal Corporation lies in the distinction between the performance of the colliery and the performance of the manager. Even though the company's MCS is thought to provide the data needed for the evaluation of managerial performance, it may only accurately reflect colliery performance (Otley, 1990, p. 115). It is Dearden (1987) who likewise claims that in the design of MCSs there are often tradeoffs between the evaluation of business performance and managerial performance. Dearden (1987, p. 85) therefore stipulates that it is in many circumstances advisable to separate the corporate control systems, i.e. to use different systems for evaluating business performance and managerial performance.

A further comprehensive survey on cost allocations which is worth referring to in this discussion on the controllability principle comes from Drury and El-Shishini (2005). Based on the works of Fremgen and Liao (1981), Merchant (1987; 1989), Ramadan (1989), and Skinner (1990), the authors identify different categories of uncontrollable costs and investigate the allocation of these costs to division managers. It is found that "a significant majority of organizations allocate all, or most, of each category of noncontrollable costs for measuring divisional managerial performance" (Drury & El-Shishini, 2005, p. 4). These results underline that the allocation of uncontrollable costs is widespread and that, with respect to cost allocations, the controllability principle is often not applied in practice.

Apart from cost allocations, uncontrollable influence on managers' performance may also stem from corporate managers' decisions on transfer pricing policies. According to Ghosh (2000, p. 13), "it is well accepted that transfer pricing policies affect both the authority and the responsibility of managers". Scholars in the field of transfer pricing (Eccles, 1986, p. 43; Emmanuel & Mehafdi, 1994, p. 51; Grabski, 1985, pp. 50-51) distinguish between negotiation and dictation as the most common policies. Negotiation means that managers are free to set transfer prices and may buy or sell in the outside market as well as within the company. The policy of dictation, on the contrary, refers to transfers and transfer prices which are mandated by a superior authority. Such vertical interdependencies in the form of mandated transactions leave managers with no or only limited control over the way in which internal transactions are handled. Empirical evidence gathered by Eccles (1986) confirms that when internal transactions are mandated (i.e. managers have to sell or purchase internally and are not allowed to search for business partners external to the company), their interdependencies increase whereas their autonomy and controllability decrease (Eccles, 1986, p. 207).

Vertical interdependencies and their relevance for the application of the controllability principle are also examined in several studies on the specific types of performance measures that superiors may choose for the evaluation of subordinate managers. Two early studies in this area come from Hirst (1983a; 1983b). In his first study, Hirst (1983a, pp. 35-36) finds that managers' perceived controllability of accounting performance measures is negatively correlated to task uncertainty, which is why superiors are advised to reduce their emphasis on such measures in settings where task uncertainty is high. In the second study, Hirst (1983b) investigates the effects of superiors' reliance on accounting performance measures on managers' job tension. He finds that increased reliance on accounting performance measures in a high uncertainty setting (with the measures here becoming perceivedly uncontrollable to managers) results in higher job tension among the managers (Hirst, 1983b, pp. 601-602).

Bushman et al. (1996) provide further empirical evidence that the application of the controllability principle is inherently related to the types of measures that are chosen for the evaluation of managers' performance. The authors differentiate between two types of measures: individual performance measures and corporate performance measures which differ in their degree of controllability since the former capture manager-specific outcomes that are deemed more controllable than the latter which refer to aggregate financial results of the company (e.g. stock-price-based measures). In their study on top managers' compensation in a large sample of US companies, Bushman et al. (1996) report that the use of individual performance measures as opposed to corporate performance measures varies significantly across the companies. Examining the determinants of the use of the different measures reveals that the importance of individual performance measures increases, among others, with the length of product development and product life cycle (Bushman et al., 1996, pp. 188-189).

Vertical interdependencies are also the central object of investigation in a related study by Bushman et al. (1995). Using evaluation data from US companies, the authors find evidence that the variable pay of business unit managers is commonly based on aggregate performance criteria measured at organizational levels higher than the managers' own business unit level. For the average division manager, Bushman et al.'s (1995, p. 103) data show that 34% of his or her annual bonus is based on group level or corporate level performance, and 96% of his or her long-term compensation is based on corporate level performance. With such compensation arrangements, business unit managers are strongly dependent on managers from higher hierarchical levels.

In a later study, Keating (1997) reports similar results to those of Bushman et al. (1995). The author analyzes the use of three alternative types of performance measures in the evaluation of division managers: company stock price, company accounting measures (e.g. company earnings), and division accounting measures (e.g. division earnings). It is found that – even though these measures differ in their degree of controllability – all three types of measures play an important part in the evaluation of division managers. In line with his theoretical development, Keating (1997) shows that the use of higher-level measures (i.e. company accounting measures instead of division accounting measures) increases with the impact of managers' actions on divisions other than their own (Keating, 1997, p. 267).

Another study on the use of different types of performance measures is provided by Ittner et al. (1997). In their investigation of the relative weight placed on financial versus nonfinancial measures in managers' bonus contracts, the authors argue on the basis of the informativeness criterion that all measures – whether being controllable by the managers or not – should be included in bonus contracts as long as they convey information about managers' actions (Ittner et al., 1997, p. 233). Relying on the informativeness criterion, Ittner et al. (1997) develop several hypotheses most of which are empirically supported by data on compensation contracts of US top managers. Ittner et al.'s (1997) results show that a lack of controllability of financial performance measures that may originate from noise in the measures leads to the decreased use of financial measures while the relative weight placed on nonfinancial measures correspondingly increases (Ittner et al., 1997, pp. 251-252). The same result is reported in a more recent study by Van Veen-Dirks (in press, p. 19). When the noise in financial performance measures increases and hence their controllability decreases, the importance attached to that type of measures is decreased in performance evaluation.

Noise as a performance measure property is also examined by Bouwens and Van Lent (2006). In their study with Dutch companies which have an incentive pay plan in place, the authors empirically test for the effort and selection effect (see also chapter B2.3.1). Noise is found to have a direct impact on both the effort and the selection functioning of incentive contracts (Bouwens & Van Lent, 2006, p. 55): More precise performance measures increase in controllability and appear to be associated with more intense incentives. In a later study, Bouwens and Van Lent (2007) relate the noise of performance measures to the degree of the measures' aggregation. They suggest that the primary function of using disaggregated types of measures is to reduce the noise in aggregated types (Bouwens & Van Lent, 2007, p. 668). Bouwens and Van Lent (2007) find empirically that disaggregated measures generally gain in importance when interdependencies between organizations' business units increase the noise in the measures. Bouwens and Van Lent (2007, pp. 690-691) propose that disaggregated types of performance measures are less susceptible to the effects of interdependencies which is why superiors choose them in complex and highly interdependent settings.

Superiors' choice of different types of performance measures is also investigated by Simons (2007). According to Simons (2007), performance measures generally vary in the degree to which they are controllable by managers and superiors intentionally choose from a wide spectrum of measures depending on the nature of the work that is performed by their subordinates. Simons (2007) hypothesizes and finds empirical support that, for routine work and functions, controllable performance measures are chosen. However, in jobs where a high degree of innovation and proactivity is expected from managers, they are confronted with less controllable performance measures (e.g. research and development managers are held accountable for products' market success) since their superiors want them to develop a sense of entrepreneurship (Simons, 2007, pp. 13-21).

Apart from cost allocation schemes, transfer pricing policies, and the choice of performance measure types, managers are vertically dependent on their superiors' decisions in terms of the allocation of resources. Ghosh and Lusch (2000) report an example of how superiors' discretion in resource allocation represents an uncontrollable factor to managers. In their field study with a US retail company, they test for the existence of the outcome effect in the subjective evaluation of store managers' performance by their superiors. Ghosh and Lusch's (2000) results provide strong empirical evidence for the outcome effect when target outcome knowledge as well as the controllable and uncontrollable determinants of managers' outcome are taken into consideration. Two of the uncontrollable determinants included in the study are the size and the location of the retail stores. Both determinants are of high importance to store managers' measured performance because the greater the size and the better the location, the higher the economic success of the stores. However, these two determinants are decided upon by the company's central management and are hence uncontrollable by the store managers (Ghosh & Lusch, 2000, p. 417). The store managers may neither decide on their stores' location nor on the size of their stores since stores are assigned to them by central management. Due to such a discretion of central management in the allocation of resources, store managers face a high degree of uncontrollable influence on their performance (Ghosh & Lusch, 2000, pp. 422-423).

Finally, it is important to point out that vertical interdependencies in the form of superiors' decision-making powers are generally paramount for the application of the controllability principle. After all, it most commonly lies in superiors' discretion whether to implement controllability filters or not. The purpose of controllability filters is to ex post remove from managers' measured performance the effects of any type of uncontrollable factors. Such filters have been shown in both field research (Bento & White, 2006; Merchant, 1987; 1989) and experimental research (Shields et al., 1989; Shields & Waller, 1988; Waller & Chow, 1985) to have a strong impact on managers' contract selection, their satisfaction with performance evaluation, effort, and gaming behaviors.

Investigating the determinants of superiors' propensity to implement controllability filters, Marginson and McAulay (2001) suggest several personality and social factors which are hypothesized to shape superiors' attitude towards the controllability principle. In their study with executives from a UK communications company, the descriptive statistics reveal that 41% of the executives expect initial budgetary targets to be achieved even though uncontrollable factors interfere with subordinate managers' performance. They opt against the establishment of controllability filters and hence show a disregard for the controllability principle. With 23% of the responses being neutral, only 36% of the executives in Marginson and McAulay's (2001) sample do implement controllability filters. Marginson and McAulay (2001) then use a regression model for hypothesis testing. They find that it is mainly two factors which determine executives' attitude towards the controllability principle and the implementation of controllability filters: social influence from other group members and executives' functional background (Marginson & McAulay, 2001, p. 20). Apart from Marginson and McAulay's (2001) work and two related studies by Ueno and Wu (1993) and Merchant et al. (1995), there is only sparse empirical evidence on which personality factors shape executives' propensity to implement controllability filters. The latter two studies indicate that there are cross-cultural differences in managers' attitude towards the controllability principle. Ueno and Wu (1993, p. 33) find that in US companies managers seek higher controllability of budgetary targets than managers in Japanese companies. The authors relate this finding to the cultural dimension of individualism versus collectivism.

3.3.2 Uncontrollable External Factors

Uncontrollable influence on managers' performance may not only stem from internal interdependencies, but also from environmental factors which are external to the company. As Moers (2000, p. 25) generally states, "environmental uncertainty decreases the controllability of . . . performance measures". Empirical studies demonstrate that it is actually a wide range of environmental factors which may produce uncertainty and a lack of controllability.

The first study which investigates the application of the controllability principle in the context of economic and competitive conditions comes from Merchant (1987). Exploring corporate practice of adjusting for uncontrollable factors in managers' performance evaluation, the author finds that all three companies in his sample hold their managers accountable for at least some uncontrollable economic and competitive factors. He indicates that there is a belief in these companies that the advantages of doing so outweigh the disadvantages. The main argument in favor of not adjusting performance for fluctuations in economic and competitive conditions is that managers are expected to react to these conditions. If they are buffered from the fluctuations, the intensity of their efforts to respond to uncontrollable conditions is likely to decrease (Merchant, 1987, pp. 333-334). Interestingly, several of the managers interviewed by Merchant (1987) were either unconcerned about, or even felt that they should be held accountable for, such uncontrollable influence – a finding which resembles those of later studies by Bourguignon and Chiapello (2005, p. 688), Frow et al. (2005, p. 280), and Giraud et al. (2008, pp. 39-41). This leads one company in Merchant's (1987) sample to totally disregard the controllability principle in performance evaluation. Merchant (1987) states that managers in this company are made to bear the same risk as the company's shareholders. In fact, their risk is even higher because the shareholders' returns are diversified across the several companies which are part of the parent company (Merchant, 1987, p. 332).

Despite some differences between the three companies in his sample, Merchant (1987) observes a similar pattern for the adjustments which are made for acts of nature. Whereas two companies occasionally tolerate adjustments for strikes or fires, the third company again does not allow any adjustments when managers suffer from unfavorable acts of nature. An important reason for this unwillingness to make adjustments is corporate management's fear that this might give rise to unnecessary and time-consuming discussions of gray areas, such as whether the effects are large enough to warrant adjustments or how the adjustments should be calculated (Merchant, 1987, p. 335).

Applying the same distinction between (a) economic and competitive conditions and (b) acts of nature, Merchant (1989) extends his investigation of the application of the controllability principle to a larger sample of US companies. He reports about the management of uncontrollable external factors in 12 companies where adjustments for the effects of economic factors appear to be fairly uncommon (Merchant, 1989, p. 122). Profit center managers often have to bear the full risk of abrupt changes in economic conditions, unexpected cost increases, or foreign currency fluctuations. Only three of the 12 companies in Merchant's (1989) sample indicate that adjustments for unfavorable economic conditions might be considered under certain circumstances, but even in these companies few such adjustments are eventually made. Adjustments for competitive factors are even rarer than those for economic factors. According to Merchant (1989), adjustments for competitive factors are only tolerated in exceptional cases where the factors are deemed to be totally uncontrollable. In this context, Merchant (1989) refers to the case of a manager operating in the liquor distribution industry. This profit center manager faces a major price war in his market with margins declining from a normal level of $6.00-7.00 per case to $1.50 per case. This margin decline makes the managers' sales unprofitable because distribution costs are $4.20 per case. The price war turns out to be particularly costly because it affects margins as well as sales volumes. However, corporate managers do not allow adjustments in the manager's year-end performance evaluation because they argue that the profit center manager might have been able to anticipate the price war and, hence, should have incorporated the sales decline in his initial budget forecast (Merchant, 1989, pp. 123-125). With regard to adjustments for acts of nature as further uncontrollable factors, Merchant (1989) describes the observed practice in his sample companies as follows: Only five companies tend to make adjustments for acts of nature (such as fires, floods, or accidents) if two conditions come together. First, the effects must be notable in magnitude since managers are expected to be able to cope with minor uncontrollable influences. Second, it must be determined that the acts of nature are truly unpredictable and uncontrollable by the managers (Merchant, 1989, pp. 125-126).

Uncontrollable changes in the external environment also entail violations of the controllability principle in Otley's (1990) case study with the British Coal Corporation. Investigating external factors which have an impact on colliery managers' results, Otley (1990) identifies the world price of coal, unexpected geological conditions, wage increases due to national wage agreements, and capital cost increases due to changes in interest rates. All of these factors are, according to Otley (1990), clearly beyond colliery managers' control. Since these factors yet affect the financial performance of the collieries, managers who wish to ensure that their colliery continues to maintain its economic viability have to adapt the way in which they operate in the light of changing circumstances. Otley (1990) argues that part of colliery managers' responsibility lies in anticipating and responding to external uncontrollable factors (Otley, 1990, p. 116).

Uncontrollable influence as induced by external stakeholder groups (i.e. customers and politicians) is investigated by Modell (1997). He conducts a case study with a dental practice in Sweden, which leads him to the insight that the primary sources of lacking controllability are often related to the patients in public sector settings. Modell (1997, pp. 324-325) mentions the diversity of patients' needs and the uncertainty in the flow of patients as complicating the application of the controllability principle in the management of the dental practice. Additionally, Modell (1997) notes that the perceived uncertainty and the lack of controllability in the public service industry is likely to be exacerbated by political decisions. Such decisions are beyond the clinic managers' control but have a profound impact on their ability to meet their targets, e.g. in terms of the length of their waiting lists (Modell, 1997, p. 328). In a later study, Modell and Lee (2001) again refer to political pressure as causing uncontrollable influence. Political pressure on cost containment is reported to produce arbitrary ex post cost allocations imposed on department heads at a Norwegian hospital (Modell & Lee, 2001, p. 213). Modell and Lee (2001) therefore conclude that the application of the controllability principle in the public sector is not necessarily subject to rationalized and discretionary managerial choice, but rather suffers from the interests of fund-granting institutions and external stakeholders (Modell & Lee, 2001, p. 193).

Budding's (2004) case study with managers from Dutch municipalities provides further evidence that political pressure and the uncertainty associated with it complicate the application of the controllability principle in public sector organizations. Participants in Budding's (2004) interviews state that local politicians' attitudes and strategies with regard to the way services have to be performed are perceived as unpredictable (Budding, 2004, p. 296). However, politicians are only one of several external stakeholders producing uncontrollable influence on municipality managers' performance. In total, Budding (2004) distinguishes between four types of stakeholders which cause managers to be held accountable for results that are not under their control: (a) local politics, (b) actions of the central government, (c) cooperation with other organizations outside of the municipality, and (d) customers' demand for services and their changing composition (Budding, 2004, pp. 293-294).

Customers and demand-related factors which are uncontrollable by managers also play an important part in the work of Ghosh and Lusch (2000). In their field study with a US retail company, one of the uncontrollable factors which store managers are confronted with is market matching. Market matching describes the extent to which the demographics of a particular store's trade area match the retail company's desired target market. It is expected that the higher a store's degree of market matching, the higher the economic performance of that store. In Ghosh and Lusch's (2000) study, market matching is indicated by the percentage of Hispanics in the trade area population because Hispanics are the primary target market of the retail company. Since store managers are assigned to their stores by central management and are not allowed to decide on which store they want to be responsible for, they cannot influence the market matching profile of their store. Market matching consequently represents an uncontrollable factor to them. In the course of their investigation, Ghosh and Lusch (2000) do not only identify the demand-related factor of market matching, but also competition-related factors which are uncontrollable from a store manager's perspective. These are the relative store size of the main competitor in a manager's trade area, store saturation as measured by the total number of retail stores in the trade area, and the general economic health of the trade area (Ghosh & Lusch, 2000, p. 417).

Further empirical insights on the uncontrollable influence that may originate from factors external to the company is provided in studies by Huffman and Cain (2000; 2001). They investigate the degree to which adjustments for uncontrollable difficulties in salespeople's territories are made by their superiors in performance appraisals and whether these adjustments have an effect on salespeople's perceptions. It is found that adjustments for uncontrollable territory difficulties not only increase their perceived usefulness of the evaluation system (Huffman & Cain, 2000, p. 823), but also perceived distributive and procedural fairness as well as satisfaction with performance ratings (Huffman & Cain, 2000, pp. 823-824; 2001, pp. 606-608). Nevertheless, far from all superiors actually make adjustments for uncontrollable territory difficulties. Huffman and Cain's (2000) survey demonstrates that almost 30% of the superiors in their sample do not adjust their subordinates' performance ratings for such uncontrollable factors (Huffman & Cain, 2000, p. 811). Specifically, the assignment of given sales territories represents an uncontrollable factor because the territories often differ substantially in terms of market potential, geographic size, and competitive strength. According to Ryans and Weinberg (1979, pp. 462-464), these types of territory differences may account for as much as 40% of the variation in salespeople's achieved sales. Obviously, since salespeople are frequently confronted with uncontrollable territory difficulties, they are rewarded or punished for results which are in parts due to their territories rather than their actions or sales strategies (Huffman & Cain, 2000, p. 800).

Uncontrollable external influence on managers' performance may also stem from capital market pressure. Recent studies by Toms (2005), Larmande and Ponssard (2007), and Pelster (2007) show that the use of performance measures derived from or associated with capital markets is often related to problems of controllability. This caveat is also found in theoretical work of Hartmann (2000, p. 469), Lynch and Perry (2003, pp. 48-49), Merchant (1985, p. 107), Milgrom and Roberts (1992, p. 404), and Simons (1995, p. 77) who argue that such measures (e.g. stock prices) may be very insensitive to the actions of any individual manager below the highest executive level of a company. Toms's (2005) empirical investigation of the historical determinants of accounting practices in the British cotton industry reveals that modern capital markets have in many places led to a "rise of accountability and decline of managerial control" (Toms, 2005, p. 639). Likewise, Pelster's (2007, pp. 248-249) interviews with managers from a publicly listed company indicate that capital market orientation tends to restrict the managers' decision latitude and may thus produce a lack of controllability. A longitudinal case study conducted by Larmande and Ponssard (2007) appears to further affirm this proposition. Larmande and Ponssard (2007) investigate a multinational corporation's efforts to align with market values and its corresponding implementation of an economic value added (EVA) compensation system. They find that the new system suffers from a lack of controllability for two reasons. First, the EVA calculations are not able to eliminate complex and arbitrary accounting treatments which introduce internal administrative noise in the evaluation process. Second, and more importantly, the process for setting targets excludes managers' exercise of influence. This is due to the general EVA methodology which provides little space for the elimination of uncontrollable factors through negotiations and subjective adjustments (Larmande & Ponssard, 2007, p. 20).

3.4 Explanations for the Limited Application of the Controllability Principle

The empirical studies reviewed in chapters B3.3.1 and B3.3.2 document that companies do not consistently apply the controllability principle. As indicated in chapter B3.1, management accounting scholars have originally designated practical reasons for the lack of application. More precisely, it has been thought that complexity and uncertainty complicate the application of the principle (Giraud et al., 2004, p. 8; Hirst, 1983a, p. 35; Moers, 2000, p. 25). These two phenomena make it difficult to pinpoint individual controllability and render the distinction between controllable and uncontrollable factors vague (Gibbs et al., 2004, p. 413; Hofstede, 1967, p. 204; Huffman & Cain, 2000, p. 827; Merchant, 1989, p. 87; Merchant & Manzoni, 1989, p. 554). Hence, it is arguably for the reasons of complexity and uncertainty that Hopwood (1972, p. 158) acknowledges the pervasive implementation of the controllable principle to be "a difficult, if not impossible, task".

However, such practical reasons cannot entirely explain the lack of the principle's application. Several of the studies reviewed in chapters B3.3.1 and B3.3.2 demonstrate that organizations often intentionally follow a rationale that differs from the prescriptions of the (traditional) controllability principle. Even if organizational realities allow the application of the controllability principle, it is not always in the organizations' interest to do so. They purposely avoid eliminating uncontrollable factors and want their managers to be confronted with it. Hence, organizational interests represent another important explanation for the limited application of the controllability principle in company practice. In the light of the empirical evidence reviewed in chapters B3.3.1 and B3.3.2, this explanation of organizational interests basically comprises three components: (a) a risk-sharing component, (b) an information-retrieving component, and (c) an attention-directing component (Cohen, Loeb, & Stark, 1992, pp. 291-292; Drury & El-Shishini, 2005, pp. 21-22).

The first organizational interest that helps to explain the nonapplication of the controllability principle in many companies is the desirability of making managers share risk with their superiors. Holding managers accountable for uncontrollable factors may discourage them from risky business decisions and so reduces the risk and uncertainty borne by their superiors alone (Demski, 1976, pp. 242-243). Empirical support for risk-sharing as one reason for the nonapplication of the controllability principle comes from various management accounting studies (e.g. Merchant (1987) or Giraud et al. (2008)).

The second argument which justifies violations of the controllability principle is informativeness. Founded in agency theory, this argument led to the formulation of the conditional controllability principle (see chapter B1.2.2). It prescribes that all data available – whether controllable or not – should be used for performance evaluation as long as it includes additional information content about managers' unobservable actions (Antle & Demski, 1988, pp. 714-716; Holmström, 1979, p. 89; Lambert, 2001, pp. 23-24). Again, several studies reviewed in chapters B3.3.1 and B3.3.2 provide empirical support for this proposition. Eccles (1986), Bushman et al. (1995), Ittner et al. (1997), Moers (2000), and most of the writers on RPE (e.g. Maher (1987) or Gibbons and Murphy (1990)) indicate that, in some places, companies do take account of information content and de facto follow the conditional controllability principle instead of the traditional controllability principle.

Apart from risk- and information-related aspects, it is the organizational interest to direct managers' attention to critical performance areas which represents the third explanation for the nonapplication of the controllability principle. According to Manzoni (2002, p. 32), "overall firm performance is unlikely to be maximized by focusing managers' efforts on dimensions and measures that are controllable by them". Organizations therefore direct managers' attention to areas which are not controllable, but which they are expected to take into consideration when performing their job (Bourguignon & Chiapello, 2005, p. 687; Giraud et al., 2008, p. 34; Merchant, 1998, p. 576; Simons, 2005, pp. 94-95). With respect to uncontrollable external factors, managers will, according to Manzoni (2002, p. 32), not be able to control acts of nature or competitors' actions, but they are expected to work as hard as necessary on anticipating and influencing such factors. If managers are fully shielded from the impact of these factors, they are unlikely to devote as much attention to these factors as they would if their measured performance included the impact of these factors. Following Manzoni (2002, p. 32), the same applies to uncontrollable internal factors (i.e. horizontal and vertical interdependencies). Overall corporate performance depends to a large extent on issues that are managed at the interface of different hierarchical levels and business units. Focusing managers only on what they can literally control is likely to lead to insufficient attention on these intersections and, hence, organizational disintegration.

Much of the empirical work introduced in chapters B3.3.1 and B3.3.2 substantiates Manzoni's (2002) proposition. There is strong support that the intention to direct managers' attention to critical performance areas often leads to the nonapplication of the controllability principle. It seems that many organizations instead follow the influenceability principle (see chapter B1.2.3) which stipulates that managers should be held accountable for factors that they can influence rather control (Merchant & Otley, 2006, p. 794). In the design of performance evaluation systems, the decisive criterion for holding managers accountable obviously is not total controllability, but managers' potential contribution to the achievement of organizations' objectives. Managers are in many cases held accountable for factors over which they have incomplete control but which they may somewhat influence. And it is this kind of influence that superiors often wish to direct managers' attention to. According to the empirical evidence, the positive effects from such accountability structures seem to be manifold: Internally, managers increase their communication, interaction, and reciprocal influence on other units (e.g. Drury and El-Shishini (2005), Fremgen and Liao (1981), or Frow et al. (2005)); externally, they are stimulated to proactively work on the management of unfavorable environmental conditions (e.g. Merchant (1987) or Otley (1990)); or, more generally, they show an increase in entrepreneurial thinking and acting (e.g. Giraud et al. (2008) or Simons (2007)). Given these empirical indications, Merchant and Otley (2006, pp. 793-794) draw the following conclusion:

> Why do we generally hold managers accountable for much more than they can control? . . . This disparity in practice has two basic causes . . . One is that it is often difficult to separate the uncontrollable and the controllable effects on the performance measures . . .

> The other basic cause is that while some factors are uncontrollable, organizations want managers to respond to changes in those factors.

As a result, the limited application of the controllability principle in company practice may be generally attributed to two underlying patterns. First, conditions of complexity and uncertainty represent practical reasons which make the application of the principle difficult. Second, organizational interests add up as a further reason why in many circumstances the principle's application is not only difficult, but even undesirable. The controllability principle clearly is not "universally applicable" (Filley & House, 1969, p. 99). However, the principle's limited application stands in contrast to the strong theoretical points that were made for the principle in chapter B2.3. This tension between the principle's theoretical rationale and its practical application has led to different opinions about the value of the controllability principle (Hartmann, 2000, p. 472; Hirst, 1983a, p. 36).

On the one hand, the controllability principle holds an intuitive logic. Motivational effects are frequently put forward in the literature as being inherently related to the principle: "When held accountable for things that they do not control, managers . . . become demotivated" (Giraud et al., 2008, p. 32). Justice theory predicts that managers perceive the nonapplication of the controllability principle as unfair, which results in decreased satisfaction with the job and deteriorating work attitudes. Expectancy theory posits that with the principle's non-application managers decrease their work endeavors because of a perceived decline in effort-reward-probabilities. Agency theory argues that when managers are held accountable for uncontrollable factors adverse effort and selection effects arise. In short, theory predicts certain costs to organizations if they opt not to apply the controllability principle in the evaluation of managerial performance (Choudhury, 1986, p. 190).

On the other hand, empirical research shows that "careful thought should be given before adhering too strictly to the controllability principle" (Kren & Liao, 1988, p. 300). Not only that complexity and uncertainty complicate the principle's application, even more importantly it seems as if "'implementing a perfect controllability principle might work against organizational effectiveness" (Besson et al., 2008, p. 6). Eliminating all uncontrollable factors reduces managers' incentives to respond to the factors in ways that would moderate their impact on the welfare of the company. The ideal evaluation should therefore filter out and neutralize only the truly uncontrollable factors, but include any factors that can be changed by managers' efforts. Doing the former reduces risk, while doing the latter stimulates managers to respond appropriately to the factors as they unfold, making use of any information as it is learned (Gibbs et al., 2004, p. 413). As one can imagine, such an ideal evaluation represents an overly difficult task for superiors (Hopwood, 1972, p. 158). Nevertheless, the key question that superiors are expected to keep in mind is: "When is the managers' influence great enough to warrant holding them at risk for something they cannot totally control?" (Merchant, 1989, p. 5).

Consequently, there appears to be some dilemma between the need to apply the controllability principle for reasons such as justice and the desire to stimulate managers to effectually respond to uncontrollable factors. Holding managers accountable for factors over which no influence can be exerted, and expecting an intelligent and adaptive response to these factors is a very fine line (Otley, 2006, pp. 299-300). It is Merchant (1998, p. 576) who points out to superiors that failures to eliminate uncontrollable factors "violate the strict controllability principle, but they are consistent with the rule presented earlier: Hold managers accountable for the performance areas you want them to pay attention to". At the same time, he warns against handling the controllability principle with too great laxity: "Do not hold employees accountable for too many things over which they have little influence" (Merchant, 1998, p. 577).

In this dilemma, management accounting scholars conclude that there can only be a tradeoff between the benefits and the costs of implementing the controllability principle (Atkinson et al., 1997, p. 84; Choudhury, 1986, pp. 196-197; Merchant, 1989, p. 130; Modell, 1997, p. 314). The appropriateness of the controllability principle should hence be approached as a combination of functional and dysfunctional consequences. This is why – as stated in the beginning of part A – the controllability principle plays such a decisive role in the struggle for organizational effectiveness and managerial motivation.

C Introduction to Role Theory

A theory is necessary "to make sense of what would otherwise be inscrutable or unmeaning empirical findings" (Kaplan, 1964, p. 302). According to Ahrens and Chapman's (2006, p. 821) definition, a theory is a set of explanatory concepts which allows the systematic ordering of such findings. It helps in guiding, structuring, and disciplining the research process (Spicer, 1992, p. 5; Zimmerman, 2001, p. 418) and, without theory, "data analysis and classification is blind" (Hempel, 1966, p. 13).

Management accounting research commonly draws from a broad range of theoretical disciplines. Economics as well as social sciences, e.g. sociology, psychology, and political science, often appear to offer equally compelling explanations for observed management accounting practices (Anderson & Widener, 2006, p. 319; Ittner, Larcker, & Meyer, 2003, p. 754). It has become increasingly evident that in order to understand these practices a multiplicity of perspectives is required rather than a purely economic point of view (Atkinson et al., 1997, p. 101; Birnberg et al., 2006, p. 132; Drury & Tayles, 1995, p. 278). Such an integrative approach differs from research in other areas of accounting, most notably financial accounting and taxation, which are almost exclusively economics-based (Merchant & Otley, 2006, p. 799).

This work relies on role theory (Kahn et al., 1964; 1966; Katz & Kahn, 1966; 1978) to formulate research questions, test hypotheses, and explain empirical findings. A strong theory is generally needed to make causal inferences in quantitative research (Modell, 2005, p. 235; Van der Stede, Young, & Chen, 2006, p. 461). As such, role theory is part of social psychology theory which has often been used by researchers to "explain and predict how management accounting practices such as budgeting and performance evaluation and their organizational context influence individuals' minds and behavior, in particular, decisions, judgments, satisfaction, and stress" (Birnberg et al., 2006, p. 114). In the light of role theory's general importance for management accounting research, it is surprising to observe that it has hardly been used in previous empirical work on the controllability principle. Instead, motivational theories (see chapters B2.3.1 to B2.3.5), which undoubtedly have a raison d'être in research on the principle, have commonly been adopted. Agency theory has proved helpful when analytically approaching the principle from an organizational perspective on the management of risk and information asymmetries (Bushman et al., 1995, pp. 123-126; Demski, 1976, pp. 242-243; Holmström, 1979, pp. 75-90). Likewise, expectancy theory and justice theory have contributed to an understanding of managers' intrapersonal desire for the application of the controllability principle (Giraud et al., 2008, pp. 38-43; Hartmann &

Slapničar, 2007, pp. 14-17). However, when juxtaposing these motivational theories to role theory, this work agrees with Frink and Klimoski (1998, p. 34), who argue that "a role theory perspective is a superior vehicle for understanding accountability forces in work organizations". As a matter of fact, the use of role theory comes along with two essential advantages over motivational theories.

First, the explanatory power of motivational theories is limited with regard to the application of the controllability principle and individuals' behavioral responses. Agency theory in particular falls short of taking behavioral aspects into consideration. Referring to the work of Jensen and Meckling (1994), Davis et al. (1997, p. 24) criticize the theory's homo economicus assumption and argue it to be an "unrealistic description of human behavior". Similarly, justice theory may help to explain individuals' preferences for the application of the controllability principle, but remains somewhat inconclusive in effectively linking perceptions of controllability to behavioral responses. By contrast, role theory provides a more suitable platform for examining the relationship between the application of the controllability principle and individuals' behavior as "role and role play seem to be so endemic to organizational behavior" (Collins, 1982, p. 117). Role theory above all proves to be less one-sided in the explanation of human behavior than most motivational theories. As will become apparent from the following chapters, role theory offers considerable explanatory power in that it allows to take both the benefits and the costs of applying the controllability principle into consideration.

Second, there are "striking similarities regarding the structure and functioning of role systems and accountability systems in organizations" (Frink & Klimoski, 1998, p. 21). It is for these similarities that role theory helps to understand the consequences of organizational accountability arrangements and in particular the consequences of the application of the controllability principle. According to Frink and Klimoski (1998, p. 28), the similarities between role systems and accountability systems stem from role theory's integration of the many components and relationships that are central to the conceptualization of organizational accountability. Collins (1982, p. 117) also argues for the adoption of a role theory perspective in research on accountability systems because it "takes into account many salient factors" needed to comprehensively understand the systems.

As a result, this work complements prior management accounting research by providing an alternative theoretical stance in the discussion on the controllability principle. Even though scholars have occasionally noticed the potential relevance of role concepts for research in this area (Choudhury, 1986, p. 190; McNally, 1980, p. 166), it is this work which for the first time employs role theory in an empirical investigation of managers' responses to the application of the controllability principle. For this purpose, the following elaboration of role theory sets the stage for the theory's use in hypothesis development (see part D). Chapter C1 provides an overview of the history of the theory and its key concepts, chapter C2 outlines more recent developments in role literature, and chapter C3 describes the theory's use in prior management accounting research.

1. Overview of Classical Role Theory

1.1 History of Role Theory

Unlike other theories, role theory did not begin with the influential contributions of a single author. Instead, role theory arose coincidentally in several social sciences. Scholars from sociology, psychology, and anthropology have contributed to the development of role theory and used the theory in their research endeavors. This parallel development of role concepts in various sciences has led to different formulations of the theory and occasional inconsistencies in its various formulations (Biddle, 1979, pp. 8-9; Turner, 1979, p. 123). Nevertheless Biddle and Thomas (1966b, p. 8) argue that "role concepts are not the *lingua franca* [emphasis in original] of the behavioral sciences, but perhaps they . . . come closer to this universal language than any other vocabulary of behavioral science".

There are a number of reasons why role theory has provoked enthusiasm among researchers from several disciplines. First, role theory represents a unifying meeting ground on which the different disciplines can come together and where scholars from these disciplines find common terms and concepts. Second, using the words of Biddle (1979, p. 12), "role theory parades as a science" since it applies to human perceptions and experiences in natural contexts, covers a variety of events the social sciences have traditionally had an interest in, and, quite generally, is predestined for empirical work on it. Third, because role concepts are based on terms having surplus meaning within the common language, role theory appears to offer a means for expressing both the concrete thoughts of subjects and the abstract notions of investigators. Hence, role theory provides a powerful framework that is also appealing to practitioners. It makes use of terms from the common language and it suggests one-to-one relationships between the overt facts of behavior and the subjective experiences of those who behave (Biddle, 1979, pp. 12-13; Shaw & Costanzo, 1982, pp. 295-296).

Three chronological stages can be discriminated in the development of role theory. The first stage was a "precursive stage" (Biddle, 1979, p. 10) which includes the preliminary work of some early scholars and marks the starting point of the gradual evolution of the theory. This stage can be dated back to the end of the 19th century and the beginning of the 20th century. During that time, authors such as James (1890), Cooley (1902; 1909), or Simmel (1920) developed several concepts which are similar to later notions of role. Since then, the use of the term role in English and many European languages has proven to be indispensable for the further development of a technical role language in the next stages of role theory's history.

In the second stage, starting in the 1930s, role concepts were formalized, elaborated, and applied to the discussion of a variety of social events. During the 1930s and later, early role concepts were joined to newly developed role terms, which resulted in a quasi-technical language of role. To this language many behavioral scientists made contributions, with the works of Mead (1934), Moreno (1934), and Linton (1936) being particularly influential. However, the diffusion of the role language was not abundantly evident in scholarly publications until the 1940s. Since that time, the language of role theory has increasingly appeared in texts from behavioral science, in integrative theories, and in the writings of professional fields concerned with behavior, action, and change.

The third stage in the history of role theory commenced in the 1950s. This stage of extensive empirical research in which role concepts are being used in various academic disciplines today's researchers are still involved in. Most of the research conducted in this stage has been concerned with practical problems rather than with basic propositions in role theory (Biddle, 1979, pp. 9-10; 1986, pp. 70-76; Biddle & Thomas, 1966b, pp. 5-19; Dahrendorf, 2006, pp. 57-76; Haug, 1994, pp. 20-25; Shaw & Costanzo, 1982, pp. 295-299).

1.2 Terminology and Basic Concepts of Role Theory

At its core, role theory is about human behavior. The behavior of individuals is examined in terms of how it is shaped by the demands and rules of others, by their sanctions, and by individuals' own understanding and conception of what their behavior should be (Biddle & Thomas, 1966b, p. 4). Put differently, role theory differentiates individuals' behavior and the phenomenal processes that presumably lie behind it (Biddle, 1979, p. 12). Due to other people's importance for shaping individuals' role perceptions and behavior, role theory is sometimes subsumed under social psychology theory (Birnberg et al., 2006, p. 121). The social psychology perspective on role theory is also applied in this work. According to Allport's (1954, p. 5) basic definition, social psychology is generally concerned with "the scientific investigation of how the thoughts, feelings and behaviors of individuals are influenced by the actual, imagined or implied presence of others" (for more recent definitions of social psychology, see Baron, Branscombe, and Byrne (2008, pp. 5-6) or Bordens and Horowitz (2001, p. 3)).

As outlined in chapter C1.1, role theory incorporates a specific language, the central terms and concepts of which will be introduced in the following chapters. Unfortunately, this vocabulary is not always consistent across the different formulations of role theory (Biddle, 1979, pp. 55-56; Shaw & Costanzo, 1982, p. 295). This work draws on the framework and corresponding vocabulary developed by Kahn et al. (1964; 1966) and Katz and Kahn (1966; 1978). Kahn and his colleagues' framework is the central reference point for role-related studies in industrial organizations (Biddle, 1986, p. 73; Sarbin & Allen, 1968, p. 488). Management accounting scholars have therefore traditionally cited Kahn and his colleagues' work when employing role theory (Collins, 1982, p. 108; Hopwood, 1972, pp. 165-166). Most notably, research related to reliance on accounting performance measures (RAPM) – which is seen as one of the most voluminous and important areas of management accounting research (Derfuss, 2009, pp. 203-204) – is predominantly based on Kahn and his colleagues' body of thought (Briers & Hirst, 1990, p. 385; Hartmann, 2000, pp. 451-452).

1.2.1 Role

The central concern of role theory is the study of roles (Biddle, 1979, p. 55). A *role* "is a set of . . . behaviors pertaining to a particular task or social function" (Collins, 1982, p. 109). Noteworthily, a role is not identical to a *job*. While a job is the component of an individual's work experience that is relatively fixed, formal, and derived from the structural properties of an organization, a role is the more emergent, dynamic, and socially defined component of the same work experience (Perrone, Zaheer, & McEvily, 2003, p. 424). A role, in fact, contains "emergent task elements plus those elements of the job that are communicated to the job incumbent through the social system and maintained in that system" (Ilgen & Hollenbeck, 1991, p. 174). Having differentiated a role from a job, it is equally important to relate these two terms to various concepts which are necessary to understand and describe role processes in organizations.

The first of these concepts is *office* which refers to an individual's "unique point in organizational space" (Kahn et al., 1964, p. 13). Here, organizational space is defined in terms of a structure of interrelated offices and the pattern of activities associated with them. Using the concept of office, Kahn and his colleagues locate individuals in the total set of organizational relationships and behaviors (Katz & Kahn, 1966, pp. 179-180).

Based on the work of Merton (1957), Kahn and his colleagues further introduce *role sets* to describe all others' offices which are related to the individual's office. Each member of an organization is directly and indirectly related to several others. Others' offices which are particularly important for the individual's office include superiors, subordinates, and members of the individual's own organizational unit with whom he or she must work closely together. All of them have a potential interest in influencing the individual's behavior on the job (Kahn et al., 1964, pp. 13-14).

Another concept of high importance for role theory is the concept of *role expectations*. They can be regarded as the "bridge between social structure and role behavior" (Sarbin & Allen,

1968, p. 497). Since most members of an individual's role set have a stake in the behavior and performance of the individual, they develop motivations, beliefs, and attitudes about what the individual should or should not do as part of his or her role. These prescriptions and proscriptions held by the members of a role set are designated as role expectations. They are evaluative standards which define behavioral requirements or limits ascribed to the role (Katz & Kahn, 1966, p. 182). These expectations are not restricted to job descriptions and instructions by superiors, although superiors and designers of organizational structures and systems are likely to be influential members of the individual's role set (Kahn et al., 1964, p. 14; Rizzo et al., 1970, p. 155). In general, role expectations may vary in their degree of scope, specificity, formality, and – what is of particular relevance for the following review of role theory – clarity as well as consistency (Sarbin & Allen, 1968, pp. 499-500).

Roles and corresponding role expectations first "exist in the minds of people" (Ilgen & Hollenbeck, 1991, p. 169). But, of course, the expectations do not remain in the minds of the members of an individual's role set. They rather tend to be communicated in many ways: sometimes directly, e.g. via superiors' instructions or their information about rewards and penalties, and sometimes indirectly, e.g. via colleagues' admiration of or disappointment with some behavior of the individual (Katz & Kahn, 1978, pp. 190-192). Because role expectations are communicated (or sent) to the individual, Kahn and his colleagues refer to such expectations as the *sent role*. The members of an individual's role set transmitting the role expectations are called *role senders*. In addition, Kahn and his colleagues use the term *focal person* for any individual who is exposed to role senders' expectations (Kahn et al., 1964, p. 15).

The numerous acts which make up the process of role sending are designated as *role pressures*. They represent influence attempts directed toward the focal person and intended to bring about conformity with role senders' expectations. As such, they imply consequences for compliance or noncompliance. Each of these sent role pressures can be regarded as arousing in the focal person a psychological force (*role force*) of some magnitude and direction. According to Merton (1949, p. 110), individuals try "to organize their behavior in terms of the structurally defined expectations". However, this is not to say that the role forces are identical in magnitude and direction with the pressures which evoked them. Especially when role pressures are interpreted as illegitimate or coercive, they are likely to trigger resistance forces which lead to outcomes different or even opposite to the behavior originally expected by the role senders. *Role behavior* is therefore defined quite broadly as the behavior of individuals that is system relevant, but not necessarily congruent with the expectations and requirements of others (Kahn et al., 1964, pp. 15-18). The motivation for the focal person's role behavior is rooted in his or her *received role* which – as outlined in the foregoing – needs to be distinguished from the sent role (Katz & Kahn, 1978, p. 203).

The basis for Kahn and his colleagues' role theory and the role processes described above is their notion of organization as an "open social system" (Kahn et al., 1964, pp. 12-13; Katz & Kahn, 1978, pp. 752-753). The essential defining characteristics of an organization are not its name, its physical boundaries, or its legal domain. An organization is rather defined by the relationships of individuals and their roles as patterns of behavior which carry out the continuing organizational process of input, transformation, and output. Social interactions that occur throughout the role system occupy a fundamental position since they appear to guide individuals' work behavior. Roles therefore emerge as a "structural unit of social systems" (Bertrand, 1972, p. 35) or – using the words of Kahn and his colleagues – as "major defining characteristics of social organizations" (Katz & Kahn, 1966, p. 70).[8]

1.2.2 Role Stress

In the next step of Kahn and his colleagues' theoretical development, the authors relate the role pressures and the role expectations held by role senders to the degree of role stress experienced by the focal person. Role stress and the implied uncertainty felt when role incumbents think that they cannot accomplish all role demands are of primary concern to role theory (Katz & Kahn, 1978, pp. 204-206). Since it depends on individuals' abilities and resources to fulfill the expectations which they are confronted with, role stress is commonly regarded as an individual difference variable in role literature (Beehr & Glazer, 2005, p. 12).

Role stress comprises two facets: role conflict and role ambiguity (Kahn et al., 1964, pp. 18-26; 1966, pp. 277-278). According to Kahn et al. (1964, p. 3), "conflict and ambiguity are among the major characteristics of our society, and we are marked by them". These two phenomena are paramount to role theory as described by Kahn et al. (1964; 1966). It is for this reason that empirical research emanating from role theory is devoted almost exclusively to the constructs of role conflict and role ambiguity (Burke & Belcourt, 1974, pp. 55-56; Ilgen & Hollenbeck, 1991, p. 203).

1.2.2.1 Role Conflict

Role conflict refers to the "simultaneous occurrence of two (or more) sets of pressures such that compliance with one would make more difficult compliance with the other" (Kahn et al., 1964, p. 19). Rizzo, House, and Lirtzman (1970, p. 155) further concretize this definition of role conflict and depict it as "conflicting expectations and organizational demands in the form of incompatible policies, requests, standards". An integral part of the concept of role conflict

---

8 Many of Kahn and his colleagues' ideas are rooted in open system theory, which permits to integrate the so-called macro approach of sociology and the so-called micro approach of psychology to the study of social phenomena (Katz & Kahn, 1966, pp. 9-13; 1978, pp. 12-16).

is the distinction between objective or sent conflict and subjective or psychological conflict. In general, the distinction between the objective environment of an individual and his or her psychological environment is important to Kahn and his colleagues' formulation of role theory. According to Kahn et al. (1964, p. 12), the objective environment of an individual consists of real objects and events, supposed to be verifiable outside his or her consciousness and experience. The conscious and unconscious representations of this supposedly objective environment then constitute the psychological environment of the person. With objective role conflict, Kahn and his colleagues hence refer to conditions of the environment whereas subjective role conflict means a state of the individual. Other authors on role theory place similar emphasis on the discrepancies between sent expectations or pressures from the environment and the corresponding information received and processed by the individual (Graen, 1976, p. 1207).

Kahn et al. (1964, pp. 19-20) identify four basic types of role conflict: (a) intra-sender conflict, (b) inter-sender conflict, (c) inter-role conflict, and (d) person-role conflict. Intra-sender conflict implies incompatible prescriptions and proscriptions from a single role sender. Inter-sender conflict relates to opposing pressures from different role senders. Inter-role conflict means that the role pressures associated with membership in one group are in conflict with the pressures stemming from membership in other groups. Person-role conflict occurs when role requirements appear to violate the individual's moral values.

All four types of role conflict have one major characteristic in common: Members of a particular role set exert influence to change the behavior of the focal person (Kahn et al., 1964, p. 21). When such pressures are generated, they do not enter an otherwise empty field. On the contrary, the focal person already performs a role and, for this reason, maintains some kind of equilibrium among the disparate forces and motives which he or she experiences. Sent role pressures to perform a new behavior tend to threaten this equilibrium and therefore have the potential to arouse role conflict. The stronger the pressures from role senders toward changes in the current behavior of the focal person, the greater the degree of role conflict experienced by the focal person. According to Sarbin and Allen (1968), high degrees of role conflict result in increased cognitive activity and cognitive strain for the focal person (Sarbin & Allen, 1968, pp. 540-541).

1.2.2.2 Role Ambiguity

Similar to role conflict, the phenomenon of role ambiguity also represents a pattern of role sending which takes inadequate account of the needs and abilities of the focal person. Role ambiguity specifically refers to the "discrepancy between the amount of information a person has and the amount he requires to perform his role adequately" (Kahn, 1974, p. 59). Role ambiguity hence occurs when the set of behaviors expected for the focal person's role is unclear or inconsistent due to a lack of information. As with role conflict, objective role ambiguity must again be distinguished from its subjective counterpart. Objective ambiguity characterizes certain properties of the social and physical environment in terms of their likely influence on the perceptual processes of the focal person. Their actual influence on the focal person then constitutes his or her subjective (or experienced) ambiguity in that particular environment (Kahn et al., 1964, p. 22).

According to Kahn and his colleagues, there are several areas of ambiguity in occupational roles. It is claimed that all too often individuals are unclear about the scope of their responsibilities, in other words they may not know what they are supposed to do as part of their role. Furthermore, in cases when individuals know what to do, they may not always know how to do it. Such uncertainties arise because the expectations defining the role are themselves vague or inconsistent. Or it may be the case that individuals are uncertain as to whose expectations they are required to meet as it sometimes appears to be difficult to distinguish between legitimate role senders and other senders whose expectations could be safely ignored. To the extent that such secondary ambiguities center around available channels of communication, individuals may not know how to resolve the primary ambiguities from which they suffer. And, finally, role ambiguity may also stem from individuals' uncertainty about their opportunities for advancement (Kahn et al., 1964, pp. 24-25, 380-381).

Subjective role ambiguity is an unwanted psychological state (Ilgen & Hollenbeck, 1991, p. 194). The focal person experiences an unpleasant lack of clarity and structure in his or her role because he or she is uncertain which role behavior is appropriate and also cannot forecast the complementary conduct of other members of the role set (Sarbin & Allen, 1968, p. 503). In general, a focal person's doubts about his or her role, about how others evaluate him or her, or about how satisfied they are with the focal person's performance are seen as intimately related to strain and anxiety (House & Rizzo, 1972, p. 467; Kahn et al., 1964, pp. 24-25).

1.2.3 Coping Efforts and Symptom Formation

It is an integral part of Kahn and his colleagues' formulation of role theory that a focal person who is confronted with role conflict or role ambiguity "must respond to it in some fashion" (Kahn et al., 1964, p. 28). However, authors in the field of role theory have noted that the theory is fairly unspecific in its description of what these responses may consist of (Burke & Belcourt, 1974, p. 56; Ilgen & Hollenbeck, 1991, p. 188; Marginson & Ogden, 2005a, p. 442). Furthermore, Kahn et al. (1964, p. 95) predict that the responses to role conflict and those to role ambiguity are very similar, which means that, in the analysis of the consequences of role stress, the two constructs are often not clearly distinguished from each other. It is generally assumed that responses to role stress can take two forms: behavioral coping efforts and affective symptom formation. A focal person can use these responses singly or in combination (Kahn et al., 1966, pp. 278-279).

Behavioral coping efforts include a focal person's attempts to regain clear, orderly, and meaningful work experiences by compliance with role expectations or – if compliance is not possible – by persuading role senders to modify incompatible or ambiguous demands. Coping may also take the form of withdrawal from role senders and other behaviors avoiding the sources of role stress. Furthermore, Kahn et al. (1964, p. 29) mention the possibility of using defense mechanisms which distort the perceived reality of a conflictual or ambiguous situation in order to relieve the strain of the undistorted experience. Kahn and his colleagues point out that most of these behavioral coping efforts tend to decrease organizational effectiveness[9] (Kahn et al., 1964, p. 72).

Symptom formation refers to an individual's affective responses when facing role conflict or role ambiguity. Again, Kahn and his colleagues describe a variety of conceivable consequences on the part of the focal person, ranging from indecision and job dissatisfaction to tension and anger (Kahn et al., 1964, pp. 28-29; 1966, p. 278). Sometimes even more intense and debilitating emotional reactions may occur. Feelings of futility as well as symptoms of hysteria and psychosomatic disorders seem to be connected to the tensions engendered by role stress (Kahn et al., 1964, p. 67). The notion that conflicting and ambiguous role expectations relate to affective states which are predominantly dysfunctional to the individual can already be found in Merton's (1949) work. Here, an individual's frustration is mentioned as a typical consequence of role conflict (Merton, 1949, p. 110).

As a result, Kahn and his colleagues suppose that "role conflict and ambiguity exact a price, both in terms of individual well-being and organizational effectiveness" (Kahn et al., 1964, p. 53). Other scholars in the field of role theory follow the proposition that it is mainly dysfunctional individual and organizational consequences which result from the existence of role conflict and role ambiguity (Ilgen & Hollenbeck, 1991, pp. 191-192; Rizzo et al., 1970, p. 150).

---

9 For an elaboration on Kahn and his colleagues' definition of organizational effectiveness, see Katz and Kahn (1966, pp. 149-170). In short, the authors define organizational effectiveness as the ratio of energic input to energic output. Only organizations which import greater amounts of energy than they return to the environment are able to survive or, as Katz and Kahn (1966, p. 150) put it, are able to "maintain negentropy".

1.2.4 Surrounding Conditions

"The study of the isolated individual per se has no place in role theory" (Sarbin & Allen, 1968, p. 490). On the contrary, apart from the variables explained in the foregoing chapters, Kahn and his colleagues incorporate three types of conditioning factors in their framework which "can be regarded as providing the context in which the basic causal sequence of conflict and response is worked out" (Kahn et al., 1964, p. 8). Labeling them as "surrounding conditions" (Kahn et al., 1964, p. 37), the authors state organizational factors, personality factors, and interpersonal relations to be important for the understanding of role processes (Kahn et al., 1964, pp. 31-33; 1966, pp. 279-281; Katz & Kahn, 1978, pp. 208-217). This consideration of contextual factors in role processes is shared by other role theorists, e.g. Bertrand (1972, pp. 204-208) or Biddle and Thomas (1966a, pp. 51-64).

1.2.4.1 Organizational Factors

Organizational factors are claimed to be antecedents of roles. The role expectations held by the members of a role set, i.e. the prescriptions and proscriptions associated with a particular role, are at least in parts determined by the broader organizational context. Kahn et al. (1964, p. 31) refer to the organizational structure, the functional specialization and division of labor, and the formal reward system as dictating the content of the focal person's role. More specifically, organizational size, an organization's products, the focal person's as well as the role senders' rank in the organization, and the number and positions of others related to the focal person may influence the development of role expectations, role pressures, and subsequent role processes (Kahn et al., 1964, pp. 31-32, 97-98; 1966, p. 279).

1.2.4.2 Personality Factors

Kahn and his colleagues use the term personality broadly to take account of all factors that describe individuals' propensity to behave in a particular way, i.e. their motives, values, sensitivities, fears, and habits. The effects of these factors on role processes are threefold. First, some of the factors may evoke or facilitate certain role-related actions and attitudes on part of the role senders. Second, personality factors are relevant to role processes because they possibly cause some focal persons to experience role pressures differently than others. This means that personality factors can act as conditioning variables in the relationship between a supposedly objective situation and the focal person's individual perception of that situation. Third, personality factors deserve attention in the analysis of role processes because the focal person's reactions to the experience of role stress, i.e. coping efforts and symptom formation, are dependent on personality predispositions. Examples of personality factors which may act as conditioning variables are ability, confidence, extroversion, and flexibility (Kahn et al., 1964, pp. 32, 223-238; 1966, p. 280).

1.2.4.3 Interpersonal Relations

Interpersonal relations comprise the more or less stable patterns of interaction between the focal person and role senders and their orientations toward each other. According to Kahn and his colleagues, these patterns may be characterized along two main dimensions, the first stemming from formal organizational arrangements, the second from informal interactions and relationships. Basically, interpersonal relations influence role processes in ways analogous to those described for personality factors (see chapter C1.2.4.2). Again, role senders' actions and attitudes depend on interpersonal relations. Next, role pressures are likely to be interpreted differently by the focal person depending on the quality of the relations between the focal person and the role senders. Also, the nature of the focal person's responses to role conflict or role ambiguity may be affected by interpersonal relations. Kahn et al. (1964; 1966) provide some examples of interpersonal relations that may act as conditioning variables. Among others, they mention the affective bonds between the focal person and the role senders, such as respect or trust in cooperativeness, and the style of communication between the two (Kahn et al., 1964, pp. 32-33, 165-166; 1966, pp. 280-281).

1.3 The Role Episode as Causal Sequence in Role Processes

The interplay of role expectations, role pressures, role conflict and role ambiguity, coping efforts, and surrounding conditions can be illustrated in one integrated framework which Kahn and his colleagues call the *role episode*. This "classic role process" (Ilgen & Hollenbeck, 1991, p. 188) represents a causal sequence (Kahn et al., 1966, p. 277) combining the role concepts and relationships outlined in the preceding chapters (see Figure 3).

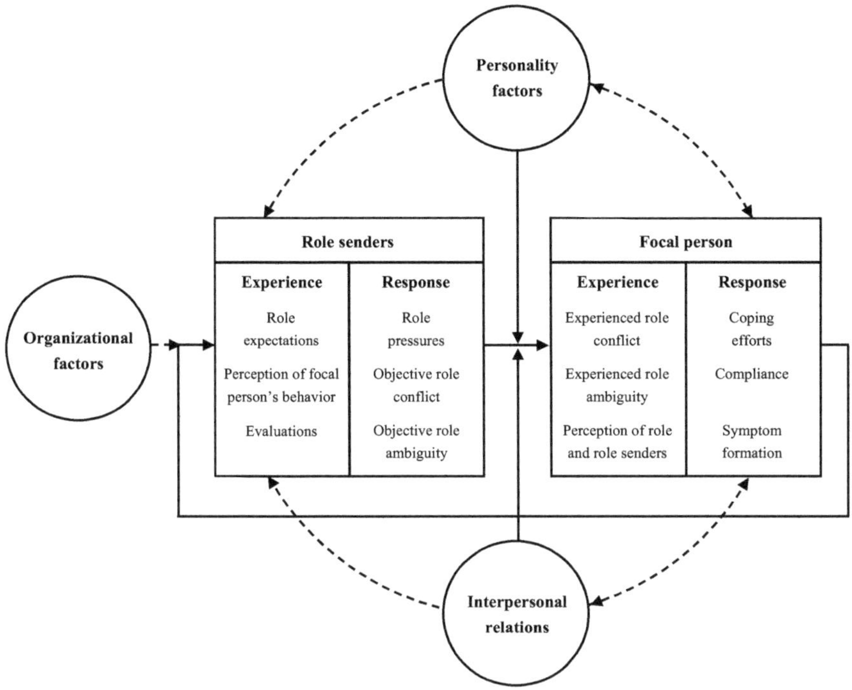

Figure 3: The Role Episode Model[10]

The basic role episode model is made up of the four boxes labeled role senders' and focal person's experience and response. These boxes depict the main events of the role episode which are causally connected. The existence of a set of role expectations on the part of the role senders represents the starting point of the episode. Role senders have certain expectations regarding the way in which the focal person should perform his or her role. They also have their own perceptions of how the focal person is actually behaving and performing. Altogether, the role senders' initial experience on the basis of which they develop their role expectations includes perceptual and evaluative components (Kahn et al., 1964, pp. 26-27).

Role senders correlate their role expectations and their perceptions of the focal person's performance. On this basis, they exert role pressures on the focal person to make his or her performance congruent with their expectations. Sometimes role senders communicate these pressures overtly to the focal person, and sometimes they apply more subtle influence attempts. It may even be the case that role senders are relatively unaware that their behavior

10 Taken (and slightly adapted) from Kahn et al. (1966, p. 280).

really is an influence attempt resulting in role pressures for the focal person. Irrespective of the intensity of the influence attempt, communications about actual and expected role performance usually carry an evaluative connotation. And even though there is no simple correspondence between role expectations being communicated and the resultant role pressures, the expectations always represent attempts to influence the behavior of the focal person (Kahn et al., 1966, pp. 277-278).

The sent role pressures generally induce a perceptual experience in the focal person (Kahn et al., 1964, p. 28). According to Kahn and his colleagues, it is indispensable to investigate the total set of all role senders' expectations which the focal person is confronted with when determining the effects of sent role pressures on the focal person. As mentioned before, Kahn and his colleagues at this point make an explicit distinction between the objective environment of the focal person and his or her psychological environment (Kahn et al., 1964, p. 12). The degree of objective role conflict and role ambiguity inherent in the role pressures depend on the configuration of the pressures actually exerted by role senders on the focal person. The focal person's subjective experience of role conflict and role ambiguity may diverge from their objective counterparts. The subjective experience depends to a certain extent on the objective magnitude of role conflict and role ambiguity; however, several conditioning variables (see chapter C1.2.4) are likely to modify the objective characteristics of the focal person's environment. The experienced degree of role conflict and role ambiguity will thus always reflect the focal person's objective situation as it interacts with relevant properties of the person, the organization, and interpersonal relations (Kahn et al., 1964, pp. 27-28).

The focal person's processing of the received role pressures and the accompanying degrees of conflict and role ambiguity produce what Kahn et al. (1964, p. 27) call adjustive or maladjustive responses. Role conflict and role ambiguity are thereby positioned as intervening variables that mediate the effects of role pressures on the resultant responses (Pearce, 1981, p. 665; Rizzo et al., 1970, pp. 154-155). As described in chapter C1.2.3, the responses to experienced role ambiguity and conflict consist of behavioral and affective components (Kahn et al., 1964, pp. 379-381). The focal person may try to effectively cope with role pressures in order to regain a gratifying work experience. However, again depending on the various conditioning variables as well as on the configuration of the role pressures, the focal person may also react by withdrawal, frustration, and dissatisfaction (Kahn et al., 1966, pp. 278-279).

The role episode does not end with the focal person's adjustive or maladjustive responses. Since the role episode model represents a complete "cycle of role sending, response by the focal person, and the effects of that response on the role sender" (Kahn et al., 1964, p. 26), it is important to note that Kahn and his colleagues incorporate a feedback loop in their theory (Katz & Kahn, 1966, p. 183; 1978, p. 195). The degree to which the focal person's responses conform to the expectations initially held by the role senders is expected to affect the state of these expectations in the next role episode. If, for example, the focal person's response is essentially a hostile counterattack on the role senders, the role senders are likely to behave to the focal person in ways quite different than if the focal person were submissively compliant. In sum, the role episode theoretically describes a cyclic and ongoing process in which the focal person's responses provide feedback to the senders of role pressures in ways that alter or reinforce the latter. The subsequent role sendings depend on the role senders' evaluation of the responses to the previous sendings, and thus a new role episode begins (Kahn et al., 1966, p. 279). That way, Kahn and his colleagues' formulation of role theory is supposed to be equally appropriate for investigating dynamic changes in role patterns and relationships as it is for illustrating stable states, e.g. states of conflict, ambiguity, or harmony (Kahn et al., 1964, p. 379).

Finally, the role episode model depicted in Figure 3 underlines the interaction of the model's core variables (i.e. role expectations, role pressures, role conflict and role ambiguity, and coping efforts) with its surrounding conditions. Organizational factors, personality factors, and interpersonal relations substantially influence the consecutive stages of the role episode. However, it is noteworthy that, according to Kahn and his colleagues, the surrounding conditions not only affect the relationships between the episode's core variables, but are, conversely, also affected themselves by results of the role process. It is stated that certain reactions to role experiences may lead to changes in interpersonal relations or personality, e.g. when the focal person's continual inability to meet the environmental demands threatens his or her confidence. The focal person's reactions to role pressures may also include immediate changes in his or her feelings toward the role senders, such as a loss of respect, which is in the long run likely to deteriorate the relationship between the two (Kahn et al., 1966, pp. 281-282).

2. Recent Developments and Expansions to Role Theory

Despite its contribution to several academic disciplines, classical role theory has at times been criticized. Scholars such as Habermas (1973, pp. 127-128), Haug (1994, pp. 124-126), and Turner (1979, p. 127) have denounced the theory because it allegedly neglects the important dimension of individuals' freedom to act. Similarly, Jackson (1998, pp. 51-52) regards role theory as insufficient in terms of a complete understanding of the many intentions underlying individuals' observable actions and of human subjectivity in general. Others have expressed their discontent with the vague and inconsistent concepts of role theory (Biddle, 1986, pp. 67-68; Duckro, Beal, & George, 1979, p. 270; Turner, 1979, pp. 124-125) and the rather prescriptive nature it suffers from (Henriksen, 2008, pp. 42-43; Tan & Moghaddam, 1999, pp. 186-187). Furthermore, Kahn and his colleagues' role theory has been criticized because of its implicit assumption that all conflicts in organizations are merely role conflicts. Some thoughts from role theory also turn out to be rather naïve in that they suggest that organizational members will inevitably be happy and productive once role conflict and role ambiguity are resolved (Biddle, 1986, p. 74). Finally, in the light of the contribution that empirical studies on role phenomena have made to the theory, it has been noted that there appears to be "a lack of integration between the efforts of theorists and researchers in the role field" (Biddle, 1986, p. 86).

Some of the above points of criticism have been addressed in later works and expansions to role theory. Of central importance to this study are the research streams on role orientation and extra-role behavior which take a broader approach as to how organizational roles emerge and to which types of role behavior can be distinguished.

2.1 Role Orientation

Role represents the product of a learning process whereby individuals apprehend how to act in their environment (Beehr & Glazer, 2005, p. 10). However, early scholars in the field of role theory were often not interested in studying role learning (Habermas, 1973, p. 126; Sarbin & Allen, 1968, p. 544). It is later generations of role theorists who have put increased emphasis on roles as evolving from the focal person's learning (Dierdorff & Morgeson, 2007, p. 1237; Ilgen & Hollenbeck, 1991, p. 169). Two of the main topics which emanate from viewing roles as the product of a learning process are role making and role orientation.

Tellingly, the central chapters on role theory in Katz and Kahn's (1966; 1978) works are entitled "The taking of organizational roles". Individuals are supposed to take or, put differently, to adopt a role, which conveys a rather passive perspective on how roles emerge (Frink & Klimoski, 1998, p. 26). As described in Kahn and his colleagues' formulation of role theory, the focal person receives role expectations from the role senders and then attempts to fulfill these expectations. This view on role processes basically means that the "shaping of role to person has already occurred" (Katz & Kahn, 1978, p. 217), either in the minds of the role senders or in formal job descriptions and the like. It severely delimits the decision-making latitude of the individual performing a role. Thus traditional role theory leaves little space for the individual to play an active part in the configuration of his or her own role (Griffin, 1987, p. 94; Griffin & McMahan, 1994, pp. 30-31).

It is Graen and his colleagues (Dansereau, Graen, & Haga, 1975; Graen, 1976; Graen & Scandura, 1987) who argue that the individual is much more anxious to shape his or her role than implied in the original formulation of role theory. Graen (1976, pp. 1205-1209) refers to Kahn et al.'s role episode as a role taking model and contrasts it with role making. Role making describes a process whereby the focal person actively influences the definition of his or her role in a way that is satisfactory both to members of the role set and to him- or herself. In particular, role making processes allow for the individual's propensity to (a) acquire knowledge about the content of demands placed upon his or her behavior and the sources of these demands, (b) receive and send persuasive communications regarding his or her behavior in the role, (c) accept a particular pattern of behavior, and (d) modify this pattern over time (Graen, 1976, pp. 1201-1202). The concept of role making integrates the focal person's job history, his or her own set of expectations about the role, as well as his or her motives and beliefs (Katz & Kahn, 1978, p. 217) and therefore represents a complementary perspective on the emergence of roles. This perspective is also reflected in the work of other role theorists (Bertrand, 1972; Ilgen & Hollenbeck, 1991; Turner, 1962). Turner (1962, p. 22) assumes that the individual "is creating and modifying roles as well as bringing them to light; the process is not only role-taking but role-making". Perrone et al. (2003, p. 424) conclude that role making together with role taking provides a more "compelling approach for highlighting the duality inherent in roles, much like two sides of a coin". Meanwhile, the role making perspective on the emergence of organizational roles has found its way into much of the contemporary role literature from social psychology (Baron et al., 2008, p. 384; Hogg & Vaughan, 2005, p. 295).

The concept of role orientation is part of the role making perspective and likewise highlights the importance of learning and individual role shaping. According to Parker (2007, p. 406), role orientation refers to how individuals define "their work role, such as how broadly they perceive their role; what types of tasks, goals, and problems they see as relevant to their role". Parker and her colleagues' work on role orientation (Parker, 2000; 2007; Parker et al., 1997) is based on Davis and Wacker's (1987) and Ilgen and Hollenbeck's (1991) distinction between roles and jobs. Following Davis and Wacker (1987, p. 433), a key difference between the two (see also chapter C1.2.1) is:

> In a narrow "job-description sense", one's job is a particular task assignment . . . ; in a broad "role" sense, one's job is to help carry out the responsibilities assigned to the team, to participate in team decisions, to cross-train, and to use one's judgment to contribute to the team's productivity, maintenance, and development.

The notion that individuals may exhibit a flexible (or broad) role orientation that goes beyond mere job descriptions implies that they are likely to perceive tasks as being part of their duties that others who have a narrow role orientation might neglect. Parker (2000; 2007) therefore depicts role orientation as a cognitive variable which reflects a proactive rather than reactive state. As such, it is shaped by the environment, as well as by the focal person's personality and individual differences (Parker, 2000, pp. 449-452; 2007, pp. 403-406).

The concept of role orientation and the role making perspective as a whole represent a valuable extension to Kahn and his colleagues' role theory since they modify the theory's passive and restrictive keynote. It is not without reason that Kahn and his colleagues admit in a concluding review of their theory that "research on role sending in organizations has thus far concentrated more on . . . particular inadequacies in the expectational pattern and sending process (conflict, ambiguity, overload) than on constructive elements" (Katz & Kahn, 1978, p. 203).

2.2 Extra-Role Behavior

Literature on extra-role behavior also attempts to enrich classical role theory. Following Van Dyne, Cummings, and McLean Parks (1995), extra-role behaviors (which are collectively often referred as extra-role performance) can be defined as behaviors which benefit the organization, which are discretionary, and which go beyond conventional job requirements. They are unlike in-role behaviors (or in-role performance), which are prescribed by formal job descriptions and corresponding tasks and duties (Van Dyne et al., 1995, pp. 218-222). From an organizational perspective, extra-role behaviors are valued because dynamic environments often do not allow specification of all desired employee behaviors in advance (Morrison, 1994, p. 1543; Van Dyne & LePine, 1998, p. 108). It is "virtually impossible . . . to anticipate all the task elements that will be necessary to make jobs work in the environment for which they are designed. Thus to make jobs work in their environment, an extra set or collection of task elements needs to be added to those that originally constituted the job" (Ilgen & Hollenbeck, 1991, p. 174).

Extra-role behavior can take many forms. A common typology of extra-role behaviors is based on the work of Van Dyne, Cummings, and McLean Parks (1995). This typology contrasts promotive and prohibitive extra-role behaviors as well as affiliative and challenging extra-role behaviors. Promotive behaviors are proactive in that they promote, encourage, or cause things to happen. Prohibitive behaviors are protective and preventative. They include interceding to protect those with less power as well as speaking out to stop inappropriate or unethical occurrences. Affiliative behaviors are interpersonal and cooperative. They strengthen relationships and are other-oriented. Challenging behaviors emphasize ideas and issues. They are change-oriented and can even damage relationships (Van Dyne et al., 1995, pp. 228-250). This typology of promotive, prohibitive, affiliative, and challenging extra-role behaviors together with exemplary constructs from prior research in this area is depicted in Figure 4.

	Affiliative	Challenging
Promotive	Example: **Organizational citizenship behavior** (Organ, 1988) = promotes the effective functioning of the organization, is discretionary and not directly or explicitly recognized by the formal reward system. Consists of five sub-dimensions	Example: **Internal influence behavior** (Bettencourt, Brown, & MacKenzie, 2005) = takes individual initiative in communications to others in order to solve organizational problems and improve operations outside one's own area of authority
Prohibitive	Example: **Stewardship** (Van Dyne et al., 1995) = protects less powerful individuals. Prevents unfair treatment, injustice, or harm	Example: **Whistle-blowing** (Near & Miceli, 1985) = discloses illegal, immoral or illegitimate practices to persons or organizations that may be able to effect action

Figure 4: Typology of Extra-Role Behaviors[11]

Despite seemingly clear-cut definitions, scholars agree that the boundaries between in-role and extra-role behaviors are often ill-defined and subject to multiple interpretations (Morrison, 1994, p. 1544). There is not only evidence that individuals differ in what they define as in-role and extra-role (Morrison, 1994, p. 1543), it is also reported that superiors often tend to view extra-role behaviors as a required part of their subordinates' jobs or define job performance more broadly to include any behaviors (whether formally required or not) that contribute to the effective functioning of the organization (MacKenzie, Podsakoff, & Fetter, 1991, p. 145; 1993, p. 78). When superiors evaluate their subordinates' performance, they may sometimes reward extra-role behaviors just like in-role aspects of performance, for the purpose of increasing the frequency of the extra-role behaviors (Podsakoff, MacKenzie, Paine, & Bachrach, 2000, p. 533). This underlines the dynamic nature of role processes – roles and role behavior evolve over time as the result of the interaction of physical and social systems in the organization (Frink & Klimoski, 1998, p. 24; Ilgen & Hollenbeck, 1991, p. 167). In many circumstances the distinction between in-role and extra-role behaviors appears to be a question of personal gusto rather than reasoning. In his seminal work on organizational citizenship behavior, Organ (1988, p. 5) therefore points out that "realistically, what we have in organization environments is a continuum" of behaviors that may be regarded as extra-role in one situation and as in-role in another. Likewise, Morrison (1994, p. 1564) suggests imagining an individual's definition of his or her role as a set of concentric circles. In the center are core behaviors (in-role behaviors), and in the outermost ring are behaviors that are

[11] Based on Van Dyne et al. (1995, p. 252).

above and beyond formal job requirements (extra-role behaviors). The boundaries between them appear to be in a constant state of flux.

3. Role Theory in Management Accounting Research

Since the early use of Kahn and his colleagues' role theory in the work of DeCoster and Fertakis (1968), the theory has had impact on both conceptual and empirical studies in the field of (management) accounting. Figure 5 provides an overview of the studies that are informed by role theory and were published in 10 leading accounting journals[12] from 1964 to 2009.

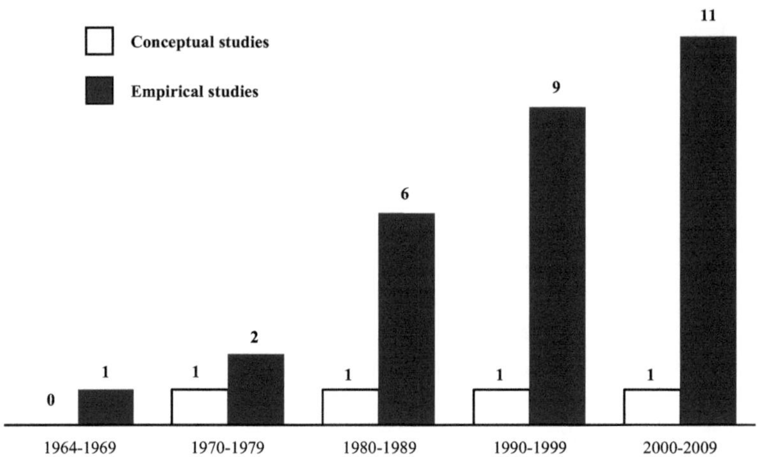

Figure 5: Management Accounting Studies Informed by Role Theory

The last decades of management accounting research are marked by a sharp increase in the use of role theory. However, only four conceptual studies that are rooted in role theory have been published so far. It becomes obvious that role theory has been more helpful in guiding

12 Including the following A+, A, and B journals (according to the VHB ranking): (a) The Accounting Review, (b) Accounting, Organizations and Society, (c) Contemporary Accounting Research, (d) Management Accounting Research, (e) Journal of Accounting Research, (f) Journal of Management Accounting Research, (g) Critical Perspectives on Accounting, (h) European Accounting Review, (i) Abacus: Journal of Accounting, and (j) Behavioral Research in Accounting. Relevant studies have first been identified with the help of a database search (in EBSCO, Sciencedirect, and other databases if the former two did not allow adequate access to the above journals) for "role theory", "role expectation", "role stress", "role conflict", or "role ambiguity" in either title, abstract, key words, or full text. In the second step, these studies have been analyzed more closely in order to ascertain that they are truly informed by role theory. In the third step, further studies applying role theory have been identified with the help of cross-references in the studies obtained during the first two steps.

empirical research endeavors. In the period from 1964 to 2009, 29 empirical studies have employed the theory. Among them, the survey method has been applied most frequently. 26 studies rely on this method whereby six of them combine survey data with additional insights gained through interviews. A case study approach has been chosen in only three of the empirical studies.

Apart from these in total 33 studies, several other management accounting works have implicitly benefited from role theory – either in their use of theoretical constructs emanating from role theory (i.e. first and foremost role conflict and role ambiguity) or in the understanding of causal processes of human perception and behavior. The following brief review of role theory in management accounting studies, however, only focuses on the identified 33 studies which explicitly refer to Kahn and his colleagues' theory in their reasoning or hypothesis development. Table 6 briefly portrays all 33 studies. A synopsis of the studies' common themes and more details on selected studies follow in the last part of this chapter.

Study and year of origin	Type	Details
DeCoster and Fertakis (1968)	Empirical	Applies role theory to explore how superiors use budgets as a way of expressing their own patterns of leadership
Hopwood (1972; 1973)	Empirical	Centers around role stress aspects of role theory; Investigates managers' responses to different supervisory styles, in particular to the use of accounting data in performance evaluation
Shenkir and Strawser (1972)	Conceptual	Employs role theory to describe potential role conflicts among certified public accountants when expected to act as auditors and management advisors for the same client
Otley (1978)	Empirical	Follows Hopwood (1972) in the examination of the effects of supervisory styles on managers' experienced job tension; Relies on role theory in terms of basic causal relationships (managers' inner states are depicted as intervening variables)
Hopper (1980)	Empirical	Examines accountants' and managers' perceptions of management accounting roles under conditions of centralization and decentralization of the management accounting function; Identifies role stress emanating from accounting workflows
Senatra (1980)	Empirical	Investigates role conflict and role ambiguity experienced by audit seniors in a large accounting company; Draws on role theory to develop a framework including consequences and sources of role conflict and role ambiguity
Hirst (1981)	Empirical	Attempts to enlarge previous studies on the use of accounting performance measures (Hopwood, 1972; Otley, 1978) by the variable of task uncertainty
Collins (1982)	Conceptual	Highlights accounting systems' usefulness in communicating role expectations, triggering motivation, and communicating organizational climate
Collins, Munter, and Finn (1987)	Empirical	Draws on role theory to develop and test a research model on managers' role stress and game playing behaviors that are related to superiors' budgetary leadership style
Chenhall and Brownell (1988)	Empirical	Examines the effects of participative budgeting on job satisfaction and performance; Depicts role ambiguity as intervening variable
Bamber, Snowball, and Tubbs (1989)	Empirical	Employs role theory to investigate the effects of audit structure (i.e. structured versus unstructured audit companies) on organizational characteristics which, in turn, are potential sources of role conflict and role ambiguity

Study and year of origin ***(cont.)***	**Type**	**Details**
Rebele and Michaels (1990)	Empirical	Examines role stress experienced by independent auditors; Uses role theory to develop a causal model including several antecedent, outcome and moderating variables
Fogarty (1992)	Conceptual	Uses key concepts from role theory to develop a framework for socialization of staff members in accounting companies
Jaworski and Young (1992)	Empirical	Explores the relationship between three contextual variables (goal congruence, perceived peer dysfunctional behavior, information asymmetry between superiors and subordinates) on subordinate dysfunctional behavior; References role theory in order to develop hypotheses about the mediating effects of role conflict and tension
Dunk (1993b)	Empirical	Attempts to validate Hopwood's (1972) finding that managers' tension negatively influences their performance
Gregson, Wendell, and Aono (1994)	Empirical	Determines whether variables frequently used in research on role theory (role conflict, role ambiguity, perceived environmental uncertainty) represent measurements of distinct constructs
Ross (1994; 1995)	Empirical	Attempts to replicate previous studies on the use of accounting performance measures (Hirst, 1981; Hopwood, 1972; Otley, 1978); Additionally examines the moderating influence of trust
Abernethy and Stoelwinder (1995)	Empirical	Investigates the conflict between the management of hospital professionals (physician and nurse subunit managers) and bureaucratic norms; Employs role theory to explain the dysfunctional effects of bureaucracy
O'Connor (1995)	Empirical	Explores the moderating effect of cultural variables on the relationship between managers' budget participation and their experienced role ambiguity
Jönsson (1998)	Empirical	Describes management as a cooperative game where communication is central to attention direction; Refers to a symbolic-interactive view of role theory that sees role concepts in a more communicative light
Abernethy and Brownell (1999)	Empirical	Discusses the importance of accounting and budgeting for implementing strategic change; Interprets CEOs as the key agents of strategic change and declares the CEOs' overt behaviors to be "enacted role"
Fisher (2001)	Empirical	Extends prior research on the effects of role stress on outcome variables by examining the moderating influence of the "Type A" behavior pattern
Lau and Buckland (2001)	Empirical	Draws on role theory and prior RAPM studies to investigate the effects of particular combinations of budget emphasis and budgetary participation on managers' tension

Study and year of origin *(cont.)*	**Type**	**Details**
McAulay, Scrace, and Tomkins (2001)	Empirical	Investigates the implementation of a transfer pricing system in a financial services company; Depicts the transfer pricing system as part of the CEO's role expectation for cost-reduction
Viator (2001)	Empirical	Employs role theory to examine the association between mentoring, three measures of role stress (role conflict, role ambiguity, perceived environmental uncertainty), and job performance as well as turnover intentions
Marginson and Ogden (2005a)	Empirical	Examines the extent to which budgets have a positive or "comforting" influence; Argues that managers confronted with role ambiguity may respond by becoming positively committed to achieving budgetary targets because budgets offer a source of structure and certainty
Marginson (2006)	Empirical	Deals with the psychology of information processing; Focuses on the acquisition of clear information about expected role behaviors through communication channels and information media
Burney and Widener (2007)	Empirical	Relies on mediating role stress variables (role conflict and role ambiguity) to explain the effect of strategic performance measurement systems (SPMS) on managerial performance
Byrne and Pierce (2007)	Empirical	Addresses the determination of the roles of management accountants; Identifies a set of antecedents, characteristics, and consequences of roles
Hall (2008)	Empirical	Argues that the effects of comprehensive performance measurement systems on managerial performance is mediated by role perceptions; Focuses on role clarity instead of role ambiguity
Hechter (2008)	Conceptual	Discusses current literature on norms and normative control; References role theory in order to argue that distinctive positions in society are often defined normatively
Maas and Matějka (2009)	Empirical	Employs role theory to explain business unit controllers' role conflict and role ambiguity when being confronted with dual responsibilities of supporting both local decision-making and corporate control over their business units
Marginson and Bui (2009)	Empirical	Relies on role theory to argue that managers experience role conflict leading to a decrease in performance when they are facing superiors' expectations that emphasize innovation and empowerment alongside budget goal attainment

Table 6: Management Accounting Studies Informed by Role Theory

Managers' role stress turns out to be the central topic of most management accounting studies that are built on role theory (Abernethy & Stoelwinder, 1995; DeCoster & Fertakis, 1968; Dunk, 1993b; Hirst, 1981; Hopwood, 1972; 1973; Lau & Buckland, 2001; Marginson & Bui, 2009; Otley, 1978; Ross, 1994; 1995). The work of DeCoster and Fertakis (1968) is the first of these studies into role stress. The authors use role theory to structure their investigation of an issue raised by Argyris (1952; 1953), namely that of how budgeting and managers' interaction with their superiors influence managers' budget-induced pressure and their own leadership style towards their subordinates. DeCoster and Fertakis (1968, p. 242) interpret communications from immediate superiors and their detailed requirements regarding budgetary matters as role expectations and as the "closest source of pressure" upon a manager. Testing their theoretical predictions, DeCoster and Fertakis (1968) find that budget-induced pressure is correlated with two particular types of leadership behavior – initiating structure (i.e. leadership behavior which is related to work performance and therefore production-oriented and structuring) and consideration (i.e. leadership behavior which is employee-oriented and indicative of friendship, mutual trust, and respect). Unlike superiors' role expectations, pressures from procedures for formulating budgets or budget administration are not related to either type of leadership behavior (DeCoster & Fertakis, 1968, pp. 245-246).

It is Hopwood (1972; 1973) who picks up the idea of superiors' emphasis on budgets as influencing managers' psychological well-being and behavior. He uses role theory to connect supervisory styles, tension, and dysfunctional behaviors. According to Hopwood (1972; 1973), there are three different supervisory styles: (a) the budget-constrained style which refers to an evaluation that is primarily based upon managers' ability to continually meet the budget on a short-term basis, (b) the profit-conscious style which means that managers are evaluated on the basis of their ability to increase the general effectiveness of their units' operations in relation to the long-term purposes of the organization, and (c) the nonaccounting style which implies that accounting data play a relatively unimportant part in superiors' evaluation of their subordinate managers' performance (Hopwood, 1972, p. 160). It is argued that, given the imperfect nature of accounting performance measures, especially a budget-constrained supervisory style leads to role conflict and role ambiguity. Role conflict and role ambiguity, in turn, cause managerial stress, tension, and anxiety. Dysfunctional behaviors, Hopwood (1972) further argues, are a consequence of managers trying to cope with such stress and tension (Hopwood, 1972, pp. 160-163). Hopwood's (1972, p. 166) findings reveal that, as hypothesized, tension among managers is highest for the budget-constrained supervisory style. Hopwood's (1972; 1973) work has provoked a series of further studies examining the effects of different supervisory styles. Commonly, it is investigated how role conflict and role ambiguity mediate these effects on tension, dysfunctional behaviors, and managerial performance (Birnberg et al., 2006, p. 122). This body of literature is referred to as the RAPM research stream. Prominent examples of later RAPM studies come from Otley

(1978), Hirst (1981), and Ross (1994; 1995). Apart from few exceptions (Brownell, 1982; Dunk, 1993a), RAPM research "shows great consistency in its basic theoretical framework, that is informed by role theory" (Hartmann, 2000, p. 467). In fact, Hartmann (2000, p. 467) and Briers and Hirst (1990, p. 395) ascribe RAPM studies' limited focus on the stressful and negative effects of RAPM to the role theory paradigm prevailing in this research stream.

Apart from the examination of role stress that is supposed to result from the use of MCSs and accounting data, there are some, but comparatively few, studies which use role theory less restrictively and unilaterally (Collins, 1982; Jönsson, 1998; Marginson, 2006; Marginson & Ogden, 2005a). Neglecting the focus on role conflict and role ambiguity that is inherent to most RAPM studies, role theory is here presented as a platform to elaborate on the relative importance of MCSs in clarifying job requirements and prescribing normative role behaviors in organizations. Collins (1982) is a proponent of this view who develops three propositions on the value of MCSs which are informed by role theory. He not only argues that (a) MCSs are useful in communicating role expectations and hence in informing role incumbents about what is expected from them, but also highlights that (b) the systems are important for motivation since they can influence the intrinsic and extrinsic desirability of performing a given task or role. According to Collins (1982), it is also noteworthy that (c) MCSs are expressive of the organizational climate and thus helpful in socialization processes. The term climate here refers to the qualitative nature of the social processes within the organization. MCSs indicate whether the organizational climate is, for example, bureaucratic, democratic, or autocratic. Collins (1982) concludes that role theory offers a very specific framework which epitomizes the relevance of MCSs for controlling organizational behavior. The theory points out that management should generally be concerned with identifying and articulating organizational purpose and also with directing organizational energy toward its achievement. It is in this context that MCSs are expected to be paramount since they provide a helpful instrument to shape individuals' beliefs about values, norms, and role requirements – in short, they can focus organizational energy (Collins, 1982, pp. 108-110).

While Collins's (1982) propositions and the findings from RAPM research appear to be primarily tailored to managers and managerial role perceptions, several other studies have originated which adopt the role theory perspective to the jobs of auditors, financial accountants, and management accountants (Byrne & Pierce, 2007; Fisher, 2001; Gregson et al., 1994; Hopper, 1980; Maas & Matějka, 2009; Rebele & Michaels, 1990; Senatra, 1980; Shenkir & Strawser, 1972). The most comprehensive study on antecedents, characteristics, and consequences of the roles of management accountants is provided by Byrne and Pierce (2007). Building on the work of Hopper (1980), the authors identify a variety of factors which influence the roles of management accountants. Particular attention is devoted to the involvement of management accountants in management processes and what causes such involvement. Byrne and Pierce (2007) consider operating managers acting as role senders and expressing their role expectations toward management accountants. Some managers are reported to be comfortable with a narrower accounting role which mainly focuses on information provision, while others expect accountants to occupy a broader partnering role which includes participation in decision-making. Next to role expectations on behalf of operating managers, Byrne and Pierce's (2007) findings show that the management accountants themselves are important drivers in the design of their own roles. It is their attitudes, personalities, and initiative that appear to determine role making processes (Byrne & Pierce, 2007, pp. 487-489). The work of Byrne and Pierce (2007) hence represents an insightful example of how role theory helps to understand the interplay of normative role expectations, role taking and role making, perceived roles, and actual role behaviors.

In conclusion, prior studies have successfully transferred key concepts of role theory into the realm of management accounting research and illustrated their value for the investigation of behavioral phenomena. Role theory has clearly proven to be "a theoretical research structure around which research on the behavioral aspects of managerial accounting may be conducted" (Collins, 1982, p. 108). It helps to remind researchers that MCSs are an essential part of the explicit mechanisms of accountability that guide individuals to perform the role behaviors that the organization prefers (Frink & Klimoski, 1998, p. 38; Graen, 1976, p. 1215; Marginson & Bui, 2009, pp. 59-60). Thus, the continued use of role theory in management accounting research seems promising because the theory is broad enough to provide researchers with a frame of reference for their research, yet specific enough to generate testable hypotheses (Collins, 1982, p. 119).

D Development of the Causal Models

Based on the findings from extant literature on the controllability principle (see part B) and deliberations derived from role theory (see part C), the following chapters develop several hypotheses addressing the research questions outlined in part A. In doing so, it is the ambition of this work to counteract the main caveats which have been raised against prior empirical research on the controllability principle (see also chapter B1.1.1.2).

First, this work aims to alleviate the "lack of prior research which was directly based on the controllability principle" (Marginson & McAulay, 2001, p. 14). Many insights into corporate practice of applying the controllability principle stem from research that has actually been devoted to topics such as decentralization or budgeting and is thus often only incidentally related to the controllability principle. In this work, however, the principle's application and its importance for organizational control represent the central objects of investigation.

Second, this work intends to contribute to existing literature in that it chooses a specific unit of analysis, namely the managers who are being confronted with the application (or nonapplication) of the controllability principle in their performance evaluation. According to Giraud et al. (2008, p. 34), it is this position of the managers evaluated that "has not been much examined". Prior research on the controllability principle has rather focused on evaluators and designers of performance evaluation systems. Their attitude towards the principle dominates the perspective of most previous empirical work. However, Ramadan (1989, p. 37) rightly argues that "their views might well differ" from those of the managers evaluated. Drury and El-Shishini (2005, p. 46) therefore call for further empirical management accounting research that is targeted at the managers themselves instead of superiors and system designers.

Third, as highlighted by many management accounting scholars (Choudhury, 1986, pp. 196-197; Merchant, 1989, p. 130; Modell, 1997, p. 314), the application of the controllability principle is a matter of costs and benefits associated with it (see also chapter B3.4). Nonetheless, most previous research endeavors focus on either the advantages or the disadvantages of the principle's application. This work attempts to combine the two perspectives in a single study. It follows Atkinson et al. (1997, p. 84), who point out that "both the costs and benefits of relying on the controllability principle to design performance evaluation systems deserve additional investigation . . . [Empirical research should] identify whether manager's strategies are functional or dysfunctional to the firm".

Fourth, and closely related to the aforementioned point, it is the objective of this work to go beyond the descriptive nature of many previous studies on the controllability principle. As Pelster (2007, p. 74) notes in his review of empirical studies on the principle, most research merely investigates the factual degree of the principle's application in practice. The functional and dysfunctional effects resulting from different levels of application are often disregarded. On that account, this study primarily investigates what Drury and El-Shishini (2005, p. 46) refer to as the "behavioral implications" of management accounting practices. It is these behavioral implications related to the application of the controllability principle that ultimately determine the principle's relevance for organizational effectiveness and managerial motivation (Marginson & Ogden, 2005b, p. 49).

1. The Basic Line of Argument

As outlined in the foregoing, this work argues that "aside from studying the technical aspects of management control systems, it is essential to consider how the system will influence the behavior of the people who use it" (Bhimani et al., 2008, p. 614). However, following psychological theories it is not likely that MCSs and their design characteristics directly affect human behavior. This work therefore adopts the viewpoint that the effects of MCSs on observable outcomes depend on mental processes, which takes account of indirect causal relationships that may be subject to complex interactions (Griffin, 1987, p. 111; Hackman & Oldham, 1976, p. 264; Ilgen, Fisher, & Taylor, 1979, p. 366).

In general, individuals' responses to MCSs and their design characteristics can be categorized as (a) cognitive, (b) affective, and (c) behavioral. Cognitive responses include individuals' perceptions, imagination, and thinking. They are typically seen as nonevaluative, they simply refer to the processes by which individuals become aware of, interpret, and assimilate information obtained by their senses. Affective responses are more evaluative in nature and include individuals' feelings, emotions, and well-being. Behavioral responses refer to actions, reactions, and efforts shown by individuals. They include the complete spectrum of organizationally relevant behaviors from which individuals may choose. Prominent among these are performance, absenteeism, and turnover (Bunge & Ardila, 1987, p. 207; Griffin, 1987, pp. 94-95; Luckett & Eggleton, 1991, pp. 375-376; Taylor, Fisher, & Ilgen, 1984, p. 100). All of the above are important components in the understanding of the implications of MCSs on the level of the individual. In fact, MCSs and the way they are designed provide information and feedback to the individual and thus represent particular types of stimuli that the individual has to address in managing his or her job (Luckett & Eggleton, 1991, p. 376).

Since this work is based on role theory, it is hypothesized that cognitive variables and specifically individuals' role perceptions mediate the effects of the stimuli provided by MCSs on affective and behavioral responses. This reasoning of indirect effects has a long tradition in behavioral research (Ajzen, 1991, p. 179; James & Brett, 1984, p. 307; Tetlock, 1985, pp. 300-301). In order to increase explanatory power and leave black-box-models of human behavior, scholars have long agreed that mental processes have to be taken into account. According to Bunge and Ardila (1987, p. 118), any research in the fields of psychology and human behavior that takes such mental processes into account is called stimulus-organism-response (S-O-R). Woodworth's (1928) S-O-R model is an early and frequently cited, even though fairly generic work on mediation. Today, many management accounting studies heavily use the mediation hypothesis in researching the effects of MCSs and their design characteristics on behavioral variables (e.g. Burney, Henle, and Widener (2009), Hartmann and Slapničar (2009), or Shields et al. (2000)). This seems to be the result of a favorable learning process in management accounting research since early studies in this area have often simply investigated whether management accounting variables directly affect outcomes such as job satisfaction or managerial performance. According to Covaleski, Evans, Luft, and Shields (2003, pp. 28-29) and Birnberg et al. (2006, p. 116), the mixed results of these early studies have led researchers to develop mediation models that help to shed light on the mental mechanisms lying behind the correlations of management accounting variables with observable outcome variables.

Apart from the integration of mediating effects, role theory also takes the existence of moderators into consideration. It recognizes that the effects of stimuli on cognitive, affective, and behavioral responses may be modified by contextual factors (Katz & Kahn, 1978, pp. 583-585). This approach is also reflected in several contemporary management accounting studies that include moderators in their investigation of causal relationships between MCSs and individuals' responses (e.g. Burney and Widener (2007), Gul and Chia (1994), Hirst and Yetton (1999), or Ross (1994)). Above all the RAPM research stream has included moderator variables to analyze the contextual appropriateness of RAPM as well as to explain differences in the findings from previous studies. Under the label of contingency approaches, RAPM studies have included a broad variety of moderators, ranging from organizational strategy to personality and cultural variables (Hartmann, 2000, pp. 468-469). This work follows role theory in the search for moderators on the basic relationships between stimuli and responses. Figure 6 depicts the S-O-R sequence that is postulated by Kahn and his colleagues and that prepares the ground for the development of moderated mediation models in this work. It is this sequence that also underlies Kahn and his colleagues' role episode model outlined in chapter C1.3.

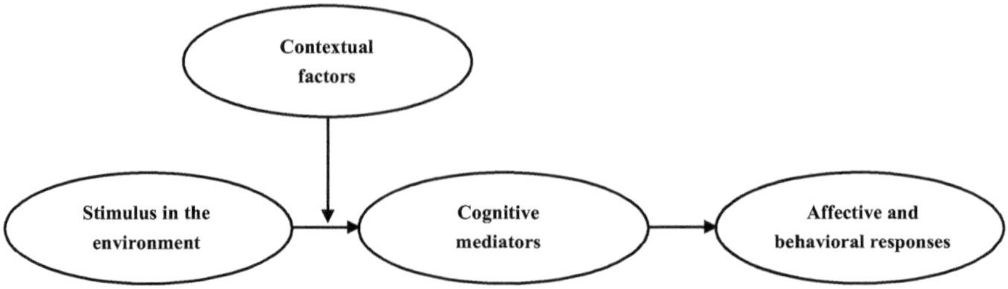

Figure 6: Stimulus-Organism-Response Sequence of Role Theory[13]

In accordance with the S-O-R sequence in Figure 6, the following chapters develop hypotheses that imply indirect effects of the application of the controllability principle on affective and behavioral outcomes among managers. It is suggested that the principle's application directly affects cognitive mediators (i.e. role conflict, role ambiguity, and role orientation) which, in turn, have an effect on this study's dependent variables (i.e. job tension, job satisfaction, in-role performance, and extra-role performance). Additionally, the following chapters include several propositions on potential moderating effects. Since literature is not developed to the extent that specific directional effects can be hypothesized, these moderator propositions are exploratory. Role theory suggests that moderating influence on the basic relationships between stimuli and responses may stem from three sources: organizational factors, personality factors, and interpersonal relations (see chapter C1.2.4). For each of the three sources, this work investigates the moderating effect of one specific contextual factor (i.e. managers' hierarchical level, self-efficacy, and trust in superior).

With regard to the many management accounting studies that have previously employed role theory in empirical research (see chapter C3), this work adopts a similar perspective on the design of MCSs. It is argued that the way superiors evaluate their subordinate managers' performance and how system designers set up performance evaluation systems rest upon their role expectations toward organization members' behavior and compliance. According to Atkinson et al. (2007, p. 363), the ways in which organizations measure performance generally send signals to its members about what the organization considers as its priorities. In particular the degree of the application of the controllability principle is indicative of specific role expectations on behalf of role senders. This central line of argument is rooted in role theory, which is unspecific as to what constitutes the content of role expectations (Frink & Klimoski, 1998, p. 22), and also finds strong support in the conclusion of chapter B3.4.

---

13 Adapted from Katz and Kahn (1978, p. 584).

In that chapter, organizational interests were identified as one of the major explanations as to whether the controllability principle is applied or not. Superiors and system designers act as representatives of these organizational interests and carry specific intentions, which determine their attitude towards the application of the principle. In some cases, role senders (i.e. superiors and system designers) opt for the strict application of the controllability principle because their intent is to ensure reliable performance of routine jobs and not to distract managers from the core of their jobs (e.g. Merchant (1998, p. 573) or Simons (2007, pp. 13-14)). In other cases, they opt not to follow the controllability principle because their expectation is to share risk with subordinates, retrieve information about their unobservable actions, or direct their attention to critical performance areas (e.g. Dent (1987, p. 133), Drury and El-Shishini (2005, p. 20), Frow et al. (2005, p. 277), or Vancil (1979, p. 105), see also chapter B3.4).

Merchant (1989) adds that superiors and system designers are usually in the position that they can choose to eliminate the distorting effects of uncontrollable factors. Even if ex ante eliminations of uncontrollable factors are not always feasible, ex post adjustments (i.e. adjustments for uncontrollables after the measurement period) should in most cases provide an effective means to protect managers from bearing the effects of uncontrollable factors. But, as Merchant (1989, p. 107) concludes, superiors and system designers often refrain from making such adjustments due to their role expectations:

> Their measurement system design choice shows they do not want to do so: they *want* [emphasis added] . . . managers to consider these factors over which they are judged to have some influence in making their decisions, even when their influence is less then complete.

The idea that it is well-defined role expectations that determine the application of the controllability principle is important to this work. It represents the link between the literature on the controllability principle (part B) and the reasoning of role theory (part C). The concept of role expectations hence allows the integration of role theory into research on the application of the controllability principle.

2. The Main Models

2.1 Proposed Effects of the Application of the Controllability Principle on Cognitive Mediators

2.1.1 Proposed Effect of the Application of the Controllability Principle on Role Conflict

Even though MCSs are generally intended to improve and assist in managerial decision-making (Maciariello & Kirby, 1994, p. 1; Rejc & Slapničar, 2004, p. 52; Zimmerman, 2009, p. 2), some design characteristics of the systems may result in conflicting representations of individuals' responsibilities (Birnberg et al., 2006, p. 113). In the following, this work suggests that the application of the controllability principle represents one of the design characteristics that are associated with role conflict among managers. Since there has so far been no empirical research on the effect of the principle's application on role conflict, this chapter first reviews related studies which investigate antecedent variables of role conflict that deserve attention when discussing design characteristics of MCSs. The majority of these studies come from the fields of organizational behavior and applied psychology. From the following review it can be concluded that design characteristics of MCSs may have an effect on managers' role conflict in terms of the degree to which they (a) allow for participative decision-making, (b) influence the intensity of communication and information asymmetry between managers and superiors, (c) establish organizational interdependencies and require boundary-spanning activities, and (d) link managers' work space to overall corporate strategy.

To begin with, evidence on the importance of MCSs for managers' experienced role conflict comes from studies on participation in decision-making processes. Organizational systems and structures that facilitate participation are hypothesized to incorporate a means of exerting influence on role expectations to the individual thereby decreasing potential conflicts among the expectations (Jackson, 1983, p. 5). Early studies in this area by Hamner and Tosi (1974) and Rizzo et al. (1970) reveal that under such systems individuals indeed feel significantly less role conflict than when they are not empowered to exert influence on decisions (Hamner & Tosi, 1974, p. 498; Rizzo et al., 1970, p. 158). This finding has been confirmed in a variety of later studies (e.g. Morris, Steers, and Koch (1979), Schuler (1980), Smith and Brannick (1990), or Daniels and Bailey (1999)). A meta-analysis of the relationship between participation and role conflict conducted by Jackson and Schuler (1985, p. 34) also supports this result. Hamner and Tosi (1974, p. 498) therefore conclude that the received role of managers in the organization seems to be generally shaped by the decision-making powers that are granted to them.

Besides, MCSs are likely to have an effect on role conflict among managers since they represent an important organizational mechanism to exchange information. An increased disclosure of information on the part of the managers may enhance their superiors' understanding of the managers' job and accordingly reduce the incidence of conflicting expectations imposed by superiors. Moreover, intensified communication is expected to lead both sides to a more informed and balanced view concerning existing procedures, rules, and work methods (Jaworski & Young, 1992, p. 23). Research by Kahn et al. (1964), Jaworski and Young (1992), and Walker (1977) confirms that increased communication between managers and superiors reduces information asymmetry and role conflict.

Next, evidence on how MCSs may affect role conflict is also provided in studies on organizational interdependencies and boundary-spanning requirements. To the extent that formal structures and the corresponding MCSs tighten interdependencies, they are likely to evoke conflicting expectations and constrain individual flexibility in achieving performance targets (Parasuraman & Alutto, 1981, p. 54). According to Wong et al. (2007, p. 288), it can be hypothesized that "the likelihood of encountering conflicting expectations is greater when there is a larger set of interdependencies to coordinate . . . Feelings of role conflict are likely to arise insofar as managers perceive that they have to struggle to reconcile opposing requirements from different interdependent parties". Empirical studies by Kahn et al. (1964), Parasuraman and Alutto (1981; 1984), and Wong et al. (2007) substantiate this hypothesis. More generally, some scholars argue that conflicting expectations may arise whenever managers are in prolonged contact with representatives from outside their own unit. Role conflict therefore appears to be related to the degree that MCSs require managers to perform boundary-spanning activities. Boundary-spanning activities refer to the "coordination of highly differentiated constituencies [that] must be borne in order to achieve successful role performance" (Miles, 1976, p. 26). Managers in boundary-spanning positions have to interact with representatives of different units who convey to them particular expectations that each unit has about the managers' role. Given that the units' values and interests may be different, the managers in such positions are likely to experience conflicting expectations of how to fulfill their role. Several empirical studies have confirmed that individuals occupying boundary-spanning positions suffer from increased levels of role conflict (e.g. Bettencourt and Brown (2003), Friedman and Podolny (1992), Kahn et al. (1964), or Lysonski (1985)). Van Sell, Brief, and Schuler (1981, p. 62) even assume that boundary-spanning activities are "one of the best-documented correlates of role conflict".

Further insights into how the design of MCSs may affect managers' experienced role conflict are provided by Burney and Widener (2007). The authors suggest that role conflict is negatively associated with the extent to which organizations' MCSs are linked to corporate strategy. They argue that when the systems are linked to strategy this creates a higher shared understanding among the managers, which then allows their superiors to better align individual actions. In such cases, it is less likely that the MCSs incorporate conflicting demands from superiors. Since the overall strategic focus of the organization is supposed to be clear, managers are, for example, less likely to be faced with one superior who asks them to enhance quality thereby increasing costs, while another superior asks them to reduce costs by any means necessary (Burney & Widener, 2007, pp. 48-49). The empirical data gathered by Burney and Widener (2007) support their hypothesis. MCSs which are more closely linked to strategy lead to less role conflict. This effect is in parts direct and in parts indirect because MCSs also influence managers' experienced role conflict through the amount of job-related information they provide to the managers (Burney & Widener, 2007, pp. 59-60).

The preceding paragraphs demonstrate that the degree of role conflict experienced by managers depends on MCSs and how they are designed. The application of the controllability principle is regarded as a further design characteristic of MCSs that is potentially associated with role conflict. Role theory defines role conflict as "conflicting expectations and organizational demands in the form of incompatible policies, requests, standards" (Rizzo et al., 1970, p. 155). It is positioned as originating from sent role expectations and resultant pressures (Kahn et al., 1964, pp. 21-24). This work argues that the nonapplication of the controllability principle is perceived by managers as an inadequately specified reward scheme (Choudhury, 1986, p. 190) and hence as an incompatible request (Rizzo et al., 1970, p. 155). It is likely to be perceived as incompatible in that managers are responsible for achieving performance targets that they do not have enough formal authority and control for. This discrepancy between responsibility and authority that is per definition inherent to the nonapplication of the principle can give rise to role conflict (McNally, 1980, p. 166). It is in their original formulation of role theory that Kahn et al. (1964, p. 123) themselves indicate that a "lack of formal authority" is expected to be an indicator of conflicting expectations and might therefore produce role conflict. Kahn and Quinn (1970, p. 69) refer to such a discrepancy as "responsibility-authority dilemma". The dilemma causes managers to see themselves as torn between what is formally required from them and what they are able to directly control. Since a lack of controllability implies that they do not have all the means necessary to achieve their targets in their own hands, managers appear to be dependent on others, either inside or outside the company. In his case study on the application of the controllability principle at a US technology company, Dent (1987, p. 135) reports that "managers find their responsibilities quite stressful" when they are dependent on others and perceive that they do not have sufficient formal authority. Obviously, violations of the controllability principle and interdependencies among managers are intimately related to each other (see chapter B3.3.1), with interdependencies being a crucial antecedent of role conflict (Wong et al., 2007, p. 297).

Research from the fields of organizational behavior and applied psychology indirectly supports the hypothesis of a relationship between the application of the controllability principle and managers' experienced role conflict. In studies investigating the effects of general perceptions of job control, it is found that the greater the perceived control among individuals, the lower their experienced role conflict (Fry & Hellriegel, 1987; Oliver & Brief, 1977; Spector, 1986). According to Daniels and Guppy (1994, p. 1527), job control may be obtained from different sources, e.g. job autonomy, participation in decision-making, and social support. Relating the general concept of job control to the application of the controllability principle, this work follows Kahn and Quinn (1970, pp. 65-66) and argues that it is not necessarily the mere lack of job control but in particular the discrepancies between role expectations and job control that may be the genesis of stressors such as role conflict. This wants to say that the lower the application of the controllability principle, the higher these discrepancies and resultant levels of role conflict. Or, conversely stated:

H1: The application of the controllability principle is negatively associated with role conflict.

2.1.2 Proposed Effect of the Application of the Controllability Principle on Role Ambiguity

Management accounting research has not only investigated how MCSs and particular design characteristics are related to role conflict, but also how they affect managers' experienced role ambiguity. In parallel, many other academic disciplines have researched the phenomenon of role ambiguity with most studies coming again from the fields of organizational behavior and applied psychology. The variable of role ambiguity is thereby more frequently studied than is the variable of role conflict (Jackson & Schuler, 1985, pp. 26-27). Three comprehensive reviews on the two constructs have shown that overlaps exist in terms of the antecedent variables of role ambiguity and role conflict (Fisher & Gitelson, 1983, pp. 323-324; Jackson & Schuler, 1985, pp. 22-25; Van Sell et al., 1981, pp. 46-58). In the light of previous research results on the antecedents of role ambiguity, MCSs may be expected to have an effect on managers' role ambiguity in that they (a) provide feedback and information, (b) allow for participative decision-making, (c) generate feelings of autonomy at work, (d) influence the degree of formalization, and (e) link managers' work space to overall corporate strategy.

Since role ambiguity is closely associated with deficient or uncertain information about the appropriateness of different role behaviors (Kahn et al., 1964, p. 23; King & King, 1990, p. 49), MCSs are of considerable importance in providing desired information and feedback to individuals. Information and feedback about the effectiveness of individuals' behaviors have long been recognized as a crucial element in work settings (Hollenbeck, Ilgen, LePine, Colquitt, & Hedlund, 1998, pp. 279-280; Ilgen et al., 1979, p. 349; London, 1995, p. 159; Taylor et al., 1984, p. 82). In their review of 96 publications on correlates of role ambiguity, Jackson and Schuler (1985, p. 22) find that the feedback provided to individuals actually represents the strongest antecedent of role ambiguity. However, this finding is not surprising because roles are primarily learned through informational clues provided by the individuals' environment (Jackson & Schuler, 1985, p. 29). Management accounting scholars have also found that the provision of information and feedback is significantly correlated with a decrease in role ambiguity (Fogarty & Kalbers, 2000; Marginson, 2006; Viator, 2001) which is consistent with the results from recent studies in the fields of organizational behavior and applied psychology (Elloy, Everett, & Flynn, 1995; Elovainio & Kivimäki, 2001; Sawyer, 1992). Marginson (2006, p. 194), for example, hypothesizes and empirically finds that information provided by MCSs in the form of written and numeric documents serves to reduce managers' experienced role ambiguity.

The use of MCSs may also attenuate role ambiguity among managers by involving them in decision-making processes. In fact, researchers often closely relate the issue of participative decision-making to the aforementioned issue of information and feedback provision. Participation in decision-making helps individuals to gain specific knowledge about more effective approaches to manage their jobs and to further clarify role expectations by providing the opportunity to appreciate those dimensions of expectations which will, or will not, be quantified financially (Chenhall & Brownell, 1988, p. 227). It therefore facilitates individuals' acquisition of information[14] which subsequently should reduce role ambiguity (Kren, 1992, p. 512). From this perspective, the most important decision-making process that has been heavily researched by management accounting scholars is budgeting. Since the work of Chenhall and Brownell (1988), several studies have been undertaken that theorize and find empirical evidence of either a positive relationship between budget participation and level of information or a negative relationship between budget participation and role ambiguity (Kren, 1992; Lau & Tan, 2003; Leach-Lopez, Stammerjohan, & McNair, 2007; Magner, Welker, & Campbell, 1996; O'Connor, 1995).

MCSs have further potential to function as reducers of role ambiguity in that they generate feelings of autonomy among individuals. Autonomy is often depicted as one source of job control (Daniels & Guppy, 1994, p. 1527; Skinner, 1996, p. 549; Spector, 1986, p. 1006) and

14 Management accounting literature typically identifies two primary types of information in organizations: Decision influencing, which is collected about managers' behavior for the purpose of performance evaluation, and decision-facilitating, which is collected to help managers to improve their action choice through better-informed effort (Baiman & Demski, 1980, pp. 184-185; Demski & Feltham, 1976, pp. 9-13; Sprinkle, 2003, p. 290; Tiessen & Waterhouse, 1983, pp. 257-258). According to Kren (1992, p. 512; 1988, pp. 294-295), most accounting information in organizations is of one or the other type. In literature on participative decision-making, the focus is on the decision-facilitating use of information.

can be defined as the degree to which a job provides substantial freedom, independence, and discretion to individuals in scheduling their work and in determining the procedures to be used in carrying it out (Hackman & Oldham, 1976, p. 258). Even though previous studies offer rather weak theoretical arguments for the existence of a negative relationship between autonomy and experienced role ambiguity, a considerable body of research from different academic disciplines provides empirical support for this hypothesis (Fogarty & Kalbers, 2000; Kalbers & Cenker, 2008; Rizzo et al., 1970; Singh, 1998; Teas, Wacker, & Hughes, 1979; Walsh, Taber, & Beehr, 1980; Yaping, Shenkar, & Yadong, 2001). The meta-analysis by Jackson and Schuler (1985, p. 29) also confirms that the higher individuals' perceptions of autonomy at work, the lower their experienced role ambiguity.

Moreover, MCSs may be designed to reduce role ambiguity by contributing to formalization. Formalization, or the existence of written rules, policies, and procedures governing work activities (Pugh, Hickson, Hinings, & Turner, 1968, p. 76), is beneficial from a role stress perspective because it helps to clarify individuals' role perceptions as well as it specifies legitimate role senders and appropriate role behaviors (Jackson & Schuler, 1985, p. 32). Empirically, the negative relationship between the degree of formalization and individuals' role ambiguity has been supported in several studies (Michaels, Cron, Dubinsky, & Joachimsthaler, 1988; Michaels, Dubinsky, Kotabe, & Lim, 1996; Rizzo et al., 1970; Rogers & Molnar, 1976). An imposing example of how MCSs may generate perceptions of formalization among managers is provided by Marginson and Ogden (2005a). The authors argue that managers confronted with role ambiguity may respond to it by becoming positively committed to achieving budgetary targets because budgets offer a source of structure and certainty to them. The empirical data gathered by the authors confirm that the use of budgets in MCSs is an important antidote to role ambiguity (Marginson & Ogden, 2005a, p. 435).

Empirical research has also shown that the design of MCSs is instrumental in decreasing role ambiguity among managers by linking their work space to overall corporate strategy. Two recent studies address this research issue. Burney and Widener (2007) are the first who hypothesize that role ambiguity is negatively associated with the extent to which the organizations' MCSs are linked to strategy. In accordance with Ittner et al. (2003, p. 719), the authors promote strategic MCSs as a means to provide managers with increased communication about the specific actions that they should pursue to achieve organizational objectives. Hence, such systems are supposed to contain more consistent and clear information about role expectations and motivate managers to perform in accordance with overall objectives (Burney & Widener, 2007, p. 48). The results of Burney and Widener's (2007) data analysis support the hypothesis that the implementation of strategic MCSs reduces role ambiguity. Further empirical support for this hypothesis comes from a second study by Hall (2008). In his examination of role clarity – a variable that is proposed to be conceptually no different from role ambiguity (Hall, 2008, p. 144) – the author argues and finds that MCSs which relate to corporate strategy help managers to better understand their role within the organization. This is because they allow them to see the "big picture" and to develop a reference point in the interpretation of their role (Hall, 2008, pp. 145-156).

In view of this knowledge about the effects of MCSs on individuals' role ambiguity, this work argues that the application of the controllability principle is a further design characteristic of MCSs that relates to the experience of role ambiguity in managerial jobs. When managers are facing uncontrollable influence on their performance, it can be expected that they do no longer feel certain about which of their behaviors and decisions are most effective in leading to positive performance evaluation. As Hirst (1981, pp. 776-777) puts it, "where performance measures are not controllable, subordinates are in an ambiguous situation because they cannot be sure what actions are likely to result in favorable performance". If this is the case, managers' knowledge about the cause-and-effect relationships that are supposed to be prescribed in formal MCSs is likely to diminish. Without certainty about such cause-and-effect relationships, managers will lack reliable and consistent information regarding possible ways to fulfill role expectations (Ilgen & Hollenbeck, 1991, p. 191; Tubre & Collins, 2000, p. 164).

It can further be argued that when managers' performance is distorted by uncontrollable factors, the feedback resulting from performance evaluation is of poor quality (Huffman & Cain, 2000, p. 825). It is often stated that one of the primary functions of evaluation systems is to provide feedback to the evaluatees (Hartmann, 2007, p. 175; Ilgen et al., 1979, p. 365; Luckett & Eggleton, 1991, p. 371; Murphy & Cleveland, 1995, p. 91). However, this function will be adversely affected when managers are being evaluated on the basis of factors beyond their control. With their performance evaluation being subject to uncontrollable influence, managers may find it difficult to derive advantage from the provided feedback when developing strategies to improve their future performance.

The role stress perspective therefore suggests that the application of the controllability principle is advisable because, benefiting from a higher degree of controllability, managers should be more certain about what is and will be required from them. They are more confident in their intended behaviors and decisions and feel greater clarity in the role expectations they are confronted with (Elovainio & Kivimäki, 2001, p. 366). This is in line with the findings of other management accounting scholars who suggest that role ambiguity can be reduced when the organizational imbalance of responsibility exceeding authority is minimized (Eccles, 1986, pp. 278-279; Ghosh, 2000, p. 13; Hopwood, 1972, p. 161; McNally, 1980, p. 166; Senatra, 1980, pp. 600-601). Additional, albeit indirect, support for this hypothesis can again be found in studies from the fields of organizational behavior and applied psychology (Fry & Hellriegel, 1987; Spector, 1986; Von Emster & Harrison, 1998). Perceived job control is here reported to be one of the organizational variables that are negatively related to role ambiguity. The foregoing discussion thus leads to the following hypothesis:

H2: The application of the controllability principle is negatively associated with role ambiguity.

2.1.3 Proposed Effect of the Application of the Controllability Principle on Flexible Role Orientation

Contrary to the large body of management accounting literature on the effects of MCSs on role conflict and role ambiguity, there is only scarce evidence on how the systems and their design may be related to managers' role orientation. This is surprising because, as Vancil (1979, p. 81) states, "management systems, designed and evolved by managers, are intended to institutionalize the way that each manager thinks about his role in the organization". Since role orientation represents an important organizational variable, further research on the shaping and promoting of managers' role orientation is recommended in the literature (Morrison, 1994, p. 1564; Parker, 2007, p. 428).

As defined in chapter C2.1, role orientation refers to the problems, tasks, and competencies individuals see as relevant to their role and effective performance of that role. It ranges from narrow to flexible, with a narrow role orientation meaning that individuals passively define their role solely based on formal job descriptions. A flexible (or broad) role orientation, however, implies that individuals define their role differently, i.e. they go beyond immediate operational requirements and perceive as part of their duties also those tasks that others who have a narrow role orientation might neglect. A narrow role orientation is for example shown by someone who sees the most important requirement as doing "what I am told", while a flexible role orientation is shown by someone who recognizes that key competencies of his or her role include being self-directed, using initiative, and knowing about issues outside his or her own area of authority (Parker, 2000, p. 450). Role orientation can thus be seen to represent the psychological boundary of a role (Parker et al., 1997, p. 902).

A small number of management accounting studies indicate that the application of the controllability principle in the design of MCSs is related to managers' role orientation. Dent (1987), Vancil (1979), and Merchant (1987; 1989) are among the first researchers to find that the application of the controllability principle has an effect on how managers see their role in the organization. In the case study conducted by Dent (1987), the author argues that the company under his investigation designs formal MCSs in order to stimulate curiosity among the managers. He depicts MCSs in which the controllability principle is not applied as "explicit motivators for action" (Dent, 1987, p. 120). When managers are confronted with a lack of controllability, this is to make them learn a different orientation towards their role. According to Dent (1987, pp. 133-137), such a different role orientation implies managers' increased interest in factors uncontrollable but relevant to them. They recognize to have a stake in issues outside their immediate area of authority. This learning process[15] includes managers' experience of being dependent on others and resultant attempts to manage these interdependencies by increasingly seeking information from and interacting with organization members external to their own units. The nonapplication of the controllability principle is therefore "advocated to activate dynamics and discovery in organizations" (Dent, 1987, p. 120).

Similarly, the studies conducted by Vancil (1979) and Merchant (1987; 1989) indicate that the nonapplication of the principle changes managers' role orientation. Both researchers find that the allocation of uncontrollable costs is related to how managers feel about their role in the organization. It is reported that when uncontrollable costs (e.g. costs of capital, interest expenses, or tax expenses) are allocated, managers realize that they are expected to manage a complete, presumably more autonomous, organizational unit (Merchant, 1987, p. 333; 1989, p. 103; Vancil, 1979, p. 304). Such cost allocations also influence managers' role perceptions in that they generate feelings of empowerment. Based on his empirical observations, Merchant (1987, p. 333) suggests that uncontrollable cost allocations and the dependencies on the units causing the costs make managers learn that they are given some legitimation to exert influence on these units.

More recently, Frow et al. (2005), Giraud et al. (2004; 2008), and Simons (2007) have put emphasis on the interaction between the application of the controllability principle and managers' received role. Giraud et al.'s (2004; 2008) large-scale study reveals that the nonapplication of the principle is associated with managers' self-image as entrepreneurs. According to Giraud et al. (2008, p. 42), managers sometimes

> have a very broad conception of their role. They assume a certain level of risk in their job and sometimes consider that they have to manage this risk; i.e., to reduce the impact of external uncontrollable factors on their performance. They consider themselves as entrepreneurs.

Following these thoughts, organizations can use a relaxation of the controllability principle to actively craft managers' self-image as entrepreneurs. Giraud et al. (2004, p. 16) and Simons

[15] As outlined in chapter C2.1, roles are generally subject to learning processes. Managers' role orientation does therefore not constitute a stable personal state, but "reflects the active process of cognitive job crafting" (Parker, 2007, p. 411). This notion implies that people are thought to continually develop new understandings of their roles and how they should be performed (Dierdorff & Morgeson, 2007, p. 1237; Parker, 2000, p. 453; Parker et al., 1997, p. 923; Wrzesniewski & Dutton, 2001, p. 179).

(2007, p. 11) suggest that role senders' attitude towards the principle's application is affected by their conception of what the managers' role in the organization should be. The principle's nonapplication thereby reflects the intention to make managers act as entrepreneurs. Managers are expected to see it as integral to their role to find new and unprescribed ways of responding to uncontrollable factors. As can be seen in Frow et al.'s (2005, p. 280) study, this may even go that far that managers learn that coping with uncontrollable factors is an ordinary part of the challenge of managing.

On this basis, it can be argued that when managers are buffered from the influence of uncontrollable factors in the evaluation of their performance, they will – apart from experiencing less role conflict and role ambiguity – show a different role orientation as compared to situations where they are not buffered from such influence. In the presence of uncontrollable factors, managers are likely to devote their attention to these factors, thus developing a more flexible role orientation (Manzoni, 2002, p. 32; Merchant, 1998, p. 571; Merchant & Van der Stede, 2007, p. 277).

The above review of prior research on the relationship between the application of the controllability principle and managers' role orientation leads to the following hypothesis:

H3: The application of the controllability principle is negatively associated with flexible role orientation.

2.2 Proposed Effects of Cognitive Mediators on Affective Outcome Variables

2.2.1 Proposed Effect of Role Conflict on Job Tension and Job Satisfaction

Management accounting scholars have frequently claimed that when the controllability principle is not applied in the evaluation of managerial performance, managers will suffer from negative affective states such as job tension and lowered job satisfaction (Dent, 1987, p. 135; Hopwood, 1972, pp. 161-162; Merchant, 1987, p. 333; 1989, pp. 103-107; Simons, 2005, pp. 94-95). Scholars in the fields of organizational behavior and applied psychology also suppose that a "low level of control paired with a high level of responsibility . . . is a likely prescription for stress and dissatisfaction" (Parker, 1993, p. 955). Since this work is based on role theory, it is hypothesized that the effect of the application of the controllability principle on job tension and job satisfaction[16] is indirect through cognitive role variables, i.e. managers' experienced role conflict and role ambiguity.

[16] According to Chenhall (2003, p. 133), "there have not been many MCS studies that have examined the effects of MCS on job satisfaction". He reckons it is job tension that is more closely related to the nature of

Prior research on individuals' affective reactions to role conflict strongly supports the notion that role conflict is positively associated with job tension and negatively associated with job satisfaction (Fisher & Gitelson, 1983, pp. 323-325; Jackson & Schuler, 1985, pp. 38-40; Van Sell et al., 1981, pp. 48-49). Kahn et al. (1964, pp. 65-67) argue that role conflict is related to the two affective variables because in situations of role conflict individuals tend to worry more about and feel more bothered by their work than do individuals whose roles involve less role conflict. More recent studies in the fields of organizational behavior and applied psychology that examine role conflict and its effects on job tension and job satisfaction have used similar reasonings and commonly report statistically significant relationships between the variables (Beehr, Walsh, & Taber, 1976; Mohr & Puck, 2007; Moncrief, Babakus, Cravens, & Johnston, 1997; Slattery, Selvarajan, & Anderson, 2008). Role conflict is thereby supposed to be more strongly related to affective variables than to behavioral variables (Beehr & Glazer, 2005, p. 22).

There is also evidence from (management) accounting settings that role conflict is positively related to job tension and negatively related to job satisfaction. Fisher (2001, p. 148) suggests that job satisfaction is the result of a job design that fulfills job-related values. Further arguing that role conflict represents more or less the opposite of job-related values, he predicts and empirically finds a negative effect of role conflict on job satisfaction (Fisher, 2001, pp. 155-156). As far as job tension is concerned, Jaworski and Young (1992, p. 24) hypothesize that role conflict leads individuals to feel that they are not allowed the necessary discretion to carry out their job activities and that individuals then impersonalize their job. The authors find that, as a consequence, individuals' attitudes toward their job deteriorates with role conflict, which increases experienced job tension (Jaworski & Young, 1992, p. 30). In a related study by Fogarty et al. (2000), the effect of role conflict on individuals' burnout tendencies is investigated. The authors argue that role conflict results in "emotionally charged role environments" (Fogarty et al., 2000, p. 37) where extreme levels of effort are required to perform job activities. Fogarty et al.'s (2000) empirical results reveal that such environments give rise to individuals' job tension and burnout tendencies. In the light of these findings, this work suggests:

MCSs than job satisfaction. In order to find out whether the application of the controllability principle in the design of MCSs has an effect on both job tension and job satisfaction or whether there are differences between the two affective outcomes, this study includes both variables in the following investigation. The study of managers' responses to MCSs in terms of job tension and job satisfaction is worthwhile because these variables are likely to have an effect on organizational functioning, e.g. on the overall acceptance of organizational systems. And, according to Cawley, Keeping, and Levy (1998, p. 616), the acceptance of systems is of high importance: "One may develop the most technically sophisticated, accurate appraisal system, but if that system is not accepted and supported by employees, its effectiveness ultimately will be limited". Further, management accounting scholars have shown interest in job tension and job satisfaction because these variables are viewed as surrogates for a variety of dysfunctional behaviors (Hirst, 1983b, p. 597; Lau & Tan, 2006, p. 173; Ross, 1994, p. 629).

H4: Role conflict is positively associated with job tension.

H5: Role conflict is negatively associated with job satisfaction.

2.2.2 Proposed Effect of Role Ambiguity on Job Tension and Job Satisfaction

According to Kahn et al. (1964, p. 95), individuals' reactions to role ambiguity resemble those to role conflict. Their early research on the effects of role stress indicates that "ambiguity leads to increased emotional tension and to decreased satisfaction with one's job" (Kahn et al., 1964, p. 85). It is stated that with high levels of role ambiguity "the world becomes not merely unknown, but hostile and dangerous" (Kahn et al., 1964, p. 84). Role ambiguity is expected to have detrimental effects on individuals' well-being because humans have a basic need for predictability, structure, and clarity, which is seriously jeopardized in the presence of role ambiguity (Elovainio & Kivimäki, 2001, p. 367; Eysenck, 1954, pp. 221-227; Kahn & Quinn, 1970, p. 60). Though scholars have since then challenged the notion that utmost clarity is maximally desirable to organizations and have accepted that role ambiguity is an inherent part of managerial jobs (Katz & Kahn, 1978, p. 206; Macintosh, 1994, p. 215), empirical research most commonly confirms the detrimental effect of role ambiguity on well-being (Abramis, 1994, p. 1418; Fisher & Gitelson, 1983, pp. 323-325; Jackson & Schuler, 1985, pp. 38-40; Van Sell et al., 1981, pp. 50-51). A multitude of studies from the fields of organizational behavior and applied psychology finds a positive effect of role ambiguity on job tension and a negative effect of role ambiguity on job satisfaction (Beehr et al., 1976; Elovainio & Kivimäki, 2001; Harris, Artis, Walters, & Licata, 2006; Klenke-Hamel & Mathieu, 1990; Yousef, 2000). As mentioned in the above chapter on role conflict, role ambiguity is likewise more strongly related to affective variables than to behavioral variables (Beehr & Glazer, 2005, p. 22).

The effect of role ambiguity on job tension and job satisfaction has also been examined in (management) accounting research. One of the first studies in this area comes from Chenhall and Brownell (1988). It depicts role ambiguity as the consequence of budgetary participation practices and reports a negative effect of role ambiguity on the study's dependent variable, i.e. job satisfaction (Chenhall & Brownell, 1988, pp. 229-230). Arguing that role ambiguity opposes job-related values, Fisher (2001, pp. 155-156) also finds a negative relationship between the two variables. Empirical support for a positive relationship between role ambiguity and job tension is provided by Collins and Killough (1992) and Fogarty (2000). In their studies, it is claimed that working under role ambiguity conditions requires excessive levels of energy and mental resources. According to Collins and Killough (1992, p. 540), this leads to an increase in job tension, according to Fogarty (2000, p. 53), to higher burnout tendencies. In the light of such empirical findings, the following hypotheses are proposed:

H6: Role ambiguity is positively associated with job tension.

H7: Role ambiguity is negatively associated with job satisfaction.

2.3 Proposed Effects of Cognitive Mediators on Behavioral Outcome Variables

2.3.1 Proposed Effect of Role Conflict on In-Role Performance

Role theorists have long argued that role conflict is detrimental to individuals' in-role performance (see chapter C2.2 for the distinction between in-role performance and extra-role performance). Following Jackson and Schuler (1985), a negative relationship between role conflict and in-role performance can generally be explained by research that focuses on cognitive and motivational processes. From a cognitive perspective, in-role performance should be hindered by role conflict because it leads individuals to perceive "an almost impossible situation for doing everything expected" (Jackson & Schuler, 1985, p. 43). Faced with role expectations that appear to be incompatible and contradictory, their decisions and behaviors are most likely to be misdirected and insufficient – regardless of how much effort individuals expend. A motivational perspective would predict that in-role performance is negatively associated with role conflict because role conflict is thought to decrease effort-to-performance and performance-to-reward expectancies (Jackson & Schuler, 1985, pp. 42-43; Jex, 1998, pp. 34-36; Kahn & Byosiere, 1992, pp. 608-610; Naylor, Pritchard, & Ilgen, 1980, pp. 142-146; Tubre & Collins, 2000, p. 157).

As far as empirical evidence is concerned, Kahn et al.'s (1964, pp. 55-71) original research on the effects of role conflict indicates that this facet of role stress might be detrimental to individuals' in-role performance because it leads to social and psychological withdrawal. Assuming that withdrawal reduces levels of commitment and influence at the workplace, individuals' effectiveness is likely to deteriorate. Seeman (1953) also provides relevant empirical clues by showing that school executives experience difficulties in making effective decisions when experiencing role conflict. Using interview data and correlation analysis among responses to interview questions, he concludes that individuals find certain decisions (which were rated as not very hard to make in previous circumstances of low role conflict) very difficult to make when their perceptions changed due to an increase in the conflict surrounding their role (Seeman, 1953, p. 380). This finding is supported by another early study on role conflict by House and Rizzo (1972). Their study, conducted with managerial and technical staff at a manufacturing company, shows that role conflict is directly and inversely related to employees' organizational effectiveness. The authors define effectiveness in terms of the ability to make timely decisions, the disclosure of undistorted information, and the adaptability to change (House & Rizzo, 1972, p. 488). Others have directly investigated the relationship between role conflict and different measures of job performance. Whereas Dubinsky and Mattson (1979) find a significant and negative effect of role conflict on self-rated performance among a sample of retail sales people, Szilagyi, Sims, and Keller (1976) encounter the same result when relying on superiors' performance ratings in a larger sample of employees from diverse backgrounds and companies.

Later studies by management accounting researchers only find mixed results for the relationship between role conflict and job performance. With the exception of Fisher's (2001) study, the works of Fogarty et al. (2000), Burney and Widener (2007), Rebele and Michaels (1990), and Viator (2001) all report a weak and insignificant relation between role conflict and self-reported measures of job performance. Likewise, meta-analyses investigating the relationship between the two variables have demonstrated that even though a negative relation exists between role conflict and job performance, the strength of the effect is found to be only moderate at best (Fisher & Gitelson, 1983, p. 323; Gilboa et al., 2008, p. 243; Jackson & Schuler, 1985, pp. 42-43; Tubre & Collins, 2000, p. 162). Tubre and Collins (2000, p. 164) and Gilboa et al. (2008, p. 252) note that the relation is supposed to be stronger at the managerial level, which is the job position under investigation in this study. For this reason and since persuasive theoretical arguments can be found for the existence of a negative effect of role conflict on in-role performance, this work hypothesizes:

H8: Role conflict is negatively associated with in-role performance.

2.3.2 Proposed Effect of Role Ambiguity on In-Role Performance

The theoretical arguments mentioned in the foregoing discussion on role conflict are equally relevant to the relationship between role ambiguity and in-role performance. Again, cognitive and motivational explanations can be referred to when theorizing about role ambiguity's supposedly detrimental effect on in-role performance (Jackson & Schuler, 1985, pp. 42-43; Tubre & Collins, 2000, p. 157). Following a cognitive reasoning, high levels of role ambiguity imply conditions of uncertainty and arousal which, in turn, may lead to a narrowing of individuals' perceptual attention. They tend to ignore performance-related cues, thus deleteriously affecting their in-role performance. This is because in situations of role ambiguity individuals are first and foremost engaged in clarifying role expectations and coping with the role stressors. Such coping is thought to reduce individuals' ability to perform by diverting their endeavors away from concentrating on core job functions (Gilboa et al., 2008, p. 230; Jamal, 1985, p. 411). Likewise, Rizzo et al. (1970, p. 151) argue that individuals will "hesitate to make decisions and will have to rely on a trial and error approach" when suffering from role ambiguity. More generally, role ambiguity is associated with deficiencies in decision-making (Burney & Widener, 2007, p. 51; Kahn et al., 1964, pp. 72-73). From a motivational perspective, role ambiguity is likely to reduce individuals' in-role performance because of the uncertainty around role expectations and the resultant decreased probability of fulfilling them. Role ambiguity is thought to diminish overall work motivation by reducing either the expectation that effort leads to performance or the expectation that performance leads to valued outcomes (Beehr et al., 1976, p. 42; Jex, 1998, pp. 34-36; Naylor et al., 1980, pp. 154-156).

Since Kahn and his colleagues' original research on the consequences of role ambiguity, there has been a multitude of empirical studies investigating the relationship between role ambiguity and in-role performance or performance-related variables. In total, there is almost unanimous support for a negative performance effect of role ambiguity that appears to be stronger in magnitude and significance than the performance effect of role conflict (Gilboa et al., 2008, p. 250; Tubre & Collins, 2000, pp. 164-165). Apart from the many studies in the fields of organizational behavior and applied psychology (e.g. Berkowitz (1980), Fried, Ben-David, Tiegs, Avital, and Yeverechyahu (1998), Von Emster and Harrison (1998), and Yaping et al. (2001)), research carried out by management accounting scholars has also addressed the allegedly causal effect of role ambiguity on job performance. Most of them reveal a significant and negative relationship between the two variables.

Positioning role ambiguity as a mediator in the relationship between budget participation and job performance, Brownell and Chenhall (1988) are among the first management accounting scholars who predict and find a negative effect of role ambiguity on job performance. Later works by Fogarty et al. (2000), Burney and Widener (2007), Rebele and Michaels (1990), and Viator (2001) confirm this effect in (management) accounting settings. Further, related to role ambiguity is goal clarity. A recent study by Hall (2008) using this variable reveals that also goal clarity is significantly associated with job performance.

Additional evidence that role ambiguity among managers is likely to have disadvantageous effects on in-role performance comes from studies on the provision of information. These studies are worth mentioning in this discussion on role ambiguity because at its core role ambiguity is about a lack of required information (Kahn, 1974, p. 59; Kahn & Quinn, 1970, p. 58; Kahn et al., 1964, p. 25). The importance of information for enabling managers to show superior performance is demonstrated in the work of Eisenhardt (1989c). In a series of case studies, the author examines strategic decision-making processes in high technology companies. She finds that managers who are exposed to more information have a better-developed intuition and, as a result, are able to respond more quickly and effectively to the information they encounter (Eisenhardt, 1989c, p. 544). In a related study by Vandenbosch and Huff (1997), the authors investigate managers' use of information systems suggesting two common modes of use: (a) scanning, or general browsing of data, and (b) focused search, or seeking answers to specific questions or well-defined problems. They find that the increased use of information is positively related to organizational effectiveness as well as efficiency. It is concluded that "without information, executives simply cannot function" (Vandenbosch & Huff, 1997, p. 82). This proposition is also reflected in the studies of Kren (1992) and Chong and Chong (2002). Arguing that large amounts of job-related information facilitate decision-making processes and hence job performance (Chong & Chong, 2002, pp. 69-70), both report a strong relationship between the provision of job-related information and resultant performance levels among managers. Likewise, findings from a study by Burkert (2008) are concerned with the relationship between the provision of information and managers' performance. He finds that a higher quality of information provided by organizations' MCSs increases the quality of managers' decisions (Burkert, 2008, p. 161).

In the light of the aforementioned empirical evidence and concordant results reported in meta-analyses on role ambiguity (Abramis, 1994, pp. 1427-1428; Gilboa et al., 2008, p. 243; Jackson & Schuler, 1985, p. 43; Tubre & Collins, 2000, p. 162), it is hypothesized:

H9: Role ambiguity is negatively associated with in-role performance.

2.3.3 Proposed Effect of Flexible Role Orientation on Extra-Role Performance

Apart from in-role performance, this study investigates whether managers' role perceptions emanating from the application of the controllability principle have an effect on other behavioral outcome variables. More specifically, it is argued that managers' role orientation is related to their extra-role performance. Among the different types of behaviors which are subsumed under extra-role performance (see chapter C2.2), internal influence behavior and its causal relationship with managers' role orientation is examined in this study.

Internal influence behavior is depicted as promotive and challenging extra-role behavior. It refers to managers taking individual initiative in communications to other managers in order to solve organizational problems and improve operations outside their own area of authority (Bettencourt et al., 2005, p. 142). As such, it represents one of the modes of behavior that organizational scholars have recommended for investigation in the debate on individuals' coping with challenging role expectations (Büssing et al., 1999, p. 1024). The call for research on such behaviors (instead of classical variables like in-role performance) is also not new to management accounting literature (Otley, 1994, p. 297). It is Hirst (1983b, p. 603) who wrote more than two decades ago that "it would be useful to consider the incidence of other forms of behavior (e.g. innovative and cooperative behaviors) associated with different evaluative situations". Likewise, Atkinson et al. (1997, p. 85) propose that "an avenue for future research is exploring the broader question of how characteristics of the management accounting system affect managers' propensity to direct change". However, management accounting research has been fairly reluctant in integrating such behaviors into contemporary research designs. The recent work of Burney et al. (2009) examining the relationship between strategic MCSs and extra-role performance is a notable exception.

Parker (2007, p. 408) predicts that it is individuals' role orientation that directs "effort towards particular behaviors rather than others". When managers exhibit a narrow role orientation, their behaviors on the job are likely to be restricted to activities that are prescribed by formal job descriptions. Correspondingly, when managers have a flexible role orientation, i.e. when they define their role as going beyond immediate operational requirements, they will be more willing to perform tasks that are designated as extra-role. More generally speaking, a close linkage can be expected between how people define their roles and which behaviors they show at the workplace (Kamdar, McAllister, & Turban, 2006, p. 841; Morrison, 1994, p. 1543; Parker, 2000, p. 464).

Empirical evidence on the relationship between individuals' role orientation and different types of extra-role behaviors comes from studies by Parker and Axtell (2001), Howell and Boies (2004), and Parker et al. (2006). The study by Parker and Axtell (2001) reports that a flexible role orientation predicts perspective taking (i.e. adopting another person's viewpoint) which, in turn, is positively related to individuals' extra-role performance (i.e. cooperative and helping behaviors towards others). Howell and Boies (2004) build on Parker and Axtell's (2001) findings and hypothesize that individuals with a flexible role orientation are more likely to include creativity and innovation as part of their role, and are thus more likely to engage in behaviors leading to idea generation. Their empirical data confirm that individuals who construe their role more broadly are indeed more involved in activities related to idea generation. In a subsequent study, Parker et al. (2006) focus on related extra-role behaviors, in particular proactive idea implementation and problem-solving. They predict and find that individuals with a flexible role orientation are more likely to engage in such proactive behaviors and the pursuit of improvement in domains beyond their narrow set of tasks. This is because they are thought to have a higher sense of personal responsibility for a broader range of goals and therefore feel a sense of accomplishment when helping to achieve these goals through their behaviors. Further empirical evidence on the importance of role perceptions for extra-role behaviors is provided by Morrison (1994), Kamdar et al. (2006), McAllister, Morrison, Kamdar, and Turban (2007). In research on role breadth and role definition – two variables which are conceptually very similar to role orientation – the authors find that the degree to which individuals engage in a variety of extra-role behaviors is significantly related to these variables.

The foregoing discussion highlights that individuals' role perceptions are likely to be important antecedents of extra-role behaviors (Podsakoff et al., 2000, p. 530). This work argues that when managers have developed a flexible role orientation, they are likely to convert such an orientation into behaviors that exceed a conventional spectrum of tasks. In particular, it is expected that with a flexible role orientation they increasingly show internal influence behavior, i.e. they actively get involved in matters outside their own area of authority. This work therefore hypothesizes:

H10: Flexible role orientation is positively associated with extra-role performance.

2.4 Summary of the Main Models

In accordance with prominent management accounting scholars who claim that both benefits and costs are associated with the application of the controllability principle (Atkinson et al., 1997, p. 84; Choudhury, 1986, pp. 196-197; Merchant, 1989, p. 130; Modell, 1997, p. 314), this work argues that the effects of applying the principle are twofold. First, it is hypothesized that the application of the controllability principle is instrumental in reducing role conflict and role ambiguity among managers, which, in turn, is supposed to have a favorable impact on their job tension, job satisfaction, and in-role performance. These supposedly functional effects of the principle's application are summarized in Figure 7 to Figure 9.

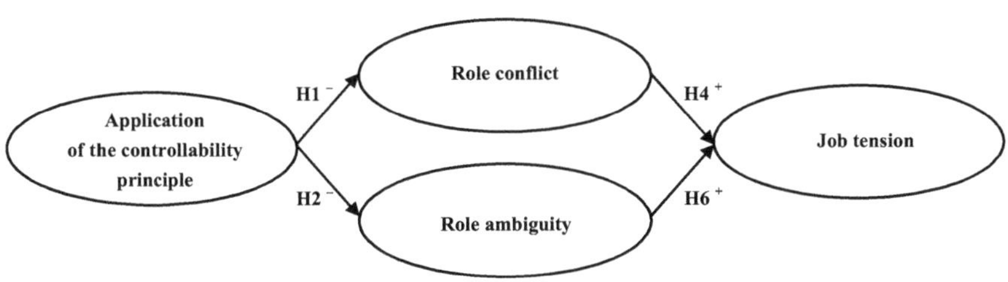

Figure 7: Proposed Effects of the Application of the Controllability Principle on Job Tension

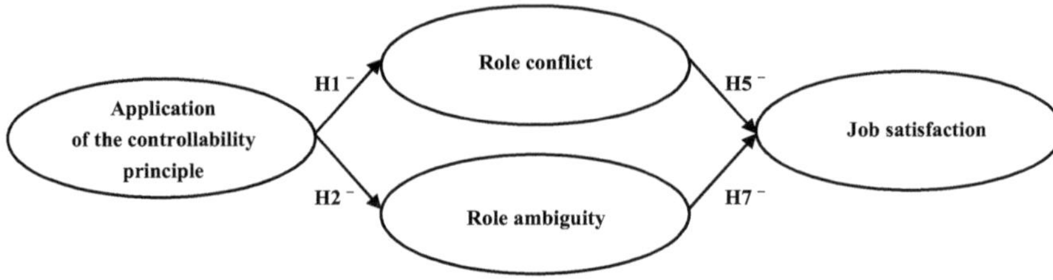

Figure 8: Proposed Effects of the Application of the Controllability Principle on Job Satisfaction

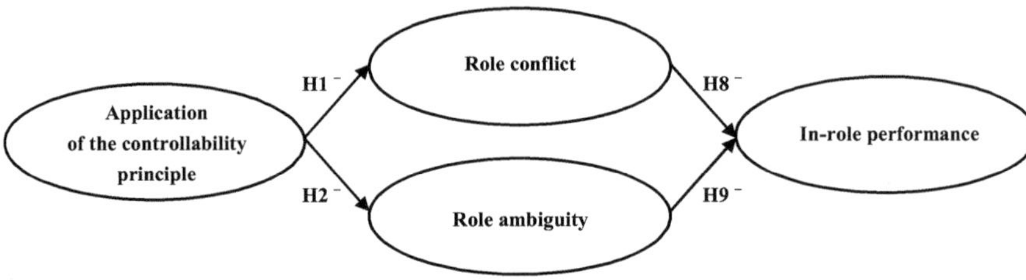

Figure 9: Proposed Effects of the Application of the Controllability Principle on In-Role Performance

Second, this work follows Giraud et al. (2008, p. 33), who have recently claimed that "managers do not always react negatively when the controllability principle is not applied". It is suggested that when the controllability principle is not implemented in the design of MCSs whereby managers are not protected from uncontrollable factors, they are incited to develop a more flexible role orientation. Flexible role orientation, in turn, is argued to be an important antecedent of extra-role performance, in this case internal influence behavior. This type of behavior is conceptually different from in-role performance in that it goes beyond conventional definitions of performance and furthers corporate success by managers taking influence on issues outside their own area of authority. The organizational importance of such influence behavior has been repeatedly emphasized in literature (Cobb, 1980, p. 159; Podsakoff et al., 2000, pp. 550-551; Yukl, Chavez, & Seifert, 2005, p. 705). Accordingly, Ronen and Livingstone (1975, p. 681) posit that "excluding from the evaluation basis activities that are partially controllable but classified as uncontrollable will direct the subordinate not to exert effort in those activities and eventually to jeopardize the accomplishment of the organization's goals". The assumed dysfunctional effect associated with the application of the controllability principle is depicted graphically in Figure 10.

Figure 10: Proposed Effects of the Application of the Controllability Principle on Extra-Role Performance

3. The Moderated Models

3.1 Proposed Effects of Hierarchical Level

Role theory predicts that the role episode is influenced by organizational factors (Kahn et al., 1964, pp. 30-32; 1966, pp. 279-280). In particular, role senders' and role incumbents' rank in the organizational hierarchy are supposed to have an impact on role processes and the experience of role stress (Frink & Klimoski, 1998, p. 36). This is because individuals' self-image, their ego motivation, and aspirations as well as their risk preferences are likely to vary across the hierarchy (Kahn et al., 1964, pp. 137-150; Sitkin & Pablo, 1992, p. 16).

Empirical evidence exists that managers' hierarchical level in the organization is an important variable when investigating their responses to the application of the controllability principle. The first study in this area comes from Marginson and McAulay (2001). They examine managers' attitude towards the controllability principle in relation to their organizational position. In a study with 125 managers from a UK communications company, the authors find that the positions occupied by the managers "were significant predictors of behavior towards the controllability principle" (Marginson & McAulay, 2001, p. 21). However, Marginson and McAulay's (2001) study is restricted to a single research site, which limits the generalizability of their findings. For a later study on managers' responses to the application of the controllability principle, Pelster (2007) gathers data from multiple research sites. He investigates the effects of the principle's application on managers' effort in their job. The analysis of Pelster's (2007) data reveals that there are differences across the organizational hierarchy. Whereas managers at lower hierarchical levels vehemently expect the controllability principle to be applied by their superiors, the application of the principle turns out to be less of an issue for managers at higher hierarchical levels. Pelster (2007, p. 272) therefore reasons that the effect of the principle's application on managers' effort is weaker at higher levels than it is at lower levels. He concludes that further research is needed on managers' attitude towards the controllability principle and the way it relates to their hierarchical level (Pelster, 2007, p. 274).

So far, individuals' hierarchical level has been mainly proposed as a moderator variable in studies from the fields of organizational behavior and applied psychology (Aquino, 2000; Schminke, Cropanzano, & Rupp, 2002; Singh, 1997; Stahl & Caligiuri, 2005). According to Barber and Simmering (2002, p. 31), "the importance of hierarchical level as a moderator of reactions in organizational contexts is widely recognized" by researchers in these fields. In particular the study of Schminke et al. (2002) supports the view that individuals' responses to organizational stimuli are qualified by their hierarchical level. Having conducted a cross-sectional survey study, the authors report that the relationships between several structural characteristics of organizations (such as formal authority and participation rights granted to individuals) and respondents' justice perceptions vary from lower hierarchical levels to higher hierarchical levels. More specifically, the structural characteristics appear not to play as strong a role in terms of their effects on justice perceptions among higher level employees as among lower level employees (Schminke et al., 2002, pp. 899-900).

The introduction of individuals' hierarchical level as a moderator is, however, not entirely new to management accounting research. In fact, the studies of Davis, Kohlmeyer, Epstein, and John (2005), Dunk (1992), and Viator (2001) all predict and find a significant moderating effect of individuals' hierarchical level on several relationships between management accounting variables and behavioral outcomes. Since the work of Viator (2001) also rests upon role theory, it is of particular interest in the context of this study. Hypothesizing that the availability of mentors reduces role stress (i.e. role conflict and role ambiguity) among accounting professionals, the author finds that these relationships depend on individuals' hierarchical level. According to Viator (2001, p. 87), mentoring is more effective in reducing role stress for employees at lower ranks than for employees at higher ranks.

In the light of these empirical findings, it seems plausible that managers' hierarchical level also has an effect on how they respond to the application of the controllability principle in their performance evaluation. However, literature is not developed to the extent that it allows specifying directional effects. Due to the exploratory nature of this study's moderator analyses, the effects are examined using the interrogative form:

E1a: Does managers' hierarchical level moderate the relationship between the application of the controllability principle and role conflict?

E1b: Does managers' hierarchical level moderate the relationship between the application of the controllability principle and role ambiguity?

E1c: Does managers' hierarchical level moderate the relationship between the application of the controllability principle and flexible role orientation?

3.2 Proposed Effects of Self-Efficacy

Apart from organizational factors, role theory emphasizes the importance of personality factors for a comprehensive understanding of the role episode (Kahn et al., 1964, p. 32; 1966, p. 280). Since it is likely that role incumbents will differ in the perception of their environment due to varying personalities, Kahn et al. (1964, p. 32) see personality factors as "conditioning variables" in the relationship between expectations imposed by role senders and role incumbents' responses. Similarly, Rizzo et al. (1970, p. 162) argue that personality factors may lead some role incumbents to perceive particular role expectations as stressful while others may experience the same expectations as rewarding. Among the many personality variables that may theoretically act as moderators in role processes (Katz & Kahn, 1978, p. 213), this study focuses on individuals' self-efficacy. Self-efficacy "refers to beliefs in one's capabilities to organize and execute the courses of action required to produce given attainments" (Bandura, 1997, p. 3). It is closely related to individuals' perceptions of their ability and operates as a central factor in self-regulatory mechanisms governing motivation and action (Bandura, 1977, pp. 193-194; 1982, pp. 122-123; Bandura & Wood, 1989, p. 806; Gist & Mitchell, 1992, pp. 183-186).

In the investigation of the potential moderating influence of self-efficacy, this work follows scholars from the fields of organizational behavior and applied psychology. Throughout their immense research on accountability in organizations, they advocate the search for moderators when examining the effects of accountability on individuals' responses (Frink & Klimoski, 1998, pp. 35-36; Lerner & Tetlock, 1999, p. 259; Mero, Guidice, & Anna, 2006, p. 798; Tetlock, 1985, p. 325; 1992, pp. 368-370). In particular, they call for an increased attention to individuals' self-efficacy since this variable is "related to how one interprets and responds to environmental cues, and might help to explain and predict behavior related to accountability perceptions" (Frink & Klimoski, 1998, p. 36).

Self-efficacy has repeatedly been shown to moderate individuals' responses to a variety of work stimuli (Brown, Ganesan, & Challagalla, 2001; Heuven, Bakker, Schaufeli, & Huisman, 2006; Jex & Bliese, 1999; Jex & Gudanowski, 1992; May, Schwoerer, Reed, & Potter, 1997; Nauta, Liu, & Li, in press; Schaubroeck & Merritt, 1997; Speier & Frese, 1997). The study by Nauta, Liu, and Li (in press) examines the interaction of job autonomy and self-efficacy in the prediction of psychological and physical strains among US employees. As hypothesized, the authors report that high self-efficacy serves as a buffer against low job autonomy in the prediction of strains. A related study by Speier and Frese (1997) provides similar empirical results. It investigates the effects between job control, self-efficacy, and individuals' initiative at work. According to Speier and Frese (1997), self-efficacy functions as a moderator of the relation between job control and initiative. It is found that highly self-efficacious individuals are less dependent on their work conditions than low self-efficacious individuals in the development of initiative. Their high self-efficacy seems to shield them from the detrimental effects of low control at work (Speier & Frese, 1997, p. 188). Another study in this area, conducted by Brown et al. (2001), deals with two forms of information seeking among employees: (a) inquiry, i.e. directly asking superiors or coworkers for information, and (b) monitoring, i.e. observing superiors' or coworkers' behavior. Both are found to be helpful for individuals in order to increase their perceived role clarity. With regard to the moderating influence of self-efficacy on the relationship between information seeking and role clarity, the authors detect that only individuals with high self-efficacy effectively seek, integrate, and use information to increase role clarity (Brown et al., 2001, pp. 1049-1050).

The empirical evidence cited above indicates that highly self-efficacious individuals can be expected to cope more successfully with challenges in the job than individuals with low self-efficacy. However, some authors warn that, in some circumstances, high self-efficacy can also have adverse effects on psychological states. Flammer (2001, p. 13812) suggests that high self-efficacy produces tension insofar as it can induce overly ambitious individuals to assume more responsibility than they are able to cope with. Similarly, Schaubroeck and Merritt (1997, p. 750) provide an explanation why high self-efficacy can turn out to be problematic in certain situations: "A lack of control may be particularly harmful for people with high self-efficacy in demanding circumstances because uncontrollable situations may challenge personal agency perceptions".

Either way, self-efficacy appears an important "moderating variable that may determine whether job control contributes positively or negatively" (Schaubroeck & Merritt, 1997, p. 738) to individuals' perceptions of their work. In the context of this study, it is therefore likely that managers' cognitive responses to the application of the controllability principle differ due to varying beliefs in self-efficacy. Because of the exploratory nature of this proposition, it is not predicted ex ante whether the strengths of the relationships will increase or decrease from managers with high self-efficacy to managers with low self-efficacy. Rather, this work attempts to examine:

E2a: Does managers' self-efficacy moderate the relationship between the application of the controllability principle and role conflict?

E2b: Does managers' self-efficacy moderate the relationship between the application of the controllability principle and role ambiguity?

E2c: Does managers' self-efficacy moderate the relationship between the application of the controllability principle and flexible role orientation?

3.3 Proposed Effects of Trust in Superior

In role theory, the third source of factors which may influence role processes is circumscribed as interpersonal relations (Kahn et al., 1964, pp. 32-33; 1966, pp. 280-281). With the term interpersonal relations, Kahn et al. (1964, p. 32) refer to "the more or less stable patterns of interaction between a person and his role senders and to their orientations toward each other". In the definition of high quality interpersonal relations, role theory attaches great importance to the degree of trust between role incumbents and their role senders. According to Katz and Kahn (1978, pp. 216-217), the moderating effect of trust in role processes may take one of three forms: interaction, buffering, or intensification.

Recently, there has been a call to examine the impact of trust on managers' attitude towards the controllability principle (Giraud et al., 2008, pp. 42-43). It is assumed that the degree of trust between managers and their superiors may influence managers' responses towards the application of the principle. This view finds support in earlier studies on the controllability principle (Budding, 2004; Choudhury, 1986). Choudhury (1986, p. 190) suggests that "a manager may value control less if he felt he could rely on his superior to 'protect' him". Similarly, Brion (1989, p. 371) indicates that trust is an important factor that has the potential to alleviate the consequences of performance evaluation. Trust – which is widely viewed as "a psychological state [consisting of] the intention to accept vulnerability based upon positive expectations of the intentions or behavior of another" (Rousseau, Sitkin, Burt, & Camerer, 1998, p. 395) – is sometimes even seen as the most important factor leading employees to have negative or positive feelings towards performance evaluation (Henderson, 1980, p. 10).

Empirical evidence for the moderating effect of trust comes mainly from selected studies in the fields of organizational behavior and applied psychology (Dirks, 1999; Kimmel, Pruitt, Magenau, Konar-Goldband, & Carnevale, 1980; Read, 1962; Robinson, 1996; Rousseau & Tijoriwala, 1999). Read (1962) is among the first scholars to investigate trust as a moderator in organizational processes. He suggests that as individuals' motivation to be promoted increases, they are less likely to share negative information about their work with their superiors. He further proposes that this relationship is moderated by trust. The tendency to withhold information is expected to be particularly acute when individuals do not trust their superiors. The data gathered by the author confirm his hypotheses (Read, 1962, p. 13). In a more recent study, Dirks (1999) finds that trust moderates the relationship between group members' motivation and group processes and outcomes. More specifically, groups with high levels of motivation are reported to direct their effort toward group goals under conditions of high interpersonal trust, whereas they tend to direct their effort toward individual goals under low-trust conditions. Similarly, it is found that motivation has a significant, positive effect on group performance under high-trust conditions, but no effect on performance under low-trust conditions (Dirks, 1999, p. 453).

In the light of these findings, organizational behavior scholars have recommended to include trust as a moderator in studies from related disciplines (Dirks & Ferrin, 2001, p. 462). However, it is in particular management accounting research that has been fairly reluctant in the integration of trust in contemporary research designs. Scapens (2006, p. 23) notes that "although the concept of trust has been well researched in the organizational literature, it is relatively under-researched in the management accounting literature." In fact, there are only very few studies examining the moderating influence of trust on relationships between management accounting variables and behavioral responses (Gibbs et al., 2004; Ross, 1994). Initial promising insights are provided by Ross (1994). In an effort to contribute to the RAPM research stream, the author examines trust as a moderator on the effect of using accounting information for performance evaluation on job tension. He finds that the use of a budget-constrained performance evaluation style (which has been shown to be associated with dysfunctional responses in earlier studies) does not always lead to high levels of job tension. Instead, job tension among managers decreases when a budget-constrained performance evaluation style is used in the presence of high levels of trust in superiors (Ross, 1994, p. 633).

In sum, research from the fields of organizational behavior and applied psychology indicates that "trust influences the impact of a range of predictors on perceptions, attitudes, behaviors and performance outcomes" (Dirks & Ferrin, 2001, p. 462). Managers' trust in their superiors emerges as a potential moderator for research on managerial coping with the application of the controllability principle. However, because of the scarce empirical evidence previously gathered in management accounting settings, this work refrains from predicting specific directional effects in the analysis of trust as a moderator. An exploratory investigation of the effects is proposed:

E3a: *Does managers' trust in superior moderate the relationship between the application of the controllability principle and role conflict?*

E3b: *Does managers' trust in superior moderate the relationship between the application of the controllability principle and role ambiguity?*

E3c: *Does managers' trust in superior moderate the relationship between the application of the controllability principle and flexible role orientation?*

3.4 Summary of the Moderated Models

Literature calls for the examination of potential moderators on the relationships between work stimuli and role stress (Gilboa et al., 2008, p. 256; Jackson & Schuler, 1985, p. 27; King & King, 1990, p. 61) as well as on the relationships between work stimuli and more proactive role concepts such as role orientation (Clegg, Unsworth, Epitropaki, & Parker, 2002, p. 411; Crant, 2000, p. 458). This call is motivated by the view that "the nature of work roles cannot be divorced from the contexts in which they are enacted" (Griffin et al., 2007, p. 328). In accordance with role theory, this study introduces three theoretically meaningful moderators: (a) managers' hierarchical level, which represents an organizational factor deemed to be important for the understanding of role processes; (b) self-efficacy as a personality factor that accounts for differences in personality structures; and (c) trust in superior, which is an indicator of the quality of interpersonal relations between role incumbents and role senders. Since literature has not yet been developed to an extent that allows predicting specific directional effects of these variables, the moderator analyses are exploratory in nature. The proposed effects are summarized in Figure 11 to Figure 13.

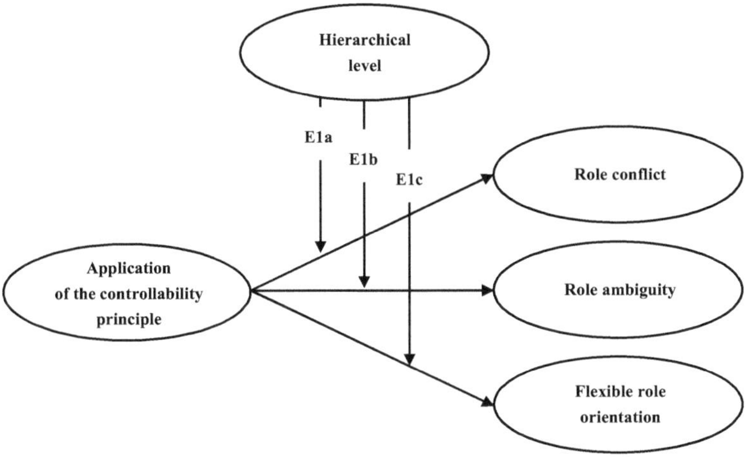

Figure 11: Proposed Moderating Effects of Hierarchical Level

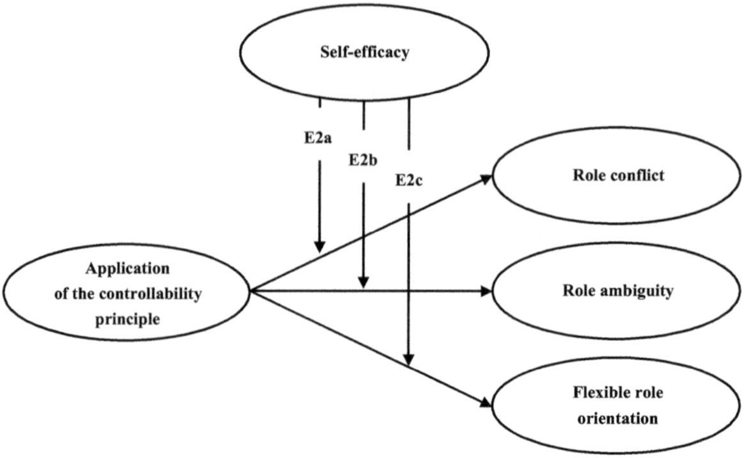

Figure 12: Proposed Moderating Effects of Self-Efficacy

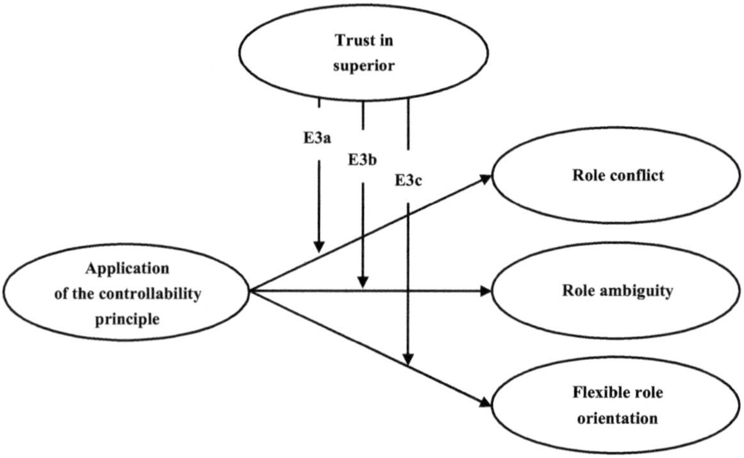

Figure 13: Proposed Moderating Effects of Trust in Superior

The main model hypotheses (see chapter D2.4) predict that the application of the controllability principle is, on the one hand, advantageous because it reduces role conflict and role ambiguity among managers. On the other hand, the principle's application is predicted to be disadvantageous because it keeps managers from developing a flexible role orientation, which would question whether applying the controllability principle was always the right decision. The objective of the moderator analyses is therefore to identify conditions under which either the application or the nonapplication of the controllability principle is particularly desirable. If managers' responses to the principle differ across the three moderating variables, this might allow a relaxation of the principle's application in certain situations.

The finding that the application of the controllability principle is not necessarily advisable in all situations would have various implications. If not applying the principle, organizations might not only find managers with a flexible role orientation among the workforce, but could also save costs because adjusting MCSs and evaluative procedures with regard to the effects of uncontrollable factors consumes considerable management resources (Merchant, 1989, pp. 130-131; 1998, pp. 582-583). Several authors support the view that the consequences of the principle's (non)application have to be investigated in relation to managers' individual contexts (Dent, 1987, pp. 131-137; Frow et al., 2005, pp. 288-289; Simons, 2005, p. 95). Dent (1987), for example, conducts a case study at a research site where the predominant management style is marked by an almost complete disregard for the controllability principle. He concludes that "the efficiency of this management style is likely to be dependent on context" (Dent, 1987, p. 142).

E Development of the Research Design

1. Elements of the Research Design

Having used role theory to generate testable hypotheses, this work proceeds and develops a corresponding research design in the following chapters. Among the main questions a researcher has to give an answer to in the research process are the issues of methodology and method (Ahrens & Chapman, 2006, pp. 821-822; Atkinson & Shaffir, 1998, p. 42; Creswell, 2003, p. 5; Richardson, 1996, pp. 3-5). Even though the two terms are sometimes used interchangeably, it is "important to distinguish between methodology and method in research" (Richardson, 1996, p. 3). While methodology means "a general approach to studying research topics", method refers to "a specific research technique" (Silverman, 2005, p. 98).

1.1 Methodology

The researcher's methodology expresses his or her "philosophy of the research process" (Bailey, 1987, p. 33). It includes assumptions and values that serve as a rationale for the research conducted and the standards or criteria the researcher uses for interpreting data and reaching conclusions. In short, it is through a particular methodology that the researcher gains knowledge of the world around him or her (Denzin & Lincoln, 2000, p. 19). The different methodologies are sometimes also referred to as "knowledge claims" (Creswell, 2003, p. 6) or "social science paradigms" (Tashakkori & Teddlie, 1998, p. 3). Following Creswell (2003, p. 6) and Sarantakos (2005, pp. 8-11), it can be distinguished between five main methodologies: positivism, postpositivism, constructivism, advocacy/participatory approach, and pragmatism.

The positivistic methodology which goes back to the work of Auguste Comte (Peel, 1996, p. 120) implies that the keys to the conduct of social science are "objectivity, distance, and control" (Greenwood & Levin, 2000, p. 92). In positivism, research questions can correctly be dealt with only in relation to empirical observations. Knowledge regarding matters of fact is to be based on the "positive" data of experience or, put differently, empirical tests must always be the final arbiter in theoretical disputes (Alexander, 1996, p. 649; Crotty, 1998, pp. 19-20). The fundamental belief underlying positivistic thinking is that "objective accounts of the real world can be given" (Denzin & Lincoln, 2000, p. 24). Accordingly, positivists see the world as commensurable and claim that scientific results are dissociated from the personality and social position of the researcher (Ahrens & Chapman, 2006, p. 822; Sarantakos, 2005, p. 34).

Postpositivism refers to the methodological approach after positivism. It holds that entirely objective accounts of the world are not feasible because all methods of examining the world are flawed. Rather, only partially objective accounts of the world can be produced by the researcher (Denzin & Lincoln, 2000, p. 24). The difference between positivists and postpositivists is therefore that positivists believe in a reality which can be studied, captured, and understood, while postpositivists contend that reality can never be fully apprehended, only approximated. Human knowledge is not seen to be unchallengeable, rather it is positioned as conjectural (Guba, 1990, p. 22). As a consequence, postpositivistic researchers often rely on a multiplicity of methods in order to capture as much of reality as possible (Denzin & Lincoln, 2000, p. 9). They follow the scientific method where the researcher begins with a theory, collects data that either support or refute theory, and then makes necessary revisions before he or she conducts additional tests. The works of postpositivists typically reflect a deterministic philosophy in which causes determine effects or outcomes. Cause-and-effect-relationships are of major interest to postpositivists. The works of postpositivists are also reductionist in that their intent is to reduce ideas into a small, discrete set of testable hypotheses (Creswell, 2003, pp. 7-8).

Unlike positivism and postpositivism, the constructivist paradigm (often combined with interpretativism) assumes a relativist ontology, meaning that there are multiple realities. In constructivism, reality is the result of a subjective interpretation of the world; it is therefore socially constructed (Crotty, 1998, pp. 42-44; Denzin & Lincoln, 2000, p. 21). Individuals develop subjective meanings of their experiences – meanings which are directed toward certain objects or things. Often, these meanings are negotiated socially and historically through individuals' interaction with others. Since the subjective meanings may be varied and multiple, researchers are to take account of this complexity rather than to narrow meanings into a few categories or ideas. The goal of constructivist research is hence to rely as much as possible on the views and opinions of the people participating in a research project. Instead of starting with a theory, researchers who follow the constructivist paradigm generate or inductively develop a theory or pattern of meaning. They also recognize that their own backgrounds influence their interpretations. Accordingly, they position themselves in the research to acknowledge how their interpretations flow from their own personal, cultural, and historical experiences (Creswell, 2003, pp. 8-9). This is why the main stances of constructivism are often interpreted as standing in contrast to positivistic ideas (Tashakkori & Teddlie, 1998, pp. 6-13).

The advocacy/participatory approach starts with the notion that (post)positivistic assumptions entail structural laws and theories that do not fit marginalized and disenfranchised individuals. Also, it is felt that the constructivist perspective does not go far enough in advocating for an action agenda to help these individuals (Creswell, 2003, p. 9). On this basis, the advocacy/

participatory approach is positioned as a methodology that allows the researcher to conduct practical and collaborative studies with individuals who are facing constraints and irrational structures in their lives. It is focused on bringing about change in practices and thus freeing individuals from their constraints. Researchers following this approach attempt to initiate change via political debates and discussions. In these attempts, they inquire "with" others rather than "on" or "to" others which is why advocacy/participatory authors engage participants as active collaborators in their research (Kemmis & Wilkinson, 1998, pp. 23-26).

In pragmatism, knowledge claims arise out of actions or situations, and not – as (post)positivism would suggest – out of ex ante defined conditions (Cherryholmes, 1992, pp. 13-14; Creswell, 2003, p. 11). As Dewey (1989, p. 32) puts it, "pragmatism . . . does not insist upon antecedent phenomena but upon consequent phenomena; not upon the precedents but upon the possibilities of action". Pragmatic researchers are primarily concerned with applications as well as with solutions to problems. They believe that problems and scientific research on these problems always have to be seen in their greater social, historical, and political context (Cherryholmes, 1992, p. 14). In their focus on research problems they apply pluralistic approaches to derive knowledge about the problems (Tashakkori & Teddlie, 1998, pp. 12-13). Pragmatists are thereby not committed to any one system of philosophy and reality (Creswell, 2003, p. 12).

In the light of the five methodologies outlined above, this work can be classified as postpositivistic. It is based on the view that rational deliberations which are based on an established theory (i.e. role theory) offer a suitable foundation for conducting empirical research. It follows the deterministic philosophy of postpositivism in suggesting causal relationships between the selected independent and dependent variables. Also, it is postpositivistic because of its reductionism in translating broad ideas from role theory into a set of testable hypotheses on the effects of the application of the controllability principle. Finally, it relies on multiple methods (i.e. the survey and interview method, see chapter E1.2) as a way of capturing as much of reality as possible.

1.2 Method

Researchers have a variety of research methods at hand. With the help of a particular method, researchers are able to gather, analyze, and present empirical evidence (Richardson, 1996, p. 3). Often, scholars in the social sciences distinguish between quantitative and qualitative empirical methods (Creswell, 2003, p. 17; Kaplan & Duchon, 1988, pp. 571-572; Silverman, 2005, p. 99).

The use of quantitative methods implies the collection of data that can be measured and expressed numerically and used for statistical data analysis, most commonly with the intent of generalizing research claims from a particular sample to its population. Quantitative methods hence allow researchers to test theories and hypothesized relationships. They are instrumental in the measurement of complex phenomena linking empirical observations to statistical expressions. The use of qualitative methods means the detailed observation of, and involvement of researchers in, the natural setting in which the research occurs. Qualitative methods are often characterized by attempts to avoid prior commitment to theoretical constructs or to hypotheses formulated before gathering data. Although qualitative methods provide less explanation of variance in statistical terms, they can produce data from which richer explanations of processes and outcomes can be developed (Anderson & Widener, 2006, pp. 321-322; Atkinson & Shaffir, 1998, pp. 43-44; Creswell, 2003, pp. 18-21; Kaplan & Duchon, 1988, pp. 572-573). The researchers' choice of method is thereby influenced by the adopted methodology (Ryan, Scapens, & Theobald, 2002, p. 223; Silverman, 2005, pp. 99-100). While quantitative methods are generally associated with a positivistic or post-positivistic methodology, qualitative methods can often be found in research following a constructivist or advocacy/participatory methodology (Creswell, 2003, p. 18; Kaplan & Duchon, 1988, p. 572).

Among the quantitative empirical methods typically used in management accounting research are experiments and surveys. Experiments represent "empirical research conducted in controlled laboratory-like conditions, using human participants as 'subjects'" (Gibbins & Salterio, 1996, p. 9). In experiments, the researcher manipulates explicitly one or more variables and assigns subjects to groups with different treatments of the variable(s). True experiments mean that the subjects are randomly assigned; quasi-experiments mean that they are non-randomly assigned. The latter is the case with econometric (archival) methods. For hypothesis testing, the researcher observes and compares causes and effects across the groups, assuming that the observed effects are the result of the prior treatments (Gibbins & Salterio, 1996, pp. 9-11; Ryan et al., 2002, pp. 129-130; Smith, 2003, pp. 100-101).

Surveys – even though being criticized by some scholars (Young, 1996, pp. 55-56) – represent the second heavily used quantitative method in management accounting research. It is estimated that 30% of all empirical management accounting studies published over the last 20 years have used this method (Van der Stede et al., 2006, p. 445). Surveys enable the researcher to gather cross-sectional data from large samples, typically by applying standardized procedures and asking identical questions. Open-ended and closed questions are often combined when using the survey method. Questionnaires are the most widely used form of data collection in survey research and can be administered in various ways: face-to-face, by telephone, by fax, by postal mail, or electronically by email (Roberts, 1999, pp. 57-58; Shields, 1997, p. 13; Smith, 2003, p. 117). According to Van der Stede et al. (2006, p. 447), surveys serve two main purposes: description and explanation. Descriptive studies help the researcher to discover characteristics of and differences between samples of a given population. The purpose of survey studies used for explanation is to test theory and expected causal relationships among a set of variables. Theory testing represents the dominant purpose in management accounting studies relying on the survey method (Van der Stede et al., 2006, pp. 447-461).

Qualitative empirical methods used in management accounting research commonly take the form of case studies, field studies, and to a minor extent ethnographies. A case study can be defined as "an empirical inquiry that investigates a contemporary phenomenon within its real-life context, especially when the boundaries between phenomenon and context are not clearly evident" (Yin, 2003, p. 13). Following this definition, the key characteristic of the case study method is its focus on the investigation of phenomena in naturally occurring settings (Birnberg, Shields, & Young, 1990, pp. 35-36; Ryan et al., 2002, pp. 142-145; Schäffer & Brettel, 2005, pp. 43-45; Shields, 1997, pp. 10-11). Case studies are conducted in a single entity in order to provide a rich description of an actual situation, activity, or process. For the most part, they tend to be used more for hypothesis-generation than for hypothesis-testing. Case study data can thereby be collected by various procedures: personal interviews, observations, descriptions, document analyses, with combinations of the aforementioned being common (Creswell, 2003, p. 181; Eisenhardt, 1989b, pp. 534-535; Kaplan, 1986, p. 442).

Field studies are often distinguished from case studies in that they are viewed as cross-sectional case studies. With a field study approach, researchers gather data across a number of organizations and research sites. In terms of the data collection procedures and the researcher's involvement into the research process, however, field studies and case studies are pretty much alike (Birnberg et al., 1990, pp. 34-35; Bruns & Kaplan, 1987, pp. 8-9; Kaplan, 1986, p. 442).

Even though they are typically conducted by anthropologists and applied less frequently in management accounting research, ethnographies represent a further important qualitative method. Ethnographies involve the intensive study of intact cultural groups in their natural settings over a prolonged time period. Providing a flexible method, they evolve contextually in response to the lived realities encountered by the researcher. The aim of ethnographies is "to produce a systematic narrative of the behavior and idea systems of the actors in a particular culture, organization, profession, or community of some sort including their conceptions, discursive practices, and interrelationships with each other" (Jönsson & Macintosh, 1997, p. 370). In ethnographies, the researcher tries to get as close as possible to the participants. This means the researcher must "live-in" with them for some time to experience in real time and space the conditions of their social existence. Accordingly, observation is the primary form of data collection used by the researcher when conducting ethnographies (Creswell, 2003, p. 14; Jönsson & Macintosh, 1997, pp. 370-375).

Each of the quantitative and qualitative methods brings along its own strengths and weaknesses (Birnberg et al., 1990, p. 51). The researcher's choice of a particular method has implications for the internal, external, and construct validity of his or her study. Internal validity refers to the rigor with which the study is conducted and the credibility of the causal relationships between the study's independent and dependent variables inferred from data. External validity describes the extent to which the research results can be generalized from the study's sample and setting to the wider population, settings, or times. Construct validity refers to whether the theoretical concepts used by the researcher are adequately reflected by the operational definitions and the measures of empirical phenomena (Abernethy, Chua, Luckett, & Selto, 1999, pp. 7-8; Modell, 2005, pp. 234-237; Ryan et al., 2002, pp. 122-124). In terms of internal validity, the experimental method has typically been considered superior, whereas the case and field study method is often criticized due to measurement difficulties and the lack of control over variables. The survey method – if applied rigorously – is expected to be particularly helpful when striving for high levels of external validity. Testing construct validity is also thought to be most advanced in survey research, but considered only a minor issue in experimental studies. Due to its greater closeness to the empirical research object, the case study method is sometimes also positioned as a sound vehicle to achieve good fit between conceptual apparatus and empirical data, thus increasing construct validity (Abernethy et al., 1999, pp. 8-23; Birnberg et al., 1990, pp. 36-42; Smith, 2003, pp. 131-134).

In the light of each method's strengths and weaknesses, Birnberg et al. (1990, p. 61) conclude that "since no research method dominates the other on all criteria, multiple research methods should be used to investigate management accounting phenomena". Similarly, Hopper and Hoque (2006, p. 482), Modell (2005, pp. 250-251), and Tashakkori and Teddlie (1998, pp. 41-42) recommend the use of a mixed-methods approach for the purpose of triangulation. Triangulating data sources helps to reduce the biases inherent in any single method, alleviates problems of generalization, and seeks convergence across quantitative and qualitative methods.

According to Creswell (2003, p. 16), there are three general procedures for the application of a mixed method approach: sequential, concurrent, and transformative procedures. Sequential procedures imply the researcher's intention to elaborate on or expand findings from one method with another method. Quantitative and qualitative methods are therefore applied in successive phases, e.g. beginning with a qualitative method for exploratory purposes and following up with a quantitative method for the generalization of findings. Concurrent procedures mean that the researcher converges data gathered with quantitative and qualitative methods aiming at a comprehensive analysis of the research question. This procedure is not sequential; the researcher rather applies different methods at the same time and then integrates the gathered data in his or her final interpretation. Transformative procedures are characterized by the researcher's use of a theoretical lens as an overarching perspective within a research design that contains both quantitative and qualitative methods. This lens represents an exhaustive framework for the topics of interest, methods for data collection, and outcomes anticipated by the study. Within this lens either a sequential or concurrent approach to the application of methods is possible (Creswell, 2003, pp. 15-17).

Acknowledging the strong points made for mixed-methods approaches in prior literature, this study employed both quantitative and qualitative methods for the collection of empirical data. More specifically, it integrates the field study method and the survey method into one research design. According to Modell (2005, p. 250), research primarily engaged in theory and hypothesis testing, which is the case here, concentrates the use of qualitative methods to the early stages of the research process. It is in these stages that the use of qualitative methods is expected to be particularly helpful (Creswell, 2003, p. 16; Silverman, 2005, p. 100; Tashakkori & Teddlie, 1998, pp. 46-47). Since the application of the controllability principle has not yet been investigated in relation to managers' role perceptions, the first phase of this study's data collection therefore consisted of semi-structured interviews with managers. The interviews allowed learning more about the research subject, refining previously formulated hypotheses, and gaining deeper insights into managers' responses to the application of the controllability, thereby sometimes also going beyond the initial research questions. The second phase of this study's sequential mixed-methods approach was made up of a cross-sectional questionnaire. This questionnaire forms the primary source of data in this work and enables testing of the causal relationships proposed in part D. Even though experimental designs are often depicted as instrumental in determining causality, this study opted against this method because the focus is on the investigation of managers in their natural settings and "the mere fact that subjects are placed in a laboratory setting may create an effect resulting in an outcome which would not have arisen outside the experimental setting" (Smith, 2003, p. 103). In particular, and with regard to the effects of accountability, Tetlock (1985, p. 306) and Lerner and Tetlock (1999, p. 270) speak out against laboratory investigations because individuals' responses to accountability are expected to differ from manipulated experiments to natural settings. Also, the use of archival data was not an option because the variables of interest to this study are manifestations of managers' cognitions, feelings, and behavior which can hardly be retrieved from existing documents and databases.

2. Operationalization of the Research Model

The hypotheses developed in part D describe causal relationships between latent variables, also termed constructs. Constructs refer to theoretical creations that can be defined in conceptual terms but cannot be observed and measured directly. Therefore they are anchored to observable reality by means of indicators. Indicators are variables that represent observable manifestations or observable facets of a construct. They are also termed manifest variables. Operationalization then describes the process of determining the indicators that represent a construct and the way in which they will be measured (Babbie, 2004, pp. 45-46; Bisbe et al., 2007, p. 790; Bollen, 1989, p. 11; Hair, Anderson, Tatham, & Black, 2006, pp. 707-708). It is generally recommended to operationalize constructs with the help of multiple indicators because the validity and reliability of constructs increases by the number and the quality of indicators (Baumgartner & Homburg, 1996, p. 144; Churchill, 1979, pp. 66-67; Hinkin, 1995, p. 972; Peter, 1979, p. 16). This study therefore relies on the measurement of at least three indicators for each construct. At the same time, it avoids using an excessive number of indicators since too many indicators reflecting the same theoretical concept can lead to fatigue, boredom, and inattention among the survey participants (Drolet & Morrison, 2001, p. 198).

Having identified a set of indicators for each construct, it is important to determine the nature and direction of the relationships between a construct and its indicators. One can thereby distinguish between reflective and formative measurement models. In a reflective measurement model, a construct is understood as an underlying concept which is manifested through a series of indicators. The indicators depend on the construct and are thus referred to as effect indicators. In a formative measurement model, however, the construct is understood to be formed by a series of constitutive indicators. Under the formative perspective, indicators are depicted as causing the construct. Therefore they are also called cause indicators (Bisbe et al., 2007, p. 792; Blalock, 1964, pp. 162-169; Bollen & Lennox, 1991, p. 306; Hair et al., 2006, pp. 786-789; Jarvis, MacKenzie, & Podsakoff, 2003, pp. 200-201). The main conceptual differences between reflective and formative measurement models are summarized in Figure 14.

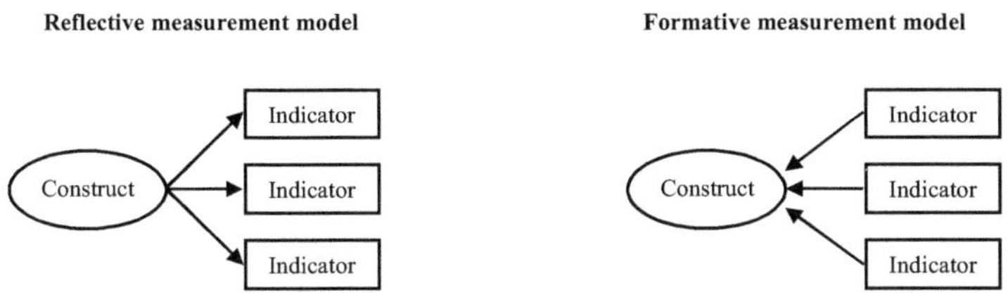

Reflective measurement model:

(a) Direction of causality is from construct to indicator.

(b) Indicators are expected to be correlated. (They should possess internal consistency reliability.)

(c) Dropping an indicator from the measurement model does not alter the meaning of the construct.

(d) Measurement error is taken into account at the indicator level.

Formative measurement model:

(a) Direction of causality is from indicator to construct.

(b) There is no reason to expect that the indicators are correlated. (Internal consistency is not implied.)

(c) Dropping an indicator from the measurement model may alter the meaning of the construct.

(d) Measurement error is taken into account at the construct level.

Figure 14: Differences between Reflective and Formative Measurement Models[17]

Figure 14 focuses on the relationships between indicators and first-order constructs. Some constructs are, however, defined conceptually at a more abstract level (Edwards, 2001, pp. 144-148; Law, Wong, & Mobley, 1998, pp. 741-746). More precisely, they may be specified as consisting of several first-order constructs (or dimensions). Such constructs are referred to as multidimensional (or second-order) constructs in that they connect several distinct but related dimensions parsimoniously and meaningfully into one single holistic concept. When integrating first-order dimensions into a second-order construct, the researcher must again specify whether the relationships between the dimensions and the overall construct are reflective or formative in nature. One can distinguish between two modes of relating dimensions to constructs: reflective second-order (or latent) measurement models and formative second-order (or emergent) measurement models. A reflective second-order (or latent) model assumes that there is a multidimensional construct that exists at a deeper and more embedded level of abstraction than its dimensions. The construct is expected to be manifested in different forms through its dimensions. The causal relationships therefore flow from the construct to its dimensions. A formative second-order (or emergent) model is defined as a combination of its dimensions. It exists at the same level of abstraction as its dimensions and the causal relationships flow from the dimensions to the construct (Bisbe et al., 2007, pp. 803-804; Diamantopoulos, Riefler, & Roth, 2008, pp. 1205-1208; Jarvis et al., 2003, pp. 204-207; MacKenzie, Podsakoff, & Jarvis, 2005, pp. 713-716).

---

[17] Adapted from Jarvis et al. (2003, p. 201).

This study uses a formative measurement model for only one construct, i.e. the application of the controllability principle. All other constructs are operationalized with the help of reflective measurement models. In order to relate the results of this study to prior research, existing measurement scales have been employed for the constructs whenever available. Since this study tests the proposed relationships using a sample of German managers, a standard translation-back-translation procedure was applied for all English measurement scales. Discrepancies in the wording of the original indicators and the back-translated indicators were solved by discussions with the translators and academic colleagues. This procedure helps to minimize semantic differences and thus ensures equivalent meaning in the German language (Brislin, 1980, pp. 426-437; Mallinckrodt & Wang, 2004, pp. 368-369; Van de Vijver & Hambleton, 1996, pp. 91-97). The indicators of all constructs used in this study were assessed with the help of a seven-point Likert scale. The Likert scale represents the most commonly used response format in survey research (DeVellis, 2003, pp. 78-79).

Particular attention was also paid to the pretesting of the survey instruments. A pretest is generally advisable to improve the quality of a questionnaire, verify construct validity, and assess the reliability of newly developed measurement scales (Anderson & Gerbing, 1991, pp. 732-733; Bagozzi, 1994a, pp. 42-43; Hunt, Sparkman, & Wilcox, 1982, pp. 269-273; Kwok & Sharp, 1998, p. 159). The aim of the pretest was to ensure that all indicators were unambiguous and captured the respective constructs of interest. In the first phase of pretesting, standard practices were employed, including the use of a panel of management accounting academics and questionnaire design experts to assess the survey instruments for understanding, style of question, length of question, and layout. The instruments were revised on the basis of comments received. The second phase of pretesting was undertaken with a convenience sample of 45 managers showing characteristics similar to those in the target population (Dillman, 2007, pp. 140-147; Singleton & Straits, 2002, pp. 64-65). They were given a copy of the questionnaire and asked to complete it as well as to assess the substance, relevance and clarity of the proposed questions. Final adjustments to the questionnaire were made on the basis of their feedback. The data set obtained through the pretest of the questionnaire allowed the application of factor analytical techniques to assess the preliminary descriptive statistics for all measurement scales.

2.1 Variables Used in the Main Models

2.1.1 Application of the Controllability Principle

Chapter B1.4 provided a conceptual specification of the controllability principle. Based on the work of Bisbe et al. (2007), it argues that the application of the controllability principle is a question of managers' perception[18]. More specifically, managers are thought to perceive the controllability principle to be applied when they feel that the measures used to evaluate their performance are (a) sensitive and (b) precise. Sensitivity thereby means that changes in the performance measures are due to managers' actions; precision implies a lack of noise or variability in the performance measures. Since Bisbe et al. (2007, p. 805) predict that managers will only perceive their performance measures as controllable when they are both sensitive and precise at the same time, it is recommended to operationalize the application of the controllability principle as a construct that combines the two constitutive facets (or dimensions) of sensitivity and precision in a formative second-order measurement model[19].

Unfortunately, management accounting research has until recently been characterized by "an uncritical reliance on reflective models" (Bisbe et al., 2007, p. 810). The application of the controllability principle has not yet been operationalized using the prescriptions of Bisbe et al. (2007). Scholars note that serious misspecification problems may arise out of wrong epistemic relationships between constructs, dimensions, and indicators (Bollen, 1989, p. 65; Bollen & Lennox, 1991, p. 307; Edwards & Bagozzi, 2000, p. 156; Jarvis et al., 2003, pp. 207-212; MacKenzie et al., 2005, pp. 716-724). This work therefore follows Bisbe et al. (2007) in the development of a new measurement scale for the application of the controllability principle. As outlined above, the resulting scale depicts the construct as a formative second-order combination of its two dimensions (i.e. sensitivity of performance measures and precision of performance measures) both of which are assessed using reflective measurement models. Reflective indicators are also added on the second-order level to make the measurement parameters more stable and less sensitive to changes in the structural relationships. This leads to a MIMIC (multiple indicators and multiple causes) model (see also Figure 20 in chapter F1.1). MIMIC models are commonly regarded as the optimal approach for solving error indeterminacy and achieving identification of formative

---

18 This work focuses on managers' perceptions concerning the application of the controllability principle instead of attempting to collect hard data that might be supposed to deliver more "objective" descriptions of the application of the controllability principle in companies' MCSs. This approach (see also chapter B1.3) is based on the belief that "employees behave based on how they perceive the system; not necessarily on the actual system design . . . Therefore, it is important for research to examine perceptions to understand subsequent employee and organizational outcomes" (Burney et al., 2009, p. 306).

19 Second-order means that the application of the controllability principle consists of the two first-order dimensions sensitivity of performance measures and precision of performance measures. Jarvis et al. (2003, p. 203) state that a multidimensional construct should be modeled as formative second-order if the following conditions prevail: (a) the dimensions are viewed as defining characteristics of the construct, (b) changes in the dimensions are expected to cause changes in the construct, (c) changes in the multidimensional construct are not expected to cause changes in the dimensions, (d) the dimensions do not necessarily share a common theme, (e) eliminating a dimension may alter the conceptual domain of the construct, (f) a change in one of the dimensions is not necessarily expected to be associated with a change in all of the other dimensions, and (g) the dimensions are not expected to have the same antecedents and consequences. Such formative second-order models are designated as "emergent models" by Bisbe et al. (2007, p. 799).

measurement models (Bagozzi, 1994b, p. 333; Bisbe et al., 2007, p. 816; Diamantopoulos & Winklhofer, 2001, p. 272; Jarvis et al., 2003, p. 213).

The final operationalization consists of eleven indicators all of which are cast on a seven-point Likert scale ranging from 1 = "strongly disagree" to 7 = "strongly agree". The two first-order dimensions sensitivity of performance measures (SENSIT1-SENSIT4) and precision of performance measures (PRECIS1-PRECIS4) are each assessed with the help of four indicators. These measurement scales are similar to the instruments developed by Moers (2006). Moers (2006, p. 908) reports Cronbach's alphas of 0.81 and 0.70, respectively, for his original scales. Moers' (2006) instruments have been revised to fit into the context of this study. The three additional reflective indicators on the second-order level are designated as CONTRO1, CONTRO2, and CONTRO3. They have been newly developed for this study using existing guidelines (DeVellis, 2003, pp. 60-99; Rossiter, 2002, pp. 305-332). Pretests involving exploratory and confirmatory factor analyses have shown that sensitivity of performance measures and precision of performance measures are two distinct facets of the overall construct.

Indicators of the construct: Application of the controllability principle

SENSIT1	Mit meinen Handlungen kann ich beeinflussen, zu welchem Grad ich meine Zielvorgaben erreiche. (With my actions I can influence my performance measures.)
SENSIT2	Mein Einsatz wirkt sich auf den Grad aus, zu dem ich meine Zielvorgaben erreiche. (My effort has an impact on my performance measures.)
SENSIT3	Die Höhe der von mir erreichten Zielvorgaben ist von meinen Handlungen abhängig. (My performance measures do depend on my actions.)
SENSIT4	Mit meinem Einsatz kann ich die Größen, anhand derer meine Leistung beurteilt wird, beeinflussen. (With my effort I can influence the measures according to which my performance is evaluated.)
PRECIS1	Es kommt zu keinen Unschärfen bei der Bewertung meiner Leistung, da ungewisse oder von mir nicht kontrollierbare Ereignisse kaum Einfluss auf meine Zielvorgaben haben. (There is no noise in the evaluation of my performance as uncertain or uncontrollable factors do not have an impact on my performance measures.)
PRECIS2	Es gibt keine Verzerrungen in meiner Leistungsbewertung, die durch nicht kontrollierbare Einflussfaktoren verursacht werden könnten. (There is no distortion in my performance evaluation that might be caused by uncontrollable factors.)
PRECIS3	Die Leistungsbewertung anhand meiner Zielvorgaben ist präzise, das heißt der Einfluss von nicht kontrollierbaren Faktoren ist minimal. (My performance measures are precise, i.e. the influence of uncontrollable factors is minimal.)
PRECIS4	Die Größen, anhand derer meine Leistung beurteilt wird, werden kaum durch von mir nicht kontrollierbare Faktoren verfälscht. (My performance measures are not blurred by factors that I cannot control.)
CONTRO1	Meine Zielvorgaben enthalten Punkte, die ich nur indirekt beeinflussen kann. (My performance measures include issues which I can only influence indirectly.) (R)
CONTRO2	Meine Zielvorgaben enthalten Punkte, die außerhalb meines Einflussbereichs liegen. (My performance measures include issues that are beyond my sphere of influence.) (R)
CONTRO3	Meine Zielvorgaben enthalten Punkte, die im Grunde von mir nicht kontrollierbar sind. (My performance measures include issues that are virtually uncontrollable by me.) (R)

Corresponding English indicators are provided in brackets. Differences in the translations are based on the feedback obtained in the pretest. (R) means that the indicator is reverse-coded.

Table 7: Operationalization of the Construct Application of the Controllability Principle

2.1.2 Role Conflict

Role conflict is operationalized with the help of the traditional eight-indicator instrument developed by Rizzo et al. (1970). Again, a seven-point Likert scale ranging from 1 =

"strongly disagree" to 7 = "strongly agree" was used in the questionnaire. Theoretically, role conflict occurs when individuals receive requests that are perceived as contradictory and incompatible (Kahn et al., 1964, pp. 18-19; Katz & Kahn, 1978, p. 204). The Rizzo et al. (1970) scale therefore asks the respondents about the existence of several sources of role conflict in their job. Even though this measurement instrument has come under scrutiny for its psychometric properties and item response characteristics (King & King, 1990, p. 62; Tracy & Johnson, 1981, pp. 467-468), Schuler, Aldag, and Brief (1977, p. 111) and House, Schuler, and Levanoni (1983, p. 334) conclude that it is on the whole a satisfactory scale. In fact, it is the most consistently used scale in studies on role conflict (Gilboa et al., 2008, p. 235; Jackson & Schuler, 1985, p. 16; Van Sell et al., 1981, p. 46). It is also widely employed in management accounting studies on role stress. Recent studies drawing upon the Rizzo et al. (1970) scale are, among others, Burney and Widener (2007), Rebele and Michaels (1990), and Viator (2001). The Cronbach's alpha for the scale as reported in these studies is always above the threshold of 0.70 (Nunnally & Bernstein, 1994, p. 245).

Indicators of the construct: Role conflict

ROLEC1	Ich habe manchmal Dinge zu tun, die eigentlich anders gemacht werden sollten. (I have to do things that should be done differently.)
ROLEC2	Ich erhalte gelegentlich Aufgaben ohne das Personal, um sie zu erledigen. (I receive assignments without the manpower to complete them.)
ROLEC3	Manchmal muss ich eine Regel oder Anweisung umgehen, um eine Aufgabe zu erledigen. (I have to buck a rule or policy in order to carry out an assignment.)
ROLEC4	Verschiedene Personen stellen an mich Anforderungen, die nicht miteinander vereinbar sind. (I receive incompatible requests from two or more people.)
ROLEC5	Ich tue Dinge, die von manchen Personen akzeptiert werden, von anderen allerdings nicht. (I do things that are apt to be accepted by one person and not accepted by others.)
ROLEC6	Manchmal erhalte ich Aufgaben ohne adäquate Ressourcen und Mittel, um sie auszuführen. (I receive assignments without adequate resources and materials to execute them.)
ROLEC7	Manchmal bearbeite ich unnötige Dinge. (I work on unnecessary things.)
ROLEC8	Ich arbeite mit mehreren Abteilungen, die ziemlich unterschiedlich agieren. (I work with two or more groups who operate quite differently.)

Original English indicators are provided in brackets. Differences in the translations are based on the feedback obtained in the pretest.

Table 8: Operationalization of the Construct Role Conflict

2.1.3 Role Ambiguity

This construct is assessed using the traditional measurement instrument developed by Rizzo et al. (1970). The response categories are Likert in format with 1 = "strongly disagree" and 7 = "strongly agree". Since the conceptual meaning of role ambiguity refers to individuals' cognition of having adequate information to define their work role (Kahn et al., 1964, pp. 21-23; Katz & Kahn, 1978, pp. 206-207), this scale comprises six indicators which directly ask the respondents about the overall clarity of their authorities, responsibilities, and objectives. Like the role conflict scale, the Rizzo et al. (1970) instrument for role ambiguity is the most frequently used one in role stress studies across many disciplines, including management accounting (Gilboa et al., 2008, p. 235; Jackson & Schuler, 1985, p. 16; Van Sell et al., 1981, p. 46). Prominent management accounting studies adopting this scale are Chenhall and Brownell (1988) and Fogarty et al. (2000). The Cronbach's alphas reported in these two studies are 0.87 and 0.73, respectively. Gregson, Wendell, and Aono (1994) provide additional evidence in an accounting setting that supports the construct validity and distinctiveness of the Rizzo et al. (1970) measures for role conflict and role ambiguity.

Indicators of the construct: Role ambiguity

ROLEA1	Ich bin mir darüber im Klaren, welche Befugnisse ich habe. (I feel certain about how much authority I have.) (R)
ROLEA2	Ich habe klare, geplante Ziele und Vorgaben für meine Aufgaben. (I have clear, planned goals and objectives for my jobs.) (R)
ROLEA3	Ich weiß, dass ich meine Zeit richtig einteile. (I know that I have divided my time properly.) (R)
ROLEA4	Ich weiß, wofür ich verantwortlich bin. (I know what my responsibilities are.) (R)
ROLEA5	Ich weiß genau, was von mir erwartet wird. (I know exactly what is expected of me.) (R)
ROLEA6	Es wird mir eindeutig erklärt, was zu tun ist. (I receive a clear explanation of what has to be done.) (R)

Original English indicators are provided in brackets. Differences in the translations are based on the feedback obtained in the pretest. (R) means that the indicator is reverse-coded.

Table 9: Operationalization of the Construct Role Ambiguity

2.1.4 Flexible Role Orientation

Since role orientation has only recently attracted attention in the literature and has not yet been operationalized in a managerial context (Parker et al., 2006, p. 646), a new measurement instrument was developed for the purpose of this study. In conceptual terms, role orientation describes the tasks, goals, and problems which individuals see as relevant to their role (Mehta, Anderson, Dubas, Dubinsky, & Liu, 1999, p. 407; Parker, 2007, p. 406). It refers to a continuum of role definitions ranging from narrow to flexible with a narrow role orientation implying that individuals tend to define their role very restrictively and work only on explicitly assigned tasks. A "that's not my job" mindset is often associated with a narrow role orientation. The notion of a flexible (or broad) role orientation, however, describes individuals' belief that their role goes beyond mere job descriptions and includes more global and far-reaching aspects of the job (Parker, 2000, p. 450; Parker & Sprigg, 1999, p. 928; Parker et al., 1997, pp. 900-901).

So far, role orientation has primarily been operationalized in a production environment. Parker et al. (1997) and Parker (2000; 2007) assess the role orientation of blue-collar employees working in manufacturing departments by determining the extent of felt ownership for issues beyond their immediate production tasks. Employees are, for example, asked to indicate whether matters of customer satisfaction are of concern to them. Employees with a narrow role orientation are expected to score low on such indicators, whereas employees with a flexible role orientation are expected to score high (Parker, 2000, p. 458). However, Parker (2000; 2007) indicates that such an operationalization does only work in this particular production environment. There is unlikely to be a straightforward, "one-size-fits all" method of assessing role orientation across different professions and contexts. For the successful operationalization of the role orientation construct in a managerial context, Parker (2007, p. 427) therefore suggests: "To assess flexible role orientation amongst managers, . . . items should assess more than ownership of departmental-level problems (which is to be expected from managers) and instead assess ownership of organizational level problems".

This study follows Parker's (2007) recommendation in the design of a new measurement instrument for role orientation among managers. Using existing guidelines for scale development (DeVellis, 2003, pp. 60-99; Rossiter, 2002, pp. 305-332), seven indicators are proposed, all of which describe work issues and problems that are beyond the level of the managers' own departments. Correspondingly, a Likert scale ranging from 1 = "of no concern to me" to 7 = "most certainly of concern to me" is employed. High scores on this scale indicate a flexible role orientation towards the respondents' managerial job; low scores display a narrow role orientation. This method of assessing role orientation is preferable to directly asking managers how broadly they view their role because it avoids problems of social desirability bias (Parker, 2007, p. 413). Expert interviews as well as exploratory and confirmatory factor analyses of the data gathered from the pretest sample indicate that the newly developed scale is valid and reliable.

Indicators of the construct: Flexible role orientation

Inwieweit sind die folgenden Aspekte und Probleme von persönlicher Bedeutung für Sie? (To what extent are the following work issues and problems of personal concern to you?)	
ROLEO1	Ein Mangel an abteilungsübergreifender Koordination aufgrund der Unternehmensstrukturen (A lack of interdepartmental coordination due to the company's structure)
ROLEO2	Neue Chancen oder Gefahren im Unternehmensumfeld, die bisher nicht beachtet wurden (New opportunities or threats in the company's environment that were not being considered)
ROLEO3	Unzulänglichkeiten in anderen Abteilungen, die nicht entschieden angegangen werden (Deficiencies in other work units that are not being addressed in a resolute manner)
ROLEO4	Übergreifende Risiken für das Unternehmen (Overall risks for the company)
ROLEO5	Angelegenheiten anderer Abteilungen, die indirekten Einfluss auf meine Abteilung haben (Issues in other work units which have an indirect impact on my work unit)
ROLEO6	Probleme und Schwachstellen auf Gesamtunternehmensebene (Problems and weaknesses on a corporate level)
ROLEO7	Ineffiziente Arbeitsabläufe in anderen Abteilungen (Inefficient procedures in other work units)
Corresponding English indicators are provided in brackets. Differences in the translations are based on the feedback obtained in the pretest.	

Table 10: Operationalization of the Construct Flexible Role Orientation

2.1.5 Job Tension

Job tension is assessed using the well-established House and Rizzo (1972) scale together with a seven-point Likert scale where 1 = "strongly disagree" and 7 = "strongly agree". This scale comprises seven indicators to measure the extent to which individuals experience symptoms of tension and anxiety resulting from work situations. In a comparison of different job tension scales, literature recommends the use of the House and Rizzo's (1972) measurement instrument. The indicators of this scale are supposed to "have more face validity because they refer to psychological or psychosomatic symptoms often associated with the concept of tension" (Jackson & Schuler, 1985, p. 40). The scale has also repeatedly found application in prior management accounting studies. Collins and Killough (1992) and Senatra (1980), for example, use the scale and both report acceptable validity and reliability for it. In the Collins and Killough (1992) study, a Cronbach's alpha of 0.89 is disclosed.

Indicators of the Construct Job Tension

TEN1	Tendenziell hat mein Job direkte Auswirkungen auf meine Gesundheit. (My job tends to directly affect my health.)
TEN2	Ich arbeite unter großer Anspannung. (I work under a great deal of tension.)
TEN3	Ich habe mich wegen meines Jobs schon unruhig oder nervös gefühlt. (I have felt fidgety or nervous as a result of my job.)
TEN4	Wenn ich einen anderen Job hätte, würde sich mein Gesundheitszustand wahrscheinlich verbessern. (If I had a different job, my health would probably improve.)
TEN5	Probleme, die mit meinem Job zu tun haben, haben mich nachts schon wach gehalten. (Problems associated with my job have kept me awake at night.)
TEN6	Vor Meetings im Unternehmen habe ich mich schon nervös gefühlt. (I have felt nervous before attending meetings in the company.)
TEN7	Ich nehme „meinen Job häufig mit nach Hause", das heißt ich denke über meine Arbeit nach, wenn ich andere Dinge tue. (I often "take my job home with me" in the sense that I think about it when doing other things.)

Original English indicators are provided in brackets. Differences in the translations are based on the feedback obtained in the pretest.

Table 11: Operationalization of the Construct Job Tension

2.1.6 Job Satisfaction

For the operationalization of the job satisfaction construct, this study relies on a scale developed by Rusbult and Farrell (1983). This instrument adopts a global approach (as opposed to a facet approach) in that it focuses on the measurement of individuals' overall job satisfaction. It includes six positively worded statements asking respondents to indicate their agreement on a seven-point Likert scale ranging from 1 = "strongly disagree" to 7 = "strongly agree". This instrument was chosen over the Minnesota satisfaction questionnaire (Weiss, Dawis, England, & Lofquist, 1967) due to its shorter length. The scale has been widely used in management accounting research demonstrating its validity and reliability. Chow, Harrison, McKinnon, and Wu (2002), Ketchand and Strawser (1998), and Pasewark and Viator (2006) all report a Cronbach's alpha of 0.85 or higher for this scale.

Indicators of the construct: Job satisfaction

SATIS1	Alles in allem bin ich sehr zufrieden mit meinem aktuellen Job. (All things considered, I am very satisfied with my current job.)
SATIS2	Im Allgemeinen mag ich meinen Job sehr gerne. (In general, I like my job very much.)
SATIS3	Mit meinem jetzigen Wissen würde ich mich sicher wieder für meinen aktuellen Job entscheiden, wenn ich nochmal wählen müsste, ob ich den Job nehme, den ich jetzt habe. (Knowing what I know now, if I had to decide all over again whether to take the job I have now, I would certainly do it.)
SATIS4	Ich würde meinen Job weiterempfehlen, wenn mir ein guter Freund bzw. eine gute Freundin sagen würde, dass er/sie sich für einen Job wie den meinen bei meinem Arbeitgeber interessiert. (If a good friend of mine told me that he/she was interested in a job like mine for my employer, I would recommend it.)
SATIS5	Mein aktueller Job kommt dem für mich idealen Job sehr nahe. (My current job compares very well to my ideal job.)
SATIS6	Mein aktueller Job erfüllt ganz die Erwartungen an einen solchen Job, die ich hatte, als ich ihn antrat. (My current job measures up very well to the sort of job I wanted when I took it.)

Original English indicators are provided in brackets. Differences in the translations are based on the feedback obtained in the pretest.

Table 12: Operationalization of the Construct Job Satisfaction

2.1.7 In-Role Performance

To measure managers' in-role performance, this work applies a scale developed by Burkert (2008) which comprises five indicators cast on a Likert scale ranging from 1 = "strongly disagree" to 7 = "strongly agree". The scale is based on the conception of the management cycle as a planning and control process thereby emphasizing the importance of the quality of managers' decisions for their in-role performance. The quality of managers' decisions can be regarded as in-role performance since it is a regular "part of performing the duties and responsibilities of the assigned role" (Van Dyne et al., 1995, p. 222) as a manager. Burkert's (2008) scale assesses managers' success in the areas of (a) decision-making, (b) implementing/enforcing decisions, and (c) monitoring the results of decisions. Such an approach to the measurement of performance is recommended by Kren and Liao (1988, p. 299) who state: "A study that focused on the quality of the decision rather than the result . . . would be enlightening". Burkert's (2008) scale has already been validated in a large sample of German managers and demonstrates high validity and reliability. Burkert (2008) reports a Cronbach's alpha of 0.87 for his scale.

As with the other constructs included in this study, self-reports are used to assess in-role performance. This kind of measurement is thought to be advantageous over superior-rated scales as it overcomes superiors' tendency to capture only one cognitive dimension ("halo error") in the evaluation of subordinates (Brownell, 1982, p. 17; Heneman, 1974, p. 642). It is also worth noting that subordinates' self-reports of their performance have been shown not only to correlate with superiors' subjective assessments but also with objective performance assessments (Bommer, Johnson, Rich, Podsakoff, & MacKenzie, 1995, pp. 596-598; Furnham & Stringfield, 1994, pp. 65-66; Heneman, 1974, p. 641). Unlike the more frequently used performance scale of Mahoney, Jerdee, and Carroll (1965) which suggests the measurement of managers' overall performance with a single indicator, the Burkert (2008) scale consists of several indicators that each measure performance. Since structural equation modeling is employed for hypothesis testing, the use of the Burkert (2008) scale is hence also advisable from a psychometric perspective.

Indicators of the construct: In-role performance

INROLE1	Mit der Umsetzung meiner Entscheidungen bin ich sehr zufrieden. (I am very satisfied with the way my decisions are implemented.)
INROLE2	Mit der Kontrolle der Umsetzung meiner Entscheidungen bin ich sehr zufrieden. (I am very satisfied with the way the execution of my decisions is monitored.)
INROLE3	Mit den Ergebnissen meiner Entscheidungen bin ich sehr zufrieden. (I am very satisfied with the results of my decisions.)
INROLE4	Mit der Durchsetzung meiner Entscheidungen im Unternehmen bin ich sehr zufrieden. (I am very satisfied with the way my decisions are accepted and adhered to in the company.)
INROLE5	Mit meinen Entscheidungen bin ich sehr zufrieden. (I am very satisfied with my decisions.)

Corresponding English indicators are provided in brackets. Differences in the translations are based on the feedback obtained in the pretest.

Table 13: Operationalization of the Construct In-Role Performance

2.1.8 Extra-Role Performance

To assess managers' extra-role performance, this study refers to the degree to which managers engage in internal influence behavior. Internal influence behavior is a type of behavior that captures managers' individual initiative in communicating to other managers about ways to solve organizational problems and improve operations outside their own area of authority. As such, it is discretionary, goes beyond conventional job requirements, and is regarded as extra-role (see also chapter C2.2). Internal influence behavior is measured by the four-indicator scale of Bettencourt et al. (2005). The scale has been slightly adapted to fit into the context of this study. Since managers are asked about the frequency of showing particular behaviors, the response categories employed for the Likert scale range from 1 = "very infrequently" to 7 = "very frequently". In the studies of Bettencourt and Brown (2003) and Bettencourt et al. (2005), Cronbach's alphas of 0.91 and 0.94, respectively, are reported for the original scale. Though the Bettencourt et al. (2005) scale has not yet been used in a management accounting setting, its indicators have a close resemblance with an instrument developed by Macintosh and Williams (1992). They use this instrument to measure what they call an "entrepreneurial profile" of effective managers. Such a profile consists of proactive behaviors like the initiation of change within the organization and the exploration of corporate opportunities (Macintosh & Williams, 1992, p. 30).

Indicators of the construct: Extra-role performance (internal influence behavior)

EXROLE1	Ich mache anderen Managern oder Abteilungen konstruktive Vorschläge für Verbesserungen. (I make constructive suggestions for improvements to other managers or departments.)
EXROLE2	Ich steuere viele Ideen zur Optimierung (von Vorgehensweisen, etc.) bei. (I contribute many ideas for optimization (of procedures, etc.).)
EXROLE3	Ich teile kreative Lösungen für Probleme mit anderen Managern oder Abteilungen. (I share creative solutions to problems with other managers or departments.)
EXROLE4	Ich ermuntere andere Manager oder Abteilungen, Ideen und Vorschläge zur Verbesserung im Unternehmen beizutragen. (I encourage other managers or departments to contribute ideas and suggestions for organizational improvement.)

Original English indicators are provided in brackets. Differences in the translations are based on the feedback obtained in the pretest.

Table 14: Operationalization of the Construct Extra-Role Performance

2.2 Variables Used in the Moderated Models

2.2.1 Hierarchical Level

An adaptation of Dunk's (1992) instrument is used in order to assess managers' hierarchical level in their organization. A generic organization chart was reproduced in the questionnaire so that managers could indicate their managerial level. It is distinguished between three levels: lower level management, middle management, and top management. The inclusion of such a generic organization chart in the questionnaire avoids the disadvantage of having respondents simply report their title, in which case the level reported may only be meaningful in the context of respondents' specific companies (Berger & Cummings, 1979, p. 180).

Indicator of the construct: Hierarchical level

LEVEL	Bitte geben Sie an, welcher Managementebene Sie angehören: (a) untere Managementebene, (b) mittlere Managementebene, (c) Top Management (Please indicate your managerial level: (a) lower management, (b) middle management, (c) top management)

Original English indicator is provided in brackets. Differences in the translations are based on the feedback obtained in the pretest.

Table 15: Operationalization of the Construct Hierarchical Level

2.2.2 Self-Efficacy

Self-efficacy which describes individuals' belief in their ability to cope, perform, and successfully execute actions (Bandura, 1997, p. 3; Stajkovic & Luthans, 1998, p. 240) varies in generality and requires different measurement instruments depending on what should be measured. As Bandura (1986, p. 396) states, "people may judge themselves efficacious only in certain domains of functioning or across a wide range of activities and situations". Psychologists therefore differentiate between (a) self-efficacy as an enduring personality trait that the individual carries around from situation to situation at a relatively constant level and (b) self-efficacy as a situation-specific state that varies in the same individual across situations (Bozeman, Hochwarter, Perrewé, & Brymer, 2001, p. 489; Eden, 1988, pp. 640-641; Eden & Kinnar, 1991, p. 771). The former is called generalized self-efficacy, the latter specific self-efficacy. Since this work interprets self-efficacy as a personality variable (see chapter D3.2), it is preferable to choose the construct of generalized self-efficacy for the purpose of operationalization. To assess generalized self-efficacy among managers, the measurement instrument of Speier and Frese (1997) is applied. It comprises six indicators that measure self-efficacy broadly so that it covers a variety of work-related issues and challenges. Responses are elicited on a seven-point Likert scale ranging from 1 = "strongly disagree" to 7 = "strongly agree". The Cronbach's alpha for the scale as reported by Speier and Frese (1997, p. 178) is 0.68.

Indicators of the construct: Self-efficacy

SELF1	Ich schätze meine Fähigkeiten als hoch ein. (I judge my abilities to be high.)
SELF2	Wenn ich etwas erreichen will, kann ich Rückschläge bewältigen ohne mein Ziel aufzugeben. (If I want to achieve something, I can overcome setbacks without giving up my goal.)
SELF3	Wenn ich mit einer neuen Aufgabe konfrontiert werde, habe ich häufig die Befürchtung, mit ihr nicht zurecht zu kommen. (When I am confronted with a new task, I am often afraid of not being able to handle it.) (R)
SELF4	Wenn ich ein Ziel erreichen will, schaffe ich es normalerweise auch. (When I want to reach a goal, I am usually able to succeed.)
SELF5	Sollte ich arbeitslos werden, bin ich davon überzeugt, dass ich aufgrund meiner Fähigkeiten bald einen neuen Job finden würde. (In case of becoming unemployed, I am convinced that, because of my abilities, I will soon find a new job.)
SELF6	Müsste ich meinen Job wechseln, bin ich sicher, dass ich den Anforderungen gewachsen wäre. (If I had to change my job, I am sure I would be up to the demands.)

Original English indicators are provided in brackets. Differences in the translations are based on the feedback obtained in the pretest. (R) means that the indicator is reverse-coded.

Table 16: Operationalization of the Construct Self-Efficacy

2.2.3 Trust in Superior

Data on this construct were collected using the instrument of Read (1962). The four items of this scale are intended to reflect respondents' trust or confidence in their superiors' motives and intentions with respect to matters relevant to the respondents' career and status in the organization. Read's (1962) instrument thereby focuses on neutral vis-à-vis specific causes of trust and directly assesses elements of trustworthiness. It employs a seven-point Likert scale ranging from 1 = "strongly disagree" to 7 = "strongly agree" and has been used in several prior management accounting studies, e.g. Otley (1978), Ross (1994), Lau and Tan (2006). Its wide application offers further support for choosing this scale. Also, the Cronbach's alphas reported in the aforementioned studies reach at least 0.78, indicating good reliability of the scale.

Indicators of the construct: Trust in superior

TRUST1	Mein Vorgesetzter nutzt aufkommende Möglichkeiten, um meine Interessen mit seinen Handlungen und Entscheidungen zu unterstützen. (My superior takes advantage of opportunities that come up to further my interests by his actions and decisions.)
TRUST2	Ich scheue mich nicht, Probleme und Schwierigkeiten, die ich in meinem Job habe, mit meinem Vorgesetzten zu besprechen, da keine Gefahr droht, dass ich damit meine Position aufs Spiel setze oder mir dies später vorgehalten wird. (I feel free to discuss with my superior the problems and difficulties I have in my job without jeopardizing my position or having it "held against" me later on.)
TRUST3	Ich vertraue darauf, dass mich mein Vorgesetzter umfassend und offen über die Dinge informiert, die für mich wichtig sein könnten. (I feel confident that my superior keeps me fully and frankly informed about things that might concern me.)
TRUST4	Wenn mein Vorgesetzter eine Entscheidung trifft, die entgegen meiner Interessen zu sein scheint, habe ich dennoch Vertrauen, dass diese Entscheidung aufgrund anderer Überlegungen gerechtfertigt ist. (If my superior makes a decision which seems to be against my interests, I still have trust that my superior's decision is justified for other considerations.)

Original English indicators are provided in brackets. Differences in the translations are based on the feedback obtained in the pretest.

Table 17: Operationalization of the Construct Trust in Superior

3. Structural Equation Modeling

To test the hypotheses proposed in this study, structural equation modeling (SEM) is applied. SEM is a family of statistical tools that seek to explain the (mostly linear) relationships between multiple variables. In doing so, it examines the structure of these relationships expressed in a series of equations, similar to a series of multiple regression equations. SEM thereby combines techniques of multiple regression analysis with techniques of factor analysis. It forms a major component of applied multivariate data analysis and is widely used across many social sciences dealing with nonexperimental and quasi-experimental data (Hair et al., 2006, pp. 711-712; Marcoulides & Schumacker, 1996, pp. 1-6; Mueller, 1996, pp. 129-130; Rigdon, 1998, pp. 251-253).

SEM has been suggested to be one of the most important and influential revolutions in recent scientific progress (Marcoulides & Schumacker, 1996, p. 1). In fact, it offers several advantages over related statistical techniques. First, SEM is designed to produce unobservable latent variables or constructs (see introduction to chapter E2). Second, it is able to simultaneously model complex causal relationships between multiple independent and dependent variables. Third, SEM techniques allow the modeling of measurement error thus recognizing the imperfect nature of measures. Fourth, SEM enables the researcher to compare a priori theoretical and measurement assumptions with empirical data. Fifth, it can handle potential correlations between independent latent variables, which makes multicollinearity less a problem in data analysis (Byrne, 1998, pp. 3-8; Chin, 1998b, p. 297; Rigdon, 1998, pp. 253-256). Due to these advantages, SEM is often designated as a second-generation multivariate technique as opposed to first-generation techniques such as regression analysis and factor analysis (Chin, 1998a, p. 1; Fornell, 1987, p. 408).

3.1 Fundamentals of Structural Equation Modeling

Generally, a structural equation model (or causal model) consists of (a) several measurement models that depict the relationships between latent variables and manifest indicators, and (b) the structural model that specifies the relations between latent independent and dependent variables (Bollen, 1989, p. 11; Byrne, 1998, pp. 11-12; Hair et al., 2006, pp. 711-713; Homburg & Hildebrandt, 1998, pp. 20-21). According to Anderson and Gerbing (1982, p. 453), "the reason for drawing a distinction between the measurement and the structural model is that proper specification of the measurement model is necessary before meaning can be assigned to the analysis of the structural model". Path diagrams are used to describe structural equation models in graphical form. An example of a path diagram that includes relationships between three latent variables can be found in Figure 15. In this example, one independent (exogenous) variable is causally related with two dependent (endogenous) variables. Each latent variable is measured by three manifest indicators.

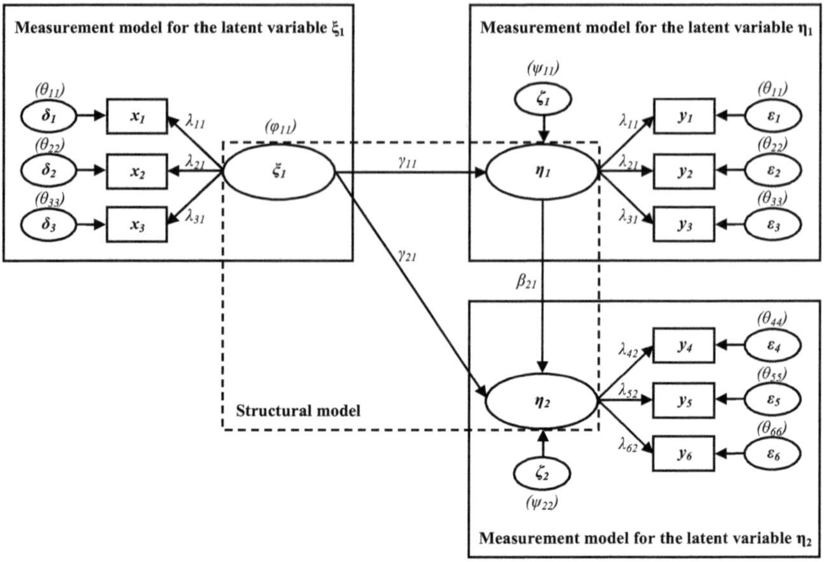

Figure 15: Exemplary Structural Equation Model[20]

The different parts of a structural equation model can also be described mathematically using a series of equations (Bagozzi & Baumgartner, 1994, pp. 386-387; Bollen, 1989, pp. 10-20; Jöreskog & Sörbom, 2001, pp. 1-3; Mueller, 1996, pp. 131-141). For the structural model, it is compactly written:

$$\eta = \mathrm{B}\eta + \Gamma\xi + \zeta \qquad [1]$$

The equation [1] is the general matrix representation of the structural equations for the latent variables included in a particular causal model. It specifies the relationships between the independent variables (ξ) and the dependent variables (η). B is a matrix of the structural coefficients for the latent endogenous variables. Its typical element is β_{ij} with i and j referring to row and column positions. Γ is a matrix of the structural coefficients linking independent variables to dependent variables. In the example from Figure 15, Γ is a 1 x 2 matrix because there are two dependent variables and one independent variable. Finally, the errors in the equations (or disturbances) are represented by the column vector ζ.

$$x = \Lambda_x \xi + \delta \qquad [2]$$

[20] Adapted from Nachtigall, Kroehne, Funke, and Steyer (2003, p. 5).

The equation [2] depicts the measurement model for the independent variables. It relates the independent manifest variables (x), or indicators, to the independent latent variables (ξ). x is the column vector of the manifest variables. They are measured as deviations from their means. Accordingly, ξ is the column vector of the latent variables. Λ_x describes a matrix that contains the λ_{ij} parameters. These parameters are the structural coefficients linking manifest and latent variables. i refers to the indicator x_i and j refers to the latent variable ξ_j that influences x_i. δ contains the vector of random influence (or measurement error terms in the manifest variables).

$$y = \Lambda_y \eta + \varepsilon \qquad [3]$$

Correspondingly, the equation [3] depicts the measurement model for the dependent variables. It relates the dependent manifest variables (y), or indicators, to the dependent latent variables (η). Thereby, y is the column vector of the manifest variables and η is the column vector of the latent variables. Λ_y refers to a matrix that contains the λ_{ij} parameters linking manifest and latent variables. ε is the column vector of the measurement error terms in the manifest variables.

$$\eta = \sum_{n=1}^{n} \lambda_i y_i + \zeta \qquad [4]$$

While equations [2] and [3] apply to reflective measurement models only, equation [4] refers to a formative measurement model. Generally, a structural model can include both reflective and formative measurement models. If – in the case of formative indicators – the latent variable is conceived as being determined by a linear combination of manifest variables, the respective measurement model must be specified differently (Bollen & Lennox, 1991, pp. 307-312; Diamantopoulos et al., 2008, pp. 1203-1215; Diamantopoulos & Siguaw, 2000, p. 21; Jarvis et al., 2003, pp. 200-207; MacCallum & Browne, 1993, pp. 535-540). As can be seen from equation [4], an index construction approach is applied for the specification of formative measurement models. In equation [4], λ_i is a coefficient capturing the effect of indicator y_i on the latent variable η. ζ is a disturbance term. This disturbance term comprises all remaining causes of the latent variable which are not represented in the indicators and are not correlated to the latter.[21]

In addition to the structural matrices Β, Γ, Λ_y, and Λ_x, a set of four covariance matrices is required for the complete specification of a hypothesized causal model (Diamantopoulos & Siguaw, 2000, pp. 39-45; Homburg & Hildebrandt, 1998, pp. 21-23; Mueller, 1996, p. 176): (a) the covariance matrix Φ of the latent independent variables (ξ), (b) the covariance matrix

21 For simplicity, Figure 15 only provides a graphical description of reflective measurement models. A description of formative measurement models and the optimal method of identifying such models can be found in chapters E2.1.1 and F1.1.

ψ of the error terms associated with the structural equations (ζ), (c) the covariance matrix Θ_δ of the measurement errors of the manifest independent variables (δ), (d) the covariance matrix Θ_ε of the measurement errors of the manifest dependent variables (ε). Under certain assumptions (Homburg, 1989, pp. 147-153), the covariance matrix Σ of the manifest variables x and y can be depicted as a function of the eight parameter matrices B, Γ, Λ_x, Λ_y, Φ, ψ, Θ_δ, and Θ_ε:

$$\Sigma = \Sigma(\mathrm{B}, \Gamma, \Lambda_y, \Lambda_x, \Phi, \Psi, \Theta_\delta, \Theta_\varepsilon) \qquad [5]$$

Denoting the parameters which are estimated in these eight matrices as vector α (Homburg & Baumgartner, 1998, p. 350), equation [5] can be simplified to equation [6]:

$$\Sigma = \Sigma(\alpha) \qquad [6]$$

3.2 Alternative Approaches to Structural Equation Modeling

Broadly speaking, there are two SEM approaches for the estimation of causal models: the covariance-based approach and the variance-based approach. The latter is also referred to as Partial Least Squares (PLS) approach. The covariance-based and variance-based approach differ in their (a) primary research objective, (b) estimates and algorithms, (c) data assumptions, (d) sample size requirements, (e) model complexity, and (f) provision of fit indices (Chin & Newsted, 1999, p. 314; Fornell & Bookstein, 1982, pp. 440-441; Scholderer & Balderjahn, 2005, pp. 87-98). Correspondingly, the approaches also have their own strengths and weaknesses.

The covariance-based approach is predominantly applied for theory testing. Its use commonly assumes that substantive theoretical and empirical knowledge already exists when investigating causal relationships (Chin, 1998b, p. 297; Fornell & Bookstein, 1982, p. 450). For theory testing, the covariance-based approach calculates a covariance matrix from the empirical data set. Parameter estimates for the specified model are selected such that the implied covariances based on the model parameter estimates are similar to those of the empirical data set. The procedure of the covariance-based approach then consists of continually estimating parameters with the aim of minimizing the fitting function between the empirical sample covariances and those implied by the parameter estimates. This procedure is performed iteratively until no further improvement can be made to the minimization of the fitting function (Chin, 1998b, pp. 299-301; Mueller, 1996, pp. 151-153; Rigdon, 1998, pp. 264-265). For this procedure, most software packages for the covariance-based approach offer different choices of estimation method. The two most widely used estimation methods are maximum likelihood (ML) and generalized least squares (GLS) which "are certainly preferred because of computational simplicity, accuracy, and correctness of statistical results" (Chou &

Bentler, 1995, p. 54). However, these methods require the sample data to be multivariate normally distributed and a large overall sample size. Depending on the number of indicators and constructs, literature suggests that at least a sample size of 150 to 200 observations is required (Bagozzi & Baumgartner, 1994, p. 392; Hair et al., 2006, pp. 740-742; Mueller, 1996; Rigdon, 1998, pp. 263-265). With smaller sample sizes, it becomes difficult to reliably estimate complex models. Fit indices and computation may be affected adversely when estimating such models (Chin, Marcolin, & Newsted, 2003, p. 197; Chin & Newsted, 1999, p. 310).

The PLS approach is less restricted to theory testing. Although it can also be used for theory testing, it is mainly applied in exploratory research where relationships might or might not exist (Chin, 1998b, p. 295). In other words, the PLS approach emphasizes data relative to theory and is thus more prediction-oriented than the covariance-based approach (Chin & Newsted, 1999, p. 12). Under the PLS perspective, causal models are therefore viewed and used differently than under the covariance-based perspective. Instead of aiming to explain the covariances of all the indicators, the PLS approach switches to minimizing the variance of all dependent variables (both latent and observed). Hence, "parameter estimates are obtained based on the ability to minimize the residual variances of dependent variables" (Chin, 1998b, p. 301). The PLS approach starts by approximating latent variables by their respective indicators. Latent variables are thereby defined as linear aggregates of their indicators and the PLS algorithm strives to obtain the best weight estimates for each block of indicators that belong to a particular latent variable. Basically, the PLS algorithm then iterates back and forth between two ways of estimating latent variables: outside approximation and inside approximation. Whereas the outside approximation provides estimates of the latent variables via aggregation of their respective indicators, the inside approximation produces estimates by combining neighboring latent variables. The PLS approach hence represents a SEM method that simultaneously models the structural paths and measurement paths of a causal model (Betzin & Henseler, 2005, pp. 50-54; Chin, 1998b, pp. 301-303; Chin et al., 2003, p. 197). Unlike the covariance-based approach, the PLS algorithm does not require multivariate normally distributed data. Because it consists of a series of ordinary least squares analyses, the algorithm actually does not presume any distributional form of the measured variables. Also, the number of observations needed for the application of the PLS approach is comparatively low. Minimal recommendations range from 30 to 100 observations. Furthermore, the PLS algorithm is capable to estimate even complex models with a moderate number of observations (Chin & Newsted, 1999, pp. 313-314). However, due to its inherent assumptions and objectives, the PLS approach does not offer as meaningful indices to test significance and model fit as the covariance-based approach does. It is seen particularly critical in literature that no proper overall goodness-of-fit measures exist for the evaluation of causal models when using the PLS approach (Chin, 1998b, p. 316; Huber, Herrmann, Meyer, Vogel, & Vollhardt, 2007, pp. 10-11; Hulland, 1999, p. 202).

3.3 The Choice of the LISREL Approach

Contrasting the covariance-based approach with the PLS approach, this study opts to employ a covariance-based approach. The reason for this choice lies in the study's primary research objective which is hypothesis testing. It builds on strong theoretical and empirical knowledge and – apart from the investigation of the moderating effects – does not follow an exploratory research strategy. Furthermore, the data gathered in this research fulfill the assumptions and sample size requirements which are commonly suggested in literature on the covariance-based approach. Also, the complexity of the causal models proposed in part D is rather low and hence does not necessitate the application of the PLS approach. Consequently, all of the distinctive criteria between the two approaches advocate the use of the covariance-based approach. As Smith (2003, p. 84) notes,

> Partial Least Squares (PLS) may be viewed as the 'poor man's' SEM in that it is the alternative sought when we cannot satisfy the stringent assumptions of SEM. PLS may be preferred when we have a weak theory, small sample size (less than 100), and data which are likely to violate assumptions of normality.

Even proponents of the PLS approach admit that if the hypothesized model is correct in the sense of explaining the covariance of its indicators and the data and sample requirements are met, "the covariance-based procedure provides optimal estimates of the model parameters" (Chin & Newsted, 1999, p. 313). Hence, the covariance-based approach must be preferred over the PLS approach in this work. Specifically, the LISREL software package is employed for data analysis and hypothesis testing. LISREL represents the most popular and widely used SEM software among the covariance-based methods (Byrne, 1998, p. 9; Hair et al., 2006, p. 743).

As outlined in the foregoing chapter, the covariance-based approach aims at minimizing the fitting function between the empirical sample covariances and those implied by the parameter estimates. Referring back to equation [6], this implies that the LISREL parameter estimation attempts to determine the vector $\hat{\alpha}$ so that the model-implied covariance matrix $\hat{\Sigma} = \Sigma(\hat{\alpha})$ most closely represents the observed covariance matrix. Mathematically, the corresponding fitting function that minimizes the discrepancies between the sample matrix S and the model-implied matrix can be described as follows (Bollen, 1989, pp. 104-107; Diamantopoulos & Siguaw, 2000, p. 12; Homburg & Hildebrandt, 1998, pp. 22-23; Mueller, 1996, pp. 151-155):

$$f_s(\alpha) = F(S, \Sigma(\alpha)) \rightarrow \min \qquad [7]$$

However, LISREL can only estimate the unknown model parameters if sufficient information is available to obtain a unique solution for the parameters. Identification is therefore necessary before the parameters can be estimated (Bollen, 1989, pp. 88-104; Diamantopoulos & Siguaw, 2000, pp. 48-54). To determine whether a particular structural model meets the minimum requirements for identification, the following formula is used:

$$t \leq s / 2 \qquad [8]$$

where t is the number of parameters to be estimated, s is the number of variances and covariances among the manifest variables calculated as $(p+q)(p+q+1)$, p is the number of manifest dependent variables, and q is the number of manifest independent variables. If $t > s / 2$, the model is underidentified (or unidentified). It cannot be estimated by LISREL. If $t = s / 2$, the model is just-identified. LISREL is able to estimate the model parameters. However, since all the information made available through model specification is used for estimation, no information remains to test the model. In other words, the degrees of freedom are zero. If $t < s / 2$, the model is overidentified. In this case, LISREL can produce more than one estimate for each parameter. The degrees of freedom are positive and equal to $s / 2 - t$. Only overidentified models offer a set of estimates to test the model. If the different estimates available for at least one of the model parameters differ significantly, such a finding provides evidence that the model is false in some respect. LISREL provides various goodness-of-fit measures to assess the data-model fit (see Table 18 in chapter E3.6.3).

3.4 Test for Mediating Effects

This work proposes indirect effects of the application of the controllability principle on affective and behavioral outcomes. In accordance with role theory, role variables are positioned as cognitive mediators in the causal relationships (see chapter D1 and D2). Statistically, mediation is present when it can be shown that the causal influence of an independent variable on a dependent variable is transmitted through one or more additional variables, referred to as mediators or intervening variables (Baron & Kenny, 1986, p. 1176; Hoyle & Kenny, 1999, p. 195; James & Brett, 1984, p. 307; Shields & Shields, 1998, p. 51). A simple mediational model is depicted in Figure 16.

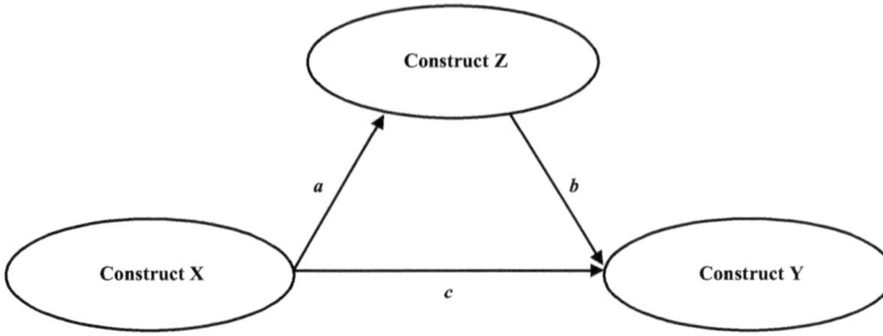

Figure 16: Mediational Model

In Figure 16, construct Z acts as a mediator on the relationship between construct X and construct Y. The total effect of X on Y is partitioned into two components: the direct effect, reflected in path *c*, and the indirect effect which can be denoted as *ab*. Statistical evidence for the existence of a mediating effect of Z requires the following: (a) variations in the independent variable X significantly account for variations in the presumed mediator Z (path *a*), (b) variations in the presumed mediator Z significantly account for variations in the dependent variable Y (path *b*), and (c) when paths *a* and *b* are controlled, the size of the direct effect between X and the Y (path *c*) decreases. Generally, two types of mediation can be distinguished: partial mediation and complete mediation. Partial mediation implies that the direct effect *c* still remains significant after the introduction of the mediator Z. Complete mediation means that whereas the mediating effect *ab* is significant, the direct effect *c* is not statistically different from zero (Baron & Kenny, 1986, p. 1176; Hoyle & Kenny, 1999, pp. 198-199; Shrout & Bolger, 2002, pp. 423-424).

To test for mediating effects, this work follows the approach developed by Baron and Kenny (1986, p. 1177) and Kenny, Kashy, and Bolger (1998, pp. 258-260). In a step-wise fashion, LISREL is used to first assess whether X directly affects Y. This initial step "establishes that there is an effect that may be mediated" (Kenny et al., 1998, p. 259). Next, the mediator Z is introduced into the structural model. For a mediation effect, Z must be related to both X and Y. Finally, the path coefficients for the direct effect from X on Y are compared across the two models from the foregoing steps. If the path coefficient is reduced from the first step to the second step, this indicates evidence for Z being a mediator on the relationship between X and Y. If the path coefficient even becomes insignificant, a complete mediation is displayed.

3.5 Test for Moderating Effects

Role theory not only predicts the existence of mediating effects in the investigation of role processes, but also highlights the moderating influence of "surrounding conditions" (Kahn et al., 1964, p. 37). This work proposed three moderating variables which might affect managers' coping with the application of the controllability principle (see chapter D1 and D3). Statistically, a moderating effect describes the influence of a variable that affects the direction and/or strength between an independent variable and a dependent variable (Baron & Kenny, 1986, p. 1174; James & Brett, 1984, p. 310; Shields & Shields, 1998, p. 51). Figure 17 provides a graphical illustration of a moderating effect.

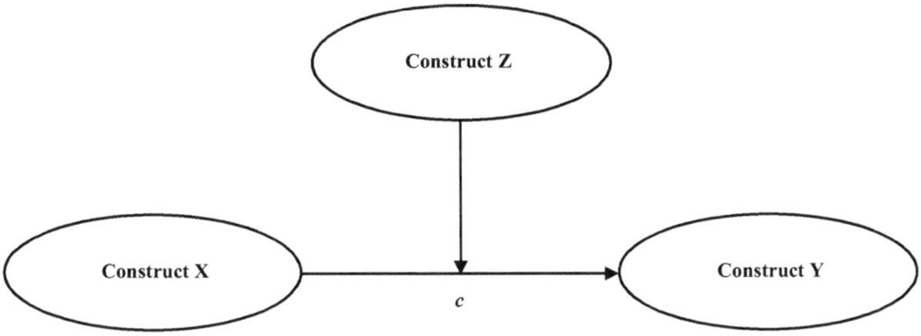

Figure 17: Moderator Model

According to Sharma, Durand, and Gur-Arie (1981, pp. 292-294), two general types of moderating variables Z which both interact with the independent variable X can be distinguished: pure moderators and quasi moderators. Whereas pure moderators are by definition not related to the independent and dependent variable, quasi moderators can be related to the independent and/or dependent variable. Luft and Shields (2003, p. 174) designate the influence of the former as moderator-variable interaction and the influence of the latter as independent-variable interaction. Most commonly, two basic methods have been used for identifying the presence of moderating variables: multisample (or subgroup) analysis and moderated regression analysis (Arnold, 1984, pp. 213-223; Sharma et al., 1981, pp. 294-296; Stone & Hollenbeck, 1984, pp. 195-197). According to Rigdon, Schumacker, and Wothke (1998, p. 2), "the multisample approach is still the most useful approach for modeling latent variable interaction effects". This work therefore prefers the multisample analysis over moderated regression analysis.

A multisample analysis involves three basic steps. First, the available sample is partitioned into subsamples based upon their scores on the suspected moderator variable. Second, the degree of association between the independent and dependent variables is determined for each subsample. Third, it is assessed whether the detected levels of association differ between the subsamples (Sharma et al., 1981, pp. 294-295; Stone & Hollenbeck, 1984, p. 196). This work uses LISREL to perform these steps in the investigation of the proposed moderating effects. LISREL thereby simultaneously estimates a model across the previously defined subsamples. Through the specification of equality constraints across the subsamples, group differences can be tested. Such equality constraints force the LISREL algorithm to derive equal estimates for the respective parameters within all subsamples. The fit of the resulting constrained model can then be compared to the fit of the unrestricted model without the equality constraints. If the fit of the constrained model is significantly worse than the fit of the unrestricted model, one can conclude that the parameters are not equal across the subsamples. The variable which initially served to form the subsamples hence appears to operate as a moderator (Bagozzi & Yi, 1988, p. 83; Jöreskog & Sörbom, 2001, pp. 277-279; Kline, 2005, pp. 289-290; Rigdon et al., 1998, pp. 1-12).

3.6 Goodness-of-Fit Measures

To assess whether a theoretical model that has been developed on the basis of a set of hypotheses fits with empirical data, LISREL offers a variety of goodness-of-fit measures. Generally, several fit assessments should be conducted to uncover potential data-model inconsistencies (Mueller, 1996, p. 163). The test of structural relationships between theoretical variables requires that the instruments applied to measure these variables fulfill certain minimum requirements in terms of reliability and validity (Anderson & Gerbing, 1982, pp. 453-454; Bagozzi & Baumgartner, 1994, pp. 401-404; Bollen, 1989, pp. 206-207; Schäffer, 2007, p. 1).

3.6.1 Reliability and Validity

Reliability means the consistency of measurement. It is a matter of whether a particular instrument or technique yields the same result when being repeatedly applied to the same object. In psychometric terms, the reliability of a measurement instrument is the proportion of the variance attributable to the true score of a latent variable (Babbie, 2004, p. 141; DeVellis, 2003, p. 24; Hair et al., 2006, p. 137; Nunnally & Bernstein, 1994, p. 225). Or, put differently, it is inversely related to the amount of random error in a measurement (Carmines & Zeller, 1979, p. 13). To ensure the reliability of their measurement instruments, researchers usually distinguish between (a) inter-rater reliability, (b) test-retest reliability, (c) parallel-forms reliability, and (d) internal consistency reliability. Inter-rater reliability refers to the degree to which different raters give consistent estimates of the same phenomenon. Test-retest reliability means the consistency of a measure from one time to another. Parallel-forms reliability assesses the equivalence of results from two tests constructed in the same way. Internal consistency reliability describes the consistency of results across several indicators within a test. The rationale of the internal consistency approach is that the individual indicators of a scale should all be measuring the same theoretical concept and thus be highly intercorrelated. This approach is commonly used in the social sciences since it overcomes difficulties which are inherent to the other approaches of assessing reliability. Whereas in particular the test-retest and the parallel-forms approach potentially suffer from carry-over effects (practice, memory, attitude) due to the time lag between measurements, an instrument's internal consistency can be assessed with only a single administration of a reliability coefficient (Bollen, 1989, pp. 209-218; Hair et al., 2006, p. 137; Mueller, 1996, pp. 112-113). To assess the reliability of measurement instruments, this work therefore relies on the internal consistency approach.

Whereas reliability is concerned with the accuracy of the researcher's measurement instrument, validity is concerned with the researcher's success at measuring what he or she set out to measure. More precisely, validity is the degree to which a measurement instrument truly reflects or assesses the specific theoretical concept that the researcher attempts to measure. As such, it refers to the amount of nonrandom error in a measurement (Babbie, 2004, p. 143; Carmines & Zeller, 1979, pp. 14-15; DeVellis, 2003, p. 43; Hair et al., 2006, p. 137; Nunnally & Bernstein, 1994, pp. 86-87). In chapter E1.2, it was broadly distinguished between three types of validity: (a) external validity, (b) internal validity, and (c) construct validity.

External validity describes the extent to which empirical findings can be generalized from a particular sample to the wider population. However, the answer to the question of generalizability is not mathematically or inductively fully attainable. While the researcher's methods of sample selection, the applied control procedures, and the general type of research design potentially strengthen inferences that research results are representative, the induction remains largely inconclusive. The replication of a certain study (in different settings and, if possible, using multiple methods) is hence required to bolster the generalizability of its results (Brewer, 2000, pp. 4-10; Cook & Campbell, 1979, pp. 70-73).

Internal validity refers to the rigor with which a study is conducted and to the credibility of the causal relationships between independent and dependent variables. The question here is whether it can be concluded that the variations in the independent variable produce the differences observed in the dependent variable. The matter of external validity is thereby dependent upon the prior demonstration of adequate internal validity (Sternberg & Powell, 1982, p. 977). Scholars commonly differentiate between different types of internal validity: content validity, face validity, and criterion-related validity. Sometimes construct validity is also regarded as one type of internal validity (Babbie, 2004, pp. 144-145; Carmines & Zeller, 1979, pp. 17-28; DeVellis, 2003, pp. 43-50; Kwok & Sharp, 1998, pp. 141-143). Content validity refers to the extent to which a measurement instrument reflects the specified content domain of a theoretical concept. Face validity, which is used synonymously to content validity by the some authors, is also concerned with how a measure appears in relation to the concept it belongs to. Yet, unlike content validity, face validity does not rely on established theory for support (Fink, 2002, p. 51). Finally, criterion-related validity requires a measurement instrument to be related to an external criterion. To assess criterion-related validity, the researcher thus needs a variable that may function as a standard to which to compare the measurement instrument under scrutiny. Criterion-related validity is sometimes also called predictive validity.

Construct validity refers to whether the theoretical concepts used by the researcher are adequately reflected by the operational definitions and the measures of empirical phenomena. It is about the agreement between a theoretical concept and a specific measurement instrument and depends on three sub-categories: convergent validity, discriminant validity, and nomological validity (Bagozzi, Yi, & Phillips, 1991, p. 425; Campbell & Fiske, 1959, pp. 83-85; Hair et al., 2006, pp. 136-137; Kwok & Sharp, 1998, p. 5). Convergent validity assesses the degree to which different measures for the same theoretical concept are correlated. As it is assumed that the underlying concept causes common variation in the measures reflecting the concept, they should be highly correlated. If the researcher does not find evidence for a high correlation between them, the measures are of poor quality and/or the correspondence between the concept and the measures is questionable. Discriminant validity refers to the degree to which measures of different theoretical concepts are distinct. Here, the focus is on finding evidence that measures are not highly correlated. Nomological validity, as the third sub-category of construct validity, means the degree to which predictions from a formal theoretical network containing the concepts under scrutiny are confirmed. Nomological validity hence assesses the degree to which constructs that should theoretically be related are indeed empirically related.

The reliability and validity of measurement instruments can be assessed using a variety of quantitative techniques. Scholars usually distinguish between (a) first-generation statistical techniques and (b) second-generation statistical techniques (Fornell, 1982, p. 217; 1987, p. 408; Homburg & Giering, 1998, pp. 118-119; Schäffer, 2007, p. 2). First-generation techniques for the assessment of reliability and validity have been introduced to the empirical research in business administration by Churchill (1979). They derive from psychometrics. Based on classical test theory (CTT), these techniques are more oriented towards an exploratory perspective. In first-generation statistical techniques, validity and reliability are assessed in separate analyses. The analyses are independent from actual hypothesis testing and do not influence the overall assessment of a model's fit to empirical data. Second-generation techniques represent extensions and generalizations of first-generation techniques. They are based on modern test theory (in particular confirmatory factor analysis) and emphasize a theory-based approach (Diamantopoulos & Siguaw, 2000, p. 4). In several respects, second-generation techniques are more powerful than their first-generation forerunners and can thus be used to complement first-generation techniques (Anderson &

Gerbing, 1988, pp. 421-422; Homburg & Giering, 1998, p. 119; Steenkamp & van Trijp, 1991, p. 284). Not only that they take account of measurement error, second-generation techniques such as SEM also allow the researcher to analyze both the measurement model and the causal model simultaneously. Accordingly, the assessment of reliability and validity directly affects the overall fit of a theoretical model to empirical data and represents an integral part of SEM (Boudreau, Ariyachandra, Gefen, & Straub, 2003, p. 22; Schäffer, 2007, p. 2).

3.6.2 Criteria of First-Generation Statistical Techniques

Among the most frequently used first-generation criteria to evaluate goodness-of-fit are (a) the explained variance within the scope of exploratory factor analysis, (b) Cronbach's alpha, and (c) item-to-total-correlation. All three criteria are calculated in this work to ensure adequate reliability and validity of the measurement instruments.

Exploratory factor analysis (EFA) serves to determine the factorial validity of variables measuring one or more underlying factors (Babbie, 2004, pp. 455-456; DeVellis, 2003, pp. 92-93). More specifically, it attempts to reduce the dimensionality of empirically gathered data and to explain the variance in observed variables by identifying latent factors behind the variables. Unlike confirmatory factor analysis (see chapter E3.6.3), EFA does not require the researcher to ex ante define the factorial structure of the observed variables (Anderson & Gerbing, 1988, p. 412; Hair et al., 2006, pp. 773-774). No theory and a priori constraints to the data are hence needed to conduct EFA which is why EFA represents an exploratory method of data analysis. EFA condenses the information contained in observed variables to as few factors as possible while at the same time trying to minimize the loss of information. For this purpose, estimates of the factors and the contributions of each variable to the factors (also termed loadings) are required. The number of factors to be extracted from the observed variables can be derived from the Kaiser criterion. This criterion refers to the eigenvalues of the correlation matrix. It describes the variance contribution of a factor with regard to the variance of all variables. The rationale behind the Kaiser criterion is that the interpretation of proportions of variance which are smaller than the variance contribution of a single variable is dubious. Since the standardized variance of a single variable is equal to 1.00, only factors with an eigenvalue greater than 1.00 are to be extracted (DeVellis, 2003, p. 97; Nunnally & Bernstein, 1994, pp. 384-385). Alternatively, the scree test criterion can be applied to identify the optimum number of factors to be extracted. Within the scree test, the eigenvalues of factors are plotted against their serial order and an inflection point of the resulting curve is determined by visual inspection. The location of the inflection point indicates the number of factors to be extracted (Backhaus, Erichson, Plinke, & Weiber, 2006, pp. 296-297; Moosbrugger & Schermelleh-Engel, 2007, p. 312). Having identified a set of latent factors on the basis of observed variables, EFA is also used to assess the measurement of one single factor. The factor under investigation should thereby explain at least 50% of the variance determined by the observed variables that are allocated to the factor. Furthermore, a variable should only be allocated to a factor when its factor loading is sufficiently high (> 0.40) and when cross-loadings on other factors are significantly lower (Hair et al., 2006, p. 129; Homburg & Giering, 1998, p. 119).

Cronbach's alpha is an internal consistency estimate which is heavily used in the social sciences to assess the reliability of multi-indicator measurement scales (Cortina, 1993, p. 98; Peterson, 1994, p. 382). It was developed by Cronbach (1951) and can be calculated as follows:

$$\alpha = \left(\frac{k}{k-1}\right)\left(1 - \frac{\sum_{i=1}^{k} \delta_i^2}{\delta_S^2}\right) \qquad [9]$$

where k is the number of indicators in the scale, δ_i^2 is the variance of indicator i, and δ_S^2 is the variance of the scale. The computed Cronbach's alpha for a measurement scale can take values ranging from 0.00 to 1.00 with higher values indicating higher reliability of the respective scale. Generally, a Cronbach's alpha of 0.70 is considered acceptable when established scales are used (Hair et al., 2006, p. 102; Homburg & Giering, 1998, p. 120; Nunnally & Bernstein, 1994, p. 245). Despite its wide application in the social sciences, Cronbach's alpha suffers from several drawbacks in that it is adversely affected by item heterogeneity, multidimensionality, and negatively worded indicators. Caution is therefore recommended when assessing the reliability of a measurement instrument solely on the basis of Cronbach's alpha (Schermelleh-Engel & Werner, 2007, pp. 126-128; Vehkalahti, 2000, pp. 12-16).

While Cronbach's alpha evaluates the reliability of a measurement scale as a total, the item-to-total correlation is calculated separately for each indicator of a particular scale. It is defined as the correlation between a single indicator (item) and the sum of all indicators (total) that belong to a particular scale (item-to total-correlation). The corrected item-to-total-correlation refers to the correlation between a single indicator and the total score of the remaining indicators after removing the considered indicator (DeVellis, 2003, pp. 82-83; Homburg & Giering, 1998, p. 120). The values for item-to-total correlations again range from 0.00 to 1.00. A high item-to-total correlation is associated with a high convergent validity of the indicator under scrutiny. To increase the Cronbach's alpha of the overall measurement scale, it is recommended to drop the scale's indicator with the lowest item-to-total-correlation (Churchill, 1979, p. 68).

3.6.3 Criteria of Second-Generation Statistical Techniques

The use of first-generation criteria for reliability and validity assessment is criticized for a couple of reasons (Homburg & Giering, 1998, pp. 120-121; Mueller, 1996, p. 62). Most of the criticism is centered around the restrictive assumptions of first-generation criteria (Gerbing & Anderson, 1988, p. 186), the fact that "no precise standards are provided for ascertaining how well the criteria are met" (Bagozzi et al., 1991, p. 428), and the inability to take account of measurement error (Homburg & Giering, 1996, p. 9). Second-generation criteria offer the possibility to remedy these issues. They are based on confirmatory factor analysis (CFA) which has been developed by Jöreskog (1966; 1967; 1969). CFA and EFA have in common that both techniques attempt to reduce empirical data to their underlying structure. However, using the CFA technique, the researcher must a priori allocate observed variables to latent factors, which requires the existence of a preconceived theory concerning the factorial structure. Thus, instead of allowing the statistical method to determine the number of factors and loadings as in EFA, CFA is a technique that enables the researcher to either confirm or reject a hypothesized factorial structure (Hair et al., 2006, p. 774; Homburg & Giering, 1998, pp. 121-123; Jöreskog & Sörbom, 2001, pp. 138-139; Moosbrugger & Schermelleh-Engel, 2007, p. 316; Schäffer, 2007, pp. 5-6). For this purpose, CFA compares the researcher's theoretical measurement model with the reality model to assess how well the data fit. Hence, the starting point for CFA is the specification of a measurement model. Referring back to equation [2], a measurement model can be generally depicted as:

$$x = \Lambda\xi + \delta \qquad [2]$$

where x is the column vector of the manifest variables, ξ is the column vector of the latent variables, Λ is the matrix that contains the factor loadings (λ parameters), and δ is the vector of the measurement errors.

Under certain assumptions, the covariance matrix Σ of the manifest variables x can be described by the three parameter matrices Λ, Φ, and Θ. The respective equation reads as follows:

$$\Sigma = \Lambda\Phi\Lambda' + \Theta_\delta \qquad [10]$$

where Λ' is the transposed matrix to Λ, Φ is the covariance matrix of the latent variables, and Θ is the covariance matrix of the measurement errors.

The objective of CFA is to estimate the unknown model parameters in a way that the model-implied covariance matrix

$$\hat{\Sigma} = \Sigma(\hat{\Lambda}, \hat{\Phi}, \hat{\Theta}_\delta) \qquad [11]$$

most closely represents the observed covariance matrix S. The fitting function that minimizes the discrepancies between the two matrices denotes as follows:

$$f_s(\Lambda,\Phi,\Theta_\delta) = F(S,\Sigma(\Lambda,\Phi,\Theta_\delta)) \rightarrow \min \qquad [12]$$

LISREL can perform several methods of estimation in order to solve the minimization problem (Jöreskog & Sörbom, 2001, pp. 17-24). As outlined in chapter E3.2, the two most widely used methods are ML and GLS which offer several advantages over alternative methods (Bollen, 1989, pp. 107-115; Chou & Bentler, 1995, p. 54; Schermelleh-Engel, Moosbrugger, & Müller, 2003, pp. 26-27). This work applies the LISREL default method of estimation which is ML. Even though ML actually requires the latent variable scores to have a multivariate normal distribution, Monte Carlo simulations by Chou and Bentler (1995), Curran, West, and Finch (1996), and Muthén and Muthén (2002) have shown that ML appears to be quite robust against moderate violations of the normality assumption. Literature therefore recommends the use of ML if skewness does not exceed a value of 2 and kurtosis is less than 7 (Curran et al., 1996, p. 26; West, Finch, & Curran, 1995, p. 74).

Following model specification and parameter estimation, the model fit can be assessed using goodness-of-fit measures. Goodness-of-fit measures generally indicate the extent to which a theoretical model fits empirical data. Because there is no single statistical significance test that identifies a correct model given the empirical data, researchers usually take multiple criteria into consideration and evaluate model fit on the basis of various measures simultaneously (Hair et al., 2006, p. 758; Schermelleh-Engel et al., 2003, p. 31; Schumacker & Lomax, 2004, pp. 81-83). In his overview of the second-generation criteria widely used in the evaluation of management accounting scales, Schäffer (2007, pp. 5-10) focuses on the following goodness-of-fit indices: the ratio of chi-square divided by the degrees of freedom (χ^2 / df), the root mean square error of approximation (*RMSEA*), the goodness-of-fit index (*GFI*), the adjusted goodness-of-fit index (*AGFI*), and the comparative fit index (*CFI*). It is this broad range of fit indices which is also used in this study to evaluate the measurement models and the structural models under investigation. In accordance with the two-step approach proposed by Anderson and Gerbing (1988, pp. 417-418) and Schumacker and Lomax (2004, pp. 106-107), the fit of the measurement models is assessed first, followed by the evaluation of the fit of the structural models.

The χ^2 test statistic is used for testing the appropriateness of a specified model. Thereby the following null hypothesis is tested: The theoretical model is correct and the empirical covariance matrix Σ is equal to the model-implied covariance matrix $\hat{\Sigma}$. If the null hypothesis holds, then the specified model is correct and fits the data. The χ^2 value is calculated as:

$$\chi^2 = (N-1)F(S,\hat{\Sigma}) \quad [13]$$

and the degrees of freedom for the χ^2 value are:

$$df = \frac{1}{2}(p+q)(p+q+1)-t \quad [14]$$

where N is the sample size, $(p+q)$ is the number of observed variables, and t is the total number of independent parameters to be estimated. The null hypothesis is commonly accepted if the p-value associated with the χ^2 value is larger than 0.05. However, there are several shortcomings associated with the χ^2 test statistic. First, the test implies a number of requirements (in particular that the empirical data are normally distributed and that the sample size is sufficiently large) which are not met in many practical applications. Second, model complexity affects the χ^2 test statistic. The χ^2 value decreases when parameters are added to the model. Thus, χ^2 values for complex models tend to be smaller than for simpler models. Third, the χ^2 test statistic depends on sample size. With increasing sample size and a constant number of degrees of freedom, the χ^2 value tends to increase. Plausible models might be rejected based on a significant χ^2 test statistic even though the discrepancies between the sample and the model-implied covariance matrix are actually irrelevant (Cudeck & Browne, 1983, pp. 149-150; Hair et al., 2006, pp. 746-747; Mueller, 1996, p. 83; Schermelleh-Engel et al., 2003, pp. 32-33). Jöreskog and Sörbom (2001, p. 28) therefore note that the "use of χ^2 is not valid in most applications" and instead recommend the application of a descriptive goodness-of-fit index in which the χ^2 value is compared to the number of associated degrees of freedom. The ratio of chi-square divided by the degrees of freedom (χ^2 / df) should be as small as possible with values ≤ 2 indicating good fit and values between 2 and 3 indicating acceptable fit (Hair et al., 2006, p. 748; Schermelleh-Engel et al., 2003, p. 33).

Due to the inherent drawbacks of the χ^2 test statistic, alternative descriptive goodness-of-fit measures have been developed. The root mean square error of approximation (*RMSEA*) is one of the measures which attempt to correct for the tendency of the χ^2 test statistic to reject models with a large sample or a large number of observed variables. It explicitly tries to correct for sample size and model complexity by including both in its computation:

$$RMSEA = \sqrt{\max\left\{\left[\frac{F(S,\hat{\Sigma})}{df}\right] - \frac{1}{N-1}\right\},0} \quad [15]$$

where $F(S,\hat{\Sigma})$ is the minimum of the fit function, df is the number of the degrees of freedom, and N is the sample size. The *RMSEA* represents a more sensible approach in that it assesses whether the model fits approximately well in the population (Kaplan, 2000, p. 111). The null hypothesis of "exact fit" is hence replaced by the null hypothesis of "close fit" (Browne & Cudeck, 1993, p. 146). *RMSEA* values of ≤ 0.05 are considered as a close or good fit, values between 0.05 and 0.08 as an adequate fit, and values between 0.08 and 0.10 as a mediocre fit, whereas values > 0.10 are not acceptable (Browne & Cudeck, 1993, p. 144; Schermelleh-Engel et al., 2003, pp. 36-37; Schumacker & Lomax, 2004, p. 82).

The goodness-of-fit index (*GFI*) represents a further measure that is less sensitive to sample size than the χ^2 test statistic. This descriptive goodness-of-fit measure is based on model comparisons. It evaluates the fit of a particular model relative to the fit of some baseline model. The *GFI* is calculated as:

$$GFI = 1 - \frac{F_t}{F_n} = 1 - \frac{\chi_t^2}{\chi_n^2} \qquad [16]$$

where χ_n^2 is the chi-square of the baseline model, χ_t^2 is the chi-square of the target model, and F is the corresponding minimum fit function value. *GFI* values of ≥ 0.95 are indicative of a good fit relative to the baseline model, while values ≥ 0.90 can be interpreted as indicating acceptable fit (Hair et al., 2006, p. 747; Homburg & Baumgartner, 1998, p. 355; Hu & Bentler, 1995, p. 92; Schermelleh-Engel et al., 2003, p. 43).

In addition, Jöreskog and Sörbom (2001, p. 29) recommend the use of the adjusted goodness-of-fit index (*AGFI*) which adjusts for a bias resulting from model complexity. For this purpose, the *AGFI* incorporates a penalty function for the inclusion of additional parameters and hence rewards simpler models with fewer parameters to be estimated. It is given by:

$$AGFI = 1 - \frac{df_n}{df_t}(1 - GFI) = 1 - \frac{\chi_t^2 / df_t}{\chi_n^2 / df_n} \qquad [17]$$

where χ_n^2 is the chi-square of the baseline model, χ_t^2 is the chi-square of the target model, df_n is the number of degrees of freedom for the baseline model, and df_t is the number of degrees of freedom for the target model. *AGFI* values ≥ 0.90 represent a good model fit, values between 0.85 and 0.90 are considered as an acceptable level of model fit (Hair et al., 2006, p. 747; Homburg & Baumgartner, 1998, p. 356; Schermelleh-Engel et al., 2003, p. 43).

Another often used measure based on model comparisons is the comparative fit index (*CFI*). It has been developed by Bentler (1990) and represents an incremental fit index that is relatively insensitive to model complexity. The *CFI* is defined as:

$$CFI = 1 - \frac{\max[(\chi_t^2 - df_t), 0]}{\max[(\chi_t^2 - df_t), (\chi_i^2 - df_i), 0]} \qquad [18]$$

where χ_i^2 is the chi-square of the baseline model, χ_t^2 is the chi-square of the target model, and *df* is the number of degrees of freedom in the respective models. A rule of thumb for this index is that values $\geq$ 0.97 are indicative of a good model fit. Values $\geq$ 0.95 may be interpreted as acceptable model fit (Diamantopoulos & Siguaw, 2000, p. 88; Schermelleh-Engel et al., 2003, p. 42).

Apart from χ^2 / *df*, *RMSEA*, *GFI*, *AGFI*, and *CFI* which all represent global goodness-of-fit indices, there are several local goodness-of-fit criteria for the assessment of measurement instruments. Local criteria enable the researcher to assess specific parts of a model, such as single indicators or factors. This work uses the following local goodness-of-fit criteria: indicator reliability (*IR*), *t*-statistic of factor loading, factor reliability (*FR*), average variance explained (*AVE*), Fornell and Larcker (1981) criterion, and χ^2 difference test.

The indicator reliability (*IR*) is computed on the level of single indicators. It reflects the percentage of variation in an indicator that is explained by the underlying factor which it is supposed to measure. Variance that cannot be explained by the factor is attributed to measurement error. Ranging from 0.00 to 1.00, the *IR* is commonly expected to reach a value of 0.40 (Bagozzi & Baumgartner, 1994, p. 402; Homburg & Baumgartner, 1998, p. 361). The mathematical equation for its calculation denotes as follows:

$$IR(x_i) = \frac{\lambda_{ij}^2 \varphi_{jj}}{\lambda_{ij}^2 \varphi_{jj} + \theta_{ii}} \qquad [19]$$

where λ_{ij} is the estimated factor loading, φ_{jj} is the estimated variance of the latent variable ξ_j, and θ_{ii} is the estimated variance of the measurement errors δ_i.

Additionally, the *t*-statistic of factor loadings is investigated to determine whether the factor loading of a particular indicator differs significantly from zero. The *t*-statistic describes the quotient of an estimated factor loading divided by its standard error. A factor loading is considered to be significantly different from zero when its *t*-value is greater than 1.645, assuming a one-tailed test at the 5% level of significance (Homburg & Giering, 1998, p. 125).

On the level of latent factors, goodness-of-fit can be assessed using the factor reliability (*FR*) and average variance explained (*AVE*). These two measures indicate how well a latent factor is measured by the totality of its indicators. Both measures can take values ranging from 0.00 to 1.00 with higher values indicating higher goodness-of-fit of the measurement instrument. *FR* is sometimes also referred to as composite reliability and can be calculated as follows:

$$FR(\xi_j) = \frac{\left(\sum_{i=1}^{q} \lambda_{ij}\right)^2 \varphi_{jj}}{\left(\sum_{i=1}^{q} \lambda_{ij}\right)^2 \varphi_{jj} + \sum_{i=1}^{q} \theta_{ii}} \qquad [20]$$

FR values $\geq$ 0.60 are recommended for an acceptable goodness-of-fit (Bagozzi & Baumgartner, 1994, p. 403; Homburg & Baumgartner, 1995, p. 170). The *AVE* for which a threshold value of 0.50 can be found in the literature (Bagozzi & Yi, 1988, p. 82; Homburg & Baumgartner, 1995, p. 172) results from the following calculation:

$$AVE(\xi_j) = \frac{\sum_{i=1}^{q} \lambda_{ij}^2 \varphi_{jj}}{\sum_{i=1}^{q} \lambda_{ij}^2 \varphi_{jj} + \sum_{i=1}^{q} \theta_{ii}} \qquad [21]$$

While the goodness-of-fit criteria discussed above are mainly intended to assess the reliability and convergent validity of one particular measurement instrument, the Fornell and Larcker (1981) criterion and the χ^2 difference test are recommended to examine discriminant validity between latent factors (Bagozzi & Phillips, 1982, p. 476; Bagozzi & Yi, 1988, pp. 90-91; Jöreskog, 1971, pp. 125-132). Recall from chapter E3.6.1 that discriminant validity refers the extent to which a given factor measured by its corresponding scale is different from other factors. To demonstrate discriminant validity, the Fornell and Larcker (1981) criterion requires the *AVE* of each factor to exceed the squared correlations between the factors (Fornell & Larcker, 1981, pp. 41-46). The χ^2 difference test opposes a constrained model (where the correlation between the two factors for which discriminant validity should be verified is fixed to 1.00) and an unconstrained model (where the correlation is released). The comparison of the χ^2 test statistic for the two models allows the researcher to evaluate whether the correlation is significantly different from 1.00 and hence whether the two factors are distinct. This is the case when the χ^2 value decreases by at least 3.84 (1 df) from the constrained model to the unconstrained model indicating a difference at the 5% level of significance.

Table 18 provides a summary of the goodness-of-fit criteria together with their respective aspiration levels. Schermelleh-Engel et al. (2003, pp. 52-53) remind the researcher that

> these rule of thumb cutoff criteria are quite arbitrary and should not be taken too seriously. Fit indices may be affected by model misspecification, small-sample bias, effects of violation of normality and independence, and estimation-method effects (Hu & Bentler, 1998). Therefore it is always possible that a model may fit the data although one or more fit measures may suggest bad fit.

Thus, when assessing the fit of a particular measurement model or structural model, the researcher needs to consider the combined picture of several measures instead of focusing on a single measure that might suggest bad fit due to the reasons stated above.

Criteria	Aspiration level
a) First-generation criteria	
Explained variance of exploratory factor analysis (EFA)	≥ 0.50
Cronbach's alpha	≥ 0.70
Item-to-total-correlation	If Cronbach's alpha < 0.70, elimination of indicator with lowest item-to-total correlation
b) Second-generation criteria	
Ratio of chi-square divided by degrees of freedom (χ^2 / df)	≤ 3.00
Root mean square error of approximation (*RMSEA*)	≤ 0.08
Goodness-of-fit index (*GFI*)	≥ 0.90
Adjusted goodness-of-fit index (*AGFI*)	≥ 0.85
Comparative fit index (*CFI*)	≥ 0.95
Indicator reliability (*IR*)	≥ 0.40
t-statistic of factor loading	≥ 1.645
Factor reliability (*FR*)	≥ 0.60
Average variance explained (*AVE*) of confirmatory factor analysis (CFA)	≥ 0.50
Fornell and Larcker (1981) criterion	*AVE* of factor exceeds squared correlations between factors
χ^2 difference test	Difference ≥ 3.84

Table 18: Overview of Goodness-of-Fit Measures[22]

It is important to note that the goodness-of-fit criteria depicted in Table 18 have been primarily developed to test reflective measurement models. Many of them cannot be used to assess the reliability and validity of formative measurement models. Bisbe et al. (2007, pp. 802-803) explain that since the indicators of formative models need not be correlated (see Figure 14) "traditional reliability evaluation tools based on internal consistency (e.g.

22 Adapted from Schäffer (2007, p. 10).

Cronbach's alpha, CFA, EFA) and others derived from classical test theory (CTT) . . . are meaningless, illogical and inappropriate". Formative measurement models hence require different tests for reliability and validity (Bagozzi, 1994b, p. 333; Bollen & Lennox, 1991, p. 312; Diamantopoulos & Winklhofer, 2001, p. 272; MacKenzie et al., 2005, p. 727). This work relies on the following criteria: significance and strength of the paths from the indicators to the composite latent construct, overall goodness-of-fit of the MIMIC model, variance inflation factor (*VIF*), and degree of discriminant and nomological validity.

According to MacKenzie et al. (2005, p. 727), the item validity of a formative indicator "is reflected in the significance and strength of the path from the indicator to the composite latent construct". Though there are no standards for judging the absolute magnitude of item validity for formative indicators, the relative magnitude can be compared using standardized path coefficients. If the path from a particular indicator to the composite latent construct turns out be insignificant, there must be very solid theoretical reasons why the indicator is still to be regarded as a constituent of the formative construct. Rather such an indicator should be considered for elimination (Bollen, 1989, p. 222; Diamantopoulos et al., 2008, p. 1215; MacKenzie et al., 2005, p. 727).

Diamantopoulos and Winklhofer (2001, pp. 272-274) recommend using a MIMIC model (see chapters E2.1.1 and F1.1) because such an approach simultaneously allows the estimation of the paths from indicators to the composite construct and the provision of overall model fit statistics. These fit statistics can be evaluated using standard goodness-of-fit criteria such as χ^2 / *df*, *RMSEA*, *GFI*, etc. (see above). If the model fit proves acceptable, this can be taken as supporting evidence for the set of indicators that has been chosen for operationalization (Diamantopoulos & Winklhofer, 2001, p. 272). However, MIMIC models, which are considered "an optimal approach for solving error indeterminacy and achieving identification" (Bisbe et al., 2007, p. 816) of formative measurement models, require the inclusion of some reflective indicators in the measurement scale (see chapter E2.1.1). Hence, the researcher needs to develop a set of both reflective and formative indicators before conducting the survey (Diamantopoulos et al., 2008, p. 1213; Jarvis et al., 2003, p. 213; Jöreskog & Sörbom, 2001, p. 185). Mathematically, MIMIC models can be described as follows:

$$y = \lambda \eta + \varepsilon \quad [22]$$

$$\eta = \gamma' x + \zeta \quad [23]$$

where y' refers to the indicators of the latent variable η and x describes the "causes" of η. From the LISREL point of view, one can regard equation [22] as the measurement model for η and equation [23] as the structural equation for η. Substituting [23] into [22] yields:

$$y = \lambda \gamma' x + \lambda \zeta + \varepsilon \quad [24]$$

The estimation of MIMIC models with LISREL is straightforward. Equations [22] and [23] correspond to [3] and [1], respectively. Equation [2] in this case simply says that $x \equiv \xi$ (Jöreskog & Goldberger, 1975, pp. 631-632; Jöreskog & Sörbom, 2001, pp. 185-186).

An issue particular to formative measurement models is that of multicollinearity among its indicators. The presence of highly correlated indicators makes the estimation of their weights in a formative model difficult and results in imprecise values for these weights (Albers & Hildebrandt, 2006, p. 13; Coltman, Devinney, Midgley, & Venaik, 2008, p. 1254; Diamantopoulos & Winklhofer, 2001, p. 272). Given a criterion variable, an estimate of the impact of collinearity should be made by regressing the indicators on this variable and computing standard diagnostics such as the variance inflation factor (*VIF*). A *VIF* value $\leq$ 10.00 is commonly considered unproblematic (Hair et al., 2006, p. 230; Kleinbaum, Kupper, & Muller, 1988, p. 210).

To further assess the validity of formative constructs, Bagozzi (1994b, p. 333) notes that "the best we can do . . . is to examine how well the index relates to measures of other variables". Hence, aspects of discriminant and nomological validity are particularly important for the assessment of formative measurement models (Coltman et al., 2008, p. 1254; Jarvis et al., 2003, p. 202). It involves linking the formative construct to (a) another construct with which it would theoretically be expected to be linked (nomological validity), and (b) another construct with which it should theoretically not be linked too closely for reasons of distinctiveness (discriminant validity). Validation along these lines requires that information is gathered for at least two more constructs than the one captured by the formative construct under scrutiny. These constructs need to be measured by means of reflective indicators (Coltman et al., 2008, p. 1254; Diamantopoulos & Winklhofer, 2001, p. 273). Nomological validity requires that the formative construct is considerably correlated with the construct it is linked to. Discriminant validity can then be demonstrated if the formative construct is less than perfectly correlated with the construct it is linked to. Of course, for consistency, the magnitude of the correlations used to establish the formative construct's nomological validity should be greater than the magnitude of the correlations used to establish discriminant validity. For both types of validity, standard procedures (such as the χ^2 difference test for discriminant validity) can be applied (MacKenzie et al., 2005, p. 728).

4. Data Collection and Sample

4.1 Data Collection Process

As outlined in chapter E1.2, this study followed a two-staged research process. In the first phase – which took place from February 2008 to April 2008 – semi-structured interviews were conducted. This initial research phase aimed at an exploratory investigation of managers' coping with the (non)application of the controllability principle. The interviews helped the researcher to verify that the application of the principle indeed represents a major issue in the evaluation of managerial performance and varies across different companies and contexts. They also provided valuable insights as to how to refine the hypotheses which had so far been generated solely on the basis of extant literature. As a basis for the interviews, a guideline had been developed (Kreiner & Mouritsen, 2005, pp. 157-158; Kvale, 1996, pp. 129-135; Warren, 2002, pp. 86-87) which ensured that all interviewees would be exposed to the same key questions. However, the exact sequence of questions was kept flexible so that the course of the interviews could be adapted to each respondent. Also, some updates and extensions to the initial version of the guideline were made in order to incorporate findings from previous interview sessions. In terms of the interview content, the guideline covered five main sections and consisted of eleven open questions. The first part of the interview guideline focused on the nature of the processes and measures which were in place to evaluate respondents' performance. The second part was intended to explore respondents' role perceptions and how they reacted cognitively to differing levels of controllability. The third section was centered around affective and behavioral phenomena. In particular, it was examined whether the respondents felt tension and mental troubles as a consequence of the established performance evaluation practices. The interview guideline also included a question prompting the respondents to elaborate on their internal influence behavior. The fourth part of the guideline consisted of questions dealing with contextual factors. The respondents were, for example, asked whether their attitude towards the application of the controllability principle was dependent on the trustworthiness of their superiors. Each of the interviews concluded with a final section for respondents' additional comments on the research study. This section provided room to mention any aspects not covered by the interview guideline or touched upon in the course of the interview.

The second research phase started in the end of April 2008 and lasted until July 2008. It included a cross-sectional survey which was web-based. An individualized e-mail was sent to each manager with (a) the request to participate, (b) some background information on the research subject, (c) a unique and anonymous link to the online questionnaire, and (d) a link to the webpage of the sponsoring university. In the design of the survey, guidelines provided by Dillman (2007, pp. 79-148) and Peterson (2000, pp. 13-120) were applied. Several measures were taken to increase both the quality of the survey instrument and the response rate. First, the website was made appealing to the respondents by using a limited number of colors and an overall attractive layout. Second, the respondents were guaranteed strict anonymity and were assured that all data would be analyzed and reported only in aggregated form. Third, the respondents were promised a final report which summarized the key findings from the study. In addition, an incentive was provided to the respondents in that they were given the opportunity to participate in a raffle. Fourth, whenever possible, the questionnaire relied on scales from extant literature to measure this study's constructs (see chapter E2.1.1 to E2.2.3). Fifth, the questionnaire was drafted in English and was then translated into German using a standard translation-back-translation procedure. Sixth, the German questionnaire was intensively pretested with management accounting academics, questionnaire design experts, and 45 managers to assess its length, understandability, and general attractiveness as well as to ensure satisfactory descriptive statistics for all measurement scales (see introduction to chapter E2). Finally, after having sent the initial e-mails to the respondents, a follow-up procedure was put in place, reminding respondents twice to participate in the survey.

4.2 Target Population and Final Sample Characteristics

To stay in line with previous research on the controllability principle (Giraud et al., 2004; 2008; Merchant, 1987; 1989; Simons, 2007), this study chose business unit and functional managers as its target population. Following Giraud et al. (2008, pp. 36-37), support function managers were excluded because their performance is supposed to be difficult to define and to measure, which makes the controllability principle less relevant. To minimize sampling error, a random selection approach was chosen to identify interview and survey participants from the available sample frames (Babbie, 2004, pp. 190-191; Dillman, 2007, pp. 196-197; Smith, 2003, p. 56).

The sample of interview partners consisted of twelve managers who matched the above criteria. They were selected and contacted via an online business contacts and networking platform. The interviews took place at the managers' workplace and lasted between 42 to 93 minutes (see Table 19). The interviews were either taped or captured in detailed notes immediately after the interview if taping was not desired by the respondent (Johnson, 2002, pp. 111-112; Kvale, 1996, pp. 160-162; Silverman, 2005, pp. 55-57).

Participant	Position	Industry	Interview duration
Manager A	Profit center manager	Financial services	45 min.
Manager B	Head of technical sales	IT	93 min.
Manager C	Branch manager	HR services	55 min.
Manager D	Production manager	Automotive	50 min.
Manager E	Head of supply chain management	Automotive	47 min.
Manager F	Branch manager	Logistics and parcel service	72 min.
Manager G	Head of real estate	Transportation	66 min.
Manager H	Purchasing manager	Automotive	67 min.
Manager I	Product manager	Retail	50 min.
Manager J	R&D manager	IT	42 min.
Manager K	Business sales manager	Telecommunications	78 min.
Manager L	Program manager	Military and defense	59 min.

Table 19: Overview of Field Interviews

The sample of survey participants was drawn from the Hoppenstedt database. Hoppenstedt is the market leading company in Germany providing professional contact details of business managers for direct marketing purposes. The questionnaire was sent to 3,500 managers from companies with more than 200 employees. This provided some degree of control over the size of the companies in the sample. Of the 3,500 managers contacted, a total of 456 participated in the survey. 24 of the received questionnaires were excluded from the study because of respondents' failure to complete all questions. This leaves the study with 432 usable responses which constitutes a response rate of 12.3%. Such a response rate appears to be comparable to other recent management accounting surveys (Homburg & Stebel, 2009; Widener, 2006). As Smith (2003, p. 125) notes, "response rates of less than 25% are common in accounting research . . . Non-response is only a problem if we can demonstrate that there are systematic differences between respondents and non-respondents, and that such differences will impact on the findings". Tests for non-response bias suggested by Armstrong and Overton (1977, pp. 379-401) were therefore undertaken. Splitting the sample into equally large parts on the basis of the return dates of the questionnaire and comparing the first 100 respondents to the last 100 respondents, no evidence of response bias was found.

The final sample was dominated by male managers (87.3%). Only 12.7% of the managers participating in the survey were female. Regarding the respondents' age, more than 70% of the respondents were older than 40 years. Almost half of the respondents (48.6%) were at the age between 41 and 50 (see Figure 18). In an attempt to test for the representativeness of this study's sample, the available demographic data of the 432 respondents were compared to the respective data of the original 3,500 managers obtained from the Hoppenstedt database. No significant differences could be found.

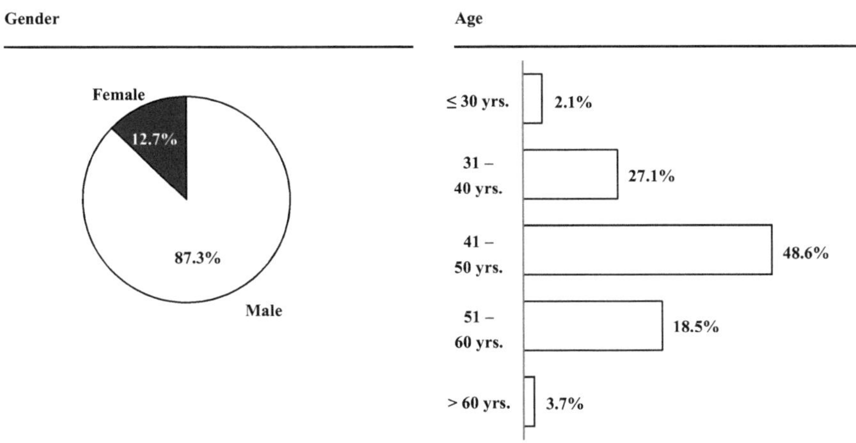

Figure 18: Sample Composition by Age and Gender

The demographic data further reveal that most of the managers (64.6%) held their position for at last three years. Also the respondents' overall tenure with their respective companies appears to be fairly long since the vast majority of managers (72.7%) worked for more than five years for the same employer. Most of the respondents (57.1%) belonged to the middle management in their companies with only 7.9% of the respondents working at lower management levels. The data on the size of the companies for which the respondents worked show that small and medium-sized companies dominate the sample. 67.6% of the managers worked for companies with less than 2,500 employees (see Figure 19). In sum, the demographic data indicate that the sample managers are highly experienced and held responsible positions in their companies.

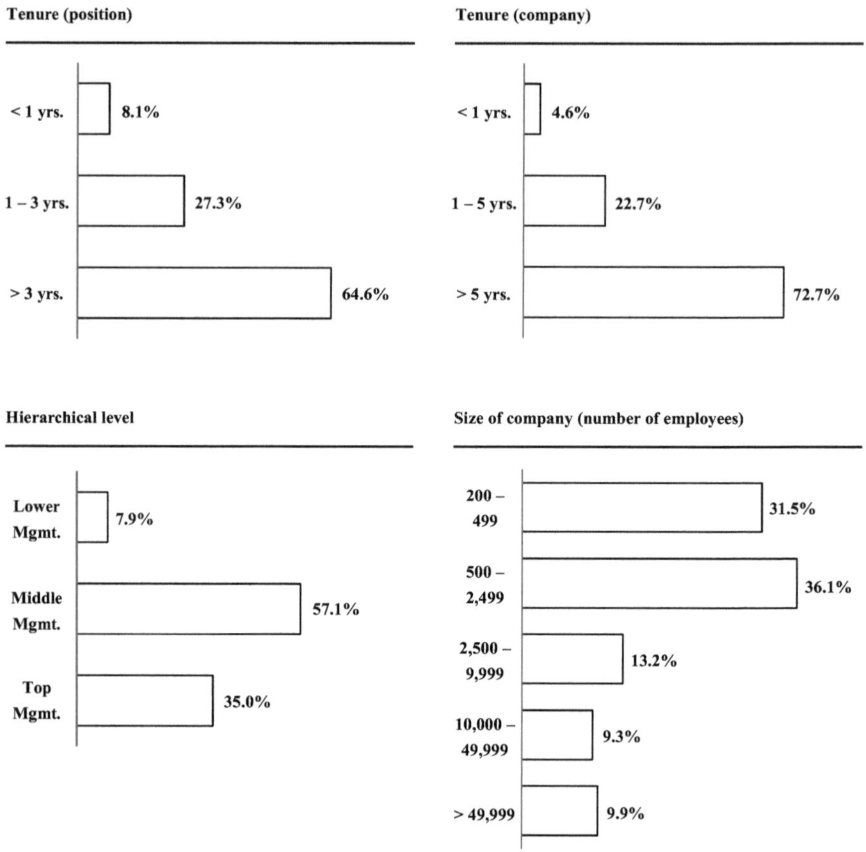

Figure 19: Sample Composition by Tenure, Hierarchical Level, and Size of Company

Before analyzing the empirical results from hypothesis testing in part F, it should be noted that the validity of the respondents' answers to the questionnaire and, hence, the causal relationships between this study's latent variables might be affected by common method variance (or common method bias). Common method variance is defined as "variance that is attributable to the measurement method rather than to the construct of interest" (Bagozzi et al., 1991, p. 426) and may result from gathering data on both independent and dependent variables from the same respondents. Potential sources of common method variance are respondents' social desirability tendency, leniency biases, or consistency motifs which do no fully mirror individual preferences and perceptions. Even though the occurrence of common method variance cannot be completely ruled out in this work, several attempts have been undertaken to minimize its influence on the causal relationships. First, independent and dependent variables were separated in the questionnaire. Second, where possible, different scale endpoints for the indicators of independent and dependent variables were chosen which should reduce method biases caused by commonalities in scale endpoints and anchoring effects. Third, the avoidance of ambiguous or unfamiliar wordings, vague concepts, complicated syntax, and double-barreled questions as well as a thorough pretesting of all survey instruments increased the overall comprehensibility of the questionnaire. Fourth, the respondents were guaranteed anonymity just as they were assured that no right or wrong answers existed. These procedures are expected to reduce respondents' evaluation apprehension and make them less likely to edit their responses to be more socially desirable, lenient, and consistent with how they think the survey designer wants them to answer (Churchill & Iacobucci, 2005, pp. 254-261; Podsakoff, MacKenzie, Lee, & Podsakoff, 2003, pp. 887-888; Tourangeau, Rips, & Rasinski, 2000, pp. 23-50, 230-264).

Having designed the survey in a way that it is as little susceptible to common method variance as possible, Harman's (1967) single-factor test as a post hoc statistical technique was conducted to evaluate the actual presence of common method variance in the data. This technique implies the assessment of the factorial structure entering all variables of a particular causal model into EFA or CFA. For the purpose of this study, the unrotated factor solution from EFA was examined to determine the number of factors that are necessary to account for the variance in the variables. It is assumed that if a substantial amount of common method variance is present, a single factor will emerge. Additionally, CFA was applied to examine the fit of a model where all variables are assigned to load on one single factor. If the fit indices for such a single-factor CFA model are satisfactory, common method variance is supposed to be responsible for the relationships among the variables (Podsakoff et al., 2003, pp. 889-890). Empirically, the EFA results for each causal model under investigation in this study revealed the presence of several distinct factors with eigenvalues greater than 1.00, rather than a single factor. Also the results from CFA showed that the single-factor model does not fit the data well, which provides some evidence that common method variance is not the main driver behind the relationships found in this study (see chapter F).

F Empirical Results

As outlined in the preceding chapters, this work applies a two-step approach to hypothesis testing (Anderson & Gerbing, 1988, pp. 417-418; Schumacker & Lomax, 2004, pp. 106-107). In the first step, the fit of the measurement models is assessed in order to ensure adequate reliability and validity of all survey instruments. This step comprises the analysis of the descriptive statistics for the latent variables used in this study (see chapter F1). In the second step, the fit of the structural models is assessed. This includes the evaluation of both the main models (see chapter F2) and the moderated models (see chapter F3).

1. Descriptive Statistics and Evaluation of the Measurement Models

Table 20 reports the descriptive statistics for the latent variable scores assuming equal weights of all items. The data on skewness and kurtosis reveal that the values for both are far below the recommended threshold values of 2 and 7, respectively (Curran et al., 1996, p. 26; West et al., 1995, p. 74). Nonnormality of empirical data is therefore not an issue in this study and the ML method can be used for LISREL parameter estimation.

Construct	Min	Max	Mean	Std. dev.	Skewness Statistic	Skewness Std. er.	Kurtosis Statistic	Kurtosis Std. er.
Sensitivity of PM*	2.00	7.00	5.273	1.027	-0.615	0.117	0.110	0.234
Precision of PM*	1.00	7.00	3.575	1.390	0.212	0.117	-0.553	0.234
Role Conflict	1.17	7.00	4.379	1.243	-0.205	0.117	-0.488	0.234
Role Ambiguity	1.00	5.75	2.153	0.905	1.128	0.117	1.735	0.234
Flexible Role Orientation	1.00	7.00	4.710	1.195	-0.628	0.117	0.058	0.234
Job Tension	1.00	7.00	4.519	1.381	-0.297	0.117	-0.745	0.234
Job Satisfaction	1.33	7.00	5.263	1.255	-0.823	0.117	0.147	0.234
In-role Performance	3.20	7.00	5.323	0.731	-0.461	0.117	0.173	0.234
Extra-role Performance	1.75	7.00	5.123	1.039	-0.749	0.117	0.593	0.234
Self-Efficacy	3.80	7.00	6.035	0.604	-0.576	0.117	0.438	0.234
Trust in Superior	1.00	7.00	4.993	1.294	-0.771	0.117	0.141	0.234

* Since the application of the controllability principle represents a second-order construct, this table depicts the descriptive statistics of its first-order dimensions, i.e. sensitivity of performance measures and precision of performance measures.

Table 20: Descriptive Statistics for the Latent Variables

1.1 Application of the Controllability Principle

The application of the controllability principle has been operationalized as a formative second-order construct (see chapter E2.1.1). The corresponding MIMIC model which is used to achieve identification is described in Figure 20. Since evaluation tools based on internal consistency do not apply to formative measurement models, the reliability and validity of the MIMIC operationalization cannot be assessed using Cronbach's alpha and other criteria informed by CTT. Instead, the following criteria are used for the evaluation of model fit (see also chapter E3.6.3): significance and strength of the paths from the first-order dimensions to the composite second-order construct, overall goodness-of-fit of the MIMIC model, variance inflation factor (*VIF*), and degree of discriminant and nomological validity.

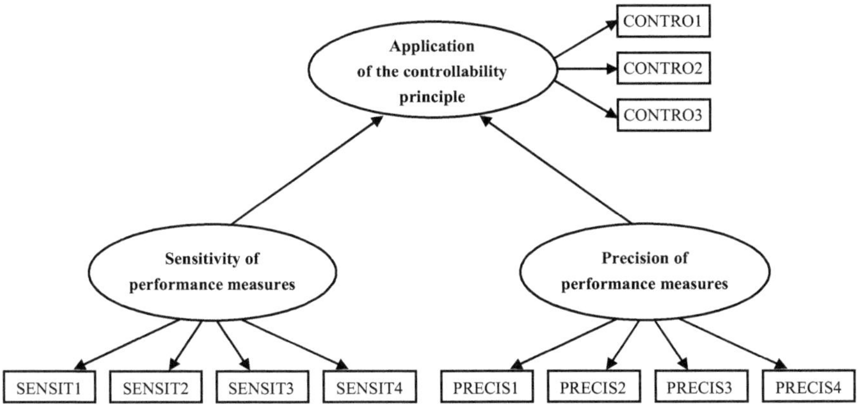

Figure 20: MIMIC Model for the Construct Application of the Controllability Principle

The paths from the first-order dimensions (i.e. sensitivity of performance measures and precision of performance measures) to the second-order construct (i.e. application of the controllability principle) are both positive and highly significant. The path from precision of performance measures to the second-order construct (0.38, t = 5.80) is thereby stronger than the respective path from sensitivity of performance measures to the second-order construct (0.18, t = 3.04).

Additionally, the goodness-of-fit criteria for the MIMIC model (see Table 21) support the successful operationalization of the application of the controllability principle. The χ^2 / *df*, *RMSEA*, *CFI*, *GFI*, and *AGFI* values indicate good model fit in that all criteria exceed the recommended aspiration levels.

To rule out that multicollinearity adversely affects the LISREL parameter estimation, the variance inflation factor (*VIF*) was assessed. For this purpose, latent variable scores for the two first-order dimensions sensitivity of performance measures (SENSIT1-SENSIT4) and precision of performance measures (PRECIS1-PRECIS4) were calculated and then regressed on the score of the three reflective indicators (CONTRO1-CONTRO3) which served as a criterion variable. The resultant *VIF* value was 1.31 and hence turned out to be considerably below 10.00 which is commonly regarded as the critical threshold when evaluating multicollinearity (Hair et al., 2006, p. 230; Kleinbaum et al., 1988, p. 210).

Information on the indicators of the construct: Application of the controllability principle

Indicator	*Item-to-total-correlation*	*Indicator reliability (IR)*	*t-value of factor loading*
Indicators of the first-order dimension: Sensitivity of performance measures			
SENSIT1	-*	-*	18.67
SENSIT2	-*	-*	16.50
SENSIT3	-*	-*	18.40
SENSIT4	-*	-*	14.92
Indicators of the first-order dimension: Precision of performance measures			
PRECIS1	-*	-*	17.41
PRECIS2	-*	-*	18.21
PRECIS3	-*	-*	22.45
PRECIS4	-*	-*	19.91
Reflective indicators on the second-order level			
CONTRO1	-*	-*	12.65
CONTRO2	-*	-*	19.90
CONTRO2	-*	-*	18.57

Information on the construct: Application of the controllability principle

Descriptive goodness-of- fit index		*Results of exploratory factor analysis (EFA)*	
Cronbach's Alpha (standardized)	-*	Variance extracted	-*
Results of confirmatory factor analysis (CFA)			
χ^2 [*df*]	63.86 [38]	χ^2 / *df*	1.68
RMSEA	0.04	*GFI*	0.97
CFI	0.99	*AGFI*	0.95
Factor reliability (*FR*)	-*	Average variance explained (*AVE*)	-*

* The application of the controllability principle is operationalized using a formative second-order measurement model. Evaluation tools based on internal consistency do not apply to such models.

Table 21: Assessment of the Instrument for Application of the Controllability Principle

In accordance with validation guidelines for formative constructs provided by MacKenzie et al. (2005, p. 728) and Diamantopoulos and Winklhofer (2001, pp. 272-274), the discriminant and nomological validity of the application of the controllability principle was further tested. The test for nomological validity implies linking the construct under scrutiny to another construct with which it should theoretically be linked. Since the literature often associates the application of the controllability principle with managers' perceptions of procedural fairness (Choudhury, 1986, p. 189; Hartmann & Slapničar, 2007, pp. 7-8; Huffman & Cain, 2001, pp. 606-607; Merchant, 1989, p. 87), procedural fairness was chosen for testing nomological validity. The instrument developed by McFarlin and Sweeney (1992) was used as a measurement scale for this variable in the questionnaire (Cronbach's alpha = 0.87). Testing the causal relationship between the application of the controllability principle and procedural fairness resulted in a reasonably well-fitting model (χ^2 / *df* = 2.49, *RMSEA* = 0.05, *CFI* = 0.96, *GFI* = 0.94, *AGFI* = 0.92). More importantly, the path from the application of the controllability principle to managers' perceived procedural fairness proved to be strong and highly significant (0.39, t = 6.76). In the light of these results, it seems legitimate to consider the measurement scale for the application of the controllability principle as nomologically valid.

The discriminant validity of the scale was assessed using the χ^2 difference test[23]. Several constrained and unconstrained models including the application of the controllability principle and the variables with which it is causally related in the structural models were compared. In all cases, the χ^2 test statistic reported significant decreases in χ^2 values for the unconstrained models providing evidence that the constructs are distinct.

Altogether, the goodness-of-fit criteria analyzed above indicate high reliability and validity of the measurement instrument used to operationalize the application of the controllability principle. The instrument and the proposed MIMIC model can hence be employed in the structural models for hypothesis testing (see chapter F2).

1.2 Role Conflict

Unlike the application of the controllability principle, the construct of role conflict was operationalized using a traditional reflective measurement model. Low indicator reliabilities of ROLEC7 and ROLEC8 led to the elimination of these items. Even though the EFA yielded a one-factor solution, the average variance explained from CFA is somewhat below the

---

[23] Since the *AVE* (which is based on the internal consistency of a scale's indicators) cannot be calculated for formative constructs (Homburg & Stebel, 2009, p. 137), the Fornell and Larcker (1981) criterion is not used to test for discriminant validity of the application of the controllability principle. For the results of the discriminant validity tests for the first-order dimensions sensitivity of performance measures and precision of performance measures, see chapter F1.11.

threshold value of 0.50. Nonetheless, the goodness-of-fit criteria for the remaining six indicators indicate satisfactory reliability and validity. For this reason and since the scale represents a well established measurement instrument, the deletion of further indicators was refused.

Information on the indicators of the construct: Role conflict

Indicator	*Item-to-total-correlation*	*Indicator reliability (IR)*	*t-value of factor loading*
ROLEC1	0.48	0.32	11.28
ROLEC2	0.58	0.31	10.84
ROLEC3	0.55	0.42	13.22
ROLEC4	0.61	0.53	15.12
ROLEC5	0.47	0.32	11.26
ROLEC6	0.65	0.39	12.58
ROLEC7	----------	eliminated	----------
ROLEC8	----------	eliminated	----------

Information on the construct: Role conflict

Descriptive goodness-of- fit index		*Results of exploratory factor analysis (EFA)*	
Cronbach's Alpha (standardized)	0.80	Variance extracted	0.50
Results of confirmatory factor analysis (CFA)			
χ^2 [*df*]	6.89 [8]	χ^2 / *df*	0.86
RMSEA	0.00	*GFI*	1.00
CFI	1.00	*AGFI*	0.99
Factor reliability (*FR*)	0.79	Average variance explained (*AVE*)	0.39

Table 22: Assessment of the Instrument for Role Conflict

1.3 Role Ambiguity

The assessment of the first- and second-generation criteria for the instrument measuring role ambiguity resulted in a final scale with four indicators. Due to low indicator reliabilities ROLEA3 and ROLEA6 were deleted. Interestingly, it is exactly these two indicators which had also shown low factor loadings in other recent management accounting studies (Burney & Widener, 2007, p. 58; Viator, 2001, p. 90). The remaining indicators of the final scale have adequate indicator reliabilities and load highly significant on the latent factor. Also the majority of the goodness-of-fit measures on the construct level (*RMSEA*, *CFI*, *GFI*, and *AGFI*) indicate good model fit. The results from EFA and CFA likewise support the scale's reliability and validity.

Information on the indicators of the construct: Role ambiguity

Indicator	*Item-to-total-correlation*	*Indicator reliability (IR)*	*t-value of factor loading*
ROLEA1	0.67	0.61	17.79
ROLEA2	0.57	0.38	13.08
ROLEA3	-----------	eliminated	-----------
ROLEA4	0.70	0.70	19.46
ROLEA5	0.67	0.56	16.82
ROLEA6	-----------	eliminated	-----------

Information on the construct: Role ambiguity

Descriptive goodness-of- fit index		*Results of exploratory factor analysis (EFA)*	
Cronbach's Alpha (standardized)	0.82	Variance extracted	0.67
Results of confirmatory factor analysis (CFA)			
χ^2 [*df*]	9.42 [2]	χ^2 / *df*	4.71
RMSEA	0.09	*GFI*	0.99
CFI	0.99	*AGFI*	0.95
Factor reliability (*FR*)	0.83	Average variance explained (*AVE*)	0.56

Table 23: Assessment of the Instrument for Role Ambiguity

1.4 Flexible Role Orientation

Due to the purification procedure which was also performed for the scale measuring flexible role orientation, the indicator ROLEO2 was dropped. All of the remaining indicators have significant *t*-values and only two of them show mediocre indicator reliabilities in that they fall below the threshold value of 0.40. All of the goodness-of-fit measures on the construct level indicate very good model fit. Additionally, the variances extracted in EFA and CFA are satisfactory with only the *AVE* value falling marginally below the recommended level of 0.50. The Cronbach's alpha for the scale is 0.84 which represents a result that is far above minimum requirements for newly developed scales (Nunnally & Bernstein, 1994, p. 245).

Information on the indicators of the construct: Flexible role orientation

Indicator	*Item-to-total-correlation*	*Indicator reliability (IR)*	*t-value of factor loading*
ROLEO1	0.49	0.33	11.82
ROLEO2	-----------	eliminated	-----------
ROLEO3	0.67	0.51	15.37
ROLEO4	0.48	0.29	10.34
ROLEO5	0.67	0.57	16.90
ROLEO6	0.69	0.56	16.58
ROLEO7	0.68	0.54	16.01

Information on the construct: Flexible role orientation

Descriptive goodness-of- fit index		*Results of exploratory factor analysis (EFA)*	
Cronbach's Alpha (standardized)	0.84	Variance extracted	0.56
Results of confirmatory factor analysis (CFA)			
χ^2 [*df*]	7.84 [6]	χ^2 / *df*	1.31
RMSEA	0.03	*GFI*	0.99
CFI	1.00	*AGFI*	0.98
Factor reliability (*FR*)	0.84	Average variance explained (*AVE*)	0.46

Table 24: Assessment of the Instrument for Flexible Role Orientation

1.5 Job Tension

After the elimination of two indicators with low standardized factor loadings and insufficient indicator reliabilities (TEN1 and TEN6), the remaining indicators measuring job tension show adequate reliability and load significantly on the latent factor. Further, the criteria for assessing the entire construct indicate a good model fit with all measures being above their respective cutoff-values. Also, the Cronbach's alpha for the scale exceeds the recommended threshold of 0.70. In sum, the measurement model results provide evidence for the successful operationalization of job tension.

Information on the indicators of the construct: Job tension

Indicator	*Item-to-total-correlation*	*Indicator reliability (IR)*	*t-value of factor loading*
TEN1	-----------	eliminated	-----------
TEN2	0.61	0.53	15.87
TEN3	0.75	0.72	19.58
TEN4	0.54	0.39	13.34
TEN5	0.65	0.53	15.46
TEN6	-----------	eliminated	-----------
TEN7	0.59	0.35	12.38

Information on the construct: Job tension

Descriptive goodness-of- fit index		*Results of exploratory factor analysis (EFA)*	
Cronbach's Alpha (standardized)	0.83	Variance extracted	0.60
Results of confirmatory factor analysis (CFA)			
χ^2 [*df*]	6.36 [3]	χ^2 / *df*	2.12
RMSEA	0.05	*GFI*	0.99
CFI	1.00	*AGFI*	0.97
Factor reliability (*FR*)	0.83	Average variance explained (*AVE*)	0.50

Table 25: Assessment of the Instrument for Job Tension

1.6 Job Satisfaction

The assessment of the goodness-of-fit criteria for the instrument measuring job satisfaction revealed that all indicator reliabilities by far exceed the recommended threshold of 0.40. Since additionally the *t*-values of all factor loadings reflect high significance, no indicator had to be dropped from the scale. On the construct level, every single goodness-of-fit criterion indicates very good model fit. In particular, the variances extracted in EFA and CFA are remarkably high. The measurement scale for job satisfaction thus demonstrates high reliability and validity.

Information on the indicators of the construct: Job satisfaction

Indicator	*Item-to-total-correlation*	*Indicator reliability (IR)*	*t-value of factor loading*
SATIS1	0.79	0.69	20.69
SATIS2	0.73	0.62	19.03
SATIS3	0.77	0.67	20.15
SATIS4	0.76	0.68	20.24
SATIS5	0.80	0.65	19.77
SATIS6	0.76	0.59	18.28

Information on the construct: Job satisfaction

Descriptive goodness-of- fit index		*Results of exploratory factor analysis (EFA)*	
Cronbach's Alpha (standardized)	0.92	Variance extracted	0.71
Results of confirmatory factor analysis (CFA)			
χ^2 [*df*]	18.13 [7]	χ^2 / *df*	2.59
RMSEA	0.06	*GFI*	0.99
CFI	0.99	*AGFI*	0.96
Factor reliability (*FR*)	0.92	Average variance explained (*AVE*)	0.65

Table 26: Assessment of the Instrument for Job Satisfaction

1.7 In-Role Performance

The five-indicator scale used to operationalize managers' in-role performance also turned out to be a reliable and valid measurement instrument. Despite two indicator reliabilities falling below 0.40, the factor loadings of all indicators are highly significant. Also the item-to-total-correlations are acceptable and hence item deletion did not appear to be necessary. The reliability and validity of the measurement scale was further supported by the goodness-of-criteria on the construct level. χ^2 / *df*, *RMSEA*, *CFI*, *GFI*, and *AGFI* values all provide evidence of a good model fit.

Information on the indicators of the construct: In-role performance			
Indicator	*Item-to-total-correlation*	*Indicator reliability (IR)*	*t-value of factor loading*
INROLE1	0.65	0.60	16.76
INROLE2	0.60	0.53	15.48
INROLE3	0.61	0.39	12.78
INROLE4	0.57	0.42	13.41
INROLE5	0.53	0.28	10.33
Information on the construct: In-role performance			
Descriptive goodness-of- fit index		*Results of exploratory factor analysis (EFA)*	
Cronbach's Alpha (standardized)	0.80	Variance extracted	0.57
Results of confirmatory factor analysis (CFA)			
χ^2 [*df*]	9.70 [4]	χ^2 / *df*	2.43
RMSEA	0.05	*GFI*	0.99
CFI	0.99	*AGFI*	0.97
Factor reliability (*FR*)	0.80	Average variance explained (*AVE*)	0.45

Table 27: Assessment of the Instrument for In-Role Performance

1.8 Extra-Role Performance

No item was dropped from the measurement scale for extra-role performance because the analysis of indicator reliabilities and item-to-total-correlations yielded acceptable results. On the construct level, the variances extracted in EFA and CFA as well as the Cronbach's alpha calculated for the scale exceed their respective cutoff-levels. Besides, the goodness-of-fit values of χ^2 / *df*, *CFI*, *GFI*, and *AGFI* are all very close to 1.00. The measurement model results hence indicate high reliability and validity of the scale.

Information on the indicators of the construct: Extra-role performance

Indicator	*Item-to-total-correlation*	*Indicator reliability (IR)*	*t-value of factor loading*
EXROLE1	0.72	0.73	19.64
EXROLE2	0.67	0.60	17.39
EXROLE3	0.68	0.45	14.39
EXROLE4	0.68	0.46	14.53

Information on the construct: Extra-role performance

Descriptive goodness-of- fit index		*Results of exploratory factor analysis (EFA)*	
Cronbach's Alpha (standardized)	0.85	Variance extracted	0.69
Results of confirmatory factor analysis (CFA)			
χ^2 [*df*]	1.30 [1]	χ^2 / df	1.30
RMSEA	0.03	*GFI*	1.00
CFI	1.00	*AGFI*	0.99
Factor reliability (*FR*)	0.84	Average variance explained (*AVE*)	0.56

Table 28: Assessment of the Instrument for Extra-Role Performance

1.9 Self-Efficacy

The evaluation of the goodness-of-fit criteria for the instrument measuring self-efficacy resulted in the elimination of the reverse-coded indicator SELF3 due to low indicator reliability. The remaining indicators show only moderate indicator reliabilities, but due to the highly significant factor loadings and acceptable item-to-total-correlations no further item deletion was deemed necessary. In the light of the goodness-of-fit results on the construct level which indicate a good model fit, the measurement scale can be considered reliable and valid. Also, the Cronbach's alpha of 0.75 exceeds the recommended threshold and compares favorably to the value reported by Speier and Frese (1997, p. 178) who used the same instrument.

Information on the indicators of the construct: Self-efficacy

Indicator	*Item-to-total-correlation*	*Indicator reliability (IR)*	*t-value of factor loading*
SELF1	0.48	0.36	11.34
SELF2	0.50	0.41	12.00
SELF3	-----------	eliminated	-----------
SELF4	0.46	0.31	10.29
SELF5	0.58	0.37	11.09
SELF6	0.58	0.37	11.07

Information on the construct: Self-efficacy

Descriptive goodness-of- fit index		*Results of exploratory factor analysis (EFA)*	
Cronbach's Alpha (standardized)	0.75	Variance extracted	0.51
Results of confirmatory factor analysis (CFA)			
χ^2 [*df*]	8.24 [4]	χ^2 / df	2.06
RMSEA	0.05	*GFI*	0.99
CFI	0.99	*AGFI*	0.97
Factor reliability (*FR*)	0.74	Average variance explained (*AVE*)	0.37

Table 29: Assessment of the Instrument for Self-Efficacy

1.10 Trust in Superior

The indicators of the measurement scale for trust in superior all have high factor loadings, acceptable indicator reliabilities, and significant *t*-values. Also the item-to-total-correlations are satisfactory and hence item deletion was not necessary. On the construct level, the goodness-of-fit criteria imply an almost perfect model fit, with the *RMSEA* value equaling 0.00 and the respective *CFI* and *GFI* values equaling 1.00. Furthermore, the variances extracted in EFA and CFA are clearly above their cutoff-values. The measurement model results thus indicate high reliability and validity of the measurement scale.

Information on the indicators of the construct: Trust in superior

Indicator	*Item-to-total-correlation*	*Indicator reliability (IR)*	*t-value of factor loading*
TRUST1	0.60	0.42	14.28
TRUST2	0.65	0.53	16.39
TRUST3	0.76	0.76	21.09
TRUST4	0.70	0.61	18.09

Information on the construct: Trust in superior

Descriptive goodness-of- fit index		*Results of exploratory factor analysis (EFA)*	
Cronbach's Alpha (standardized)	0.84	Variance extracted	0.68
Results of confirmatory factor analysis (CFA)			
χ^2 [*df*]	1.34 [2]	χ^2 / *df*	0.67
RMSEA	0.00	*GFI*	1.00
CFI	1.00	*AGFI*	0.99
Factor reliability (*FR*)	0.84	Average variance explained (*AVE*)	0.58

Table 30: Assessment of the Instrument for Trust in Superior

1.11 Test for Discriminant Validity

Subsequent to the assessment of the measurement models, discriminant validity of all constructs was analyzed using the Fornell and Larcker (1981) criterion. This criterion suggests that if the average variance explained (*AVE*) for a particular construct is greater than the squared correlations between this construct and all other constructs, then discriminant validity is obtained for the construct under scrutiny. As can be seen from Table 31, this is the case for all constructs used in this study.

Construct	1	2	3	4	5	6	7	8	9	10	11
1 Sensitivity of PM*	**0.65**										
2 Precision of PM*	0.24	**0.62**									
3 Role Conflict	0.08	0.21	**0.39**								
4 Role Ambiguity	0.22	0.16	0.15	**0.56**							
5 Flexible Role Orientation	0.01	0.09	0.24	0.04	**0.46**						
6 Job Tension	0.00	0.06	0.14	0.02	0.09	**0.50**					
7 Job Satisfaction	0.17	0.15	0.15	0.20	0.08	0.05	**0.65**				
8 In-role Performance	0.13	0.15	0.12	0.20	0.03	0.02	0.17	**0.45**			
9 Extra-role Performance	0.01	0.00	0.02	0.00	0.05	0.00	0.00	0.01	**0.56**		
10 Self-Efficacy	0.07	0.02	0.00	0.07	0.01	0.01	0.02	0.16	0.04	**0.37**	
11 Trust in Superior	0.10	0.17	0.15	0.19	0.05	0.05	0.26	0.09	0.00	0.02	**0.58**

The average variance extracted (*AVE*) for each construct is reported on the diagonal.
The squared correlations between the constructs (Pearson, equal weights for all items) are reported below the diagonal.
* Since the application of the controllability principle represents a second-order construct, this table depicts the AVE and the squared correlations for its first-order dimensions, i.e. sensitivity of performance measures and precision of performance measures.

Table 31: Assessment of Discriminant Validity (AVE vs. Squared Correlations)

2. Evaluation of the Main Models

The following chapters report the results of hypothesis testing. In chapter D2, several direct and indirect effects of the application of the controllability principle on cognitive, affective, and behavioral variables were proposed. The evaluation of the main models is structured around this study's dependent variables. First, the indirect effects of the application of the controllability principle on job tension are analyzed (chapter F2.1). Subsequently, it is investigated whether the application of the controllability principle is causally related to job satisfaction (chapter F2.2). Next, the consequences of the principle's application for managers' in-role performance are examined (chapter F2.3). Finally, a causal model is analyzed that tests the effects of the principle's application on managers' extra-role performance (chapter F2.4).

2.1 Effects of the Application of the Controllability Principle on Job Tension

Based on role theory, this work hypothesized that the application of the controllability principle represents a job-related stimulus which only indirectly affects managers' job tension via role conflict and role ambiguity. More specifically, it was proposed that the principle's application is negatively related to role conflict (H1) and role ambiguity (H2). Role conflict, in turn, was hypothesized to have a positive effect on job tension (H4). Likewise, a positive relationship between role ambiguity and job tension was expected (H6). Figure 21 reports the structural model analyzing these four relationships.

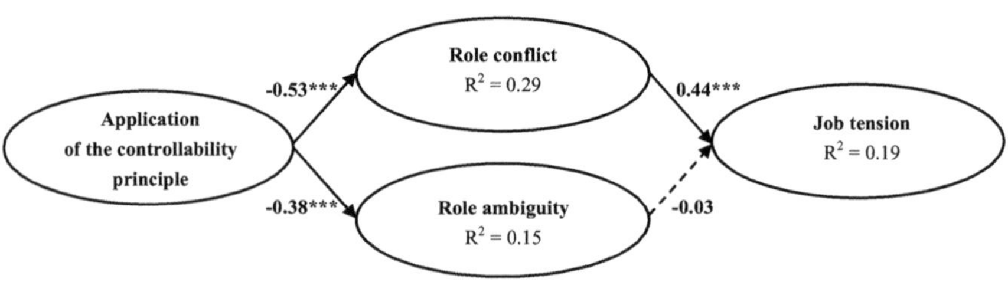

§ $p < 0.1$, * $p < 0.05$, ** $p < 0.01$, *** $p < 0.001$ (two-tailed)

Figure 21: SEM Results for the Effects of the Application of the Controllability Principle on Job Tension

For the structural model in Figure 21, LISREL reports a χ^2 / *df* value of 2.00, a *RMSEA* value of 0.05, a *GFI* value of 0.91, an *AGFI* value of 0.89, and a CFI value of 0.94. Hence, with the exception of the CFI value, all goodness-of-fit criteria indicate acceptable to good model fit. The CFI value which falls marginally below the threshold of 0.95 can be neglected because in large samples such as the one analyzed in this study "cutoff values of 0.95 on key GOF [goodness-of-fit measures] are unrealistic" (Hair et al., 2006, p. 758). Homburg and Baumgartner (1998, p. 357) and Hair et al. (2006, p. 749) therefore propose a threshold of 0.90 for the CFI. Taking further into consideration that the covariance-based approach of LISREL generally yields a decrease in model fit when formative constructs are included (Wilcox, Howell, & Breivik, 2008, pp. 1225-1226), the above SEM results provide sufficiently high confidence to accept the theoretical model.

Based on the model, H1 and H2 can both be confirmed. The application of the controllability principle has highly significant and negative effects on role conflict and role ambiguity. Remarkably, with an R^2 of 29% and 15%, respectively, the application of the controllability principle also explains considerable parts of the variances in the two role constructs. Hence, the more managers perceive the controllability principle to be applied in their performance evaluation, the lower their experienced role conflict and role ambiguity. Or, conversely stated, confronting managers with a lack of controllability represents a substantial source of role stress. Role stress, in turn, is empirically in parts related to managers' job tension. The model yields a strong and highly significant positive path (0.44, t = 6.50) from role conflict to job tension, and a negligible path from role ambiguity to job tension, with the latter being far from significance (-0.03, t = -0.52). H4 can therefore be confirmed, whereas H6 has to be rejected.

To verify whether role conflict effectively operates as a mediator between the application of the controllability principle and job tension, the Baron and Kenny (1986) test outlined in chapter E3.4 is applied. The step-wise approach of this test reveals that the application of the controllability principle initially has a direct and significant effect (-0.18, t = -3.21) on managers' job tension, which then is rendered insignificant (0.07, t = 1.01) by the introduction of the intervening role construct. Consequently, the relationship between the principle's application and job tension is completely mediated by role conflict.

2.2 Effects of the Application of the Controllability Principle on Job Satisfaction

Job satisfaction is the second affective outcome with which the application of the controllability principle was hypothesized to be causally related. As it was again proposed that the effect is indirect through role conflict and role ambiguity, the structural model depicted in Figure 22 only includes direct paths from the application of the controllability principle to role conflict (H1) and role ambiguity (H2), together with direct paths from role conflict to job satisfaction (H5) and from role ambiguity to job satisfaction (H7).

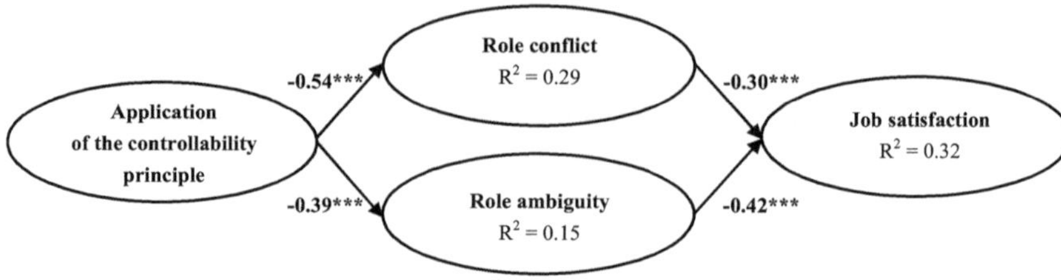

Figure 22: SEM Results for the Effects of the Application of the Controllability Principle on Job Satisfaction

LISREL reports an acceptable to good model fit with a χ^2 / *df* value of 2.10, a *RMSEA* value of 0.05, a *GFI* value of 0.90, an *AGFI* of 0.88, and a *CFI* value of 0.94 for the model in Figure 22. All of the relationships turn out to be strong and highly significant. Overall, the SEM results reported by LISREL indicate high validity of the theoretical model.

In detail, H1 and H2 can again be confirmed. Commensurate with the findings from the foregoing structural model, the application of the controllability principle emerges as an important antecedent variable of both role conflict and role ambiguity. Each of the two role constructs is, in turn, causally related to job satisfaction with the path from role ambiguity being stronger and more significant (0.42, t = -7.36) than the respective path from role conflict (0.30, t = -5.38). Hence, H5 and H7 are both confirmed. In sum, almost one third of the variance (R^2 = 0.32) in job satisfaction can be explained by the two role constructs.

The Baron and Kenny (1986) test is again employed to assess the mediating effect of role conflict and role ambiguity. Excluding the two role constructs in the structural model results in a strong and highly significant direct path from the application of the controllability principle to job satisfaction (0.32, t = 5.69). This path subsequently becomes virtually meaningless and insignificant (0.02, t = 0.36) when role conflict and role ambiguity are included in the model displaying a complete mediation effect.

2.3 Effects of the Application of the Controllability Principle on In-Role Performance

On grounds of role theory, a third model is tested suggesting that the application of the controllability principle positively affects managers' in-role performance. The effect was proposed to operate through role conflict (H1, H8) and role ambiguity (H2, H9). The corresponding structural model is visualized in Figure 23.

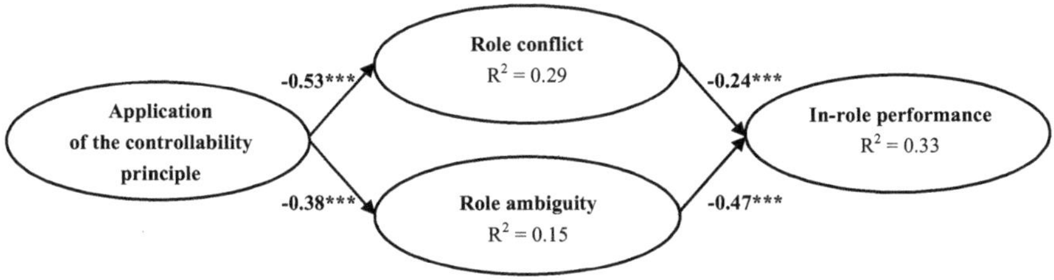

§ p < 0.1, * p < 0.05, ** p < 0.01, *** p < 0.001 (two-tailed)

Figure 23: SEM Results for the Effects of the Application of the Controllability Principle on In-Role Performance

The goodness-of-fit measures for the model in Figure 23 again indicate acceptable to good model fit. LISREL reports a χ^2 / *df* value of 2.05, a *RMSEA* value of 0.05, a *GFI* value of 0.91, an *AGFI* of 0.88, and a *CFI* value of 0.94.

In line with the two previous structural models confirming H1 and H2, the application of the controllability principle strongly and significantly affects role conflict (-0.53, t = -7.26) and role ambiguity (-0.38, t = 6.03) with the former effect being stronger than the latter. The results from SEM further confirm H8 and H9 in that both role constructs exert considerable influence on managers' in-role performance. The path from role conflict to in-role performance (-0.24, t = -4.16) is strong and highly significant, just as is the path from role ambiguity to in-role performance (-0.47, t = -7.35). With an R^2 of 33%, the two role constructs also explain a noteworthy part of the variance in managers' in-role performance.

The results from the mediation test (Baron & Kenny, 1986) again reveal a complete mediation. The effect of the application of the controllability principle on in-role performance is only through role conflict and role ambiguity. In detail, the initially significant direct relationship (0.25, t = 4.22) between the independent variable and the dependent variable is rendered insignificant (-0.08, t = -1.08) when the two role constructs are introduced into the structural model.

2.4 Effects of the Application of the Controllability Principle on Extra-Role Performance

The final main model to be tested complements the previous models in that it investigates whether the application of the controllability principle affects managers' role perceptions beyond role conflict and role ambiguity. H3 predicted that the principle's application is causally related to managers' flexible role orientation whereupon it was suggested that the higher the application of the principle, the less flexible the managers' role orientation. In H10, it was further hypothesized that flexible role orientation is, in turn, related to managers' extra-role performance.

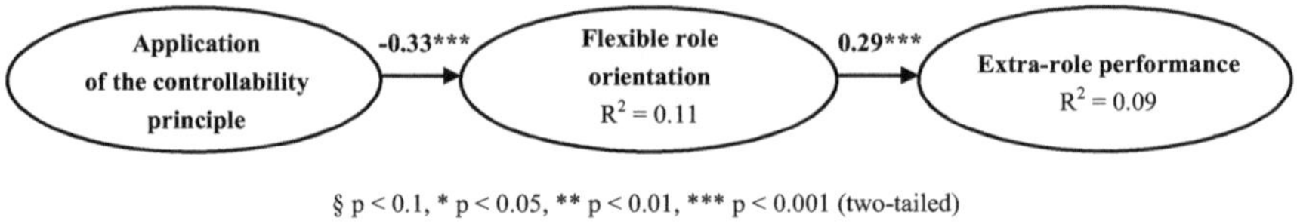

Figure 24: SEM Results for the Effects of the Application of the Controllability Principle on Extra-Role Performance

With a χ^2 / *df* value of 1.67, a *RMSEA* value of 0.04, a *GFI* value of 0.94, an *AGFI* value of 0.92, and a *CFI* value of 0.97, the statistics provided by LISREL indicate very good fit of the structural model depicted in Figure 24. All of the five goodness-of-fit criteria are clearly above their respective cutoff-values.

With regard to H3 and H10, both hypotheses can be confirmed. The path from the application of the controllability principle to flexible role orientation is negative and turns out to be strong and significant (-0.33, t = -4.89). This result substantiates that the stricter the principle's application, the less likely it is for managers to develop a flexible role orientation. The explained variance in flexible role orientation still adds up to 11%. The subsequent path from flexible role orientation to extra-role performance reaches a similar magnitude and level of significance (0.29, t = 4.80) indicating that – once having developed a flexible role orientation – managers increasingly show extra-role performance. The explained R^2 for managers' extra-role performance is 9%.

Testing whether flexible role orientation operates as a mediator in the relationship between the application of the controllability principle and managers' extra-role performance reveals that there is no significant direct relationship between the independent variable and the dependent variable (-0.08, t = -1.41). Albeit taking an intermediary position in the causal chain depicted in Figure 24, flexible role orientation does therefore not constitute a mediator in the strictest sense.

2.5 Summary of the Main Models

Table 32 summarizes the results of hypothesis testing. With the exception of H6, all main model hypotheses can be confirmed. The proposed relationships are in the predicted direction and prove to be highly significant.

	Hypothesized relationship	Empirical support	Significance
H1	The application of the controllability principle is negatively associated with role conflict.	YES	$p < 0.001$
H2	The application of the controllability principle is negatively associated with role ambiguity.	YES	$p < 0.001$
H3	The application of the controllability principle is negatively associated with flexible role orientation.	YES	$p < 0.001$
H4	Role conflict is positively associated with job tension.	YES	$p < 0.001$
H5	Role conflict is negatively associated with job satisfaction.	YES	$p < 0.001$
H6	Role ambiguity is positively associated with job tension.	NO	$p > 0.1$
H7	Role ambiguity is negatively associated with job satisfaction.	YES	$p < 0.001$
H8	Role conflict is negatively associated with in-role performance.	YES	$p < 0.001$
H9	Role ambiguity is negatively associated with in-role performance.	YES	$p < 0.001$
H10	Flexible role orientation is positively associated with extra-role performance.	YES	$p < 0.001$

Table 32: Overview of the Results of Hypothesis Testing

3. Evaluation of the Moderated Models

As hypothesized, the application of the controllability principle affects managers' role perceptions. The paths from the application of the controllability principle to role conflict, role ambiguity, and flexible role orientation are strong and highly significant. The subsequent moderator analyses are intended to examine whether these relationships hold across different contexts or whether some of the effects are – as predicted by role theory – contingent upon their "surrounding conditions" (Kahn et al., 1964, p. 37). In accordance with theory, three types of moderators are proposed for the exploratory moderation tests: the managers' hierarchical level in the organization, their self-efficacy, and their trust in the superior.

Technically, the multisample analysis described in chapter E3.5 is employed to detect potential moderating effects. This procedure has recently been applied in other management accounting studies as well (Burney & Widener, 2007; Marginson & Bui, 2009; Viator, 2001). In the first step, two subsamples are formed for the test of each moderator. For managers' hierarchical level, a first group of 151 top managers is drawn as opposed to a second group of 281 lower level and middle managers. For managers' self-efficacy and trust in their superior, two equally large groups are identified with each 216 managers scoring low respectively high in their ratings of the two measurement scales. The second step of the multisample approach compares the strength and the significance of the relationships under scrutiny across the subsamples. In the third and final step, a χ^2 difference test is used to assess whether the differences between the subsamples that were found in the second step prove to be significant. The difference in the χ^2 value is calculated on the basis of two competing models. While the first model restricts the parameter for the relationships under scrutiny to be equal ("invariant") across the subsamples, the same parameter is allowed to vary across the subsamples in the second model. An improvement of 3.84 in the χ^2 value (1 *df*) from the constrained model to the unconstrained model indicates a difference at the 5% level of significance. Correspondingly, improvements of 6.63 and 10.83 in the χ^2 value indicate a difference at the 1% level of significance and the 0.1% level of significance, respectively.

3.1 Effects of Hierarchical Level

Table 33 provides the statistical results for the moderating influence of managers' hierarchical level on the relationships between the application of the controllability principle and the three role variables.

Path	**Hierarchical level**		**χ^2 difference ($\Delta df = 1$)**
	Lower/Middle	**Top**	
Application of the controllability principle → Role conflict	$\gamma = -0.55^{***}$ $t = -6.50$	$\gamma = -0.50^{***}$ $t = -4.98$	$\Delta\chi^2 = 1.79$
Application of the controllability principle → Role ambiguity	$\gamma = -0.51^{***}$ $t = -6.48$	$\gamma = -0.14$ $t = -1.62$	$\Delta\chi^2 = 12.66^{***}$
Application of the controllability principle → Flexible role orientation	$\gamma = -0.38^{***}$ $t = -4.67$	$\gamma = -0.24^{*}$ $t = -2.41$	$\Delta\chi^2 = 2.84^{§}$

§ p < 0.1, * p < 0.05, ** p < 0.01, *** p < 0.001

Table 33: SEM Results for Multisample Analysis with Hierarchical Level as Moderator

Among the three relationships which are tested for a moderating influence of managers' hierarchical level, it appears that in particular the relationship between the application of the controllability principle and role ambiguity is highly dependent ($\Delta\chi^2 = 12.66$, $df = 1$, $p < 0.001$) on this moderator. For managers in top management positions, the direct effect of the principle's application on role ambiguity even turns out to be insignificant ($\gamma_{top} = -0.14$, $t = -1.62$). By contrast, the same effect sharply increases in magnitude and significance for managers in lower and middle hierarchical positions ($\gamma_{lower/middle} = -0.51$, $t = -6.48$). A similar pattern can be observed for the relationship between the application of the principle and role conflict. Again, the relationship is weaker for top managers (γ_{top} = -0.50, t = -4.98) than for lower level and middle managers ($\gamma_{lower/middle}$ = -0.55, t = -6.50). However, for the role conflict relationship, the differences between the two groups are only marginal and the moderating effect turns out to be insignificant ($\Delta\chi^2$ = 1.79, df = 1, p > 0.1). Finally, analyzing the influence of managers' hierarchical level on the relationship between the application of the controllability principle and flexible role orientation reveals another moderating effect which, however, is barely significant ($\Delta\chi^2$ = 2.84, df = 1, p < 0.1). Albeit the negative relationship between the principle's application and flexible role orientation holds across both groups, the effect is stronger and more significant in lower and middle management positions ($\gamma_{lower/middle}$ = -0.38, t = -4.67) than it is in top management positions (γ_{top} = -0.24, t = -2.41).

3.2 Effects of Self-Efficacy

The analysis of the moderating impact of managers' self-efficacy (see Table 34) shows that neither the relationship between the application of the controllability principle and role conflict nor the relationship between the principle's application and role ambiguity is dependent on this personality variable. However, it is found that managers' self-efficacy strongly influences the effect of the principle's application on flexible role orientation ($\Delta\chi^2$ = 9.94, df = 1, p < 0.01). Among managers with low self-efficacy, the effect between the two variables is rendered weak and insignificant (γ_{low} = -0.14, t = -1.72), whereas the same effect turns out to be strong and very significant among managers with high self-efficacy (γ_{high} = -0.50, t = -5.13).

Path	**Self-efficacy**		**χ^2 difference**
	Low	**High**	**(Δdf = 1)**
Application of the controllability principle → Role conflict	γ = -0.43*** t = -5.11	γ = -0.62*** t = -6.47	$\Delta\chi^2$ = 2.21
Application of the controllability principle → Role ambiguity	γ = -0.37*** t = -4.46	γ = -0.37*** t = -4.50	$\Delta\chi^2$ = 0.05
Application of the controllability principle → Flexible role orientation	γ = -0.14 t = -1.72	γ = -0.50*** t = -5.13	$\Delta\chi^2$ = 9.94**

* p < 0.05, ** p < 0.01, *** p < 0.001

Table 34: SEM Results for Multisample Analysis with Self-Efficacy as Moderator

3.3 Effects of Trust in Superior

The final contextual variable which is tested for a moderating influence is managers' trust in their superior. A comparison of the path coefficients across the two subgroups in Table 35 leads to the finding that the application of the controllability principle is more important for managers with low trust in their superior than it is for managers with high trust in their superior. The relationships between the principle's application and both role conflict and role ambiguity are stronger and more significant for managers in low trust relationships (γ_{low} = -0.55, t = -5.79 for role conflict and γ_{low} = -0.43, t = -4.94 for role ambiguity) than for managers in high trust relationships (γ_{high} = -0.43, t = -4.90 for role conflict and γ_{high} = -0.21, t = -2.58 for role ambiguity). Despite the differences in the path coefficients, the χ^2 test statistic shows that the detected differences do not reach levels of significance. But with a χ^2 decrease of 2.67, the moderating effect of managers' trust in their superior on the role ambiguity relationship falls only marginally below the 10% level of significance. Hence, there seems to be weak empirical support for trust in superior operating as a moderator in the relationship between the application of the controllability principle and role stress. For completeness, it is also tested for a potential moderation of the relationship between the principle's application and flexible role orientation. However, the corresponding effect of managers' trust in their superior on this relationship is far from being significant ($\Delta\chi^2 = 0.75$, $df = 1$, $p > 0.1$) and hence not meaningful.

Path	Trust in superior		χ^2 difference
	Low	High	($\Delta df = 1$)
Application of the controllability principle → Role conflict	γ = -0.55*** t = -5.79	γ = -0.43*** t = -4.90	$\Delta\chi^2 = 2.04$
Application of the controllability principle → Role ambiguity	γ = -0.43*** t = -4.94	γ = -0.21* t = -2.58	$\Delta\chi^2 = 2.67$
Application of the controllability principle → Flexible role orientation	γ = -0.23** t = -2.67	γ = -0.33*** t = -3.67	$\Delta\chi^2 = 0.75$

* $p < 0.05$, ** $p < 0.01$, *** $p < 0.001$

Table 35: SEM Results for Multisample Analysis with Trust in Superior as Moderator

3.4 Summary of the Moderated Models

The findings from the moderated models are summarized in Table 36. Even though "moderator effects are generally difficult to detect" (Schminke et al., 2002, p. 894), three of the nine effects proposed by role theory hold empirically.

	Research question	Empirical result	Significance
E1a	Does managers' hierarchical level moderate the relationship between the application of the controllability principle and role conflict?	NO	$p > 0.1$
E1b	Does managers' hierarchical level moderate the relationship between the application of the controllability principle and role ambiguity?	YES	$p < 0.001$
E1c	Does managers' hierarchical level moderate the relationship between the application of the controllability principle and flexible role orientation?	YES	$p < 0.1$
E2a	Does managers' self-efficacy moderate the relationship between the application of the controllability principle and role conflict?	NO	$p > 0.1$
E2b	Does managers' self-efficacy moderate the relationship between the application of the controllability principle and role ambiguity?	NO	$p > 0.1$
E2c	Does managers' self-efficacy moderate the relationship between the application of the controllability principle and flexible role orientation?	YES	$p < 0.01$
E3a	Does managers' trust in superior moderate the relationship between the application of the controllability principle and role conflict?	NO	$p > 0.1$
E3b	Does managers' trust in superior moderate the relationship between the application of the controllability principle and role ambiguity?	NO	$p > 0.1$
E3c	Does managers' trust in superior moderate the relationship between the application of the controllability principle and flexible role orientation?	NO	$p > 0.1$

Table 36: Overview of the Results of Moderator Tests

G Discussion

Following the statistical analysis of the survey results in part F, the next part provides a discussion of the findings in the light of previous literature on the controllability principle. In addition, it is examined how the qualitative knowledge that has been gathered from the interviews conducted in the first stage of this research project complements the survey findings. Since role theory is the underlying perspective of this work, the following chapters attempt to relate the empirical findings to the role episode model and assess the theory's explanatory power in the interpretation of the findings. The next chapters are structured around the application of the controllability principle as a corporate practice (chapter G1), the cognitive mechanisms induced by the principle's application, and the way the basic role relationships are influenced by contextual factors (chapter G2), and finally the affective (chapter G3) and behavioral (chapter G4) responses resulting from these cognitive mechanisms.

1. The Application of the Controllability Principle as Corporate Practice

It is not only the survey statistics, but also insights gained from the interviews which reveal that companies differ in the degree to which they apply the controllability principle in the evaluation of their managers. Along this continuum, there are companies which put considerable effort into the adjustment for uncontrollable factors, striving for an almost complete implementation of the principle. Among the twelve managers, two interviewees (managers A and I, see Table 19) indicate that the principle represents a central theme in their performance evaluation and that it strictly guides the appraisal process. However, based on the interview data, it seems to be corporate practice in most other companies to deliberately disregard the controllability principle. The ten remaining interviewees thereby report varying degrees of the principle's application in their companies.

The strict application of the controllability principle as reported by manager A certainly represents an exception. According to manager A, "there is virtually no uncontrollable influence on my performance measures . . . because we have a very extensive reporting system here". The use of such a detailed MCS has also been suggested in management accounting literature (McNally, 1980, pp. 170-171; Merchant & Van der Stede, 2007, pp. 539-540; Solomons, 1965, pp. 71-76) since it enables evaluators to explicitly take matters of controllability into consideration and classify cost and revenue items along their degree of controllability. Even though the implied increase in the refinement of reports may not always be justified and useful for economic decision-making, it helps to separate controllable from uncontrollable variances and thus forms the basis for a more complete application of the controllability principle (Merchant & Van der Stede, 2007, p. 539; Modell, 1997, p. 314). The high degree of sophistication in the reporting system is complemented by two other aspects which make manager A praise the application of the controllability principle in his company: First, manager A is allowed to intensively participate in the initial target setting process in that his superior allows him to make suggestions concerning the performance measures generally controllable by him and the absolute height of the performance measures. Second, manager A is in the position to call for ex post adjustments of his performance measures. Such ex post adjustments have to be approved by his superior, but, according to manager A, this is commonly the case if manager A can bring forward convincing arguments why there are uncontrollable factors that necessitate ex post adjustment.

In sharp contrast to the situation of manager A, the performance evaluation for manager G comprises a strong influence of uncontrollable factors. Manager G explains that

> basically I only have marginal impact on all of my performance measures. I cannot accomplish any of the objectives I receive from my superior on my own . . . I always have an indirect influence only. In fact, I never have the opportunity to directly influence the measures.

Even though manager G declares that ex post adjustments might be considered in exceptional cases where the uncontrollable factors are unduly onerous, he puts particular emphasis on the general discrepancy between his responsibility as a profit center manager and the corresponding authority granted by corporate management. Manager G is seen as an entrepreneur fully responsible for the success of his business unit, but at the same time he is not allowed to independently decide on issues such as staffing, resource allocation, or capital investment. Accordingly, it is mainly internal constraints including both vertical and horizontal interdependencies that strongly impede the application of the controllability principle in the company of manager G. It is a common pattern emerging throughout the interviews that managers perceive the influence from internal interdependencies as more uncontrollable and troublesome than influence from external factors. The classification of uncontrollable factors which was introduced in chapter B3.2 and which distinguishes between horizontal interdependencies, vertical interdependencies, and external factors (Giraud et al., 2008, p. 36) is used in the following to describe differences in corporate practice of adjusting for uncontrollable factors.

Not unexpectedly, horizontal interdependencies appear to be most relevant to managers of production and sales departments since they often rely on upstream business units in the timely delivery of high quality and reasonably priced products and services. Manager D who works as a production manager for an automotive supplier describes his horizontal dependencies on managers of other departments as follows:

> My performance measures are not controllable by me. Not at all . . . If I miss my BBE ["Brutto-Betriebsergebnis"] target by merely 1%, I do not get anything. But there is construction, purchasing, and sales that play along. I personally can hardly take any influence on the target. What I can do is take care of the number of workers on the shop floor, work productively, and minimize rectification of defects. However, this has only a marginal effect on the target . . . If the purchasing manager says 'No, I do not get you anything [i.e. discounts, cost savings, etc.]!' – and materials represent up to 55% of overall costs, for some products even 70% – I will never hit my target!

Since the BBE target for his business unit, which accounts for 20% of his variable pay, is heavily influenced by other managers' effort, manager D regards this target as uncontrollable by him. According to manager D, it is corporate practice in his company that such uncontrollable factors are not taken into consideration in year-end decisions on pay and promotion. Manager D, who has only recently joined the company, acknowledges that this practice of no adjustments takes a bit of getting used to:

> Things were different with my former employer. There, I received six or seven performance measures all of which were controllable by me and adjusted for uncontrollable influence if necessary . . . This was a more subtle approach . . . But that surely is a question of corporate philosophy.

Nevertheless, the interviews with managers from other companies and industries indicate that such a practice of no adjustments is not unique to manager D's employer. Manager K reports a very similar evaluation practice. He works for a large telecommunications company, where he is in charge of regional business sales. As a sales manager, he is highly dependent on product development in order to acquire new customers and operate successfully in a very competitive market:

> If a product is not available on time – or if it does not have competitive quality – you really get egg on your face . . . It is currently one of our hot topics. At the moment, our product 'Business-DSL' does not possess a voice option, but only comes with an ordinary internet access option. Our competitors, however, offer this feature. Hence, no customer is interested in our product. . . . Nonetheless, one of my targets says that I have to make sales of more than 100.000 Euros with the 'Business-DSL' product. Nobody knows how to do it . . . I don't get that thing sold, no matter how hard I try.

Manager K admits that, in the sales forecast made at the beginning of the year, the target of 100.000 Euros seemed reasonable to him because the 'Business-DSL' product was deemed to use state-of-the-art technology and hence to be competitive. However, due to technical problems, the respective product development unit had to launch the product with a delay of several weeks and also failed to integrate the voice option. The latter turned out to be a critical success factor in the telecommunications market. Manager K therefore tried to persuade his superiors that ex post adjustments of the initial sales targets were appropriate:

> In that year, I was in deep trouble . . . They said to me: 'Look, on January 1st you committed to that target. Of course, it is tough luck that the product was not available on the due date . . . But that's not relevant to us' . . . Nobody said they would reduce the sales target because the launch date was postponed und because the product does not work perfectly. That simply does not happen here!

The two examples above demonstrate that horizontal interdependencies – if they are not adjusted for – represent an uncontrollable factor. Not all companies subject their managers to bearing this influence. Altogether, the interviews provide some indication that corporate practice of categorically not adjusting for horizontal interdependencies is rather uncommon. Most interviewees report a less drastic influence of horizontal interdependencies than this is the case for managers D and K. In particular managers A, H, and I state that they are almost totally buffered from horizontal interdependencies. Additionally, it is worth noting that not all managers do necessarily expect horizontal interdependencies to be eliminated. On the contrary, one of the interviewees (manager J) declares that he generally accepts the situation of being dependent on the effort of others. Manager J works as an R&D manager with an IT company and a considerable part of his variable pay is based on the sales figures of an external business unit. Even though manager J categorizes the sales figures as fairly uncontrollable by him and acknowledges that it is uncommon to link an R&D manager's pay to sales, he relates this evaluation practice to the broader organizational context. Since interdependencies can be found all over the organization, manager J regards them as being inevitable and predictable, which makes it easier to put up with them:

> All of our targets can only be achieved if we work together in teams. There are hardly any targets which I can completely control by myself . . . However, one knows that everybody is dependent on somebody else. So it is not always a bilateral thing. One simply learns that everybody is dependent and hence we rely on others to work cooperatively.

Next to horizontal interdependencies, it is vertical interdependencies that may contribute to a lack of controllability in managerial jobs. Vertical interdependencies refer to decisions made by superiors with cost allocation schemes, transfer pricing policies, and the choice of performance measures being the most influential decisions (see chapter B3.3.1.2). In the company of manager E, a rather uncommon evaluation practice has been chosen. Instead of individualized performance measures, the company's overall net income is used by corporate management to assess the variable pay of all middle and senior managers:

> Over here, we don't have individual targets. Of course, it is customary in our industry that 50% of a manager's variable pay is based on individual targets and 50% is based on overall corporate profit . . . However, we say that our managers have to identify with the company and hence there are no individual targets. This means that we only have targets that are exclusively based on the company's net income result.

This evaluation practice however is a rare exception. In all the other companies under investigation, individualized performance measures are chosen that are calculated on the level of local business units. But here again, considerable differences can be found in company practice. The interviews reveal that it is particularly for profit center managers that different bottom-line measures are used for evaluation. The use of different bottom-line measures goes hand in hand with different cost allocation philosophies. Some profit center managers are regarded as running their business unit independently. Hence, as many indirect costs and overhead costs as possible are pushed down to the operating unit level, including corporate headquarter costs, costs for centralized administrative functions, interest expenses, currency expenses, or taxes. Managers D, F, and G are faced with net income measures used for evaluation purposes that include many of these uncontrollable cost elements. Other profit center managers are intentionally protected from such uncontrollable cost elements. They are evaluated on profit before taxes, interest expenses, currency expenses, and other corporate allocations. Managers A, C, and K are faced with such performance measures in which operating profit and earnings before interest and tax (EBIT) are most commonly used.

The comparison of the transfer pricing policies established at the twelve companies discloses further differences in corporate practice of applying the controllability principle. While some companies allow their managers to freely negotiate transfer pricing agreements including the opportunity to choose contractual partners from outside the company, other companies are far more restrictive. Managers F and G point out that they are obliged to purchase goods and services from internal sources wherever possible. Such mandated internal transfers are seen as uncontrollable and disadvantageous by managers F and G because they are confronted with fixed transfer prices, which in some cases exceed comparable prices that can be obtained in the outside market. Manager G, who is head of real estate with a regional airport company, provides the following example:

> What do I have to pay in the outside market when I purchase winter gritting and snow-clearing services? I have to pay about 8 Euros per hour. But the internal transfer price is 48 Euros for our worker who is doing that . . . And that's what I have to pay. The price we charge our customer, however, is 8 Euros. This means that we pass on these 8 Euros

> and the remaining 40 Euros increase the operating costs for this building. This makes the building very expensive to me and I am not allowed to pass on these costs . . . We really have a very strong obligation to contract internally.

Managers F and G further mention a lack of controllability with regard to staffing decisions. Even though their business units are seen as independent entities with net income representing the main basis for evaluation, they are dependent on their superiors in terms of the allocation of personnel. Manager F even reports the existence of a corporate "blueprint" that precisely specifies the maximum costs of personnel for his business unit. He holds the view that "such restrictions strongly constrain my entrepreneurial freedom".

Apart from horizontal and vertical interdependencies, the interviewees also mention external factors that represent an uncontrollable influence to them. However, it is interesting to note that – albeit being aware of uncontrollable external factors – many managers have come to terms with them in a positive sense. It appears that managers are less reluctant to bear the risk arising from uncontrollable external factors than they are with regard to uncontrollable internal factors. Among the uncontrollable external factors mentioned during the interviews are customer decisions (managers B, C, E, F, and I), competitor decisions (managers F and K), changes in the economy (managers D, H, and J), regulatory restrictions (managers D and G), and acts of nature (managers F and K). Most managers declare customer decisions to be the uncontrollable factor with the greatest impact on their performance. In spite of this, they do not necessarily wish the controllability principle to be applied for uncontrollable external factors. It seems that they assume certain risks in their job and – in particular with regard to external factors – they consider that they have to manage these risks. When asked why he does not want his performance to be adjusted for uncontrollable customer decisions, manager E, for example, states the following: "That's because we are highly-paid managers. This is part of our responsibility . . . After all, it is our job to deal with these things." Similar views are expressed by managers I and G. Obviously, some managers tend to regard themselves as entrepreneurs and accept that they should not be fully protected from uncontrollable external factors. Correspondingly, only one of the interviewees (manager D) mentions that adjustments are actually made for external factors. Not only are managers willing to bear the risk from external factors, corporate practice also refrains from making adjustments for them. Hence, as far as uncontrollable external factors are concerned, corporate practice seems to coincide with managers' preferences.

These findings are also reflected in related studies on the controllability principle. Results from Drury and El-Shishini (2005) and Merchant (1987; 1989) support the notion that the principle is often applied to certain uncontrollable factors, but not to others. More specifically, Merchant (1987, pp. 330-331; 1989, pp. 114-115) observes a difference between internal and external uncontrollable factors. His results reveal that in the twelve companies in his study, neutralization of the effects of economic or competitive factors is comparatively rare, while the consequences of vertical interdependencies are eliminated in most of the companies. Unlike Merchant's (1987; 1989) studies, which are concerned with corporate practice and adjustment policies, the more recent work by Giraud et al. (2008) focuses on managers' preferences concerning the application of the controllability principle. They find that "managers adopt a different position depending on the types of uncontrollable factors, segregating internal from external factors. The percentage of managers wanting the impact of internal factors to be completely neutralized is far higher than that for external factors" (Giraud et al., 2008, p. 41).

The foregoing paragraphs show that corporate practice of adjusting for uncontrollable factors varies across companies and types of uncontrollable factors. As Merchant (1987, p. 335) states, "although it is obvious that . . . firms exhibit considerable diversity in the extent to which they implement the controllability principle, explaining why these differences exist is not easy". In this discussion, role theory contributes a helpful perspective in suggesting that differing role expectations on the part of role senders (i.e. superiors and designers of MCSs) represent a plausible reason for the differences in observed corporate practice. In order to shed empirical light on this issue, the interviewees were asked whether they observed some rationale behind the (non)application of the controllability principle in their company. The interview results broadly suggest three tentative explanations: (a) sharing risk, (b) handling complexity, and (c) directing managers' attention. Interestingly, these explanations resemble those that have also been identified in the literature review on the controllability principle in chapter B3.4.

Several interviewees express the opinion that one of the main reasons whether or not their superiors apply the controllability principle in performance evaluation lies in the superiors' intention to share risk. If the superiors themselves are confronted with either controllable or uncontrollable performance measures, they are likely to pass on these measures in an attempt to share the implied risk with their subordinates. Manager D holds this view when searching for a reason why the managing director of his business unit (who is his immediate superior) confronts him with uncontrollable performance targets:

> Well, I think that the managing director also received this kind of target . . . And he passes it on to the plants under his supervision. So, I guess, he cascades his own targets down in a very tight manner so that he himself has the best chance of hitting his targets.

Similarly, managers I and K regard risk sharing as an explanation for the nonapplication of the controllability principle. Both of them refer to external investors who expect a certain return on their investment. According to managers I and K, investors would not accept the existence of uncontrollable influence as an excuse if the company as a whole did not come up with a satisfactory interest payment. Therefore, corporate management passes on this external pressure and does not consider the controllability principle in internal performance evaluation.

The second explanation for the differences observed in the application of the controllability principle can be found in companies' approaches to handling complexity. Managers F and J, who both work for large corporations in dynamic markets, view a relaxation of the controllability principle as a means to cope with high organizational complexity. They think that in particular in complex organizations a strict application of the controllability principle is detrimental in that it reduces interaction and cooperation. Manager J explains the nonapplication of the controllability principle in his company as follows:

> It clearly is a deliberate decision made at top levels that performance measures are defined in such a manner that they necessitate cooperation across intraorganizational boundaries. I think this is a strategy that has been chosen because our business is so complex. If we operated in a different industry, let's say if we produced light bulbs, then we would most probably have structured our company differently, with more transparency and clearer hierarchies and without all these interdependencies. But our business simply is different . . . And such a strategy is thought to be best to handle this enormous complexity.

This quote indicates that organizational complexity makes corporate managers and designers of MCSs carefully assess the appropriateness of the controllability principle. It may be the case that companies opt not to follow the principle, but rather establish far-reaching interdependencies due to wider organizational requirements. A similar finding is reported by Frow et al. (2005), who conducted a case study with a large US technology company and conclude that "the existence of these interdependencies is therefore 'hugely intentional' . . . Interdependency is necessary not only as a consequence of current operating conditions but also as a means of facilitating the collaboration and knowledge sharing" (Frow et al., 2005, p. 277).

The third explanation, which has been brought forward by two interviewees (managers B and E), refers to corporate endeavors to direct managers' attention, in particular to foster managers' entrepreneurial thinking and acting. Manager B regards the nonapplication of the controllability principle in his company as instrumental in "educating" managers to become entrepreneurs:

> Our company is undergoing a transformation . . . Currently, considerable attention is being paid to what kind of people we need . . . They [the company's corporate managers] clearly say that we need people who take care of their own enterprise, who think 'That's my business. It's me who is responsible for it.' Such people do not step back saying 'Hey, I do not have control over the whole thing'. Instead, they have to try

> and exert as much influence as possible. That's on our agenda right now . . . It is entrepreneurship that they are trying to establish at the moment. And this is also communicated from above. In our last meeting, my vice president for Northern Europe said very clearly: 'Guys, it's your business. You have to take care of it . . . That's what I expect and that's what I'll use when evaluating your performance.'

Recent studies by Simons (2007) and Giraud et al. (2008) support this finding. Both identify corporate managers' desire for entrepreneurship as a rationale for the nonapplication of the controllability principle. Stevenson and Jarillo's (1990, p. 23) definition of entrepreneurship thereby proves helpful when linking entrepreneurship to the controllability principle: "Entrepreneurship is a process by which individuals – either on their own or inside organizations – pursue opportunities without regard to the resources they currently control." In a multi-case study with US companies, Simons (2007, p. 14) finds that the application of the controllability principle "depended on the degree of innovation and entrepreneurship that was required for each specific job or function". More specifically, he reports that some corporate managers relax the application of the controllability principle when they want their subordinates to act as entrepreneurs who are innovative and proactively start initiatives. A relaxation of the controllability principle is proposed as being part of a "specific strategy" (Kuratko, Hornsby, Naffziger, & Montagno, 1993, p. 29) to foster entrepreneurship in established organizations. In cases when corporate managers' primary focus is less on entrepreneurship but on reducing innovation and increasing efficiency, Simons (2007, pp. 13-23) finds that the controllability principle is applied more strictly.

In sum, there appears to be strong evidence that the application or nonapplication of the controllability principle is not a question of coincidence. On the contrary, all three explanations provided above indicate that there are organizational interests (see also chapter B3.4) which guide the principle's application in company practice. In other words, whether superiors and designers of MCSs apply or do not apply the controllability principle depends on their role expectations.

2. The Application of the Controllability Principle and Managers' Cognitive Responses

As hypothesized in chapter D2.1, the application of the controllability principle has diverse effects on managers' cognition. On the one hand, it reduces their role stress. Managers who perceive the controllability principle to be applied experience significantly less role conflict and role ambiguity than managers who perceive the principle not to be applied. On the other hand, the application of the controllability principle also reduces managers' flexible role orientation. The higher the managers' perceived controllability in their job, the narrower the role orientation they develop.

2.1 Role Stress

The results of hypothesis testing confirm that the negative effects of the application of the controllability principle on role conflict and role ambiguity are both substantial and highly significant. If managers find the controllability principle to be applied, they regard organizational demands as being consistent and well-aligned (i.e. a decrease in role conflict) and they seem to gain a better understanding of what is expected from them (i.e. a decrease in role ambiguity). The interviews further substantiate these results. In the interview data for managers who declare that their respective superiors show a high regard for the controllability principle, hardly any indication of role conflict and role ambiguity can be found. For example manager A, the manager in the interview sample whose performance evaluation is characterized by the strictest application of the controllability principle, vehemently denies the existence of any ambiguous or conflicting task elements in his job. He states that "I have experienced this in another company . . . But over here we simply don't have that. Such conflicts are avoided. Our measures are clear and in line with each other".

The situation is different for managers whose superiors apply the controllability principle less strictly. The interview data for managers B, D, F, H, and K reveal that certain levels of role conflict and role ambiguity are the consequence when the controllability principle is not implemented. Manager G, who is responsible for real estate at his company, provides a vivid example of conflicting role expectations in his job. He is evaluated on the basis of his profit center's year-end results with sales growth representing one of the key performance measures. In order to boost sales, manager G intends to increase the head count in his advertisement department. However, corporate management and the company's works council make it almost impossible to hire new employees. These opposing positions lead to role conflict for manager G as sales growth turns out to be an uncontrollable target for him:

> Take the advertisement department as an example . . . Today, I have four people working there and we generate a sales volume of something between 4.5 and 5.0 million Euros with these four people. That's what we make today. But we could make 1 million more with every additional employee we recruit for this department. This is totally transparent, the development of the sales figures during the previous years clearly supports this reasoning . . . And now my superior has set the target for me to raise the sales of my business unit. But to hire new personnel in a company like ours is very difficult. There has to be a personnel requisition. Then this new position has to be officially approved. Then there has to be an internal job posting – somebody might be

> interested in this job, so I cannot simply go outside and search for applicants. And then, with our wage agreements, it is not easy to find someone who wants to be responsible for a sales volume of 1 million Euros and who wants to be evaluated on the basis of his performance. This means that I am completely dependent on everybody in the company saying 'Yes, that's the one we want for this job'.

Apart from role conflict that appears to be related to the confrontation with uncontrollable performance targets, the interview data also reveal that role ambiguity arises out of the nonapplication of the controllability principle. Being asked whether he is totally clear about his role and his responsibilities in the company, manager D admits that "most definitely, if you make people responsible for things that are not under their control, you get unclear responsibilities". Similarly, manager F associates role ambiguity with his job. Manager F works as a branch manager for a large logistics company where he is highly dependent on the performance of several related business units. The measures used to evaluate his performance are intimately coupled with the results of these units. Due to such dependencies, he spends considerable time exerting influence on the related units and managing the interfaces between the units. This goes that far that manager F feels uncertain about the range of the duties encompassed by his job. He wonders whether his actual job is running his own business unit or taking charge of other units. The following quote mirrors the ambiguity manager F experiences: "Sometimes, there is not enough transparency. It is like driving on the highway without knowing what the speed limit is. This leads to irritations."

With regard to the survey statistics, the effect of the application of the controllability principle on role conflict is stronger than the effect on role ambiguity. Correspondingly, the principle's application also explains higher proportions of the variance in role conflict than in role ambiguity. The analysis of the moderating effects additionally reveals that the role conflict relationship is robust across the three moderators. Regardless of managers' hierarchical level, self-efficacy, and trust in superior, role conflict is greatly diminished when the controllability principle is applied. None of the three moderators turns out to have a significant effect on the relationship between the application of the controllability principle and role conflict. By contrast, the strength of the relationship between the principle's application and role ambiguity varies with at least one of the moderators. Hence, the application of the controllability principle is not necessarily associated with reductions in role ambiguity. The observed difference between the effects of the principle's application on the two role stress variables is in accordance with extant literature. Reviewing a large body of research on organizational role processes, Fisher and Gitelson (1983, p. 327) point out that "ambiguity may be easier to control or reduce through changed organizational practices than conflict". In the following, the moderating effects are discussed in more detail.

In particular managers' hierarchical level has a strong moderating effect on the relationship between the application of the controllability principle and role ambiguity. It is found that for top managers the association between the two variables is nonexistent while for lower level and middle managers the association is strong and highly significant. The principle's application is hence more effective in reducing role ambiguity among managers at lower hierarchical levels than it is among managers at higher hierarchical levels. Though being insignificant, the moderating effect of managers' hierarchical level on the relationship between the principle's application and role conflict shows a similar pattern. Again, the association between the two variables is weaker for top managers than it is for lower level and middle managers. It can therefore be concluded that the application of the controllability principle is of higher importance in lower and middle management positions than it is at top management level. Top managers seem to be more capable of coping with a lack of controllability than are lower level and middle managers. Literature provides some indication why this is the case. Managers' self-image, motivation, and in particular their risk attitude vary across the hierarchy (Kahn et al., 1964, pp. 137-150; Macko & Tyszka, 2009, pp. 469-470; Sitkin & Pablo, 1992, p. 16). The results from a study by Grey and Gordon (1978, pp. 11-13) suggest that managers at higher hierarchical levels are more risk-oriented and deal more effectively with risk than managers at lower hierarchical levels. This finding corresponds to assumptions in agency theory that principals rather than agents are commonly modeled to bear the risk arising from uncontrollable factors (Eisenhardt, 1989a, p. 58; Frederickson, 1992, p. 651; Shields & Waller, 1988, p. 584). Other studies investigating attitudes and self-perceptions across the hierarchy reveal that managers also place a different emphasis on entrepreneurship depending on their level in the hierarchy. Applying Mintzberg's (1980) distinction between different managerial roles, Alexander (1979, pp. 186-187) and Paolillo (1981, p. 46) both find that the managerial profile of an entrepreneur significantly increases in importance with hierarchical level. Obviously, managers at higher levels are characterized by a more distinctive entrepreneurial attitude than managers at lower levels. Hence, hierarchical level most probably represents a moderator in this study because managers' self-image as entrepreneurs who have to bear the risk of uncontrollable influence on their performance is more pronounced at top management level than at lower and middle management level. This explanation also finds some support in the interview data. Manager E, who belongs to the top management in his company, expresses the following view:

> It is my firm conviction: 'Cling together, swing together!' That's the way I see things. We all have to face our responsibility towards the company and our employees. After all, we want to be responsible for the success of our company and we do almost anything to be successful . . . There is some risk in our job and we have to get along with it.

As far as the moderating effect of managers' self-efficacy is concerned, the statistical results reveal that neither the relationship between the application of the controllability principle and role conflict nor the relationship between the principle's application and role ambiguity is influenced by this personality construct. This is surprising because, theoretically, personality constructs represent important conditioning variables in the relationship between expectations imposed by role senders and role incumbents' responses (Kahn et al., 1964, p. 32; Katz & Kahn, 1978, p. 213). However, despite role theory's strong emphasis on the moderating influence of personality constructs, empirical evidence has generally been rather weak. In the meta-analytical study by Jackson and Schuler (1985, p. 37), it is therefore concluded that there is "little support for the importance of personality variables as important moderators" in role stress relationships. In an attempt to explain why self-efficacy does not operate as a moderator in this research, it may be theorized that self-efficacy has opposing effects on the relationship between the application of the controllability principle and role stress. On the one hand, one might argue that self-efficacy acts as a buffer against role stress with highly self-efficacious managers being less dependent on the principle's application than low self-efficacious managers (Bandura & Wood, 1989, p. 812; Jerusalem & Schwarzer, 1992, pp. 209-210; Speier & Frese, 1997, p. 188). This would imply a positive moderating effect of self-efficacy. On the other hand, it might be the case that in particular managers with high self-efficacy are especially reliant on the principle's application because it is consistent with their general expectation of being in control of their own destiny (Schaubroeck & Merritt, 1997, p. 750). Highly self-efficacious managers could then be eminently vulnerable to breaches of the controllability principle. Following this line of argument, a negative moderating effect of self-efficacy would be expected. Possibly, these two opposing effects cancel each other out across the total sample of managers, which is why no significant moderating effect has been found in this study.

For trust in superior as the third potential moderator, the interview data provide strong indication that managers' attitude towards the application of the controllability principle is influenced by this interpersonal variable. Manager K states that for him "trust is one of the fundamental values. If you don't trust your superior, you will call into question every performance measure you are given by him." It appears from the interview data that managers with high trust in their superior are more willing to accept a relaxation of the controllability principle. The reason for this attitude lies in their confidence that – should they suffer from uncontrollable influence on their performance – superiors will subjectively and ex post take this influence into consideration when deciding on pay and promotion at the year-end. The following quote from manager H reflects this position and highlights the importance of subjectivity:

> If you don't hit your target even though you have worked very hard and more intensively than others, this would still mean 'No bonus!' . . . Subjectivity is a very important criterion. Subjectivity is always associated with something negative, but in the end it [performance evaluation] can only be related to subjective perceptions. For me personally, subjectivity has always turned out to be advantageous and I regard it as a good means because I do not believe in mathematical pseudo-accuracy. I don't think that it is better for managers if their superiors evaluate their performance solely with the help of mathematics and formulas . . . I need trust in my superior in that he listens to me and accepts and considers my opinion and how I see things . . . I need to be certain that he stands behind me.

Similar quotes emphasizing the importance of trust and subjectivity can also be found in the interview data for managers A, B, C, G, and I. Trust and subjectivity seem to compensate for a lack of controllability because trustworthy superiors somewhat relieve managers of the mental discomfort that is associated with a lack of controllability. This finding is closely related to Manzoni's (2002) "new paradigm of management control". In his study with high performance companies, Manzoni (2002) observes the trend towards setting challenging targets and making managers accountable for them without holding on too tightly to ex ante specified, supposedly controllable performance targets. According to Manzoni (2002, p. 41), this balancing act requires a certain degree of trust and subjectivity when evaluating managers' performance: "Performance evaluation and reward is understood to require some managerial judgment, it is understood to be a subjective process." The positive effect that results from a high trust relationship with one's superior is also mirrored in the following quote from manager C. He reports about the consequences when missing his targets due to uncontrollable factors:

> You don't get hanged for that. Of course, you are held responsible for the results. But there are discussions with your superior. These discussions are very solution-oriented. They are focused on how the sinking ship can be saved and put on the right track again.

Despite the strong support for the importance of managers' trust in their superior that emanates from the interview data, the survey statistics provide only weak evidence for a moderating influence of trust. Neither the relationship between the application of the controllability principle and role conflict nor the relationship between the principle's application and role ambiguity is significantly moderated by the trust variable. However, it should be noted that the moderating effect of trust on the role ambiguity relationship only falls marginally below recommended levels of significance. And, content-wise, the moderating effects of trust on both relationships are in agreement with the tentative results from the interviews. Managers in high trust relationships experience less role stress resulting from the nonapplication of the controllability principle than managers in low trust relationships. Put differently, the application of the controllability principle seems to be more important for managers with low trust in their superior than it is for managers with high trust in their superior. In the light of these results and the previous disregard for the concept of trust in management accounting literature (Baldvinsdottir, Hagberg, Johansson, Jonäll, & Marton, 2009, pp. 30-31; Scapens, 2006, p. 23), further research is warranted that explores the interaction of controllability, trust, and subjectivity (Giraud et al., 2008, p. 43).

2.2 Role Orientation

Apart from its effects on role conflict and role ambiguity, the application of the controllability principle is also related to managers' role orientation. The empirical results reveal that the degree of the principle's application has a strong and highly significant impact on how flexible or narrow managers define their role. Role orientation, which describes the psychological boundary of a role (Parker et al., 1997, p. 902), depends on the way the controllability principle is applied. The stricter the principle's application, the narrower the managers' role orientation. If managers are protected from uncontrollable factors in their performance evaluation, they apparently decrease the attention devoted to matters outside their own area of authority and focus their role on managing only those matters that are controllable by them. This finding is in accordance with recent experimental research by Ullrich and Tuttle (2004, pp. 101-102), who report that managers generally tend to shift their attention from areas that are not measured and rewarded to areas that are. In short, if the controllability principle is applied in performance evaluation, managers tend to define their role rather restrictively.

However, literature often accentuates that from an organizational perspective it is desirable to establish a more flexible role orientation among the workforce (Howell & Boies, 2004, pp. 124-125; Parker, 2007, p. 426; Parker et al., 1997, p. 902). Morrison (1994, p. 1563) suggests that it is "an important management function . . . to reduce the perception 'that's not my job'" among organization members. The results of this study indicate that the nonapplication of the controllability principle represents a means of doing so. Not only the survey statistics, but also the interview data support this view. Several interviewees explicitly relate the way they see their role in the company to the controllability of their job. Manager E who experiences a lack of controllability because of strong dependencies on engineering and operations departments describes the effects on his role orientation as follows:

> In the end, it [the way in which performance is evaluated in the company] also serves to broaden one's professional horizon, e.g. with respect to engineering or quality issues . . . One should not shut oneself from such issues . . . Of course, it cannot be the case that

one intervenes in these issues on a daily basis because one does not have enough capacity for that. But one definitely interprets one's role more flexibly, I can tell you.

Recently, management accounting literature has shown an increased interest in this attention-directing effect of holding managers accountable for more than they can directly control (Manzoni, 2002, p. 32; Merchant & Van der Stede, 2007, p. 284; Simons, 2005, pp. 23-26). Empirical support for this effect is provided by Frow et al. (2005). In accordance with the results of this study, they find that when managers are confronted with uncontrollable factors they feel that it is "integral to their role" (Frow et al., 2005, p. 280) to draw their attention to these factors, thus attempting to manage and respond to them.

The analysis of the moderating effects reveals that the relationship between the application of the controllability principle and managers' role orientation depends on two conditioning variables: managers' hierarchical level and their self-efficacy. While the moderating effect of hierarchical level only shows weak significance, the respective effect of self-efficacy is highly significant. Trust in superior as the third potential moderator does not influence the relationship.

With regard to managers' hierarchical level, it turns out that the relationship between the application of the controllability principle and role orientation is stronger for lower level and middle managers than it is for top managers. This implies that for top managers the stimulus of the principle's (non)application is only of minor importance in shaping their role orientation. One possible explanation for this finding is provided by Mehta et al. (1999). They suggest that general managerial philosophy differs across hierarchical levels and empirically find that as "managers are promoted, their perceived role orientation will likely undergo significant change" (Mehta et al., 1999, p. 419). More specifically, Mehta et al.'s (1999) results show that managers at lower levels primarily define their role in terms of their immediate job requirements while managers at higher levels adopt a wider approach to the definition of their role and place greater importance on strategic and more global objectives. These findings relate to this study insofar as they indicate that managers at higher levels regard a flexible role orientation as an integral requirement of their job. Hence, confronting them with a certain degree of controllability probably has a lesser effect (as compared to managers at lower levels) on their role orientation because high-ranking managers display a flexible role orientation anyway. Put differently, the nonapplication of the controllability principle seems less effective in evoking a flexible role orientation for top managers than it is for lower level and middle managers. However, given the weak significance of the moderating effect of managers' hierarchical level, this finding should not be overinterpreted.

A higher level of significance is found for the moderating influence of managers' self-efficacy. Analyzing the relationship between the application of the controllability principle and role orientation in dependence on managers' self-efficacy, the moderator tests reveal a very significant influence of this personality variable. Its moderating influence is particularly strong because for managers with low self-efficacy the effect of the principle' application on role orientation is insignificant whereas the same effect turns out to be strong and very significant for managers with high self-efficacy. When highly self-efficacious managers are confronted with a strict application of the controllability principle, this makes them adopt a very narrow role orientation. Conversely, a relaxation of the controllability principle is especially appropriate in the evaluation of highly self-efficacious managers because it is only them who respond to this stimulus by reinterpreting their role. Highly self-efficacious managers seem to be able to cope more effectively with a perceived lack of controllability than low self-efficacious managers. They are more likely to undergo a "learning process" (Parker, 2000, p. 453) and develop a flexible role orientation in response to the nonapplication of the principle. This learning process is based on the belief of highly self-efficacious managers that they "may compensate for a lack of control because they will assume to be able to influence things despite the lack of situational support" (Speier & Frese, 1997). Related research by Bandura and Wood (1989, pp. 806-813) and Parker (1993, pp. 951-956) supports the notion that high self-efficacy leads individuals to be confident in their capability of managing, through ingenuity and perseverance, the uncontrollable factors they are confronted with. Since managers with low self-efficacy lack this confidence, they suffer more severely from the nonapplication of the controllability principle and are not capable of developing a flexible orientation as part of a coping mechanism. Interestingly, when managers respond to a lack of controllability by adapting the way they see their role, such changes in their role orientation also seem to result in personally advantageous side-effects. Results from a study by Frow et al. (2005, p. 283) indicate that a conscious mental effort to deal with uncontrollable factors "allows the individual manager to retain some sense of 'being in control' in situations where there is only partial controllability". Having internalized such a flexible role orientation, managers are in some instances even reported not to want the controllability principle to be applied any more (Frow et al., 2005, p. 289; Giraud et al., 2008, p. 41). However, the results of this study indicate that such a positive approach to coping with the principle's nonapplication is only feasible for managers with high self-efficacy.

Unlike managers' self-efficacy and hierarchical level, trust in superior does not moderate the relationship between the application of the controllability principle and role orientation. There is some tentative indication in the literature (Clegg et al., 2002, p. 411; Crant, 2000, pp. 449-450; Kassing, 1998, p. 204) suggesting that superiors' support and trustworthiness might have an influence on whether job characteristics affect individuals' role perceptions. However neither the interview data nor the survey statistics provide empirical evidence for this conjecture.

3. The Application of the Controllability Principle and Managers' Affective Responses

The empirical results of this study confirm that the application of the controllability principle is associated with both decreased job tension and heightened job satisfaction. In accordance with role theory, these effects are completely mediated by role conflict and role ambiguity. This is an important finding because it suggests that the application of the principle is not per se beneficial to managers' psychological well-being, but operates only through the two role stress variables.

3.1 Job Tension

Qualitative evidence for a relationship between the application of the controllability principle and job tension is found in the interview data. In particular, the data provide support for a stress-inducing effect of the principle's nonapplication in performance appraisals. Several interviewees (managers C, D, E, F, J, and K) acknowledge feelings of tension and pressure that arise from the confrontation with uncontrollable performance measures. Manager C states that "this implies stress because one is confronted with these measures every month". The fact that their measured performance depends on factors beyond their control with potentially adverse effects on pay and promotion seems to be of considerable concern to managers.

In this context, it is interesting to note that managers almost unanimously refer to uncontrollable factors as having disadvantageous effects on their measured performance. They fear suffering from "bad luck". This suggests that, in managers' minds, the controllability principle is first and foremost relevant to unfavorable influence. Apparently, this view is rather asymmetric because managers seem to ignore that uncontrollable factors can also affect their performance positively. Managers seem to blank out situations of "good luck", which are de facto related to the controllability principle the same way as situations of "bad luck". Such a finding is consistent with the results provided by Giraud et al. (2008). They report that out of 260 comments gathered from managers with regard to the perceived effects of uncontrollable factors, only one referred to "good luck" situations. Since management accounting literature has not yet investigated this phenomenon in depth (Giraud et al., 2008, p. 36), additional research is warranted here.

When relating the qualitative interview findings to the survey statistics, it turns out that the effect of the application of the controllability principle on managers' job tension is indirect. The principle's application has an immediate effect on levels of role stress which, in turn, is associated with job tension. Noteworthily, the effect of the principle's application on job tension is only mediated by role conflict whereas role ambiguity has no significant impact on managers' job tension. This finding is unexpected and challenges prior research on role stress (Fisher & Gitelson, 1983, p. 324; Jackson & Schuler, 1985, p. 23) since it has commonly been reported that role ambiguity represents a meaningful antecedent variable of job tension. One explanation for this finding might be that the subjects of most previous studies examining the role ambiguity – job tension relationship have been nurses, educators, social workers, and other nonmanagerial staff (Jackson, Turner, & Brief, 1987; Lloyd, King, & Chenoweth, 2002; Martin, 1984; Schwab & Iwanicki, 1982). Possibly, managers perceive role ambiguity as less stressful than other occupational groups. Van Sell, Brief, and Schuler's (1981, p. 50) observation that the effects of role ambiguity on affective outcomes depend on individuals' professional backgrounds further supports this explanation.

Among the studies that have investigated the consequences of role stress in a managerial context, some detect a strong effect of role ambiguity on job tension (e.g. Hamner and Tosi (1974) or Singh (1998)) whilst others only find a comparatively weak effect (e.g. Moncrief, Babakus, Cravens, and Johnston (1997)). Others again report an insignificant effect (e.g. Tosi (1971)). Apart from the use of a diverse set of measurement scales, compelling reasons for these variations in empirical results have so far not been provided in literature (Jackson & Schuler, 1985, p. 40). One of the few patterns that seems to be consistent throughout prior research and that also shows up in this study is that role conflict is more strongly related to job tension than role ambiguity (Fogarty et al., 2000, p. 56; Jackson & Schuler, 1985, p. 40; Moncrief et al., 1997, p. 794). Altogether, it appears that in particular the effect of role ambiguity on job tension is less clear than previously thought, which recommends further empirical investigation into managers' coping with this type of role stress.

3.2 Job Satisfaction

In accordance with McNally (1980, p. 168), who proposes that "dissatisfaction may occur" when responsibility is at variance with authority, the empirical results confirm that the application of the controllability principle affects managers' job satisfaction. This is reflected in the following quote from the interview with manager H, who elaborates on his feelings towards the lack of controllability of his performance targets:

> Initially, there is frustration. And this frustration then makes me ignore such performance targets . . . This isn't constructive anymore. I really have to rein myself in . . . I mean I don't get gastric ulcer, but my satisfaction with this job decreases.

Managers D, F, and K share this view. Manager K even mentions that some colleagues of his left the company due to corporate practice of not adjusting for uncontrollable factors in year-end performance appraisals. It appears that the application of the controllability principle is an important determinant of job satisfaction among managers.

The survey statistics provide further support for this conjecture. The application of the controllability principle has a considerable and highly significant effect on job satisfaction. However, as for job tension, this effect is completely mediated by role stress. Hence, the principle's application only indirectly affects job satisfaction through role conflict and role ambiguity with both role stress variables capturing discrete parts of the direct effect. As proposed by theory, role conflict and role ambiguity are each an important antecedent variable of managers' job satisfaction. This is in line with previous research on job satisfaction which has shown that individuals have a certain need for clarity and consistency in superiors' role expectations, which accounts for variations in levels of satisfaction (Benson, Kemery, Sauser, & Tankesley, 1985, pp. 127-129; Thakur, Burton, & Srivastava, 1997, pp. 222-223; Warr, 2007, pp. 371-372). Managers usually want their superiors to assist them in dealing with uncertainties implicated in their job. If however the expectations held by superiors are themselves ambiguous and conflicting, dissatisfaction with the job is likely to occur (Spector, 1997, pp. 39-40; Thakur et al., 1997, p. 223).

4. The Application of the Controllability Principle and Managers' Behavioral Responses

This study's empirical results show that the application of the controllability principle does not only have effects on managers' job tension and job satisfaction, but also entails behavioral responses. From an organizational perspective, these behavioral responses imply both functional and dysfunctional consequences. On the one hand, the principle's application is causally related to an increase in managers' in-role performance, measured as the quality of their decisions. On the other hand, it has a negative effect on managers' extra-role performance, measured in terms of their internal influence behavior. These findings reflect why there has been such an intensive discussion of the controllability principle in extant literature (Drury & El-Shishini, 2005, pp. 20-25; Giraud et al., 2008, pp. 33-34; Manzoni, 2002, pp. 32-33). Obviously, it cannot be generally concluded whether applying or not applying the controllability principle is the better recommendation (Merchant, 1989, p. 130; Modell, 1997, p. 314).

4.1 In-Role Performance

It is well accepted that "how individuals in organizations make decisions and the quality of their final choices are largely influenced by their perceptions" (Robbins, 2003, p. 131). Management accounting literature has traditionally associated managers' perceived lack of controllability with the risk of inferior decision-making and dysfunctional behaviors (Choudhury, 1986, p. 192; Modell, 1997, p. 313). Manzoni (2002, p. 33), for example, suggests that holding managers accountable for uncontrollable factors "may lead them to make sub-optimal decisions".

The interview data gathered within this study provide some support for this conjecture. Manager H points out that it is common practice in his company to intentionally build unnecessary slack into initial performance targets – behavior which is commonly regarded as dysfunctional in literature (Davis et al., 2006, p. 21; Douglas et al., 2007, p. 93). According to manager H, the creation of slack represents a means to buffer managers against uncontrollable factors which come up during the year and which might not be adjusted for by superiors. This is in accordance with the results from a study by Kren (2003). He analyzes several motives which might lead managers to create slack and finds empirically that the desire to hedge against uncertainties in the environment is the strongest predictor of slack (Kren, 2003, pp. 158-162). Further dysfunctional behaviors associated with the nonapplication of the controllability principle are reported by managers B, D, and J. They describe the development of an "excuse culture" as the result of holding managers accountable for uncontrollable factors. According to manager D, "there are basically always thousands of possible excuses. And with all these excuses, one can get away pretty comfortably if one wants to grow old here". Time-consuming discussions with superiors, lamentations, and politicking among the managerial staff are frequently mentioned throughout the interviews, which is very similar to the empirical evidence provided in case studies undertaken by Merchant (1989, pp. 135-137). Manager K depicts the behavior of his subordinate sales managers confronted with performance measures that seem uncontrollable to them as follows:

> They say 'No, I can't manage that!'. Then they start writing applications, . . . or have a moan, or wander around in my team and tell everybody how upset they are . . . Employees spend so much time on such things and, while they are doing that, they are not productive in sales.

Further evidence for an effect of the application of the controllability principle on managers' in-role performance comes from the quantitative survey results. As hypothesized, the principle's application is causally related to higher in-role performance with the entire effect operating through role conflict and role ambiguity. When managers perceive the controllability principle to be applied, they experience less role stress which, in turn, increases the quality of their decisions and hence their in-role performance. While both role conflict and role ambiguity are negatively associated with in-role performance, the statistical results reveal that the relationship between role ambiguity and in-role performance is stronger and more significant than the relationship between role conflict and in-role performance. This finding is consistent with previous research on the consequences of the two role stress variables (Burney & Widener, 2007, p. 60; House & Rizzo, 1972, pp. 500-501; Miles, 1976, pp. 32-33; Tubre & Collins, 2000, pp. 164-165; Viator, 2001, pp. 84-85). Obviously, high in-role performance is hindered more fiercely by perceptions of ambiguous role expectations than by perceptions of conflicting role expectations. This confirms Jackson and Schuler's (1985, p. 43) and Gilboa et al.'s (2008, pp. 250-251) proposition that – especially due to ambiguous role expectations – decisions are most likely to be misdirected and inefficient, which results in a deterioration of in-role performance. It is also congruent with transactional stress theory (Lazarus & Folkman, 1984) which regards role ambiguity as most detrimental to performance.

4.2 Extra-Role Performance

Despite detrimental effects of the nonapplication of the controllability principle on in-role performance, prominent management accounting scholars such as Merchant and Van der Stede (2007, p. 284) suggest that "sometimes managers are held accountable for financial line items over which they have no direct authority because the accountability empowers them to influence the actions of those who do have direct authority". Internal influence behavior as one type of extra-role performance is hence supposed to be related to the nonapplication of the controllability principle.

Several cues pointing in this direction can be found in the interview data. The majority of the interviewees (managers B, C, D, E, F, G, J, and K) indicate that their exertion of influence on other departments and cross-departmental cooperation are rooted in the nature of their performance measures and, in particular, in the controllability of the measures. They state that since their controllability over performance measures is less then 100%, internal influence behavior arises as an informal way of compensating for the lack of formal authority. As suggested by organizational behavior scholars (Ashford & Black, 1996; Crant, 2000; Frese & Fay, 2001), it seems that through such proactive behavior "work then becomes . . . more controllable" (Frese & Fay, 2001, p. 162). This finding compares to case study results reported by Marginson (1999) and Frow et al. (2005). They conducted case studies in companies where interdependencies are generally high and individual controllability correspondingly low. In conditions where the strict application of the controllability principle is hardly feasible, Marginson (1999, p. 217) recognizes that "social pressure was acting as a substitute for formal authority". Frow et al. (2005, p. 270) similarly come to the conclusion that "managers use . . . social interaction, both formally and informally, to address the lack of individual controllability". In the light of these findings, Berry et al. (2009, p. 11) observe that there is a trend in performance evaluation towards the "deliberate violation of the controllability principle to create tensions which encourage unit managers to engage in informal social interaction beyond their functional boundaries".

Social interaction can thereby take different forms. Some interviewees put strong emphasis on aspects of cooperation and mutual support. Manager C, who works as a branch manager for an HR services company, mentions such behavioral effects. In his company, the measures which are used to evaluate branch managers' performance appear to be uncontrollable by the managers because the measures are subject to influence from interdependent branches and headquarter departments. Manager C declares that if the controllability principle was more strictly applied and if branch managers were only held accountable for performance measures which are entirely controllable by them,

> the collaboration between the branches would decline. Then everybody would find it easier to achieve their targets . . . But the gains are, of course, much larger when we have to collaborate and communicate intensively. Unfortunately, some colleagues don't understand that. Many of them only see their own branches and care for their own matters . . . And [due to the lack of individual controllability] it's them who are compelled – in a positive sense – to broaden their horizon and to search for new opportunities . . . I think there is a relationship between the intensity of collaboration between our branches and the manner in which performance is measured here.

Other interviewees describe their influence behavior as being more challenging. Manager K, a sales manager faced with a lack of controllability because of a high dependency on the product development department, states that "we exchange our opinions and our colleagues are not always pleased to see us because we really take them [the product development managers] under fire". Manager B, who finds himself in similar strong dependencies, even regards the exertion of influence on others as an integral part of his managerial position: "It's the core of my job to kick other people's asses!" Manager E chooses a different wording to describe his influence attempts. He sees himself as fulfilling the function of a "watchdog", meaning that the perceived lack of controllability makes him keep an eye on how other managers do their job:

> I look more closely at other business units and play the role of a watchdog for them. And the managers of these business units do the same with regard to my own unit. In the end, this has led to an approach where we do not monitor each other because we mean mischief or impute mismanagement to others. It is rather a control mechanism ensuring that everybody keeps in line in order not to endanger the overall corporate target . . . That way we are more flexible because things lie on the shoulders of more than one individual . . . And I truly regard this as a competitive advantage.

A more subtle form of taking influence is mentioned by manager G. He highlights the importance of persuasion through persistent discussions and negotiations:

> I think I can cope with that [a lack of controllability] fairly well . . . The things I do can be best described as taking indirect influence. This implies discussing with colleagues, . . . influencing work groups, and convincing managing directors . . . It's an indirect and

> informal approach that implies using all means available to exert influence . . . It's about trying to persuade people without going the formal and organizationally directed way . . . So one has the best chance of getting things done.

Obviously, there are different approaches to exert influence. What they have in common is that managers proactively attempt to manage uncontrollable factors without relying on formal authority given to them. It appears that managers increasingly switch from formal authority to informal authority (see also chapter B2.2) in order to fulfill their responsibilities. Falling back to informal authority and taking influence on issues that are not totally controllable by them, managers seem to adhere to what has been designated as the influenceability principle in chapter B1.2.3.

The survey statistics provide further support for this conjecture. They reveal that the application of the controllability principle is causally related to managers' internal influence behavior and that this effect is indirect through role orientation. Managers' perception of the controllability principle being (not) applied changes their role orientation which, in turn, has an effect on their internal influence behavior. More specifically, it is only when managers are confronted with the principle's nonapplication that they develop a more flexible role orientation. A flexible role orientation then represents the cognitive prerequisite for an activation of internal influence behavior. This is an important contribution to research in this area because the antecedents of such proactive extra-role behaviors are currently not well understood (Frese & Fay, 2001, p. 167; Griffin et al., 2007, p. 343; Parker et al., 2006, p. 636).

As Lawler (1994, p. 5) describes, organizations need to "develop individuals to perform in new and more complex ways". Proactive extra-role behaviors such as internal influence behavior are supposed to become more critical determinants of organizational success (Crant, 2000, p. 435). Hence, companies are advised to focus on correcting organizational structures and systems that minimize and mitigate individual initiative (Frohman, 1997, p. 52). This study indicates that the decreased emphasis on the controllability principle in the design of MCSs might be a suitable approach in signaling to managers that they are expected to show individual initiative and act on seemingly uncontrollable factors. This is also reflected in Otley's (1994, p. 296) demand on how contemporary MCSs should direct managers' behavior:

> The objective of the control system now becomes the encouragement of work groups at all levels to take control into their own hands to a much greater extent than has been traditional, and to take responsibility for maintaining the viability of their part of the organization relative to its environment.

H Conclusion

This part summarizes the key findings of this study and its contribution to management accounting theory (chapter H1). Following the discussion of this study's theoretical implications, managerial implications are derived as to when and why the controllability principle should be (or should not be) applied in the design of MCSs (chapter H2). Finally, a number of limitations to this study need to be mentioned in order to provide guidance and suggestions for future research (chapter H3).

1. Summary of the Results

The starting point for this study was the lack of empirical research on managers' responses to the application of the controllability principle in their performance evaluation. Two decades ago, it was Merchant (1987), who expressed his concern with the state of knowledge and called for further management accounting research in this area: "What are the consequences, both favorable and unfavorable, of holding managers accountable for uncontrollables?" (Merchant, 1987, p. 317). Research on the controllability principle has since made only little progress and Merchant's question remains to be answered on the grounds of empirical data. For this reason, contemporary management accounting scholars still show their discontent with what is known about the effects of applying (or not applying) the principle (Atkinson et al., 1997, p. 84; Drury & El-Shishini, 2005, p. 5; Drury & Tayles, 1995, p. 276; Ghosh, 2005, p. 56; Giraud et al., 2008, p. 33; Simons, 2007, p. 3).

Unlike previous research on the controllability principle that has been dominated by the perspective of evaluators and system designers (Giraud et al., 2008, p. 34), this study focused on the managers who are themselves confronted with a certain degree of controllability. It is argued that their responses to the application of the controllability principle ultimately determine the principle's relevance for organizational effectiveness and managerial motivation (Marginson & Ogden, 2005b, p. 49). The purpose of this study was therefore to comprehensively investigate managers' cognitive, affective, and behavioral responses to the application of the controllability principle bearing in mind that the principle's application should be understood as a question of benefits and costs associated with it (Atkinson et al., 1997, p. 84; Choudhury, 1986, pp. 196-197; Merchant, 1989, p. 130; Modell, 1997, p. 314).

In the investigation of managers' responses to the application of the controllability principle, this study was guided by role theory (Kahn et al., 1964; 1966; Katz & Kahn, 1966; 1978) which led to the development of moderated mediation models. Based on role theory, the application of the controllability principle was thought to have indirect effects on affective and behavioral outcome variables. These effects were proposed to operate through cognitive role variables representing the mental mechanisms that underlie the relationships between the principle's application and its observable implications.

To test the proposed relationships, a postpositivistic research methodology was followed. In a two-staged research process, interview and survey data were sequentially gathered. In the first phase of data collection, 12 semi-structured interviews with business unit and functional managers were used to gain preliminary insights into the research subject and to refine the formulated hypotheses. In the second research phase, a questionnaire was distributed among a random sample of 3,500 managers providing the quantitative data for hypothesis testing. The final sample consisted of 432 managers, yielding an effective response rate of 12.3%. SEM was subsequently used to analyze the data and to investigate if the hypothesized relationships hold empirically. The resultant key findings of this study are summarized as follows, using the order in which the research questions were posed:

Research question 1: Does the application of the controllability principle have an effect on managers' behavior?

According to Merchant and Simons (1986, p. 193), management accounting research "should focus on problems that are widely appreciated by managers to be costly in organizational terms, on problems where benefits and costs can be considered simultaneously". Following this logic, the application of the controllability principle is a problem that qualifies for academic discourse in management accounting. It is one of this study's key findings that the application of the controllability principle represents a design characteristic of MCSs which invokes both functional and dysfunctional behavioral responses. The study insofar confirms the view of several management accounting scholars that the principle's application comes along with benefits as well as costs. On the one hand, the principle's application is causally related to an increase in managers' in-role performance, measured as the quality of their decisions. According to the survey data, managers confronted with the application of the principle tend to make better decisions. Correspondingly, the interview data indicate that the principle's application is associated with advantageous responses in that managers are less prone to succumb to opportunistic behaviors such as creating slack or adopting a mentality of excuses. On the other hand, the principle's application is causally related to a decrease in managers' extra-role performance, measured as the degree of their internal influence behavior. In accordance with predictions by Atkinson et al. (1997, p. 84) and Bento and White (1998, p. 51), the strict application of the controllability principle turns out to be a constraint to innovative and proactive employee behavior. As Kennedy and Schleifer (2006, p. 126) suggest, "the controllability principle may reduce innovation . . . by restricting actions and decisions". When the controllability principle is followed with all uncontrollable influence being eliminated, managers are induced to lessen the attention they would otherwise devote to factors that are outside their immediate area of authority: "Holding managers accountable for only those variables directly under their control does not give them an incentive to take actions that can affect the consequences of the uncontrollable event" (Zimmerman, 2009, p. 189).

In accordance with Catasús, Ersson, Gröjer, and Wallentin (2007, p. 506) and Ullrich and Tuttle (2004, p. 101), the empirical results of this study prove that performance measurement and evaluation are powerful mechanisms for influencing behavior. Otley (2003, p. 319) states that what gets measured also gets managed and what is not measured may suffer in comparison. The aphorism of "what gets measured, gets managed" also applies to the interpretation of this study's results. If performance is measured and evaluated solely on the basis of variables that are deemed controllable, managers are likely to focus their effort on these aspects of performance. If performance is however evaluated in a way that managers are not protected from uncontrollable factors, they are likely to realign their effort in an attempt to respond to these factors. This is why "decisions regarding implementation of the controllability principle boil down to striking a relatively complex tradeoff between the costs and benefits of doing so" (Modell, 1997, p. 314). The appropriateness of the controllability principle appears to be situation-specific and depends on role senders' respective expectations. When role senders' focus is on ensuring optimal decision-making within each area of authority, then the strict application of the controllability principle seems the best recommendation. However, when role senders' intention is to motivate the exertion of reciprocal influence, knowledge exchange, and stimulation across departmental boundaries, then the relaxation of the principle's application seems opportune.

Research question 2: Does the application of the controllability principle have an effect on managers' psychological well-being?

The empirical results for research question 1 reveal that, from an organizational perspective, the application of the controllability principle yields a complex set of behavioral responses that include both desirable and undesirable components. From an individual perspective, the conclusion that can be drawn from the empirical results appears to be less complex. The analysis of research question 2 indicates that the principle's application fosters managers' psychological well-being. They experience less tension and are also more satisfied with their job when the principle is observed in the evaluation of their performance. This study's results therefore provide some support for the view that "workers intuitively prefer accounting systems that hold them responsible for only outcomes over which they have control" (Frederickson & Waller, 2005, p. 710). Despite some indication in previous research that managers may not always want the controllability principle to be applied (Frow et al., 2005, pp. 288-289; Giraud et al., 2008, pp. 40-41; Merchant, 1987, p. 334), the large-scale results of this study highlight the principle's importance for the provision of a gratifying job experience to managers. Since job tension and job satisfaction are often found to be strongly related to critical outcomes such as voluntary employee turnover (Carsten & Spector, 1987, pp. 376-377; Harter, Schmidt, & Hayes, 2002, p. 273; Judge, 1993, p. 399; Warr, 2005, p. 565), the application of the controllability principle seems to emerge as an important predictor of managers' overall attitude towards their work.

Research question 3: Do managers' role perceptions mediate the proposed relationships between the application of the controllability principle and managers' behavior and psychological well-being?

In an effort to investigate and explain the mental mechanisms that underlie the relationships between the application of the controllability principle and its observable implications, this study proposed managers' role perceptions as mediators. The empirical results confirm that the effects of the principle's application on affective and behavioral outcomes are indirect through role conflict, role ambiguity, and role orientation.

When managers perceive the controllability principle to be applied, they experience both less role conflict and less role ambiguity. As proposed by Huffman and Cain (2000, p. 804), applying the controllability principle and hence "adjusting for uncontrollable factors may help make evaluation systems more useful" because managers then perceive a higher degree of clarity and consistency in the role expectations they are confronted with. This decrease in role conflict and role ambiguity in turn positively affects managers' in-role performance, reduces their job tension, and heightens their job satisfaction. Noteworthily, the three relationships between the application of the controllability principle and in-role performance, job tension, and job satisfaction are all completely mediated by role conflict and role ambiguity. When controlling for role conflict and role ambiguity, the principle's application does not exert any significant direct effect on the outcome variables. This is in accordance with other contemporary management accounting studies which provide strong evidence that design characteristics of MCSs seldom have direct effects on observable outcomes. Instead, it is commonly found that these effects operate through cognitive variables (e.g. Burney and Widener (2007), Hall (2008), or Marginson and Bui (2009)).

As far as the causal effect of the principle's application on managers' extra-role performance is concerned, the empirical results reveal that this relationship is also indirect in nature. Role orientation intervenes in the relationship between the application of the controllability principle and internal influence behavior. When managers perceive the strict application of the controllability principle, they adopt a fairly narrow role orientation. Conversely, with the nonapplication of the controllability principle managers develop a more flexible role orientation as the result of a learning process. Hence, it turns out that the way in which managers define their role in the organization is shaped by the degree of applying (or not applying) the principle in their performance evaluation. A flexible role orientation which describes individuals' propensity to go beyond narrow job descriptions and to devote attention to matters outside their own area of authority is often considered a desirable employee trait (Howell & Boies, 2004, pp. 124-125; Morrison, 1994, p. 1563; Parker et al., 1997, p. 902) because it "will motivate proactive behaviors, such as pursuing improvements in domains beyond one's immediate job" (Parker, 2007, p. 411). In fact, this study's empirical results confirm that the way managers define their role influences their subsequent behavior. Once having adopted a more flexible role orientation, they increase their extra-role performance, measured as the degree of internal influence behavior. As a consequence, and in accordance with many organizational scholars who emphasize the importance of such behavior (Cobb, 1980, p. 159; Podsakoff et al., 2000, pp. 550-551; Yukl et al., 2005, p. 705), "the generality of the traditional view that performance appraisal should exclude noncontrollable factors is questionable" (Choudhury, 1986, p. 197).

Research question 4: Do organizational factors, personality factors, and interpersonal relations moderate the proposed relationships between the application of the controllability principle and managers' role perceptions?

Management accounting scholars such as Modell (1997, p. 314) claim the appropriateness of the controllability principle to "be related to a broader contextual frame of reference". Likewise, Atkinson et al. (1997, p. 84) put situational emphasis on the principle's appropriateness by advising researchers to "develop and test theories that predict advantageous conditions for assigning responsibility for events not directly controllable by the manager". In the light of this study's results, showing that the application of the principle is associated with both functional and dysfunctional consequences, it stands to reason that further empirical insights are needed as to identify conditions under which the principle's application (or nonapplication) is particularly desirable. This notion is rooted in a contingency perspective on the design of MCSs: "There is a pressing need for studies into situations in which contemporary MCS [*sic*] may be best suited" (Chenhall, 2003, p. 130). Moderating variables (managers' hierarchical level, self-efficacy, and trust in superior) were therefore introduced to examine if managers' responses to the controllability principle vary across different contexts. Since it was hypothesized and empirically confirmed that the application of the controllability principle has direct effects only on the three role variables (i.e. role conflict, role ambiguity, and role orientation), it is these relationships that were tested for moderation.

The moderator analyses reveal that in particular managers' hierarchical level plays an important part in the elaboration on the appropriateness of the controllability principle. It is found that managers at higher hierarchical levels (as opposed to managers at lower hierarchical levels) experience less role stress when being confronted with the nonapplication of the principle. It is only to a minor extent that high-ranking managers expect the principle to be applied, which is presumably due to their distinct self-image. The complementary interview data and prior research indicate that a more pronounced entrepreneurial attitude together with a higher readiness to assume risk are characteristic of managers in top positions (Grey & Gordon, 1978, pp. 11-13; Paolillo, 1981, p. 46).

Self-efficacy as the second moderating variable under investigation has an influence on the relationship between the application of the controllability principle and managers' role orientation. More specifically, the empirical results indicate that only for managers with high self-efficacy there is a significant impact of the principle's application on role orientation. Unlike managers with low self-efficacy, they adapt their role orientation in an attempt to deal with a particular degree of controllability they are confronted with. Hence, corporate practice of not applying the controllability principle appears to be more suitable in the appraisal of highly self-efficacious managers. A relaxation of the principle is especially appropriate here because highly self-efficacious managers are able to cope more effectively with the principle's nonapplication and respond to this stimulus by reinterpreting their role.

For trust in superior as the third potential moderator, no significant influence is found in the quantitative survey data. Neither the relationships between the application of the controllability principle and the role stress variables nor the relationship between the principle's application and role orientation are subject to a significant moderating effect of trust. This is somewhat surprising since the qualitative interview data provide strong indication that managers' trust in their superior represents an important variable in the explanation of managers' attitude toward the principle. Several interviewees emphasize a positive interpersonal relationship with their superior as being a critical factor in performance appraisals. Managers seem to attach considerable importance to their superiors' trustworthiness because it relieves some of the mental discomfort that is associated with the nonapplication of the controllability principle. However, in the light of both the quantitative survey data and the qualitative interview data, this study's empirical support for an interaction effect of trust remains only tentative.

In reply to the above research questions, this study was guided by role theory. While most previous research on the controllability principle has been dominated by motivational theories (see chapters B2.3.1 to B2.3.5), the empirical results highlight the meaningful contribution that role theory can make in this field. According to Kaplan (1986, p. 444), a multitude of theories is not an obstacle to scientific progress; it mirrors researchers' exhaustive attempts to comprehensively cover a particular research topic: "Because of the complexity and ambiguity of social/managerial phenomena, it seems more likely that we will continue to have competing theories co-existing, as a function of researchers' varying perceptions of the critical issues in the phenomena they observe".

Role theory contributes to this study in the following ways: First, it provides a suitable vehicle to simultaneously examine the benefits and the costs of applying the controllability principle in the evaluation of managerial performance. The theoretical constructs of role conflict and role ambiguity on the one hand, and role orientation on the other hand, have considerable explanatory power in the analysis of the functional and dysfunctional implications that are associated with the principle. Second, and closely related to the aforementioned point, role theory helps to improve our understanding of the cognitive mechanisms that explain the effects of work stimuli on observable outcomes. Design characteristics of MCSs (such as the application of the controllability principle), and job design in general, seldom have direct effects on affective and behavioral variables. Instead, the effects often seem to be indirect through individuals' cognition and, in particular, their role perceptions (Hall, 2008, p. 142; Shields et al., 2000, pp. 197-198). Third, role theory puts emphasis on the basic role processes being embedded in what Kahn et al. (1964, p. 37) refer to as "surrounding conditions". Organizational factors, personality factors, and interpersonal relations are suggested by role theory to have a moderating influence on how individuals cope with the role expectations they are confronted with. This study succeeds in identifying two contextual variables (managers' hierarchical level and their self-efficacy) which have a strong moderating influence on the role processes under investigation. Fourth, role theory is helpful in the interpretation of why the application of the controllability principle as a corporate practice varies in organizations. It appears that superiors and designers of MCSs have differing role expectations on the basis of which they make intentional decisions as to whether applying or not applying the principle is more appropriate. The interview data gathered for this study as well as findings from prior research (Berry et al., 2009, p. 11; Dent, 1987, p. 139; Frow et al., 2005, pp. 276-277; Simons, 2007, pp. 13-23) confirm that the implementation of a certain degree of controllability most often is not a matter of coincidence, but rests upon a set of organizational interests. In sum, there are strong arguments for employing role theory in management accounting research on the controllability principle. This study hence concurs with Frink and Klimoski (1998, p. 21) in stating that "a role theory perspective adds value to any treatment of accountability in work settings".

2. Practical Implications

Relating their theoretical framework to the practice of management and leadership, Katz and Kahn (1966, p. 388) specify different types of behavior which are necessary for overall organizational effectiveness and which should therefore be encouraged by corporate structures and systems:

> Three categories of behavior are required to achieve high levels of organizational effectiveness. People must *join and remain* in the organization; they must *perform dependably* the roles assigned to them; and they must *engage in occasional innovative and cooperative behavior* beyond the requirements of role but in the service of organizational objectives [emphasis in original].

The empirical results of this study reveal that with the application of the controllability principle organizations have a stimulus at hand which may be used to activate these three types of behavior. However, the principle's application affects the different behaviors in rather opposing ways. On the one hand, the application of the principle is positively associated with the first two types of behavior. When managers are confronted with a high degree of controllability, they experience lower job tension and higher job satisfaction, which presumably increases their intention to join and remain in the organization. They also show superior in-role performance or, as Katz and Kahn (1966, p. 388) put it, they dependably perform the roles assigned to them. On the other hand, the application of the controllability principle is inversely related to the third type of behavior. A high degree of controllability has detrimental effects on managers' role orientation and subsequent extra-role performance. Managers do not feel the need to go beyond their prescribed role and to engage in innovative and cooperative behavior when the controllability principle is applied. As noted by Morrison and Phelps (1999, p. 403), "extra-role behaviors are not motivated by the same factors as traditional, role-prescribed activities". Clearly, it is an important practical implication that organizations should become aware of different stimuli being required in order to maximize the three different types of behavior (Katz & Kahn, 1978, p. 760).

In the practitioner literature, there is often a strong and somewhat unreflected emphasis on the desirability of choosing controllable performance measures (e.g. Orens and Elliott (1997, pp. 46-53), Heneman (2001, p. 250), or Niven (2002, pp. 207-210)). The empirical results reported here are to remind corporate managers and system designers that the intuitive appeal of the controllability principle and the supposed generality of its appropriateness may be misleading. It is unlikely that it can be stated in a general and normative way whether applying or not applying the controllability principle is the better recommendation. Instead, situational emphasis should be placed on the principle's relevance (Choudhury, 1986, p. 197). When organizations consist of self-contained units where the focus is on operating efficiency with innovation being less of an issue, the application of the controllability principle helps to ensure smooth working. However, when organizations are dependent on proactive and innovative staff initiatives with employees acting as entrepreneurs and working across the silos that can frequently be found in complex organizations, the nonapplication of the controllability principle is likely to foster organizational effectiveness. Confronting managers with a lack of controllability can be seen as a means of signaling that they are expected to show individual initiative and that it is their job to act on factors that are not totally controllable by them. As Bourguignon and Chiapello (2005, p. 688) state, "instead of looking for an evaluation aligned with the controllability principle, it would be more fruitful to come to an agreement on the definition of the manager's job". Corporate philosophy regarding the boundaries of the manager's job certainly represents one of the driving forces behind the (non)application of the controllability principle.

However, a word of caution is necessary. When organizations opt not to apply the controllability principle because the associated extra-role merits are valued over the in-role drawbacks, they are likely to do so at the cost of managers' mental health. While the nonapplication of the controllability principle makes managers adopt a more flexible role orientation, it entails an increase in role conflict and role ambiguity at the same time. An important challenge of MCS design, and job design in general, is therefore to reconcile organizational needs for flexibly oriented managers with individuals' needs for reduced role stress (Singh, Verbeke, & Rhoads, 1996, p. 84; Wong et al., 2007, p. 300). In this dilemma, Kahn et al. (1964, p. 387) propose the following:

> The issue, then, is not the elimination of conflict and ambiguity from organizational life; it is the containment of these conditions at levels and in forms which are at least humane, tolerable, and low in cost, and which at best might be positive in contribution to individual and organization . . . Research implies four ways in which this goal might be approached: by introducing direct structural changes into organizations, by introducing new criteria of selection and placement, by increasing the tolerance and coping abilities of individuals, and by strengthening the interpersonal bonds among organizational members.

From an organizational design perspective, structural changes intended to relieve managers from role stress and to facilitate the development of a flexible role orientation can take different forms (Gong, Shenkar, Luo, & Nyaw, 2001, pp. 770-771; McAllister et al., 2007, p. 1209; Robbins, 2003, pp. 584-585). Organizations should thereby devote particular attention to the design of their communication structures in order to ascribe clear roles to managers: "Increasing formal organization communication with employees reduces uncertainty by lessening role ambiguity and role conflict. Given the importance that perceptions play in moderating the stress-response relationship, management can also use effective communications as a means to shape employee perceptions" (Robbins, 2003, p. 585). Further, organizations are advised to decrease the fractionation of jobs. When managers learn how their job relates to the jobs of others and how their doings affect the surrounding organization, it is likely that they gain a clearer picture of what their role in the organization should be. As a consequence, jobs are meant to be organized in such a way as to facilitate stable interaction between managers in the performance of various tasks (Beehr & Glazer, 2005, p. 9; Hurrell, 2005, pp. 635-636; Katz & Kahn, 1978, pp. 762-763; McKenna, 2006, p. 680; Ruben, 1986, pp. 122-123). Following the empirical results of this study, such structural changes to the organization are particularly beneficial at lower and middle hierarchical levels. Unlike top managers, it is managers from these levels who experience the greatest role stress arising out of the nonapplication of the controllability principle. Accordingly, they should benefit most from organizational initiatives that are intended to clarify managerial roles.

Since individuals differ in their susceptibility to role stress and in their propensity to develop a flexible role orientation, selecting and placing the "right" employees in jobs with low controllability is another practical implication that can be inferred from this study. Managers with high self-efficacy seem to be able to cope more effectively with the nonapplication of the controllability principle than managers with low self-efficacy. They are more likely to develop a flexible role orientation in response to a lack of controllability, which should be taken into consideration in staffing decisions. Apart from self-efficacy, other individual characteristics such as job experience and tolerance for ambiguity have been shown to determine how managers cope with challenges in the job and can be expected to make managers less prone to stress (Chong, 1998, pp. 338-339; Harigopal, 1995, p. 80; Hartline & Bejou, 2004, pp. 33-34; Keenan & McBain, 1979, p. 284). Obviously, organizations should not restrict hiring and promotion to experienced individuals with high self-efficacy and tolerance for ambiguity exclusively, but such managers may adapt better to low controllability jobs and perform those jobs more effectively (Robbins, 2003, p. 584).

Apart from selecting and placing employees on the basis of their existing skills and dispositions, organizations should provide adequate assistance and training to managers so that they are enabled to increase their tolerance and coping abilities over time. The insights gained from the interview data suggest that subjectivity in performance evaluation is often appreciated by managers because it helps them to develop tolerance for the nonapplication of the controllability principle. With high uncertainty and low controllability in managerial jobs, it seems worthwhile for organizations to switch from a formulaic evaluation system to an approach that allows a higher degree of subjectivity. Despite its disadvantages (see chapter B1.3), subjective performance evaluation is easy to implement, provides evaluators with greater discretion, and permits a more complete picture of performance (Frink & Klimoski, 1998, p. 40; Govindarajan, 1984, p. 125; Manzoni, 2002, p. 41; Merchant et al., 1995, pp.

624-631; Modell & Lee, 2001, p. 213; Otley, 1994, p. 297). Another organizational intervention to mitigate dysfunctional effects associated with the nonapplication of the controllability principle is to manipulate managers' perceptions of what is controllable by them. Controllability too often seems to be "understood in terms of 'having administrative control' over the issue, i.e. being the one within the firm who can make the decision at issue" (Manzoni, 2002, p. 30). Since the notion of being in control is perceptual in nature, training and guidance should be available so that managers are induced to adopt of a broader interpretation of control (Choudhury, 1986, p. 192; McNally, 1980, pp. 172-173). Further, organizations may introduce stress management programs to buffer managers against those levels of stress that most probably come along with a relaxation of the controllability principle. Stress need not necessarily lead to adverse side effects. Research has shown that stress is amenable to intervention, i.e. implementing programs to diminish its detrimental consequences. Sabbaticals, workplace counseling, or recreational facilities are possible means to counteract stress among managers (Ivancevich & Matteson, 1987, pp. 240-243; Ivancevich, Matteson, Freedman, & Phillips, 1990, pp. 255-256; McKenna, 2006, pp. 681-683; Robbins, 2003, p. 584).

Lastly, a strengthening of the interpersonal bonds among the workforce is likely to alleviate some of the detrimental consequences that are associated with the nonapplication of the controllability principle. This study provides tentative indication that managers' trust in their superior makes them less susceptible to role stress. Likewise, individuals' confidence in that social support is available from coworkers is often regarded as a source of control that might compensate for a lack of formal authority (Beehr & Glazer, 2005, pp. 16-17; Daniels & Guppy, 1994, pp. 1525-1526; Hurrell, 2005, p. 639; Ruben, 1986, p. 124). Organizations are therefore advised to establish a culture of mutual trust and cooperativeness in order to make the nonapplication of the controllability principle as tolerable as possible.

3. Limitations and Future Research Directions

Although this study makes several theoretical and methodological contributions to existing literature on the controllability principle, there are some limitations which must be kept in mind when drawing conclusions from the reported results.

First, the survey approach chosen in this study faces the usual limitations of questionnaire-based research employing self-reported measures. As delineated in chapter E4.2, common method variance may have inflated the strengths of the relationships under investigation (Podsakoff et al., 2003, pp. 879-880). Despite the results of Harman's single-factor test and various attempts, such as a thorough pretesting of the questionnaire instruments, which have been undertaken to minimize the influence of common method variance, its occurrence cannot be completely ruled out. Future research should therefore try to adopt a dyadic approach where the dependent variables, in particular in-role and extra-role performance, are assessed by a different rater, e.g. the managers' superiors. In this context, it would be interesting to examine if the application of the controllability principle is also related to other types of extra-role behaviors (see Figure 4 for a typology of extra-role behaviors). It would further add to our understanding of what causes these behaviors if future research continued to consider the possibility of indirect effects that operate through cognitive and motivational variables (Crant, 2000, p. 457; Griffin et al., 2007, p. 343).

Second, this study used a newly developed instrument for measuring the application of the controllability principle. Even though existing management accounting literature was built upon and state-of-the-art guidelines were followed in the development of the corresponding measurement scale, future studies are recommended to further establish the construct's usefulness and validity. Future studies might also investigate how controllability relates to other design characteristics of MCSs. Simons (1995, p. 77) states that there is a more or less pronounced conflict between the controllability and the completeness of performance measures in that the more complete the measures the less controllable they are to the individual manager. Management accounting research should therefore investigate into whether and how a combination of complete and controllable performance measures can be achieved (Modell, 1997, p. 328).

Third, to assess the application of the controllability principle, this study focused on managers' own perceptions of their performance measures' controllability. It does not address specific management accounting practices (e.g. cost allocation and transfer pricing policies) that cause managers' perceptions of controllability nor does it investigate the personality variables that are likely to influence these perceptions (Marginson & McAulay, 2001, pp. 22-24; Pelster, 2007, pp. 269-270). Similarly, since managers differ in personality variables such as their attitude towards risk (Hillson & Murray-Webster, 2007, pp. 39-41; Sitkin & Pablo, 1992, pp. 12-13), this study's results on managers' preferences for a high degree of controllability should be treated with some caution. Hence, research that relates (a) managers' perceptions of controllability to the "objective" reality of management accounting practices and (b) managers' perceptions of and preferences for controllability to personality variables surely represents another promising avenue for future studies.

Fourth, this study pioneered in the investigation of three moderators influencing the basic role processes. It is likely that further contextual variables have an effect on these relationships, which is why future studies should allow for theoretically plausible moderators such as entrepreneurial attitude, emotional stability, or organizational culture variables. Role theory might prove helpful in the identification of such potential moderators. Furthermore, future research should in particular attempt to validate this study's somewhat ambiguous findings as to the moderating impact of managers' trust in their superior. Since the survey results are not in accordance with the insights gained from the interviews, it would be worthwhile to dig deeper into the role of trust and test different facets of trust (Ebert, 2009, pp. 66-69) for an interaction effect.

Fifth, the analysis of the interview data revealed an asymmetric perspective on the controllability principle among managers that cannot be explained with the help of role theory and this study's empirical data. Managers most often seem to fear "bad luck" and almost unanimously regard uncontrollable factors as having disadvantageous effects on their measured performance thereby neglecting that the nonapplication of the controllability principle may also make them benefit from "good luck". With this in mind, it might be that the detected effects of the application of the controllability principle on managers' role perceptions mainly apply to situations of "bad luck". As proposed by Giraud et al. (2008, p. 36), future research on the controllability principle should address this issue since "the case of favorable uncontrollable factors, i.e., the situation of 'good luck', is not really considered" in prior literature. Possibly, such a selective perception among the participants in this study is related to an internal locus of control (Rotter, 1966), which might help to explain their preference for a high degree of controllability and their denial to recognize the potentially favorable influence of uncontrollable factors on their measured performance. Locus of control describes one's generalized belief that behavioral outcomes are under personal control (internal locus) rather than depending on outside forces, luck, or powerful others (external locus) (Rotter, 1966, pp. 1-2) whereby prior research indicates that it influences individuals' perceptions of their job in general and their perceived job control latitude in particular (Daniels & Guppy, 1994, pp. 1532-1537; Rodríguez, Bravo, Peiró, & Schaufeli, 2001, pp. 105-106; Spector & O'Connell, 1994, pp. 8-9). The constructs of locus of control and job control latitude should therefore be taken into consideration in future studies investigating this phenomenon.

Finally, despite role theory guiding the development of the hypotheses, this study cannot demonstrate cause-and-effect relations empirically. Suggestions of causation are primarily based on theoretical positions. However, the interview data do provide some indication as to the direction of the relationships and, in addition, there is also no theoretical grounding for the reverse causal relationships. Nevertheless, future tests of the proposed hypotheses in an experimental setting would be beneficial as to further validate the findings. Similarly, a longitudinal research method would be helpful to overcome potential problems associated with causal directions (Nouri & Kyj, 2008, p. 1449).

Notwithstanding the aforementioned limitations, this study contributes to management accounting theory and practice. It demonstrates that the controllability principle is an important determinant of organizational effectiveness and managerial motivation. Understanding managers' responses to the application of the controllability principle is therefore of high relevance to any organization. As Merchant states, "significant problems can arise if uncontrollables are not dealt with properly. Managers must continue to struggle with these issues" (Merchant, 1998, p. 583).

References

Abernethy, M. A., Bouwens, J., & Van Lent, L. (2004). Determinants of control system design in divisionalized firms. *The Accounting Review, 79*(3), 545-570.

Abernethy, M. A., & Brownell, P. (1999). The role of budgets in organizations facing strategic change: An exploratory study. *Accounting, Organizations and Society, 24*(3), 189-204.

Abernethy, M. A., Chua, W. F., Luckett, P. F., & Selto, F. H. (1999). Research in managerial accounting: Learning from others' experiences. *Accounting and Finance, 39*(1), 1-27.

Abernethy, M. A., & Stoelwinder, J. U. (1995). The role of professional control in the management of complex organizations. *Accounting, Organizations and Society, 20*(1), 1-17.

Abernethy, M. A., & Vagnoni, E. (2004). Power, organization design and managerial behaviour. *Accounting, Organizations and Society, 29*(3-4), 207-225.

Abramis, D. J. (1994). Work role ambiguity, job satisfaction, and job performance: Meta-analyses and review. *Psychological Reports, 75*(3), 1411-1433.

Abramson, L. Y., Seligman, M. E. P., & Teasdale, J. D. (1978). Learned helplessness in humans: Critique and reformulation. *Journal of Abnormal Psychology, 87*(1), 49-74.

Adams, J. S. (1963). Toward an understanding of inequity. *Journal of Abnormal and Social Psychology, 67*(5), 422-436.

Adams, J. S. (1965). Inequity in social exchange. In L. Berkowitz (Ed.), *Advances in experimental social psychology* (Vol. 2, pp. 267-299). New York: Academic Press.

Aghion, P., & Tirole, J. (1997). Formal and real authority in organizations. *Journal of Political Economy, 105*(1), 1-29.

Ahrens, T., & Chapman, C. S. (2006). Doing qualitative field research in management accounting: Positioning data to contribute to theory. *Accounting, Organizations and Society, 31*(8), 819-841.

Ajzen, I. (1991). The theory of planned behavior. *Organizational Behavior and Human Decision Processes, 50*(2), 179-211.

Albers, S., & Hildebrandt, L. (2006). Methodische Probleme der Erfolgsfaktorenforschung: Messfehler, formative versus reflektive Indikatoren und die Wahl des Strukturgleichungsmodells. *Zeitschrift für betriebswirtschaftliche Forschung, 58*(2), 2-33.

Alexander, J. C. (1996). Positivism. In A. Kuper & J. Kuper (Eds.), *The social science encyclopedia* (2 ed., pp. 649-651). London: Routledge.

Alexander, L. D. (1979). The effect level in the hierarchy and functional area have on the extent Mintzberg's roles are required by managerial jobs. *Academy of Management Proceedings*, 186-189.

Alford, L. P. (1928). *Laws of management applied to manufacturing*. New York: Ronald Press.

Allport, G. W. (1954). The historical background of modern social psychology. In G. Lindzey (Ed.), *Handbook of social psychology* (Vol. 1, pp. 3-56). Reading: Addison-Wesley.

Ambrose, M. L. (2002). Contemporary justice research: A new look at familiar questions. *Organizational Behavior and Human Decision Processes, 89*(1), 803-812.

Amey, L. R. (1979). Towards a new perspective on accounting control. *Accounting, Organizations and Society, 4*(4), 247-258.

Ancona, A. G., & Caldwell, D. F. (1992). Bridging the boundary: External activity and performance in organizational teams. *Administrative Science Quarterly, 37*(4), 634-665.

Anderson, J. C., & Gerbing, D. W. (1982). Some methods for respecifying measurement models to obtain unidimensional construct measurement. *Journal of Marketing Research, 19*(4), 453-460.

Anderson, J. C., & Gerbing, D. W. (1988). Structural equation modeling in practice: A review and recommended two-step approach. *Psychological Bulletin, 103*(3), 411-423.

Anderson, J. C., & Gerbing, D. W. (1991). Predicting the performance of measures in a confirmatory factor analysis with a pretest assessment of their substantive validities. *Journal of Applied Psychology, 76*(5), 732-740.

Anderson, S. W., & Widener, S. K. (2006). Doing quantitative field research in management accounting. In C. S. Chapman, A. G. Hopwood & M. D. Shields (Eds.), *Handbook of management accounting research* (Vol. 1, pp. 319-342). Amsterdam et al.: Elsevier.

Ansari, S. L. (1979). Towards an open systems approach to budgeting. *Accounting, Organizations and Society, 4*(3), 149-161.

Anthony, R. N. (1989). Reminiscences about management accounting. *Journal of Management Accounting Research, 1*, 1-20.

Antle, R., & Demski, J. S. (1988). The controllability principle in responsibility accounting. *The Accounting Review, 63*(4), 700-718.

Antle, R., & Smith, A. (1986). An empirical investigation of the relative performance evaluation of corporate executives. *Journal of Accounting Research, 24*(1), 1-39.

Aquino, K. (2000). Structural and individual determinants of workplace victimization: The effects of hierarchical status and conflict management style. *Journal of Management, 26*(2), 171-193.

Argyris, C. (1952). *The impact of budgets on people*. New York: Controllership Foundation.

Argyris, C. (1953). Human problems with budgets. *Harvard Business Review, 31*(1), 97-110.

Armstrong, J. S., & Overton, T. S. (1977). Estimating nonresponse bias in mail surveys. *Journal of Marketing Research, 14*(3), 396-402.

Armstrong, M., & Baron, A. (2005). *Managing performance: Performance management in action*. London: Chartered Institute of Personnel and Development.

Armstrong, P. (2008). Calling out for more: Comment on the future of interpretive accounting research. *Critical Perspectives on Accounting, 19*(6), 867-879.

Arnold, H. J. (1984). Testing moderator variables hypotheses: A reply to Stone and Hollenbeck. *Organizational Behavior and Human Performance, 34*(2), 214-224.

Arya, A., Fellingham, J., & Glover, J. (1997). Teams, repeated tasks, and implicit incentives. *Journal of Accounting and Economics, 23*(1), 7-30.

Arya, A., Glover, J., & Radhakrishnan, S. (2007). The controllability principle in responsibility accounting: Another look. In R. Antle, F. Gjesdal & P. J. Liang (Eds.), *Essays in accounting theory in honour of Joel S. Demski* (pp. 183-198). New York: Springer.

Ashford, S. J., & Black, J. S. (1996). Proactivity during organizational entry: The role of desire for control. *Journal of Applied Psychology, 81*(2), 199-214.

Atkinson, A. A., Balakrishnan, R., Booth, P., Cote, J. M., Groot, T., Malmi, T., et al. (1997). New directions in management accounting research. *Journal of Management Accounting Research, 9*, 79-108.

Atkinson, A. A., Kaplan, R. S., Matsumura, E. M., & Young, S. M. (2007). *Management accounting* (5 ed.). Upper Saddle River: Prentice Hall.

Atkinson, A. A., & Shaffir, W. (1998). Standards for field research in management accounting. *Journal of Management Accounting Research, 10*, 41-68.

Babbie, E. R. (2004). *The practice of social research* (10 ed.). Belmont: Wadsworth.

Backhaus, K., Erichson, B., Plinke, W., & Weiber, R. (2006). *Multivariate Analysemethoden* (11 ed.). Berlin: Springer.

Bagozzi, R. P. (1994a). Measurement in marketing research: Basic principles of questionnaire design. In R. P. Bagozzi (Ed.), *Principles of marketing research* (pp. 1-49). Cambridge: Blackwell Business.

Bagozzi, R. P. (1994b). Structural equation models in marketing research: Basic principles. In R. P. Bagozzi (Ed.), *Principles of marketing research* (pp. 317-385). Cambridge: Blackwell Business.

Bagozzi, R. P., & Baumgartner, H. (1994). The evaluation of structural equation models and hypothesis testing. In R. P. Bagozzi (Ed.), *Principles of marketing research* (pp. 386-422). Cambridge: Blackwell Business.

Bagozzi, R. P., & Phillips, L. W. (1982). Representing and testing organizational theories: A holistic construal. *Administrative Science Quarterly, 27*(3), 459-489.

Bagozzi, R. P., & Yi, Y. (1988). On the evaluation of structural equation models. *Journal of the Academy of Marketing Science, 16*(1), 74-94.

Bagozzi, R. P., Yi, Y., & Phillips, L. W. (1991). Assessing construct validity in organizational research. *Administrative Science Quarterly, 36*(3), 421-458.

Bailey, K. D. (1987). *Methods of social research* (3 ed.). New York et al.: Free Press.

Baiman, S. (1982). Agency research in managerial accounting: A survey. *Journal of Accounting Literature, 1*, 154-213.

Baiman, S. (1990). Agency research in managerial accounting: A second look. *Accounting, Organizations and Society, 15*(4), 341-371.

Baiman, S., & Demski, J. S. (1980). Economically optimal performance evaluation and control systems. *Journal of Accounting Research, 18*(Supplement), 184-220.

Baiman, S., & Noel, J. (1985). Noncontrollable costs and responsibility accounting. *Journal of Accounting Research, 23*(2), 486-501.

Baker, G., Gibbons, R., & Murphy, K. J. (1994). Subjective performance measures in optimal incentive contracts. *Quarterly Journal of Economics, 109*(4), 1125-1156.

Baker, G., Gibbons, R., & Murphy, K. J. (1999). Informal authority in organizations. *Journal of Law, Economics and Organization, 15*(1), 56-73.

Baker, G., Jensen, M. C., & Murphy, K. J. (1988). Compensation and incentives: Practice vs. theory. *Journal of Finance, 43*(3), 593-616.

Baldvinsdottir, G., Hagberg, A., Johansson, I.-L., Jonäll, K., & Marton, J. P. (2009). *The trust research in accounting: Where do we go from here?* Paper presented at the Annual Meeting and Conference on Teaching and Learning in Accounting, New York.

Bamber, E. M., Snowball, D., & Tubbs, R. M. (1989). Audit structure and its relation to role conflict and role ambiguity: An empirical investigation. *The Accounting Review, 64*(2), 285.

Bamber, L. S., Braun, K. W., & Harrison, W. T. (2008). *Managerial accounting* (3 ed.). Upper Saddle River: Prentice Hall.

Bandura, A. (1977). Self-efficacy: Toward a unifying theory of behavioral change. *Psychological Review, 84*(2), 191-215.

Bandura, A. (1982). Self-efficacy mechanism in human agency. *American Psychologist, 37*(2), 122-147.

Bandura, A. (1986). *Social foundations of thought and action: A social cognitive theory.* Englewood Cliffs: Prentice Hall.

Bandura, A. (1997). *Self-efficacy: The exercise of control.* New York: Freeman.

Bandura, A., & Wood, R. (1989). Effect of perceived controllability and performance standards on self-regulation of complex decision making. *Journal of Personality and Social Psychology, 56*(5), 805-814.

Banker, R. D., & Datar, S. M. (1989). Sensitivity, precision, and linear aggregation of signals for performance evaluation. *Journal of Accounting Research, 27*(1), 21-39.

Banker, R. D., Seok-Young, L., Potter, G., & Srinivasan, D. (2001). An empirical analysis of continuing improvements following the implementation of a performance-based compensation plan. *Journal of Accounting and Economics, 30*(3), 315-350.

Barber, A. E., & Simmering, M. J. (2002). Understanding pay plan acceptance: The role of distributive justice theory. *Human Resource Management Review, 12*(1), 25-42.

Barker, J. (2008). Control and authority in organizations. In W. Donsbach (Ed.), *The international encyclopedia of communication* (pp. 980-984). Malden et al.: Blackwell.

Barnard, C. I. (1968). *The functions of the executive*. Cambridge: Harvard University Press.

Baron, J., & Hershey, J. C. (1988). Outcome bias in decision evaluation. *Journal of Personality and Social Psychology, 54*(4), 569-579.

Baron, R. A., Branscombe, N. R., & Byrne, D. E. (2008). *Social psychology* (12 ed.). Boston: Pearson.

Baron, R. M., & Kenny, D. A. (1986). The moderator-mediator variable distinction in social psychological research: Conceptual, strategic, and statistical considerations. *Journal of Personality and Social Psychology, 51*(6), 1173-1182.

Baumgartner, H., & Homburg, C. (1996). Applications of structural equation modeling in marketing and consumer research: A review. *International Journal of Research in Marketing, 13*(2), 139-161.

Beehr, T. A., & Glazer, S. (2005). Organizational role stress. In J. Barling, E. K. Kelloway & M. R. Frone (Eds.), *Handbook of work stress* (pp. 7-35). Thousand Oaks et al.: Sage Publications.

Beehr, T. A., Walsh, J. T., & Taber, T. D. (1976). Relationship of stress to individually and organizationally valued states: Higher order needs as a moderator. *Journal of Applied Psychology, 61*(1), 41-47.

Beer, M., Voelpel, S. C., Leibold, M., & Tekie, E. B. (2005). Strategic management as organizational learning: Developing fit and alignment through a disciplined process. *Long Range Planning, 38*(5), 445-465.

Benson, P. G., Kemery, E. R., Sauser, W. I., & Tankesley, K. E. (1985). Need for clarity as a moderator of the role ambiguity-job satisfaction relationship. *Journal of Management, 11*(3), 125-130.

Bentler, P. M. (1990). Comparative fit indexes in structural models. *Psychological Bulletin, 107*(2), 238-246.

Bento, A., & White, L. F. (2006). Budgeting, performance evaluation, and compensation: A performance management model. *Advances in Management Accounting, 15*, 51-79.

Bento, R. F., & White, L. F. (1998). Participants' values and incentive plans. *Human Resource Management, 37*(1), 47-59.

Berger, C. J., & Cummings, L. L. (1979). Organizational structure, attitudes, and behaviors. In L. L. Cummings & B. M. Staw (Eds.), *Research in organizational behavior* (Vol. 1, pp. 169-208). Greenwich: JAI Press.

Berkowitz, E. N. (1980). Role theory, attitudinal constructs, and actual performance: A measurement issue. *Journal of Applied Psychology, 65*(2), 240-245.

Berry, A. J., Coad, A. F., Harris, E. P., Otley, D. T., & Stringer, C. (2009). Emerging themes in management control: A review of recent literature. *The British Accounting Review, 41*(1), 2-20.

Bertrand, A. L. (1972). *Social organization: A general systems and role theory perspective.* Philadelphia: Davis.

Besson, M., Löning, H., & Mendoza, C. (2008). Dual use of budgeting in uncertainty contexts: Explorative study of senior sales and marketing managers (Working paper). SSRN.

Bettencourt, L. A., & Brown, S. W. (2003). Role stressors and customer-oriented boundary-spanning behaviors in service organizations. *Journal of the Academy of Marketing Science, 31*(4), 394-408.

Bettencourt, L. A., Brown, S. W., & MacKenzie, S. B. (2005). Customer-oriented boundary-spanning behaviors: Test of a social exchange model of antecedents. *Journal of Retailing, 81*(2), 141-157.

Betzin, J., & Henseler, J. (2005). Einführung in die Funktionsweise des PLS-Algorithmus. In F. W. Bliemel, A. Eggert, G. Fassott & J. Henseler (Eds.), *Handbuch PLS-Pfadmodellierung: Methode, Anwendung, Praxisbeispiele* (pp. 49-70). Stuttgart: Schäffer-Poeschel.

Bhimani, A., Horngren, C. T., Datar, S. M., & Foster, G. (2008). *Management and cost accounting* (4 ed.). Harlow et al.: Prentice Hall.

Biddle, B. J. (1979). *Role theory: Expectations, identities, and behaviors.* New York: Academic Press.

Biddle, B. J. (1986). Recent developments in role theory. *Annual Review of Sociology, 12*(1), 67-92.

Biddle, B. J., & Thomas, E. J. (1966a). Basic concepts for the variables of role phenomena. In B. J. Biddle & E. J. Thomas (Eds.), *Role theory: Concepts and research* (pp. 51-64). New York: Wiley.

Biddle, B. J., & Thomas, E. J. (1966b). The nature and history of role theory. In B. J. Biddle & E. J. Thomas (Eds.), *Role theory: Concepts and research* (pp. 3-20). New York: Wiley.

Bies, R. J., & Moag, J. F. (1986). Interactional justice: Communication criteria of fairness. In R. J. Lewicki, B. H. Sheppard & M. H. Bazerman (Eds.), *Research on negotiations in organizations* (Vol. 1, pp. 43-55). Greenwich: JAI Press.

Bies, R. J., & Shapiro, D. L. (1987). Interactional fairness judgments: The influence of causal accounts. *Social Justice Research, 1*(2), 199-218.

Birnberg, J. G., Luft, J., & Shields, M. D. (2006). Psychology theory in management accounting research. In C. S. Chapman, A. G. Hopwood & M. D. Shields (Eds.), *Handbook of management accounting research* (Vol. 1, pp. 113-135). Amsterdam et al.: Elsevier.

Birnberg, J. G., & Shields, M. D. (1989). Three decades of behavioral accounting research: A search for order. *Behavioral Research in Accounting, 1*, 23-74.

Birnberg, J. G., Shields, M. D., & Young, S. M. (1990). The case for multiple methods in empirical management accounting research. *Journal of Management Accounting Research, 2*, 33-66.

Bisbe, J., Batista-Foguet, J.-M., & Chenhall, R. H. (2007). Defining management accounting constructs: A methodological note on the risks of conceptual misspecification. *Accounting, Organizations and Society, 32*(7-8), 789-820.

Blalock, H. M. (1964). *Causal inferences in nonexperimental research*. Chapel Hill: University of North Carolina Press.

Bloom, M., & Milkovich, G. T. (1998). Relationships among risk, incentive pay, and organizational performance. *Academy of Management Journal, 41*(3), 283-297.

Bollen, K. (1989). *Structural equations with latent variables*. New York: Wiley.

Bollen, K., & Lennox, R. (1991). Conventional wisdom on measurement: A structural equation perspective. *Psychological Bulletin, 110*(2), 305-314.

Bommer, W., Johnson, J., Rich, G., Podsakoff, P. M., & MacKenzie, S. B. (1995). On the interchangeability of objective and subjective measures of employee performance: A meta analysis. *Personnel Psychology, 48*(3), 587-605.

Bordens, K. S., & Horowitz, I. A. (2001). *Social psychology*. Mahwah: Erlbaum.

Boudreau, M.-C., Ariyachandra, T., Gefen, D., & Straub, D. W. (2003). Validating IS positivist instrumentation: 1997-2001. In M. E. Whitman & A. B. Woszczynski (Eds.), *The handbook of information systems research* (pp. 15-26). Hershey: Idea Group Publications.

Bourguignon, A., & Chiapello, E. (2005). The role of criticism in the dynamics of performance evaluation systems. *Critical Perspectives on Accounting, 16*(6), 665-700.

Bouwens, J., & Van Lent, L. (2006). Performance measure properties and the effect of incentive contracts. *Journal of Management Accounting Research, 18*, 55-75.

Bouwens, J., & Van Lent, L. (2007). Assessing the performance of business unit managers. *Journal of Accounting Research, 45*(4), 667-697.

Bozeman, D. P., Hochwarter, W. A., Perrewé, P. L., & Brymer, R. A. (2001). Organizational politics, perceived control, and work outcomes: Boundary conditions on the effects of politics. *Journal of Applied Social Psychology, 31*(3), 486-503.

Brehm, J. W. (1966). *A theory of psychological reactance*. New York: Academic Press.

Brehm, S. S., & Brehm, J. W. (1981). *Psychological reactance: A theory of freedom and control*. New York: Academic Press.

Brewer, P. (2000). Research design and issues of validity. In H. T. Reis & C. M. Judd (Eds.), *Handbook of research methods in social and personality psychology* (pp. 3-17). Cambridge: Cambridge University Press.

Briers, M. L., & Hirst, M. K. (1990). The role of budgetary information in performance evaluation. *Accounting, Organizations and Society, 15*(4), 373-397.

Brion, J. M. (1989). *Organizational leadership of human resources: The knowledge and the skills*. Greenwich: JAI Press.

Brislin, R. (1980). Translation and content analysis of oral and written material. In H. C. Triandis & J. W. Berry (Eds.), *Handbook of cross-cultural psychology* (Vol. 2, pp. 398-444). Boston: Allyn & Bacon.

Brown, C. E., & Solomon, I. (1987). Effects of outcome information on evaluations of managerial decisions. *The Accounting Review, 62*(3), 564-577.

Brown, C. E., & Solomon, I. (1993). An experimental investigation of explanations for outcome effects on appraisals of capital-budgeting decisions. *Contemporary Accounting Research, 10*(1), 83-111.

Brown, S. P., Ganesan, S., & Challagalla, G. (2001). Self-efficacy as a moderator of information-seeking effectiveness. *Journal of Applied Psychology, 86*(5), 1043-1051.

Browne, M. W., & Cudeck, R. (1993). Alternative ways of assessing model fit. In K. Bollen & J. S. Long (Eds.), *Testing structural equation models*. Newbury Park et al.: Sage Publications.

Brownell, P. (1982). The role of accounting data in performance evaluation, budgetary participation, and organizational effectiveness. *Journal of Accounting Research, 20*(1), 12-27.

Bruns, W. J., & Kaplan, R. S. (1987). Field studies in management accounting. In W. J. Bruns & R. S. Kaplan (Eds.), *Accounting and management: Field study perspectives* (pp. 1-16). Boston: Harvard Business School Press.

Budde, J. (2009). Variance analysis and linear contracts in agencies with distorted performance measures. *Management Accounting Research*, *20*(3), 166-176.

Budding, G. T. (2004). Accountability, environmental uncertainty and government performance: Evidence from Dutch municipalities. *Management Accounting Research, 15*(3), 285-304.

Bukszar, E., & Connolly, T. (1988). Hindsight bias and strategic choice: Some problems in learning from experience. *Academy of Management Journal, 31*(3), 628-641.

Bunge, M. A., & Ardila, R. (1987). *Philosophy of psychology*. New York: Springer.

Burke, R. J., & Belcourt, M. L. (1974). Managerial role stress and coping responses. *Journal of Business Administration, 5*(2), 55-68.

Burkert, M. (2008). *Qualität von Kennzahlen und Erfolg von Managern: Direkte, indirekte und moderierende Effekte*. Wiesbaden: Deutscher Universitäts-Verlag.

Burney, L., Henle, C. A., & Widener, S. K. (2009). A path model examining the relations among strategic performance measurement system characteristics, organizational justice, and extra- and in-role performance. *Accounting, Organizations and Society, 34*(3-4), 305-321.

Burney, L., & Widener, S. K. (2007). Strategic performance measurement systems, job-relevant information, and managerial behavioral responses - role stress and performance. *Behavioral Research in Accounting, 19*, 43-69.

Burns, R. B. (1997). *Psychology for effective managers: Understanding and managing human behaviour in the workplace*. Chatswood: Business & Professional Publishing.

Bushman, R. M., Indjejikian, R. J., & Smith, A. (1995). Aggregate performance measures in business unit manager compensation: The role of intrafirm interdependencies. *Journal of Accounting Research, 33*(Supplement), 101-128.

Bushman, R. M., Indjejikian, R. J., & Smith, A. (1996). CEO compensation: The role of individual performance evaluation. *Journal of Accounting and Economics, 21*(2), 161-193.

Büssing, A., Bissels, T., Fuchs, V., & Perrar, K.-M. (1999). A dynamic model of work satisfaction: Qualitative approaches. *Human Relations, 52*(8), 999-1028.

Byrne, B. M. (1998). *Structural equation modeling with LISREL, PRELIS, and SIMPLIS: Basic concepts, applications, and programming*. Mahwah: Erlbaum.

Byrne, S., & Pierce, B. (2007). Towards a more comprehensive understanding of the roles of management accountants. *European Accounting Review, 16*(3), 469-498.

Campbell, D. T., & Fiske, D. (1959). Convergent and discriminant validation by the multitrait-multimethod matrix. *Psychological Bulletin, 56*(2), 81-105.

Caplan, E. H. (1966). Behavioral assumptions of management accounting. *The Accounting Review, 41*(3), 496-509.

Carmines, E., & Zeller, R. (1979). *Reliability and validity assessment*. Newbury Park: Sage Publications.

Carsten, J. M., & Spector, P. E. (1987). Unemployment, job satisfaction, and employee turnover: A meta-analytic test of the Muchinsky model. *Journal of Applied Psychology, 72*(3), 374-381.

Catasús, B., Ersson, S., Gröjer, J.-E., & Wallentin, F. Y. (2007). What gets measured gets . . . on indicating, mobilizing and acting. *Accounting, Auditing and Accountability Journal, 20*(4), 505-521.

Cawley, B. D., Keeping, L. M., & Levy, P. E. (1998). Participation in the performance appraisal process and employee reactions: A meta-analytic review of field investigations. *Journal of Applied Psychology, 83*(4), 615-633.

Chandler, A. D., McCraw, T. K., & Tedlow, R. S. (1996). *Management: Past and present: A casebook on the history of American business*. Cincinnati: South-Western College Publishing.

Chenhall, R. H. (2003). Management control systems design within its organizational context: Findings from contingency-based research and directions for the future. *Accounting, Organizations and Society, 28*(2-3), 127-168.

Chenhall, R. H. (2005). Integrative strategic performance measurement systems, strategic alignment of manufacturing, learning and strategic outcomes: An exploratory study. *Accounting, Organizations and Society, 30*(5), 395-422.

Chenhall, R. H., & Brownell, P. (1988). The effect of participative budgeting on job satisfaction and performance: Role ambiguity as an intervening variable. *Accounting, Organizations and Society, 13*(3), 225-233.

Chenhall, R. H., & Langfield-Smith, K. (2007). Multiple perspectives of performance measures. *European Management Journal, 25*(4), 266-282.

Chenhall, R. H., & Morris, D. (1986). The impact of structure, environment, and interdependencies of the perceived usefulness of management accounting systems. *The Accounting Review, 61*(1), 16-35.

Cherryholmes, C. H. (1992). Notes on pragmatism and scientific realism. *Educational Researcher, 21*(6), 13-17.

Chia, Y. M. (1995). Decentralization, management accounting systems (MAS) information characteristics and their interaction effects on managerial performance: A Singapore study. *Journal of Business Finance & Accounting, 22*(6), 811-830.

Chin, W. W. (1998a). Issues and opinion on structural equation modeling. *MIS Quarterly, 22*(1), 1-10.

Chin, W. W. (1998b). The partial least squares approach to structural equation modeling. In G. A. Marcoulides (Ed.), *Modern methods for business research* (pp. 295-336). Mahwah: Erlbaum.

Chin, W. W., Marcolin, B. L., & Newsted, P. R. (2003). A partial least squares latent variable modeling approach for measuring interaction effects: Results from a Monte Carlo simulation study and an electronic-mail emotion/adoption study. *Information Systems Research, 14*(2), 189-217.

Chin, W. W., & Newsted, P. R. (1999). Structural equation modeling analysis with small samples using partial least squares. In R. H. Hoyle (Ed.), *Statistical strategies for small sample research* (pp. 307-342). Thousand Oaks: Sage Publications.

Chong, V. K. (1998). Testing the contingency 'fit' between management accounting systems and managerial performance: A research note on the moderating role of tolerance for ambiguity. *The British Accounting Review, 30*(4), 331-342.

Chong, V. K., & Chong, K. M. (2002). Budget goal commitment and informational effects of budget participation on performance: A structural equation modeling approach. *Behavioral Research in Accounting, 14*, 65-84.

Chou, C.-P., & Bentler, P. M. (1995). Estimates and tests in structural equation modeling. In R. H. Hoyle (Ed.), *Structural equation modeling: Concepts, issues, and applications* (pp. 37-55). Thousands Oaks: Sage Publications.

Choudhury, N. (1986). Responsibility accounting and controllability. *Accounting and Business Research, 16*(63), 189-198.

Chow, C. W., Harrison, G. L., McKinnon, J. L., & Wu, A. (2002). The organizational culture of public accounting firms: Evidence from Taiwanese local and US affiliated firms. *Accounting, Organizations and Society, 27*(4-5), 347-360.

Chow, C. W., & Van der Stede, W. A. (2006). The use and usefulness of nonfinancial performance measures. *Management Accounting Quarterly, 7*(3), 1-8.

Churchill, G. A. (1979). A paradigm for developing better measures of marketing constructs. *Journal of Marketing Research, 16*(1), 64-73.

Churchill, G. A., & Iacobucci, D. (2005). *Marketing research: Methodological foundations*. Mason: Thomson.

Clegg, C., Unsworth, K., Epitropaki, O., & Parker, G. (2002). Implicating trust in the innovation process. *Journal of Occupational and Organizational Psychology, 75*(4), 409-422.

Cobb, A. T. (1980). Informal influence in the formal organization: Perceived sources or power among work unit peers. *Academy of Management Journal, 23*(1), 155-161.

Cohen-Charash, Y., & Spector, P. E. (2001). The role of justice in organizations: A meta-analysis. *Organizational Behavior and Human Decision Processes, 86*(2), 278-321.

Cohen, S. I., Loeb, M. P., & Stark, A. W. (1992). Separating controllable performance from non-controllable performance: The case of optimal procurement contracting. *Management Accounting Research, 3*(4), 291-306.

Collier, P. M., & Agyei-Ampomah, S. (2006). *Risk and control strategy*. Oxford: Chartered Institute of Management Accountants/Elsevier.

Collins, F. (1978). The interaction of budget characteristics and personality variables with budgetary response attitudes. *The Accounting Review, 53*(2), 324-335.

Collins, F. (1982). Managerial accounting systems and organizational control: A role perspective. *Accounting, Organizations and Society, 7*(2), 107-122.

Collins, F., Munter, P., & Finn, D. W. (1987). The budgeting games people play. *The Accounting Review, 62*(1), 29-49.

Collins, K. M., & Killough, L. N. (1992). An empirical examination of stress in public accounting. *Accounting, Organizations and Society, 17*(6), 535-547.

Colquitt, J. A. (2001). On the dimensionality of organizational justice: A construct validation of a measure. *Journal of Applied Psychology, 86*(3), 386-400.

Coltman, T., Devinney, T. M., Midgley, D. F., & Venaik, S. (2008). Formative versus reflective measurement models: Two applications of formative measurement. *Journal of Business Research, 61*(12), 1250-1262.

Cook, T. D., & Campbell, D. T. (1979). *Quasi-experimentation: Design and analysis issues for field settings*. Chicago: Rand McNally.

Cooley, C. H. (1902). *Human nature and the social order*. New York: Scribner's.

Cooley, C. H. (1909). *Social organization: A study of the larger mind*. New York: Scribner's.

Cortina, J. (1993). What is coefficient alpha? An examination of theory and applications. *Journal of Applied Psychology, 78*(1), 98-104.

Covaleski, M. A., Evans, J. H., Luft, J. L., & Shields, M. D. (2003). Budgeting research: Three theoretical perspectives and criteria for selective integration. *Journal of Management Accounting Research, 15*, 3-49.

Crant, J. M. (2000). Proactive behavior in organizations. *Journal of Management, 26*(3), 435-462.

Creswell, J. W. (2003). *Research design: Qualitative, quantitative, and mixed method approaches*. Thousand Oaks: Sage Publications.

Cronbach, L. (1951). Coefficient alpha and the internal structure of tests. *Psychometrika, 16*(3), 297-334.

Cropanzano, R., Prehar, C. A., & Chen, P. Y. (2002). Using social exchange theory to distinguish procedural from interactional justice. *Group and Organization Management, 27*(3), 324-351.

Crotty, M. (1998). *The foundations of social research: Meaning and perspective in the research process*. London: Sage Publications.

Cudeck, R., & Browne, M. W. (1983). Cross-validation of covariance structures. *Multivariate Behavioral Research, 18*(2), 147.

Curran, P. J., West, S. G., & Finch, J. F. (1996). The robustness of test statistics to nonnormality and specification error in confirmatory factor analysis. *Psychological Methods, 1*(1), 16-29.

Cyert, R. M., & March, J. G. (1963). *A behavioral theory of the firm*. Englewood Cliffs: Prentice Hall.

Dahl, R. (1957). The concept of power. *Behavioral Science, 2*(3), 201-215.

Dahrendorf, R. (2006). *Homo Sociologicus: Ein Versuch zur Geschichte, Bedeutung und Kritik der Kategorie der sozialen Rolle*. Wiesbaden: Verlag für Sozialwissenschaften.

Dalton, G. W. (1971). Motivation and control in organizations. In G. W. Dalton & P. R. Lawrence (Eds.), *Motivation and control in organizations* (1 ed., pp. 1-35). Homewood: Irvin and the Dorsey Press.

Daniels, K., & Bailey, A. (1999). Strategy development processes and participation in decision making: Predictors of role stressors and job satisfaction. *Journal of Applied Management Studies, 8*(1), 27-42.

Daniels, K., & Guppy, A. (1994). Occupational stress, social support, job control, and psychological well-being. *Human Relations, 47*(12), 1523-1544.

Dansereau, F., Graen, G., & Haga, W. (1975). A vertical dyad linkage approach to leadership within formal organizations: A longitudinal investigation of the role making process. *Organizational Behavior and Human Performance, 13*(1), 46-78.

Datar, S. M., Kulp, S. C., & Lambert, R. A. (2001). Balancing performance measures. *Journal of Accounting Research, 39*(1), 75-92.

Davidson, S., & Weil, R. L. (1978). *Handbook of cost accounting*. New York: McGraw-Hill.

Davis, J. H., Schoorman, F. D., & Donaldson, L. (1997). Toward a stewardship theory of management. *Academy of Management Review, 22*(1), 20-47.

Davis, L. E., & Wacker, G. J. (1987). *Job design*. New York: Wiley.

Davis, S., DeZoort, F. T., & Kopp, L. S. (2006). The effect of obedience pressure and perceived responsibility on management accountants' creation of budgetary slack. *Behavioral Research in Accounting, 18*, 19-35.

Davis, S., Kohlmeyer, J. M., Epstein, M. J., & John, Y. L. (2005). The impact of employee rank on the relationship between attitudes, motivation, and performance. *Advances in Management Accounting, 14*, 233-252.

Dearden, J. (1987). Measuring profit center managers. *Harvard Business Review, 65*(5), 84-88.

DeCoster, D. T., & Fertakis, J. P. (1968). Budget-induced pressure and its relationship to supervisory behavior. *Journal of Accounting Research, 6*(2), 237-246.

Demski, J. S. (1976). Uncertainty and evaluation based on controllable performance. *Journal of Accounting Research, 14*(2), 230-245.

Demski, J. S. (1981). Cost allocation games. In S. Moriarity (Ed.), *Joint cost allocations* (pp. 142-173). Norman: Center for Economic and Management Research.

Demski, J. S. (1994). *Managerial uses of accounting information*. Boston et al.: Kluwer.

Demski, J. S., & Feltham, G. A. (1976). *Cost determination: A conceptual approach*. Ames: Iowa State University Press.

Demski, J. S., & Feltham, G. A. (1978). Economic incentives in budgetary control systems. *The Accounting Review, 53*(2), 336-359.

Demski, J. S., & Sappington, D. E. M. (1989). Hierarchical structure and responsibility accounting. *Journal of Accounting Research, 27*(1), 40-58.

Dent, J. F. (1987). Tensions in the design of formal control systems: A field study in a computer company. In W. J. Bruns & R. S. Kaplan (Eds.), *Accounting and management: Field study perspectives* (pp. 119-145). Boston: Harvard Business School Press.

Denzin, N. K., & Lincoln, Y. S. (2000). The discipline and practice of qualitative research. In N. K. Denzin & Y. S. Lincoln (Eds.), *Handbook of qualitative research* (2 ed., pp. 1-29). Thousand Oaks: Sage Publications.

Derfuss, K. (2009). The relationship of budgetary participation and reliance on accounting performance measures with individual-level consequent variables: A meta-analysis. *European Accounting Review, 18*(2), 203-239.

DeVellis, R. F. (2003). *Scale development: Theory and applications* (2 ed.). Thousand Oaks: Sage Publications.

Dewey, J. (1989). The development of American pragmatism. In H. S. Thayer (Ed.), *Pragmatism: The classic writings* (pp. 23-40). Indianapolis: Hackett.

Diamantopoulos, A., Riefler, P., & Roth, K. P. (2008). Advancing formative measurement models. *Journal of Business Research, 61*(12), 1203-1218.

Diamantopoulos, A., & Siguaw, J. A. (2000). *Introducing LISREL*. London et al.: Sage Publications.

Diamantopoulos, A., & Winklhofer, H. M. (2001). Index construction with formative indicators: An alternative to scale development. *Journal of Marketing Research, 38*(2), 269-277.

Dierdorff, E. C., & Morgeson, F. P. (2007). Consensus in work role requirements: The influence of discrete occupational context on role expectations. *Journal of Applied Psychology, 92*(5), 1228-1241.

Dillman, D. A. (2007). *Mail and internet surveys: The tailored design method*. Hoboken: Wiley.

Dirks, K. T. (1999). The effects of interpersonal trust on work group performance. *Journal of Applied Psychology, 84*(3), 445-455.

Dirks, K. T., & Ferrin, D. L. (2001). The role of trust in organizational settings. *Organization Science, 12*(4), 450-467.

Douglas, P. C., HassabElnaby, H., Norman, C. S., & Wier, B. (2007). An investigation of ethical position and budgeting systems: Egyptian managers in US and Egyptian firms. *Journal of International Accounting, Auditing and Taxation, 16*(1), 90-109.

Drolet, A. L., & Morrison, D. G. (2001). Do we really need multiple-item measures in service research? *Journal of Service Research, 3*(3), 196-204.

Drucker, P. F. (1962). *The practice of management*. London: Mercury Books.

Drucker, P. F. (1993). *Post-capitalist society*. Boston: Butterworth-Heinemann.

Drury, C. (2005). *Management accounting for business decisions* (3 ed.). London: Thomson.

Drury, C. (2007). *Management and cost accounting* (7 ed.). London: Thomson.

Drury, C., & El-Shishini, H. (2005). *Divisional performance measurement: An examination of the potential explanatory factors*. London: The Chartered Institute of Management Accountants (CIMA).

Drury, C., & Tayles, M. (1995). Issues arising from surveys of management accounting practice. *Management Accounting Research, 6*(3), 267-280.

Dubinsky, A. J., & Mattson, B. E. (1979). Consequences of role conflict and ambiguity experienced by retail salespeople. *Journal of Retailing, 55*(4), 70-86.

Duckro, P. N., Beal, D., & George, C. E. (1979). Research on the effects of disconfirmed client role expectations in psychotherapy: A critical review. *Psychological Bulletin, 86*(2), 260-275.

Dunk, A. S. (1992). The effects of managerial level on the relationship between budgetary participation and job satisfaction. *The British Accounting Review, 24*(3), 207-218.

Dunk, A. S. (1993a). The effect of budget emphasis and information asymmetry on the relation between budgetary participation and slack. *The Accounting Review, 68*(2), 400-410.

Dunk, A. S. (1993b). The effects of job-related tension on managerial performance in participative budgetary settings. *Accounting, Organizations and Society, 18*(7-8), 575-585.

Dutton, J. E., Ashford, S. J., O'Neill, R. M., Hayes, E., & Wierba, E. E. (1997). Reading the wind: How middle managers assess the context for selling issues to top managers. *Strategic Management Journal, 18*(5), 407-423.

Ebert, T. A. (2009). Facets of trust in relationships: A literature synthesis of highly ranked trust articles. *Journal of Business Market Management, 3*(1), 65-84.

Eccles, R. G. (1986). *The transfer pricing problem: A theory for practice*. Massachusetts: Lexington.

Eccles, R. G. (1991). The performance measurement manifesto. *Harvard Business Review, 69*(1), 131-137.

Eden, D. (1988). Pygmalion, goal setting, and expectancy: Compatible ways to boost productivity. *Academy of Management Review, 13*(4), 639-652.

Eden, D., & Kinnar, J. (1991). Modeling Galatea: Boosting self-efficacy to increase volunteering. *Journal of Applied Psychology, 76*(6), 770-780.

Edwards, J. R. (2001). Multidimensional constructs in organizational behavior research: An integrative analytical framework. *Organizational Research Methods, 4*(2), 144-192.

Edwards, J. R., & Bagozzi, R. P. (2000). On the nature and direction of relationships between constructs and measures. *Psychological Methods, 5*(2), 155-174.

Eisenhardt, K. M. (1989a). Agency theory: An assessment and review. *Academy of Management Review, 14*(1), 57-74.

Eisenhardt, K. M. (1989b). Building theories from case study research. *Academy of Management Review, 14*(4), 532-550.

Eisenhardt, K. M. (1989c). Making fast strategic decisions in high-velocity environments. *Academy of Management Journal, 32*(3), 543-576.

Eisenhardt, K. M., Kahwajy, J. L., & Bourgeois, L. J. (1997). How management teams can have a good fight. *Harvard Business Review, 75*(4), 77-85.

El-Sehity, T., Haumer, H., Helmenstein, C., Kirchler, E., & Maciejovsky, B. (2002). Hindsight bias and individual risk attitude within the context of experimental asset markets. *Journal of Psychology and Financial Markets, 3*(4), 227-235.

Elloy, D. F., Everett, J. E., & Flynn, W. R. (1995). Multidimensional mapping of the correlates of job involvement. *Canadian Journal of Behavioural Science, 27*(1), 79-91.

Elovainio, M., & Kivimäki, M. (2001). The effects of personal need for structure and occupational identity in the role stress process. *Journal of Social Psychology, 141*(3), 365-378.

Emmanuel, C. R., & Mehafdi, M. (1994). *Transfer pricing*. London, San Diego: Academic Press.

Ewert, R., & Wagenhofer, A. (2005). *Interne Unternehmensrechnung* (5 ed.). Berlin et al.: Springer.

Eysenck, H. J. (1954). *The psychology of politics*. London: Routledge.

Fandt, P. M. (1991). The relationship of accountability and interdependent behavior to enhancing team consequences. *Group and Organization Studies, 16*(3), 300-312.

Feltham, G. A., & Xie, J. (1994). Performance measure congruity and diversity in multi-task principal/agent relations. *The Accounting Review, 69*(3), 429-453.

Ferrara, W. L. (1967). Responsibility reporting vs. direct costing - is there a conflict? *Management Accounting, June*, 43-54.

Ferris, G. R., Dulebohn, J. H., Frink, D. D., George-Falvy, J., Mitchell, T. R., & Matthews, L. M. (1997). Job and organizational characteristics, accountability, and employee influence. *Journal of Managerial Issues, 9*(2), 162-175.

Filley, A. C., & House, R. J. (1969). *Managerial process and organizational behavior.* Glenview: Scott, Foresman & Company.

Fink, A. (2002). *The survey handbook* (2 ed.). Thousand Oaks: Sage Publications.

Fischhoff, B. (1975). Hindsight is not equal to foresight: The effect of outcome knowledge on judgment under uncertainty. *Journal of Experimental Psychology: Human Perception and Performance, 1*(3), 288-299.

Fischhoff, B., & Beyth, R. (1975). "I knew it would happen": Remembered probabilities of once-future things. *Organizational Behavior and Human Performance, 13*(1), 1-16.

Fisher, C. D., & Gitelson, R. (1983). A meta-analysis of the correlates of role conflict and ambiguity. *Journal of Applied Psychology, 68*(2), 320-333.

Fisher, J. G. (1998). Contingency theory, management control systems and firm outcomes: Past results and future directions. *Behavioral Research in Accounting, 10*, 47-64.

Fisher, J. G., & Selling, T. I. (1993). The outcome effect in performance evaluation: Decision process observability and consensus. *Behavioral Research in Accounting, 5*, 58-77.

Fisher, R. T. (2001). Role stress, the type A behavior pattern, and external auditor job satisfaction and performance. *Behavioral Research in Accounting, 13*, 143-170.

Flammer, A. (2001). Self-efficacy. In N. J. Smelser & P. B. Baltes (Eds.), *International encyclopedia of the social and behavioral sciences* (pp. 13812-13815). Amsterdam, New York: Elsevier.

Fogarty, T. J. (1992). Organizational socialization in accounting firms: A theoretical framework and agenda for future research. *Accounting, Organizations and Society, 17*(2), 129-149.

Fogarty, T. J., & Kalbers, L. P. (2000). An empirical evaluation of the interpersonal and organisational correlates of professionalism in internal auditing. *Accounting and Business Research, 30*(2), 125-136.

Fogarty, T. J., Singh, J., Rhoads, G. K., & Moore, R. K. (2000). Antecedents and consequences of burnout in accounting: Beyond the role stress model. *Behavioral Research in Accounting, 12*, 31-67.

Fornell, C. (1982). *A second generation of multivariate analysis*. New York: Praeger.

Fornell, C. (1987). A second generation of multivariate analysis: Classification of methods and implications for marketing research. In M. J. Houston (Ed.), *Review of marketing* (pp. 407-450). Chicago: American Marketing Association.

Fornell, C., & Bookstein, F. L. (1982). Two structural equation models: LISREL and PLS applied to consumer exit-voice theory. *Journal of Marketing Research, 19*(4), 440-452.

Fornell, C., & Larcker, D. F. (1981). Evaluating structural equation models with unobservable variables and measurement error. *Journal of Marketing Research, 18*(1), 39-50.

Fox, M. L., Dwyer, D. J., & Ganster, D. C. (1993). Effects of stressful job demands and control on physiological and attitudinal outcomes in a hospital setting. *Academy of Management Journal, 36*(2), 289-318.

Frederickson, J. R. (1992). Relative performance information: The effects of common uncertainty and contract type on agent effort. *The Accounting Review, 67*(4), 647-669.

Frederickson, J. R., & Waller, W. S. (2005). Carrot or stick? Contract frame and use of decision-influencing information in a principal-agent setting. *Journal of Accounting Research, 43*(5), 709-733.

Freeman, J. (1999). Efficiency and rationality in organizations. *Administrative Science Quarterly, 44*(1), 163-175.

Fremgen, J. M., & Liao, S. S. (1981). *The allocation of corporate indirect costs*. New York: National Association of Accountants.

French, J. R. P., Caplan, R. D., & Van Harrison, R. (1982). *The mechanisms of job stress and strain*. Chichester et al.: Wiley.

Frese, M., & Fay, D. (2001). Personal initiative: An active performance concept for work in the 21st century. In L. L. Cummings & B. M. Staw (Eds.), *Research in organizational behavior* (Vol. 23, pp. 133-187). Greenwich: JAI Press.

Frese, M., Kring, W., Soose, A., & Zempel, J. (1996). Personal initiative at work: Differences between East and West Germany. *Academy of Management Journal, 39*(1), 37-63.

Fried, Y., Ben-David, H. A., Tiegs, R. B., Avital, N., & Yeverechyahu, U. (1998). The interactive effect of role conflict and role ambiguity on job performance. *Journal of Occupational and Organizational Psychology, 71*(1), 19-27.

Friedman, R. A., & Podolny, J. (1992). Differentiation of boundary spanning roles: Labor negotiations and implications for role conflict. *Administrative Science Quarterly, 37*(1), 28-47.

Frink, D. D., & Klimoski, R. J. (1998). Toward a theory of accountability in organization and human resource management. In G. R. Ferris (Ed.), *Research in personnel and human resources management* (Vol. 16, pp. 1-52). Greenwich: JAI Press.

Frohman, A. L. (1997). Igniting organizational change from below: The power of personal initiative. *Organizational Dynamics, 25*(3), 39-53.

Frow, N., Marginson, D., & Ogden, S. (2005). Encouraging strategic behaviour while maintaining management control: Multi-functional project teams, budgets, and the negotiation of shared accountabilities in contemporary enterprises. *Management Accounting Research, 16*(3), 269-292.

Fry, L. W., & Hellriegel, D. (1987). The role and expectancy participation model: An empirical assessment and extension. *Journal of Occupational Behavior, 8*(4), 295-309.

Furnham, A., & Stringfield, P. (1994). Congruence of self and subordinate ratings of managerial practices as a correlate of superior evaluation. *Journal of Occupational and Organizational Psychology, 67*(1), 57-67.

Garfinkel, H. (1967). *Studies in ethnomethodology*. Englewood Cliffs: Prentice Hall.

Gerbing, D. W., & Anderson, J. C. (1988). An updated paradigm for scale development incorporating unidimensionality and its assessment. *Journal of Marketing Research, 25*(2), 186-192.

Ghosh, D. (2000). Organizational design and manipulative behavior: Evidence from a negotiated transfer pricing experiment. *Behavioral Research in Accounting, 12*, 1-30.

Ghosh, D. (2005). Alternative measures of managers' performance, controllability, and the outcome effect. *Behavioral Research in Accounting, 17*, 55-70.

Ghosh, D., & Lusch, R. F. (2000). Outcome effect, controllability and performance evaluation of managers: Some field evidence from multi-outlet businesses. *Accounting, Organizations and Society, 25*(4-5), 411-425.

Gibbins, M., & Salterio, S. (1996). Experimental accounting research: Current methodological issues and debates. In A. J. Richardson (Ed.), *Research methods in accounting: Issues and debates* (pp. 9-24). Vancouver: Canada Research Foundation.

Gibbons, R. (1998). Incentives in organizations. *Journal of Economic Perspectives, 12*(4), 115-132.

Gibbons, R., & Murphy, K. J. (1990). Relative performance evaluation for chief executive officers. *Industrial and Labor Relations Review, 43*(3), 30-51.

Gibbs, M., Merchant, K. A., Van der Stede, W. A., & Vargus, M. E. (2004). Determinants and effects of subjectivity in incentives. *The Accounting Review, 79*(2), 409-436.

Gibbs, M., Merchant, K. A., Van der Stede, W. A., & Vargus, M. E. (2009). Performance measure properties and incentive system design. *Industrial Relations, 48*(2), 237-264.

Gilboa, S., Shirom, A., Fried, Y., & Cooper, C. L. (2008). A meta-analysis of work demand stressors and job performance: Examining main and moderating effects. *Personnel Psychology, 61*(2), 227-271.

Giraud, F., Langevin, P., & Mendoza, C. (2004). *The controllability principle: A survey of managers' opinions*. Paper presented at the 27th annual congress of the European Accounting Association, Prague.

Giraud, F., Langevin, P., & Mendoza, C. (2008). Justice as a rationale for the controllability principle: A study of managers' opinions. *Management Accounting Research, 19*(1), 32-44.

Gist, M. E., & Mitchell, T. B. (1992). Self-efficacy: A theoretical analysis of its determinants and malleability. *Academy of Management Review, 17*(2), 183-211.

Gong, Y., Shenkar, O., Luo, Y., & Nyaw, M.-K. (2001). Role conflict and ambiguity of CEOs in international joint ventures: A transaction cost perspective. *Journal of Applied Psychology, 86*(4), 764-773.

Goodman, P. S., & Friedman, A. (1975). An examination of Adam's theory of inequity. In R. M. Steers & L. W. Porter (Eds.), *Motivation and work behavior* (1 ed., pp. 155-179). New York et al.: McGraw-Hill.

Govindarajan, V. (1984). Appropriateness of accounting data in performance evaluation: An empirical examination of environmental uncertainty as an intervening variable. *Accounting, Organizations and Society, 9*(2), 125-135.

Grabski, S. V. (1985). Transfer pricing in complex organizations: A review and integration of recent empirical and analytical research. *Journal of Accounting Literature, 4*, 33-75.

Graen, G. (1976). Role making processes in complex organizations. In M. D. Dunnette (Ed.), *Handbook of industrial and organizational psychology* (2 ed., pp. 1201-1245). Chicago: Rand McNally.

Graen, G., & Scandura, T. A. (1987). Toward a psychology of dyadic organizing. In L. L. Cummings & B. M. Staw (Eds.), *Research in organizational behavior* (Vol. 9, pp. 175-208). Greenwich: JAI Press.

Greenberg, J. (1990). Organizational justice: Yesterday, today, and tomorrow. *Journal of Management, 16*(2), 399-432.

Greenberg, J., Colquitt, J. A., & Zapata-Phelan, C. P. (2005). What is organizational justice? A historical overview. In J. Greenberg & J. A. Colquitt (Eds.), *Handbook of organizational justice* (pp. 3-58). Mahwah et al.: Erlbaum.

Greenberger, D. B., Strasser, S., Cummings, L. L., & Dunham, R. B. (1989). The impact of personal control on performance and satisfaction. *Organizational Behavior and Human Decision Processes, 43*(1), 29-51.

Greenwald, H. P. (1972). Patterns of authority in two herding societies: An ecological approach. *Administrative Science Quarterly, 17*(2), 207-217.

Greenwood, D. J., & Levin, M. (2000). Reconstructing the relationships between universities and society through action research. In N. K. Denzin & Y. S. Lincoln (Eds.), *Handbook of qualitative research* (2 ed., pp. 85-106). Thousand Oaks: Sage Publications.

Gregson, T., Wendell, J., & Aono, J. (1994). Role ambiguity, role conflict, and perceived environmental uncertainty: Are the scales measuring separate constructs for accountants? *Behavioral Research in Accounting, 6*, 144-159.

Grey, R. J., & Gordon, G. G. (1978). Risk-taking managers: Who gets the top jobs? *Management Review, 67*(11), 8.

Griffin, M. A., Neal, A., & Parker, S. K. (2007). A new model of work role performance: Positive behavior in uncertain and interdependent contexts. *Academy of Management Journal, 50*(2), 327-347.

Griffin, R. W. (1987). Toward an integrated theory of task design. In L. L. Cummings & B. M. Staw (Eds.), *Research in organizational behavior* (Vol. 9, pp. 79-120). Greenwich: JAI Press.

Griffin, R. W., & McMahan, G. C. (1994). Motivation through job design. In J. Greenberg (Ed.), *Organizational behaviour: State of the science* (pp. 23-43). Hillsdale: Erlbaum.

Guba, E. G. (1990). The alternative paradigm dialogue. In E. G. Guba (Ed.), *The paradigm dialogue*. Newbury Park: Sage Publications.

Gul, F. A., & Chia, Y. M. (1994). The effects of management accounting systems, perceived environmental uncertainty and decentralization on managerial performance: A test of three way interaction. *Accounting, Organizations and Society, 19*(4-5), 413-426.

Habermas, J. (1973). Stichworte zur Theorie der Sozialisation. In J. Habermas (Ed.), *Kultur und Kritik: Verstreute Aufsätze* (pp. 118-195). Frankfurt: Suhrkamp.

Hackman, J. R., & Oldham, G. R. (1976). Motivation through the design of work: Test of a theory. *Organizational Behavior and Human Performance, 16*(2), 250-279.

Hair, J. F., Anderson, R. E., Tatham, R. L., & Black, W. C. (2006). *Multivariate data analysis*. Upper Saddle River: Prentice Hall.

Hall, M. (2008). The effect of comprehensive performance measurement systems on role clarity, psychological empowerment and managerial performance. *Accounting, Organizations and Society, 33*(2-3), 141-163.

Hall, R. J., & Lord, R. G. (1998a). Multi-level information-processing explanations of followers' leadership perceptions. In F. Dansereau & F. J. Yammarino (Eds.), *Leadership: The multiple-level approaches, Part B* (Vol. 24, pp. 159-183). Stamford: JAI Press.

Hall, R. J., & Lord, R. G. (1998b). The role of within-individual cognitive structures in determining higher-level effects. In F. Dansereau & F. J. Yammarino (Eds.), *Leadership: The multiple-level approaches, Part B* (Vol. 24, pp. 205-214). Stamford: JAI Press.

Hamner, W. C., & Tosi, H. L. (1974). Relationship of role conflict and role ambiguity to job involvement measures. *Journal of Applied Psychology, 59*(4), 497-499.

Harigopal, K. (1995). *Organizational stress: A study of role conflict*. London: Sangam.

Harman, H. H. (1967). *Modern factor analysis*. Chicago: University of Chicago Press.

Harris, E. G., Artis, A. B., Walters, J. H., & Licata, J. W. (2006). Role stressors, service worker job resourcefulness, and job outcomes: An empirical analysis. *Journal of Business Research, 59*(4), 407-415.

Harter, J. K., Schmidt, F. L., & Hayes, T. L. (2002). Business-unit-level relationship between employee satisfaction, employee engagement, and business outcomes: A meta-analysis. *Journal of Applied Psychology, 87*(2), 268-279.

Hartline, M. D., & Bejou, D. (2004). *Internal relationship management*. Binghamton: Best Business Books.

Hartmann, F. G. H. (2000). The appropriateness of RAPM: Toward the further development of theory. *Accounting, Organizations and Society, 25*(4-5), 451-482.

Hartmann, F. G. H. (2007). Do accounting performance measures indeed reduce managerial ambiguity under uncertainty? *Advances in Management Accounting, 16*, 159-180.

Hartmann, F. G. H., & Slapničar, S. (2007). Evaluation process justice: Relevance and consequences (Working paper). SSRN.

Hartmann, F. G. H., & Slapničar, S. (2009). How formal performance evaluation affects trust between superior and subordinate managers. *Accounting, Organizations and Society, 34*(6-7), 722-737.

Hatry, H. P., & Wholey, J. S. (1999). *Performance measurement: Getting results*. Washington: Urban Institute Press.

Haug, F. (1994). *Kritik der Rollentheorie* (5 ed.). Hamburg: Argument.

Hawkins, S. A., & Hastie, R. (1990). Hindsight: Biased judgments of past events after the outcomes are known. *Psychological Bulletin, 107*(3), 311-327.

Hayes, J. (1992). Expectations regarding the controllability of outcomes in organizations: Implications for management and organization development. *Management Decision, 30*(6), 156-165.

Hechter, M. (2008). The rise and fall of normative control. *Accounting, Organizations and Society, 33*(6), 663-676.

Heider, F. (1958). *The psychology of interpersonal relations*. New York et al.: Wiley.

Hempel, C. G. (1966). *Philosophy of natural science*. Englewood Cliffs: Prentice Hall.

Henderson, R. I. (1980). *Performance appraisal: Theory to practice*. Reston: Reston.

Heneman, H. C. (1974). Comparison of self and superior ratings of managerial performance. *Journal of Applied Psychology, 59*(5), 638-642.

Heneman, R. L. (2001). *Business-driven compensation policies: Integrating compensation systems with corporate strategies*. New York: Amacom.

Henri, J. F. (2006). Management control systems and strategy: A resource-based perspective. *Accounting, Organizations and Society, 31*(6), 529-558.

Henriksen, T. D. (2008). Liquidating roles and crystallising positions: Investigating the road between role and positioning theory. In F. M. Moghaddam, R. Harré & N. Lee (Eds.), *Global conflict resolution through positioning analysis* (pp. 41-64). New York: Springer.

Heuven, E., Bakker, A. B., Schaufeli, W. B., & Huisman, N. (2006). The role of self-efficacy in performing emotion work. *Journal of Vocational Behavior, 69*(2), 222-235.

Higgins, J. A. (1952). Responsibility accounting. *The Arthur Andersen Chronicle, 12*, 93-113.

Hillson, D., & Murray-Webster, R. (2007). *Understanding and managing risk attitude* (2 ed.). Aldershot: Gower Publishing.

Hilton, R. W. (2008). *Managerial accounting: Creating value in a dynamic business environment* (7 ed.). Boston: McGraw-Hill.

Hinkin, T. R. (1995). A review of scale development practices in the study of organizations. *Journal of Management, 21*(5), 967-988.

Hiroto, D. S. (1974). Locus of control and learned helplessness. *Journal of Experimental Psychology, 102*(2), 187-193.

Hirst, M. K. (1981). Accounting information and the evaluation of subordinate performance: A situational approach. *The Accounting Review, 56*(4), 771-784.

Hirst, M. K. (1983a). The controllability of financial outcomes. *Abacus, 19*(1), 29-38.

Hirst, M. K. (1983b). Reliance on accounting performance measures, task uncertainty, and dysfunctional behavior: Some extensions. *Journal of Accounting Research, 21*(2), 596-605.

Hirst, M. K., & Yetton, P. W. (1999). The effects of budget goals and task interdependence on the level of and variance in performance: A research note. *Accounting, Organizations and Society, 24*(3), 205-216.

Hofstede, G. H. (1967). *The game of budget control: How to live with budgetary standards and yet be motivated by them*. Assen: Van Gorcum.

Hogg, M. A., & Vaughan, G. M. (2005). *Social psychology* (4 ed.). Harlow: Pearson.

Hollenbeck, J. R., Ilgen, D. R., LePine, J. A., Colquitt, J. A., & Hedlund, J. (1998). Extending the multilevel theory of team decision making: Effects of feedback and experience in hierarchical teams. *Academy of Management Journal, 41*(3), 269-282.

Holmström, B. (1979). Moral hazard and observability. *Bell Journal of Economics, 10*(1), 74-91.

Holmström, B. (1982). Moral hazard in teams. *Bell Journal of Economics, 13*(2), 324-340.

Holmström, B., & Milgrom, P. (1987). Aggregation and linearity in the provision of intertemporal incentives. *Econometrica, 55*(2), 303-328.

Holmström, B., & Milgrom, P. (1994). The firm as an incentive system. *American Economic Review, 84*(4), 972-991.

Hölzl, E., Kirchler, E., & Rodler, C. (2002). Hindsight bias in economic expectations: I knew all along what I want to hear. *Journal of Applied Psychology, 87*(3), 437-443.

Homburg, C. (1989). *Exploratorische Ansätze der Kausalanalyse als Instrument der Marketingplanung*. Frankfurt et al.: Lang.

Homburg, C., & Baumgartner, H. (1995). Beurteilung von Kausalmodellen: Bestandsaufnahme und Anwendungsempfehlungen. *Marketing - Zeitschrift für Forschung und Praxis, 17*(3), 162-176.

Homburg, C., & Baumgartner, H. (1998). Beurteilung von Kausalmodellen: Bestandsaufnahme und Anwendungsempfehlungen. In L. Hildebrandt & C. Homburg (Eds.), *Die Kausalanalyse* (pp. 343-369). Stuttgart: Schäffer-Poeschel.

Homburg, C., & Giering, A. (1996). Konzeptualisierung und Operationalisierung komplexer Konstrukte. *Marketing - Zeitschrift für Forschung und Praxis, 18*(1), 5-24.

Homburg, C., & Giering, A. (1998). Konzeptualisierung und Operationalisierung komplexer Konstrukte: Ein Leitfaden für die Marketingforschung. In L. Hildebrandt & C. Homburg (Eds.), *Die Kausalanalyse* (pp. 111-146). Stuttgart: Schäffer-Poeschel.

Homburg, C., & Hildebrandt, L. (1998). Die Kausalanalyse: Bestandsaufnahme, Entwicklungsrichtungen, Problemfelder. In L. Hildebrandt & C. Homburg (Eds.), *Die Kausalanalyse* (pp. 15-43). Stuttgart: Schäffer-Poeschel.

Homburg, C., & Stebel, P. (2009). Determinants of contract terms for professional services. *Management Accounting Research, 20*(2), 129-145.

Hopper, T. M. (1980). Role conflicts of management accountants and their position within organisation structures. *Accounting, Organizations and Society, 5*(4), 401-411.

Hopper, T. M., & Hoque, Z. (2006). Triangulation approaches to accounting research. In Z. Hoque (Ed.), *Methodological issues in accounting research: Theories, methods, issues* (pp. 477-486). London: Spiramus.

Hopwood, A. G. (1972). An empirical study of the role of accounting data in performance evaluation. *Journal of Accounting Research, 10*(3), 156-182.

Hopwood, A. G. (1973). *An accounting system and managerial behavior*. London: Lexington.

Hopwood, A. G., & Young, S. M. (1998). Call for papers: Accounting, organizational transformation and new organizational forms. *Management Accounting Research, 9*(4), 357-358.

Horvath, M., & Andrews, S. B. (2007). The role of fairness perceptions and accountability attributions in predicting reactions to organizational events. *Journal of Psychology, 141*(2), 203-222.

House, R. J., & Rizzo, J. R. (1972). Role conflict and ambiguity as critical variables in a model of organizational behavior. *Organizational Behavior and Human Performance, 7*(3), 467-505.

House, R. J., Schuler, R. S., & Levanoni, E. (1983). Role conflict and ambiguity scales: Reality or artifacts? *Journal of Applied Psychology, 68*(2), 334-337.

Howell, J. M., & Boies, K. (2004). Champions of technological innovation: The influence of contextual knowledge, role orientation, idea generation, and idea promotion on champion emergence. *Leadership Quarterly, 15*(1), 123-143.

Hoyle, R. H., & Kenny, D. A. (1999). Sample size, reliability, and tests of statistical mediation. In R. H. Hoyle (Ed.), *Statistical strategies for small sample research* (pp. 195-222). Thousand Oaks: Sage Publications.

Hu, L.-T., & Bentler, P. M. (1995). Evaluating model fit. In R. H. Hoyle (Ed.), *Structural equation modeling: Concepts, issues, and applications* (pp. 76-100). Thousands Oaks: Sage Publications.

Huber, F., Herrmann, A., Meyer, F., Vogel, J., & Vollhardt, K. (2007). *Kausalmodellierung mit Partial Least Squares: Eine anwendungsorientierte Einführung*. Wiesbaden: Gabler.

Huffman, C., & Cain, L. B. (2000). Effects of considering uncontrollable factors in sales force performance evaluation. *Psychology and Marketing, 17*(9), 799-833.

Huffman, C., & Cain, L. B. (2001). Adjustments in performance measures: Distributive and procedural justice effects on outcome satisfaction. *Psychology and Marketing, 18*(6), 593-615.

Hulland, J. (1999). Use of partial least squares (PLS) in strategic management research: A review of four recent studies. *Strategic Management Journal, 20*(2), 195-204.

Hunt, S. D., Sparkman, R., & Wilcox, J. B. (1982). The pre-test in survey research: Issues and preliminary findings. *Journal of Marketing Research, 19*(2), 269-273.

Hurrell, J. J. (2005). Organizational stress interventions. In J. Barling, E. K. Kelloway & M. R. Frone (Eds.), *Handbook of work stress* (pp. 623-646). Thousand Oaks et al.: Sage Publications.

Ilgen, D. R., Fisher, C. D., & Taylor, M. S. (1979). Consequences of individual feedback on behavior in organizations. *Journal of Applied Psychology, 64*(4), 349-371.

Ilgen, D. R., & Hollenbeck, J. R. (1991). The structure of work: Job design and roles. In M. D. Dunnette & L. M. Hough (Eds.), *Handbook of industrial and organizational psychology* (2 ed., pp. 165-207). Palo Alto: Consulting Psychologists Press.

Indjejikian, R. J. (1999). Performance evaluation and compensation research: An agency perspective. *Accounting Horizons, 13*(2), 147-157.

Inkson, J. H. K., Pugh, D. S., & Hickson, D. J. (1970). Organization context and structure: An abbreviated replication. *Administrative Science Quarterly, 15*(3), 318-329.

Ittner, C. D., & Larcker, D. F. (1998). Innovations in performance measurement: Trends and research implications. *Journal of Management Accounting Research, 10*, 205-238.

Ittner, C. D., & Larcker, D. F. (2002). Determinants of performance measure choices in worker incentive plans. *Journal of Labor Economics, 20*(2), 58-90.

Ittner, C. D., Larcker, D. F., & Meyer, M. W. (2003). Subjectivity and the weighting of performance measures: Evidence from a balanced scorecard. *The Accounting Review, 78*(3), 725-758.

Ittner, C. D., Larcker, D. F., & Rajan, M. V. (1997). The choice of performance measures in annual bonus contracts. *The Accounting Review, 72*(2), 231-255.

Ittner, C. D., Larcker, D. F., & Randall, T. (2003). Performance implications of strategic performance measurement in financial services firms. *Accounting, Organizations and Society, 28*(7-8), 715-741.

Ivancevich, J. M., & Matteson, M. T. (1987). Organizational level stress management interventions. *Journal of Organizational Behavior Management, 8*(2), 229-248.

Ivancevich, J. M., Matteson, M. T., Freedman, S. M., & Phillips, J. S. (1990). Worksite stress management interventions. *American Psychologist, 45*(2), 252-261.

Jackson, J. (1998). Contemporary criticisms of role theory. *Journal of Occupational Science, 5*(2), 49-55.

Jackson, M. (2009). Responsibility versus accountability in the Friedrich-Finer debate. *Journal of Management History, 15*(1), 66-77.

Jackson, S. E. (1983). Participation in decision making as a strategy for reducing job-related strain. *Journal of Applied Psychology, 68*(1), 3-19.

Jackson, S. E., & Schuler, R. S. (1985). A meta-analysis and conceptual critique of research on role ambiguity and role conflict in work. *Organizational Behavior and Human Decision Processes, 36*(1), 16-78.

Jackson, S. E., Turner, J. A., & Brief, A. P. (1987). Correlates of burnout among public service lawyers. *Journal of Occupational Behavior, 8*(4), 339-349.

Jamal, M. (1985). Relationship of job stress to job performance: A study of managers and blue-collar workers. *Human Relations, 38*(5), 409-424.

James, L. R., & Brett, J. M. (1984). Mediators, moderators, and tests for mediation. *Journal of Applied Psychology, 69*(2), 307-321.

James, L. R., & Mazerolle, M. D. (2002). *Personality in work organizations*. Thousand Oaks: Sage Publications.

James, W. (1890). *The principles of psychology*. New York: Holt.

Janakiraman, S. N., Lambert, R. A., & Larcker, D. F. (1992). An empirical investigation of the relative performance evaluation hypothesis. *Journal of Accounting Research, 30*(1), 53-69.

Jarvis, C. B., MacKenzie, S. B., & Podsakoff, P. M. (2003). A critical review of construct indicators and measurement model misspecification in marketing and consumer research. *Journal of Consumer Research, 30*(2), 199-218.

Jaworski, B. J., & Young, S. M. (1992). Dysfunctional behavior and management control: An empirical study of marketing managers. *Accounting, Organizations and Society, 17*(1), 17-35.

Jensen, M. C., & Meckling, W. H. (1976). Theory of the firm: Managerial behavior, agency costs and ownership structure. *Journal of Financial Economics, 3*(4), 305-360.

Jensen, M. C., & Meckling, W. H. (1994). The nature of man. *Journal of Applied Corporate Finance, 2*(7), 4-19.

Jerusalem, M., & Schwarzer, R. (1992). Self-efficacy as a resource factor in stress appraisal processes. In R. Schwarzer (Ed.), *Self-efficacy: Thought control of action*. Washington, London Hemisphere.

Jex, S. M. (1998). *Stress and job performance: Theory, research, and implications for managerial practice*. Thousand Oaks: Sage Publications.

Jex, S. M., & Bliese, P. D. (1999). Efficacy beliefs as a moderator of the impact of work-related stressors: A multilevel study. *Journal of Applied Psychology, 84*(3), 349-361.

Jex, S. M., & Gudanowski, D. M. (1992). Efficacy beliefs and work stress: An exploratory study. *Journal of Organizational Behavior, 13*(5), 509-517.

Johnson, J. (2002). In-depth interviewing. In J. F. Gubrium & J. A. Holstein (Eds.), *Handbook of interview research: Context and method* (pp. 103-120). Thousands Oaks et al.: Sage Publications.

Jönsson, S. (1998). Relate management accounting research to managerial work! *Accounting, Organizations and Society, 23*(4), 411-434.

Jönsson, S., & Macintosh, N. B. (1997). CATS, RATS and EARS: Making the case for the ethnographic accounting research. *Accounting, Organizations and Society, 22*(3-4), 367-386.

Jöreskog, K. G. (1966). Testing a simple structure hypothesis in factor analysis. *Psychometrika, 31*(2), 165-178.

Jöreskog, K. G. (1967). Some contributions to maximum likelihood factor analysis. *Psychometrika, 32*(4), 443-482.

Jöreskog, K. G. (1969). A general approach to confirmatory maximum likelihood factor analysis. *Psychometrika, 34*(2), 183-202.

Jöreskog, K. G. (1971). Statistical analysis of congeneric tests. *Psychometrika, 36*(2), 109-133.

Jöreskog, K. G., & Goldberger, A. S. (1975). Estimation of a model with multiple indicators and multiple causes of a single latent variable. *Journal of the American Statistical Association, 70*(1), 631–639.

Jöreskog, K. G., & Sörbom, D. (2001). *LISREL 8: User's reference guide* (2 ed.). Lincolnwood: Scientific Software International.

Judge, T. A. (1993). Does affective disposition moderate the relationship between job satisfaction and voluntary turnover? *Journal of Applied Psychology, 78*(3), 395-401.

Jun Lin, Z., & Yu, Z. (2002). Responsibility cost control system in China: A case of management accounting application. *Management Accounting Research, 13*(4), 447-467.

Kahn, R. L. (1974). Conflict, ambiguity and overload: Three elements in job stress. In A. A. McLean (Ed.), *Occupational stress* (pp. 47-61). Springfield et al.: Thomas Publishing.

Kahn, R. L., & Byosiere, P. (1992). Stress in organisations. In M. D. Dunnette & L. M. Hough (Eds.), *Handbook of industrial and organisational psychology* (2 ed., pp. 571-650). Palo Alto: Consulting Psychologists Press.

Kahn, R. L., & Quinn, R. P. (1970). Role stress: A framework for analysis. In A. A. McLean (Ed.), *Mental health and work organizations* (pp. 50-115). Chicago: Rand McNally.

Kahn, R. L., Wolfe, D. M., Quinn, R. P., & Snoeck, J. D. (1964). *Organizational stress: Studies in role conflict and ambiguity*. New York: Wiley.

Kahn, R. L., Wolfe, D. M., Quinn, R. P., & Snoeck, J. D. (1966). Adjustment to role conflict and ambiguity in organizations. In B. J. Biddle & E. J. Thomas (Eds.), *Role theory: Concepts and research* (pp. 277-281). New York: Wiley.

Kalbers, L. P., & Cenker, W. J. (2008). The impact of exercised responsibility, experience, autonomy, and role ambiguity on job performance in public accounting. *Journal of Managerial Issues, 20*(3), 327-347.

Kaler, J. (2002). Responsibility, accountability and governance. *Business Ethics: A European Review, 11*(4), 327-334.

Kamdar, D., McAllister, D. J., & Turban, D. B. (2006). 'All in a day's work': How follower individual differences and justice perceptions predict OCB role definitions and behavior. *Journal of Applied Psychology, 91*(4), 841-855.

Kaplan, A. (1964). *The conduct of inquiry: Methodology for behavioral science*. San Francisco: Chandler.

Kaplan, B., & Duchon, D. (1988). Combining qualitative and quantitative methods in information systems research: A case study. *MIS Quarterly, 12*(4), 571-586.

Kaplan, D. (2000). *Structural equation modeling: Foundation and extensions*. Thousand Oaks: Sage Publications.

Kaplan, R. S. (1984). The evolution of management accounting. *The Accounting Review, 59*(3), 390-418.

Kaplan, R. S. (1986). The role for empirical research in management accounting. *Accounting, Organizations and Society, 11*(4-5), 429-452.

Kaplan, R. S., & Atkinson, A. A. (1998). *Advanced management accounting* (3 ed.). Upper Saddle River: Prentice Hall.

Kaplan, R. S., & Norton, D. P. (1992). The balanced scorecard: Measures that drive performance. *Harvard Business Review, 70*(1), 71-79.

Kaplan, R. S., & Norton, D. P. (1996). *The balanced scorecard: Translating strategy into action*. Boston: Harvard Business School Press.

Karasek, R. A. (1979). Job demands, job decision latitude, and mental strain: Implications for job redesign. *Administrative Science Quarterly, 24*(2), 285-308.

Karasek, R. A., & Theorell, T. (1990). *Healthy work: Stress, productivity, and the reconstruction of working life*. New York: Basic Books.

Kassing, J. W. (1998). Development and validation of the organizational dissent scale. *Management Communication Quarterly, 12*(2), 183.

Katz, D., & Kahn, R. L. (1966). *The social psychology of organizations* (1 ed.). New York et al.: Wiley.

Katz, D., & Kahn, R. L. (1978). *The social psychology of organizations* (2 ed.). New York et al.: Wiley.

Keating, A. S. (1997). Determinants of divisional performance evaluation practices. *Journal of Accounting and Economics, 24*(3), 243-273.

Keenan, A., & McBain, G. D. M. (1979). Effects of Type A behavior, intolerance of ambiguity, and locus of control on the relationship between role stress and work-related outcomes. *Journal of Occupational Psychology, 52*(4), 277-285.

Kelley, H. H. (1971). *Attributions in social interaction*. New York: General Learning Press.

Kelley, H. H. (1973). The processes of causal attribution. *American Psychologist, 28*(2), 107-128.

Kellogg, K. C., Orlikowski, W. J., & Yates, J. (2006). Life in the trading zone: Structuring coordination across boundaries in postbureaucratic organizations. *Organization Science, 17*(1), 22-44.

Kemmis, S., & Wilkinson, M. (1998). Participatory action research and the study of practice. In B. Atweh, S. Kemmis & P. Weeks (Eds.), *Action research in practice: Partnerships for social justice in education* (pp. 21-36). London: Routledge.

Kennedy, F. A., & Schleifer, L. (2006). Innovation: Achieving balance among empowerment, accountability and control. *Advances in Interdisciplinary Studies of Work Teams, 12*, 113-135.

Kenny, D. A., Kashy, D. A., & Bolger, N. (1998). Data analysis in social psychology. In D. Gilbert, S. T. Fiske & G. Lindzey (Eds.), *Handbook of social psychology* (4 ed., Vol. 1, pp. 233–265). New York: McGraw-Hill.

Kesselman, G. A., Hagen, E. L., & Wherry, R. J. (1974). A factor analytic test of the Porter-Lawler expectancy model of work motivation. *Personnel Psychology, 27*(4), 569-579.

Ketchand, A. A., & Strawser, J. R. (1998). The existence of multiple measures of organizational commitment and experience-related differences in a public accounting setting. *Behavioral Research in Accounting, 10*, 109-137.

Kimmel, M. J., Pruitt, D. G., Magenau, J. M., Konar-Goldband, E., & Carnevale, P. J. D. (1980). Effects of trust, aspiration, and gender on negotiation tactics. *Journal of Personality and Social Psychology, 38*(1), 9-22.

King, L. A., & King, D. W. (1990). Role conflict and role ambiguity: A critical assessment of construct validity. *Psychological Bulletin, 107*(1), 48-64.

Kleinbaum, D. G., Kupper, L. L., & Muller, K. E. (1988). *Applied regression analysis and other multivariable methods* (2 ed.). Belmont: Duxbury Press.

Klenke-Hamel, K. E., & Mathieu, J. E. (1990). Role strains, tension, and job satisfaction influences on employees' propensity to leave: A multi-sample replication and extension. *Human Relations, 43*(8), 791-807.

Kline, R. B. (2005). *Principles and practice of structural equation modeling* (2 ed.). New York, London: Guilford Press.

Kofta, M. (1993). Uncertainty, mental models, and learned helplessness: An anatomy of control loss. In G. Weary, F. Gleicher & K. L. Marsh (Eds.), *Control motivation and social cognition* (pp. 122-156). New York et al.: Springer.

Kreiner, K., & Mouritsen, J. (2005). The analytical interview: Relevance beyond reflexivity. In S. Tengblad, R. Solli & B. Czarniawska (Eds.), *The art of science* (pp. 153-176). Malmö: CBS Press.

Kren, R. L. (1992). Budgetary participation and managerial performance: The impact of information and environmental volatility. *The Accounting Review, 67*(3), 511-526.

Kren, R. L. (2003). Effects of uncertainty, participation, and control system monitoring on the propensity to create budget slack and actual budget slack created. *Advances in management accounting 11*, 143-167.

Kren, R. L., & Liao, W. M. (1988). The role of accounting information in the control of organizations: A review of the evidence. *Journal of Accounting Literature, 7*, 280-309.

Krishnan, R., Luft, J., & Shields, M. D. (2005). Effects of accounting-method choices on subjective performance-measure weighting: Experimental evidence on precision and error covariance (Working paper). SSRN.

Kristof, A. L. (1996). Person-organization fit: An integrative review of its conceptualizations, measurement, and implications. *Personnel Psychology, 49*(1), 1-49.

Küpper, H.-U. (2005). *Controlling. Konzeption, Aufgaben und Instrumente* (4 ed.). Stuttgart: Schäffer-Poeschel.

Kuratko, D. F., Hornsby, J. S., Naffziger, D. W., & Montagno, R. V. (1993). Implement entrepreneurial thinking in established organizations. *SAM Advanced Management Journal, 58*(1), 28-39.

Kvale, S. (1996). *InterViews: An introduction to qualitative research interviewing*. Thousand Oaks: Sage Publications.

Kwok, W. C. C., & Sharp, D. J. (1998). A review of construct measurement issues in behavioral accounting research. *Journal of Accounting Literature, 17*, 137-174.

Lambert, R. A. (2001). Contracting theory and accounting. *Journal of Accounting and Economics, 32*(1-3), 3-87.

Langfield-Smith, K. (1997). Management control systems and strategy: A critical review. *Accounting, Organizations and Society, 22*(2), 207-232.

Larmande, F., & Ponssard, J. P. (2007). *EVA compensation schemes and controllability issues: An empirical investigation*. Paper presented at the Midyear Meeting of the American Accounting Association, Management Accounting Section, Fort Worth.

Lau, C. M., & Buckland, C. (2001). Budgeting - the role of trust and participation: A research note. *Abacus, 37*(3), 369-388.

Lau, C. M., & Tan, S. L. C. (2003). The effects of participation and job-relevant information on the relationship between evaluative style and job satisfaction. *Review of Quantitative Finance and Accounting, 21*(1), 17-34.

Lau, C. M., & Tan, S. L. C. (2006). The effects of procedural fairness and interpersonal trust on job tension in budgeting. *Management Accounting Research, 17*(2), 171-186.

Lau, C. M., Wong, K. M., & Eggleton, I. R. C. (2008). Fairness of performance evaluation procedures and job satisfaction: The role of outcome-based and non-outcome-based effects. *Accounting and Business Research, 38*(2), 121-135.

Law, K. S., Wong, C.-S., & Mobley, W. H. (1998). Toward a taxonomy of multidimensional constructs. *Academy of Management Review, 24*(4), 24-72.

Lawler, E. E. (1971). *Pay and organizational effectiveness: A psychological view*. New York: McGraw-Hill.

Lawler, E. E. (1990). *Strategic pay: Aligning organizational strategies and pay systems*. San Francisco: Jossey-Bass Publishers.

Lawler, E. E. (1994). From job-based to competency-based organizations. *Journal of Organizational Behavior, 15*(1), 3-15.

Lawler, E. E., & Rhode, J. G. (1976). *Information and control in organizations*. Pacific Palisades: Goodyear Publishing Company.

Lazarus, R. S., & Folkman, S. (1984). *Stress, appraisal, and coping*. New York: Springer.

Leach-Lopez, M. A., Stammerjohan, W. W., & McNair, F. M. (2007). Differences in the role of job-relevant information in the budget participation-performance relationship among U.S. and Mexican managers: A question of culture or communication. *Journal of Management Accounting Research, 19*, 105-136.

Lerner, J. S., & Tetlock, P. E. (1999). Accounting for the effects of accountability. *Psychological Bulletin, 125*(2), 255-275.

Leventhal, G. S. (1980). What should be done with equity theory? New approaches to the study of fairness in social relationships. In K. J. Gergen, M. S. Greenberg & R. H. Willis (Eds.), *Social exchange: Advances in theory and research* (pp. 27-55). New York: Plenum.

Lewin, K. (1936). *Principles of topological psychology*. New York et al.: McGraw-Hill.

Lind, E. A., & Tyler, T. R. (1988). *The social psychology of procedural justice*. New York: Plenum Press.

Lindkvist, L., & Llewellyn, S. (2003). Accountability, responsibility and organization. *Scandinavian Journal of Management, 19*(2), 251-273.

Lindquist, T. M. (1995). Fairness as an antecedent to participative budgeting: Examining the effects of distributive justice, procedural justice and referent cognitions on satisfaction and performance. *Journal of Management Accounting Research, 7*, 122-147.

Linton, R. (1936). *The study of man*. New York: Appleton-Century.

Lipe, M. G. (1993). Analyzing the variance investigation decision: The effects of outcomes, mental accounting, and framing. *The Accounting Review, 68*(4), 748-764.

Lipshitz, R. (1989). 'Either a medal or a corporal': The effects of success and failure on the evaluation of decision. *Organizational Behavior and Human Decision Processes, 44*(3), 380-395.

Llewellyn, S. (1998). Pushing budgets down the line: Ascribing financial responsibility in the UK social services. *Accounting, Auditing and Accountability Journal, 11*(3), 292-308.

Lloyd, C., King, R., & Chenoweth, L. (2002). Social work, stress and burnout: A review. *Journal of Mental Health, 11*(3), 255-265.

London, M. (1995). Giving feedback: Source-centered antecedents and consequences of constructive and destructive feedback. *Human Resource Management Review, 5*(3), 159-188.

Lowe, D. J., & Reckers, P. M. J. (1994). The effects of hindsight bias on jurors' evaluations of auditor decisions. *Decision Sciences, 25*(3), 401-426.

Lowe, D. J., & Reckers, P. M. J. (2000). The use of foresight decision aids in auditors' judgments. *Behavioral Research in Accounting, 12*, 97.

Lucey, T. (2003). *Management accounting* (5 ed.). London: Continuum.

Luckett, P. F., & Eggleton, I. R. C. (1991). Feedback and management accounting: A review of research into behavioral consequences. *Accounting, Organizations and Society, 16*(4), 371-394.

Luft, J., & Shields, M. D. (2003). Mapping management accounting: Graphics and guidelines for theory-consistent empirical research. *Accounting, Organizations and Society, 28*(2-3), 169-249.

Lussier, R. N. (2000). *Management fundamentals: Concepts, applications, skill development*. Cincinnati: South Western College.

Lynch, L. J., & Perry, S. E. (2003). An overview of management compensation. *Journal of Accounting Education, 21*(1), 43-60.

Lysonski, S. (1985). A boundary theory investigation of the product manager's role. *Journal of Marketing, 49*(1), 26-40.

Maas, V. S., & Matějka, M. (2009). Balancing the dual responsibilities of business unit controllers: Field and survey evidence. *The Accounting Review, 84*(4), 1233-1253.

MacCallum, R. C., & Browne, M. W. (1993). The use of causal indicators in covariance structure models: Some practical issues. *Psychological Bulletin, 114*(3), 533-541.

Maciariello, J. A., & Kirby, C. J. (1994). *Management control systems: Using adaptive systems to attain control*. Englewood Cliffs: Prentice Hall.

Macintosh, N. B. (1994). *Management accounting and control systems: An organizational and behavioral approach*. Chichester: Wiley.

Macintosh, N. B., & Williams, J. J. (1992). Managerial roles and budgeting behaviour. *Behavioral Research in Accounting, 4*, 23-48.

MacKenzie, S. B., Podsakoff, P. M., & Fetter, R. (1991). Organizational citizenship behavior and objective productivity as determinants of managerial evaluations of salespersons' performance. *Organizational Behavior and Human Decision Processes, 50*(1), 123-150.

MacKenzie, S. B., Podsakoff, P. M., & Fetter, R. (1993). The impact of organizational citizenship behavior on evaluations of salesperson performance. *Journal of Marketing, 57*(1), 70-80.

MacKenzie, S. B., Podsakoff, P. M., & Jarvis, C. B. (2005). The problem of measurement model misspecification in behavioral and organizational research and some recommended solutions. *Journal of Applied Psychology, 90*(4), 710-730.

Macko, A., & Tyszka, T. (2009). Entrepreneurship and risk taking. *Applied Psychology: An International Review, 58*(3), 469-487.

Magee, R. P. (1986). *Advanced managerial accounting*. New York et al.: Harper & Row.

Magner, N., Welker, R. B., & Campbell, T. L. (1996). Testing a model of cognitive budgetary participation processes in a latent variable structural equations framework. *Accounting and Business Research, 27*(1), 41-50.

Maher, M. W. (1987). The use of relative performance evaluation in organizations. In W. J. Bruns & R. S. Kaplan (Eds.), *Accounting and management: Field study perspectives* (pp. 295-315). Boston: Harvard Business School Press.

Mahoney, T. A., Jerdee, T. H., & Carroll, S. J. (1965). The job(s) of management. *Industrial Relations, 4*(2), 97-110.

Maier, S. F., & Seligman, M. E. P. (1976). Learned helplessness: Theory and evidence. *Journal of Experimental Psychology: General, 105*(1), 3-46.

Malina, M. A., & Selto, F. H. (2004). Choice and change of measures in performance measurement models. *Management Accounting Research, 15*(4), 441-469.

Mallinckrodt, B., & Wang, C.-C. (2004). Quantitative methods for verifying semantic equivalence of translated research instruments: A Chinese version of the experiences in close relationships scale. *Journal of Counseling Psychology, 51*(3), 368-379.

Manzoni, J.-F. (2002). Management control: Toward a new paradigm? In M. J. Epstein & J.-F. Manzoni (Eds.), *Performance measurement and management control: A compendium of research* (Vol. 12, pp. 15–46). Amsterdam et al.: Elsevier.

Marcoulides, G. A., & Schumacker, R. E. (1996). Introduction to advanced structural equation modeling. In G. A. Marcoulides & R. E. Schumacker (Eds.), *Advanced structural equation modeling: Issues and techniques* (pp. 1-6). Mahwah: Erlbaum.

Marginson, D. (1999). Beyond the budgetary control system: Towards a two-tiered process of management control. *Management Accounting Research, 10*(3), 203-230.

Marginson, D. (2006). Information processing and management control: A note exploring the role played by information media in reducing role ambiguity. *Management Accounting Research, 17*(2), 187-197.

Marginson, D., & Bui, B. (2009). Examining the human cost of multiple role expectations. *Behavioral Research in Accounting, 21*(1), 59-81.

Marginson, D., & McAulay, L. (2001). *Determinants of executive observance of the controllability principle: Personal and social factors*. Paper presented at the 5th International Management Control Systems Research Conference, London.

Marginson, D., & Ogden, S. (2005a). Coping with ambiguity through the budget: The positive effects of budgetary targets on managers' budgeting behaviours. *Accounting, Organizations and Society, 30*(5), 435-456.

Marginson, D., & Ogden, S. (2005b). Managers, budgets and organisational change: Unbundling some of the paradoxes. *Journal of Accounting and Organizational Change, 1*(1), 45-61.

Martin, T. N. (1984). Role stress and inability to leave as predictors of mental health. *Human Relations, 37*(11), 969-983.

Masterson, S. S., Lewis, K., Goldman, B. M., & Taylor, M. S. (2000). Integrating justice and social exchange: The differing effects of fair procedures and treatment on work relationships. *Academy of Management Journal, 43*(4), 738-748.

May, D. R., Schwoerer, C. E., Reed, K., & Potter, P. (1997). Employee reactions to ergonomic job design: The moderating effects of health locus of control and self-efficacy. *Journal of Occupational Health Psychology, 2*(1), 11-24.

McAllister, D. J., Morrison, E. W., Kamdar, D., & Turban, D. B. (2007). Disentangling role perceptions: How perceived role breadth, discretion, instrumentality, and efficacy relate to helping and taking charge. *Journal of Applied Psychology, 92*(5), 1200-1211.

McAulay, L., Scrace, A., & Tomkins, C. R. (2001). Transferring priorities: A three-act play on transfer pricing. *Critical Perspectives on Accounting, 12*(1), 87-113.

McAulay, L., & Tomkins, C. R. (1992). A review of the contemporary transfer pricing literature with recommendations for future research. *British Journal of Management, 3*(2), 101-122.

McCann, J. E., & Ferry, D. L. (1979). An approach for assessing and managing inter-unit interdependence. *Academy of Management Review, 4*(1), 113-119.

McFarlin, D. B., & Sweeney, P. D. (1992). Distributive and procedural justice as predictors of satisfaction with personal and organizational outcomes. *Academy of Management Journal, 35*(3), 626-637.

McKenna, E. F. (2006). *Business psychology and organisational behaviour*. New York: Psychology Press.

McNair, C. J., & Carr, L. P. (1994). Responsibility redefined: Changing concepts of accounting-based control. *Advances in Management Accounting, 3*, 85-117.

McNally, G. M. (1980). Responsibility accounting and organisational control. *Journal of Business Finance and Accounting, 7*(2), 165-181.

Mead, G. H. (1934). *Mind, self, and society: From the standpoint of a social behaviourist*. Chicago: University of Chicago Press.

Mehta, R., Anderson, R., Dubas, K., Dubinsky, A. J., & Liu, S. S. (1999). How do sales managers perceive their roles? *Journal of Managerial Issues, 11*(4), 406-426.

Merchant, K. A. (1982). The control function of management. *Sloan Management Review, 23*(4), 43-55.

Merchant, K. A. (1985). *Control in business organizations*. Boston et al.: Ballinger.

Merchant, K. A. (1987). How and why firms disregard the controllability principle. In W. J. Bruns & R. S. Kaplan (Eds.), *Accounting and management: Field study perspectives* (pp. 316-338). Boston: Harvard Business School Press.

Merchant, K. A. (1989). *Rewarding results: Motivating profit center managers*. Boston: Harvard Business School Press.

Merchant, K. A. (1998). *Modern management control systems: Text and cases*. Upper Saddle River: Prentice Hall.

Merchant, K. A. (2006). Measuring general managers' performances. *Accounting, Auditing and Accountability Journal, 19*(6), 893-917.

Merchant, K. A., Chow, C. W., & Wu, A. (1995). Measurement, evaluation and reward of profit center managers: A cross-cultural field study. *Accounting, Organizations and Society, 20*(7-8), 619-638.

Merchant, K. A., & Manzoni, J.-F. (1989). The achievability of budget targets in profit centers: A field study. *The Accounting Review, 64*(3), 539-558.

Merchant, K. A., & Otley, D. T. (2006). A review of the literature on control and accountability. In C. S. Chapman, A. G. Hopwood & M. D. Shields (Eds.), *Handbook of management accounting research* (Vol. 2, pp. 785-804). Amsterdam et al.: Elsevier.

Merchant, K. A., & Simons, R. (1986). Research and control in complex organizations: An overview. *Journal of Accounting Literature, 5*, 183-203.

Merchant, K. A., & Van der Stede, W. A. (2007). *Management control systems: Performance measurement, evaluation and incentives* (2 ed.). Harlow et al.: Prentice Hall.

Mero, N. P., Guidice, R. M., & Anna, A. L. (2006). The interacting effects of accountability and individual differences on rater response to a performance-rating task. *Journal of Applied Social Psychology, 36*(4), 795-819.

Merton, R. K. (1949). *Social theory and social structure: Toward the codification of theory and research.* Glencoe: Free Press.

Merton, R. K. (1957). The role-set: Problems in sociological theory. *British Journal of Sociology, 8*(2), 106-120.

Messner, M. (2009). The limits of accountability. *Accounting, Organizations and Society, 34*(8), 918-938.

Michaels, R. E., Cron, W. L., Dubinsky, A. J., & Joachimsthaler, E. A. (1988). Influence of formalization on the organizational commitment and work alienation of salespeople and industrial buyers. *Journal of Marketing Research, 25*(4), 376-383.

Michaels, R. E., Dubinsky, A. J., Kotabe, M., & Lim, C. U. (1996). The effects of organizational formalization on organizational commitment and work alienation in US, Japanese and Korean industrial salesforces. *European Journal of Marketing, 30*(7), 8-24.

Miles, R. H. (1976). A comparison of the relative impacts of role perceptions of ambiguity and conflict by role. *Academy of Management Journal, 19*(1), 25-35.

Milgrom, P., & Roberts, J. (1992). *Economics, organization and management.* Upper Saddle River: Prentice Hall.

Milkovich, G. T., Newman, J. M., & Milkovich, C. (2008). *Compensation.* Boston: McGraw-Hill.

Miller, S. M. (1979). Controllability and human stress: Method, evidence and theory. *Behaviour Research and Therapy, 17*(4), 287-304.

Mintzberg, H. (1980). *The nature of managerial work*. Englewood Cliffs: Prentice Hall.

Mitchell, T. R., & Kalb, L. S. (1981). Effects of outcome knowledge and outcome valence on supervisors' evaluations. *Journal of Applied Psychology, 66*(5), 604-612.

Modell, S. (1997). A progress-oriented contingency approach to responsibility in professional services. *International Journal of Service Industry Management, 8*(4), 306-335.

Modell, S. (2005). Triangulation between case study and survey methods in management accounting research: An assessment of validity implications. *Management Accounting Research, 16*(2), 231-254.

Modell, S., & Lee, A. S. (2001). Decentralization and reliance on the controllability principle in the public sector. *Financial Accountability and Management, 17*(3), 191-218.

Moers, F. (2000). The role of performance measure characteristics in the design of incentive systems: An empirical analysis (MARC Working Paper MARC-WP/3/2000-14).

Moers, F. (2005). Discretion and bias in performance evaluation: The impact of diversity and subjectivity. *Accounting, Organizations and Society, 30*(1), 67-80.

Moers, F. (2006). Performance measure properties and delegation. *The Accounting Review, 81*(4), 897-924.

Mohr, A. T., & Puck, J. F. (2007). Role conflict, general manager job satisfaction and stress and the performance of IJVs. *European Management Journal, 25*(1), 25-35.

Moncrief, W. C., Babakus, E., Cravens, D. W., & Johnston, M. (1997). Examining the antecedents and consequences of salesperson job stress. *European Journal of Marketing, 31*(11-12), 786-798.

Moon, P., & Fitzgerald, L. (1996). Delivering the goods at TNT: The role of the performance measurement system. *Management Accounting Research, 7*(4), 431-457.

Mooney, J. D. (1998). The principles of organization. *International Journal of Public Administration, 21*(2-4), 535-544.

Moosbrugger, H., & Schermelleh-Engel, K. (2007). Exploratorische (EFA) und konfirmatorische Faktorenanalyse (CFA). In H. Moosbrugger & A. Kelava (Eds.), *Testtheorie und Fragebogenkonstruktion* (pp. 307-324). Heidelberg: Springer.

Moreno, J. L. (1934). *Who shall survive? A new approach to the problem of human interrelations*. Washington: Nervous and Mental Disease Publication Company.

Morris, J. H., Steers, R. M., & Koch, J. L. (1979). Influence of organization structure on role conflict and ambiguity for three occupational groupings. *Academy of Management Journal, 22*(1), 58-71.

Morrison, E. W. (1994). Role definitions and organizational citizenship behavior: The importance of the employee's perspective. *Academy of Management Journal, 37*(6), 1543-1567.

Morrison, E. W., & Phelps, C. C. (1999). Taking charge at work: Extrarole efforts to initiate workplace change. *Academy of Management Journal, 42*(4), 403-419.

Mowday, R. T. (1991). Equity theory predictions of behaviour in organizations. In R. M. Steers & L. W. Porter (Eds.), *Motivation and work behavior* (5 ed., pp. 111-131). New York et al.: McGraw-Hill.

Muchinsky, P. M. (2006). *Psychology applied to work* (8 ed.). Belmont: Thomson-Wadsworth.

Mueller, R. (1996). *Basic principles of structural equation modeling*. New York et al.: Springer.

Murphy, K. R., & Cleveland, J. (1995). *Understanding performance appraisal: Social, organizational, and goal-based perspectives*. Thousand Oaks: Sage Publications.

Muthén, L. K., & Muthén, B. O. (2002). How to use a Monte Carlo study to decide on sample size and determine power. *Structural Equation Modeling, 9*(4), 599-620.

Nachtigall, C., Kroehne, U., Funke, F., & Steyer, R. (2003). (Why) should we use SEM? Pros and cons of structural equation modeling. *Methods of Psychological Research Online, 8*(2), 1-22.

Nauta, M. M., Liu, C., & Li, C. (in press). A cross-national examination of self-efficacy as a moderator of autonomy/job strain relationships. *Applied Psychology: An International Review*.

Naylor, J. C., Pritchard, R. D., & Ilgen, D. R. (1980). *A theory of behavior in organizations*. London, New York: Academic Press.

Near, J. P., & Miceli, M. P. (1985). Organizational dissidence: The case of whistle-blowing. *Journal of Business Ethics, 4*(1), 1-16.

Neely, A., Gregory, M., & Platts, K. (2005). Performance measurement system design: A literature review and research agenda. *International Journal of Operations and Production Management, 25*(12), 1128-1263.

Nikias, A. D., Schwartz, S., & Young, R. A. (2005). Optimal performance measures with task complementarity. *Journal of Management Accounting Research, 17*, 53-73.

Nirel, N., Schmid, H., & Stern, Z. (1994). Formal and informal authority of hospital directors. *Journal of Management in Medicine, 8*(5), 37-48.

Nisar, T. M. (2006). Subjective performance measures in bonus payouts. *Performance Improvement, 45*(8), 34-40.

Niven, P. R. (2002). *Balanced scorecard step by step: maximizing performance and maintaining results*. New York: Wiley.

Nouri, H., & Kyj, L. (2008). The effect of performance feedback on prior budgetary participative research using survey methodology: An empirical study. *Critical Perspectives on Accounting, 19*(8), 1431-1453.

Nunnally, J. C., & Bernstein, I. H. (1994). *Psychometric theory* (3 ed.). New York et al.: McGraw-Hill.

O'Connor, N. G. (1995). The influence of organizational culture on the usefulness of budget participation by Singaporean-Chinese managers. *Accounting, Organizations and Society, 20*(5), 383-403.

Odiorne, G. S. (1965). *Management by Objectives: A System of Managerial Leadership*. New York et al.: Pitman.

Öhman, A., & Bohlin, G. (1989). The role of controllability in cardiovascular activation and cardiovascular disease: Help or hindrance? In A. Steptoe & A. Appels (Eds.), *Stress, personal control, and health* (pp. 257-276). Chichester et al.: Wiley.

Oliver, R. L., & Brief, A. P. (1977). Determinants and consequences of role conflict and ambiguity among retail sales managers. *Journal of Retailing, 53*(4), 47-59.

Orens, M. R., & Elliott, V. J. (1997). Variable pay programs: Pay for results. In P. T. Chingos & P. Marwick (Eds.), *Paying for performance: A guide to compensation management* (pp. 25-57). New York: Wiley.

Organ, D. W. (1988). *Organizational citizenship behavior: The good soldier syndrome*. Lexington: Lexington Books.

Örtqvist, D., & Wincent, J. (2006). Prominent consequences of role stress: A meta-analytic review. *International Journal of Stress Management, 13*(4), 399-422.

Østergren, K., & Stensaker, I. (2008). Management control without budgets: A field study of 'beyond budgeting' in practice (Working paper).

Otley, D. T. (1978). Budget use and managerial performance. *Journal of Accounting Research, 16*(1), 122-149.

Otley, D. T. (1990). Issues in accountability and control: Some observations from a study of colliery accountability in the British Coal Association. *Management Accounting Research, 1*(1), 101-123.

Otley, D. T. (1994). Management control in contemporary organizations: Towards a wider framework. *Management Accounting Research, 5*(3-4), 289-299.

Otley, D. T. (2003). Management control and performance management: Whence and whither? *The British Accounting Review, 35*(4), 309-326.

Otley, D. T. (2006). Trends in budgetary control and responsibility accounting. In A. Bhimani (Ed.), *Contemporary issues in management accounting* (pp. 291-307). Oxford: Oxford University Press.

Paolillo, J. G. P. (1981). Manager's self assessments of managerial roles: The influence of hierarchical level. *Journal of Management, 7*(1), 43-52.

Parasuraman, S., & Alutto, J. A. (1981). An examination of the organizational antecedents of stressors at work. *Academy of Management Journal, 24*(1), 48-67.

Parasuraman, S., & Alutto, J. A. (1984). Sources and outcomes of stress in organizational settings: Toward the development of a structural model. *Academy of Management Journal, 27*(2), 330-350.

Parker, L. F. (1993). When to fix it and when to leave: Relationships among perceived control, self-efficacy, dissent, and exit. *Journal of Applied Psychology, 78*(6), 949-959.

Parker, S. K. (2000). From passive to proactive motivation: The importance of flexible role orientations and role breadth self-efficacy. *Applied Psychology: An International Review, 49*(3), 447-469.

Parker, S. K. (2007). 'That is my job': How employees' role orientation affects their job performance. *Human Relations, 60*(3), 403-434.

Parker, S. K., & Axtell, C. M. (2001). Seeing another viewpoint: Antecedents and outcomes of employee perspective taking. *Academy of Management Journal, 44*(6), 1085-1100.

Parker, S. K., & Sprigg, C. A. (1999). Minimizing strain and maximizing learning: The role of job demands, job control, and proactive personality. *Journal of Applied Psychology, 84*(6), 925-939.

Parker, S. K., Wall, T. D., & Jackson, P. R. (1997). 'That's not my job': Developing flexible employee work orientations. *Academy of Management Journal, 40*(4), 899-929.

Parker, S. K., Williams, H. M., & Turner, N. (2006). Modeling the antecedents of proactive behavior at work. *Journal of Applied Psychology, 91*(3), 636-652.

Parkes, K. R. (1989). Personal control in an occupational context. In A. Steptoe & A. Appels (Eds.), *Stress, personal control, and health* (pp. 21-48). Chichester et al.: Wiley.

Parsons, T. (1958). Authority, legitimation, and political action. In C. J. Friedrich (Ed.), *Authority* (pp. 197-221). Cambridge: Harvard University Press.

Pasewark, W. R., & Viator, R. E. (2006). Sources of work-family conflict in the accounting profession. *Behavioral Research in Accounting, 18*, 147-165.

Pearce, J. L. (1981). Bringing some clarity to role ambiguity research. *Academy of Management Review, 6*(4), 665-674.

Pearce, J. L., & Gregersen, H. B. (1991). Task interdependence and extrarole behavior: A test of the mediating effects of felt responsibility. *Journal of Applied Psychology, 76*(6), 838-844.

Peel, J. D. Y. (1996). Auguste Comte. In A. Kuper & J. Kuper (Eds.), *The social science encyclopedia* (2 ed., pp. 120-121). Londen, New York: Routledge.

Pelster, C. (2007). *Das Controllability-Prinzip im Spannungsfeld von Theorie und Praxis: Eine empirische Untersuchung zur Verantwortung von Managern*. Wiesbaden: Deutscher Universitäts-Verlag.

Perlow, L. A. (1999). The time famine: Toward a sociology of work time. *Administrative Science Quarterly, 44*(1), 57-81.

Perrone, V., Zaheer, A., & McEvily, B. (2003). Free to be trusted? Organizational constraints on trust in boundary spanners. *Organization Science, 14*(4), 422-439.

Peter, J. P. (1979). Reliability: A review of psychometric basics and recent marketing practices. *Journal of Marketing Research, 16*(1), 6-17.

Peterson, R. (1994). A meta-analysis of Cronbach's alpha. *Journal of Consumer Research, 21*(2), 381-391.

Peterson, R. (2000). *Constructing effective questionnaires*. Thousand Oaks: Sage Publications.

Pfeffer, J. (1992). *Managing with power: Politics and influence in organizations*. Boston: Harvard Business School Press.

Podsakoff, P. M., MacKenzie, S. B., Lee, J.-Y., & Podsakoff, N. P. (2003). Common method biases in behavioral research: A critical review of the literature and recommended remedies. *Journal of Applied Psychology, 88*(5), 879-903.

Podsakoff, P. M., MacKenzie, S. B., Paine, J. B., & Bachrach, D. G. (2000). Organizational citizenship behaviors: A critical review of the theoretical and empirical literature and suggestions for future research. *Journal of Management, 26*(3), 513-563.

Porter, L. W., & Lawler, E. E. (1968). *Managerial attitudes and performance*. Homewood: Irwin.

Prendergast, C. (1999). The provision of incentives in firms. *Journal of Economic Literature, 37*(1), 7-63.

Pugh, D. S., Hickson, D. J., Hinings, C. R., & Turner, C. (1968). Dimensions of organization structure. *Administrative Science Quarterly, 13*(1), 65-105.

Rajan, M. V. (1992). Cost allocation in multiagent settings. *The Accounting Review, 67*(3), 527-545.

Ramadan, S. (1989). The rationale for cost allocation: A study of UK divisionalised companies. *Accounting and Business Research, 20*(77), 31-37.

Read, W. H. (1962). Upward communication in industrial hierarchies. *Human Relations, 15*(3), 3-15.

Rebele, J. E., & Michaels, R. E. (1990). Independent auditors' role stress: Antecedent, outcome, and moderating variables. *Behavioral Research in Accounting, 2*, 124-153.

Reichelstein, S. (Ed.) (2002) Handwörterbuch Unternehmensrechnung und Controlling (4 ed.). Stuttgart: Schäffer-Poeschel.

Reitzug, U. C. (1987). *Efficacy and accountability in organizations*. Paper presented at the Annual Meeting of the American Educational Research Association, Washington.

Rejc, A., & Slapničar, S. (2004). Determinants of performance measurement system design and corporate financial performance. In M. J. Epstein & J.-F. Manzoni (Eds.),

Performance measurement and management control: Superior organizational performance (Vol. 14, pp. 47-74). Amsterdam et al.: Elsevier.

Richardson, A. J. (1996). Introduction: Research methods in accounting. In A. J. Richardson (Ed.), *Research methods in accounting: Issues and debates* (pp. 1-7). Vancouver: Canada Research Foundation.

Rigdon, E. E. (1998). Structural equation modeling. In G. A. Marcoulides (Ed.), *Modern methods for business research* (pp. 251-294). Mahwah: Erlbaum.

Rigdon, E. E., Schumacker, R. E., & Wothke, W. (1998). A comparative review of interaction and nonlinear modeling. In R. E. Schumacker & G. A. Marcoulides (Eds.), *Interaction and nonlinear effects in structural equation modeling* (pp. 1-16). Mahwah: Erlbaum.

Rizzo, J. R., House, R. J., & Lirtzman, S. I. (1970). Role conflict and ambiguity in complex organizations. *Administrative Science Quarterly, 15*(2), 150-163.

Robbins, S. P. (2003). *Organizational behavior*. Upper Saddle River: Prentice Hall.

Roberts, E. S. (1999). In defence of the survey method: An illustration from a study of user information satisfaction. *Accounting and Finance, 39*(1), 53-77.

Roberts, J. (1991). The possibilities of accountability. *Accounting, Organizations and Society, 16*(4), 355-368.

Roberts, J., & Scapens, R. (1985). Accounting systems and systems of accountability: Understanding accountability practices in their organisational contexts. *Accounting, Organizations and Society, 10*(4), 443-456.

Robinson, S. L. (1996). Trust and breach of the psychological contract. *Administrative Science Quarterly, 41*(4), 574-599.

Rodríguez, I., Bravo, M. J., Peiró, J., & Schaufeli, W. B. (2001). The demands-control-support model, locus of control and job dissatisfaction: A longitudinal study. *Work and Stress, 15*(2), 97-114.

Rogers, D. L., & Molnar, J. (1976). Organizational antecedents of role conflict and ambiguity in top-level administrators. *Administrative Science Quarterly, 21*(4), 598-610.

Ronen, J., & Livingstone, J. L. (1975). An expectancy theory approach to the motivational impacts of budgets. *The Accounting Review, 50*(4), 671-685.

Ross, A. (1994). Trust as moderator of the effect of performance evaluation style on job-related tension: A research note. *Accounting, Organizations and Society, 19*(7), 629-635.

Ross, A. (1995). Job related tension, budget emphasis and uncertainty: A research note. *Management Accounting Research, 6*(1), 1-11.

Rossiter, J. (2002). The C-OAR-SE procedure for scale development in marketing. *International Journal of Research in Marketing, 19*(4), 305-335.

Rotter, J. B. (1966). Generalised expectancies for internal versus external control of reinforcement. *Psychological Monographs, 80*(1), 1-28.

Rousseau, D. M., Sitkin, S. B., Burt, R. S., & Camerer, C. (1998). Not so different after all: A cross-discipline view of trust. *Academy of Management Review, 23*(3), 393-404.

Rousseau, D. M., & Tijoriwala, S. A. (1999). What's a good reason to change? Motivated reasoning and social accounts in promoting organizational change. *Journal of Applied Psychology, 84*(4), 514-528.

Ruben, D. H. (1986). The management of role ambiguity in organizations. *Journal of Employment Counseling, 23*(3), 120-130.

Rusbult, C. E., & Farrell, D. (1983). A longitudinal test of the investment model: The impact on job satisfaction, job commitment, and investments. *Journal of Applied Psychology, 68*(3), 429-438.

Ryan, B., Scapens, R., & Theobald, M. (2002). *Research method and methodology in finance and accounting* (2 ed.). London: Thomson.

Ryans, A. B., & Weinberg, C. B. (1979). Territory sales response. *Journal of Marketing Research, 16*(4), 453-465.

Sandt, J. (2004). *Management mit Kennzahlen und Kennzahlensystemen: Bestandsaufnahme, Determinanten und Erfolgsauswirkungen*. Wiesbaden: Deutscher Universitäts-Verlag.

Sarantakos, S. (2005). *Social research* (3 ed.). New York: Macmillan.

Sarbin, T. R., & Allen, V. L. (1968). Role theory. In G. Lindzey & E. Aronson (Eds.), *Handbook of social psychology* (2 ed., Vol. 1, pp. 488-567). Reading et al.: Addison-Wesley.

Sawyer, J. E. (1992). Goal and process clarity: Specification of multiple constructs of role ambiguity and a structural equation model of their antecedents and consequences. *Journal of Applied Psychology, 77*(2), 130-142.

Scapens, R. (1985). *Management accounting: A review of contemporary developments*. Basingstoke, London: Macmillan.

Scapens, R. (2006). Understanding management accounting practices: A personal journey. *The British Accounting Review, 38*(1), 1-30.

Schäffer, U. (2007). *Management accounting and control scales handbook*. Wiesbaden: Deutscher Universitäts-Verlag.

Schäffer, U., & Brettel, T. (2005). Ein Plädoyer für Fallstudien. *Zeitschrift für Controlling und Management, 49*(1), 43-46.

Schäffer, U., & Pelster, C. (2007). Zur Relevanz des Controllability-Prinzips für die Unternehmenspraxis. *Zeitschrift für Controlling und Management, 51*(6), 422-436.

Schaubroeck, J., & Merritt, D. E. (1997). Divergent effects of job control on coping with work stressors: The key role of self-efficacy. *Academy of Management Journal, 40*(3), 738-754.

Schermelleh-Engel, K., Moosbrugger, H., & Müller, H. (2003). Evaluating the fit of structural equation models: Tests of significance and descriptive goodness-of-fit measures. *Methods of Psychological Research Online, 8*(2), 23-74.

Schermelleh-Engel, K., & Werner, C. (2007). Methoden der Reliabilitätsbestimmung. In H. Moosbrugger & A. Kelava (Eds.), *Testtheorie und Fragebogenkonstruktion* (pp. 113-134). Heidelberg: Springer.

Schminke, M., Cropanzano, R., & Rupp, D. E. (2002). Organization structure and fairness perceptions: The moderating effects of organizational level. *Organizational Behavior and Human Decision Processes, 89*(1), 881-905.

Scholderer, J., & Balderjahn, I. (2005). PLS versus LISREL: Ein Methodenvergleich. In F. W. Bliemel, A. Eggert, G. Fassott & J. Henseler (Eds.), *Handbuch PLS-Pfadmodellierung: Methode, Anwendung, Praxisbeispiele* (pp. 87-98). Stuttgart: Schäffer-Poeschel.

Schuler, R. S. (1977). Role perceptions, satisfaction and performance moderated by organizational level and participation in decision making. *Academy of Management Journal, 20*(1), 159-165.

Schuler, R. S. (1980). A role and expectancy perception model of participation in decision making. *Academy of Management Journal, 23*(2), 331-340.

Schuler, R. S., Aldag, R. J., & Brief, A. P. (1977). Role conflict and ambiguity: A scale analysis. *Organizational Behavior and Human Performance, 20*(1), 111-128.

Schumacker, R. E., & Lomax, R. G. (2004). *A beginner's guide to structural equation modeling* (2 ed.). Mahwah: Erlbaum.

Schwab, R. L., & Iwanicki, E. F. (1982). Perceived role conflict, role ambiguity, and teacher burnout. *Educational Administration Quarterly, 18*(1), 60-74.

Scott, T. W., & Tiessen, P. (1999). Performance measurement and managerial teams. *Accounting, Organizations and Society, 24*(3), 263-285.

Seeman, M. (1953). Role conflict and ambivalence in leadership. *American Sociological Review, 18*(4), 373-380.

Seligman, M. E. P. (1975). *Helplessness: On depression, development, and death.* San Francisco: Freeman.

Senatra, P. T. (1980). Role conflict, role ambiguity, and organizational climate in a public accounting firm. *The Accounting Review, 55*(4), 594-603.

Sharma, S., Durand, R. M., & Gur-Arie, O. (1981). Identification and analysis of moderator variables. *Journal of Marketing Research, 18*(3), 291-300.

Shavell, S. (1979). Risk sharing and incentives in the principal and agent relationship. *Bell Journal of Economics, 10*(1), 55-73.

Shaw, M. E., & Costanzo, P. R. (1982). *Theories of social psychology* (2 ed.). New York et al.: McGraw-Hill.

Shea, G. P., & Guzzo, R. A. (1987). Group effectiveness: What really matters? *Sloan Management Review, 28*(3), 25-31.

Shearer, T. (2002). Ethics and accountability: From the for-itself to the for-the-other. *Accounting, Organizations and Society, 27*(6), 541-573.

Shenkir, W. G., & Strawser, R. H. (1972). Auditing and management advisory services: A conflict of roles? *Abacus, 8*(1), 13-20.

Shields, J. F., & Shields, M. D. (1998). Antecedents of participative budgeting. *Accounting, Organizations and Society, 23*(1), 49-76.

Shields, M. D. (1997). Research in management accounting by North Americans in the 1990s. *Journal of Management Accounting Research, 9*, 3-61.

Shields, M. D., Birnberg, J. G., & Frieze, I. H. (1981). Attributions, cognitive processes and control systems. *Accounting, Organizations and Society, 6*(1), 69-93.

Shields, M. D., Chow, C. W., & Whittington, O. R. (1989). The effects of state risk and controllability filter on compensation contract and effort choice. *Abacus, 25*(1), 39-55.

Shields, M. D., Deng, F. J., & Kato, Y. (2000). The design and effects of control systems: Tests of direct- and indirect-effects models. *Accounting, Organizations and Society, 25*(2), 185-202.

Shields, M. D., & Waller, W. S. (1988). A behavioral study of accounting variables in performance-incentive contracts. *Accounting, Organizations and Society, 13*(6), 581-594.

Shrout, P. E., & Bolger, N. (2002). Mediation in experimental and nonexperimental studies: New procedures and recommendations. *Psychological Methods, 7*(4), 422-445.

Siegrist, J. (1996). Adverse health effects of high-effort/low-reward conditions. *Journal of Occupational Health Psychology, 1*(1), 27-41.

Silverman, D. (2005). *Doing qualitative research: A practical handbook* (2 ed.). London et al.: Sage Publications.

Simmel, G. (1920). Zur Philosophie des Schauspielers. *Logos, 9*, 339-362.

Simon, H. (1951). A formal theory of the employment relationship. *Econometrica, 19*(3), 293-305.

Simons, R. (1995). *Levers of control*. Boston: Harvard Business School Press.

Simons, R. (2005). *Levers of organization design: How managers use accountability systems for greater performance and commitment*. Boston: Harvard Business School Press.

Simons, R. (2007). *Revisiting the controllability principle in the twenty-first century*. Paper presented at the American Accounting Association Annual Meeting, Chicago.

Singh, J. (1998). Striking a balance in boundary-spanning positions: An investigation of some unconventional influences of role stressors and job characteristics on job outcomes of salespeople. *Journal of Marketing, 62*(3), 69-86.

Singh, J., Verbeke, W., & Rhoads, G. K. (1996). Do organizational practices matter in role stress processes? A study of direct and moderating effects for marketing-oriented boundary spanners. *Journal of Marketing, 60*(3), 69-86.

Singh, R. P. (1997). Hierarchical level as a moderator of the relationship between occupational stress and strain. *Psycho-lingua, 27*(2), 95-98.

Singleton, R. A., & Straits, B. (2002). Survey interviewing. In J. F. Gubrium & J. A. Holstein (Eds.), *Handbook of interview research: Context and method* (pp. 59-82). Thousands Oaks et al.: Sage Publications.

Sitkin, S. B., & Pablo, A. L. (1992). Reconceptualizing the determinants of risk behavior. *Academy of Management Review, 17*(1), 9-38.

Skinner, E. A. (1996). A guide to constructs of control. *Journal of Personality and Social Psychology, 71*(3), 549-570.

Skinner, R. C. (1990). The role of profitability in divisional decision making and performance evaluation. *Accounting and Business Research, 20*(78), 135-141.

Slattery, J. P., Selvarajan, T. T., & Anderson, J. E. (2008). The influences of new employee development practices upon role stressors and work-related attitudes of temporary employees. *International Journal of Human Resource Management, 19*(12), 2268-2293.

Sloan, A. P. (1963). *My years with General Motors*. New York: Doubleday/Currency.

Smith, C. S., & Brannick, M. T. (1990). A role and expectancy model of participative decision-making: A replication and theoretical extension. *Journal of Organizational Behavior, 11*(2), 91-104.

Smith, M. (2003). *Research methods in accounting*. London: Sage Publications.

Solomons, D. (1965). *Divisional performance: Measurement and control*. Homewood: Irwin.

Spector, P. E. (1986). Perceived control by employees: A meta-analysis of studies concerning autonomy and participation at work. *Human Relations, 39*(11), 1005-1017.

Spector, P. E. (1997). *Job satisfaction: Application, assessment, cause, and consequences*. Thousand Oaks: Sage Publications.

Spector, P. E., & O'Connell, B. J. (1994). The contribution of personality traits, negative affectivity, locus of control and Type A to the subsequent reports of job stressors and job strains. *Journal of Occupational & Organizational Psychology, 67*(1), 1-12.

Speier, C., & Frese, M. (1997). Generalized self efficacy as a mediator and moderator between control and complexity at work and personal initiative: A longitudinal field study in East Germany. *Human Performance, 10*(2), 171-192.

Spicer, B. H. (1992). The resurgence of cost and management accounting: A review of some recent developments in practice, theories and case research methods. *Management Accounting Research, 3*(1), 1-37.

Sprinkle, G. B. (2003). Perspectives on experimental research in managerial accounting. *Accounting, Organizations and Society, 28*(2-3), 287-318.

Stahl, G. K., & Caligiuri, P. (2005). The effectiveness of expatriate coping strategies: The moderating role of cultural distance, position level, and time on the international assignment. *Journal of Applied Psychology, 90*(4), 603-615.

Stajkovic, A. D., & Luthans, F. (1998). Self-efficacy and work-related performance: A meta-analysis. *Psychological Bulletin, 124*(2), 240-261.

Steenkamp, J.-B. E. M., & van Trijp, H. (1991). The use of LISREL in validating marketing constructs. *International Journal of Research in Marketing, 8*(4), 283-299.

Sternberg, R. J., & Powell, J. S. (1982). Theories of intelligence. In R. J. Sternberg (Ed.), *Handbook of human intelligence* (pp. 975-1006). Cambridge: Cambridge University Press.

Stevenson, H. H., & Jarillo, J. C. (1990). A paradigm of entrepreneurship: Entrepreneurial management. *Strategic Management Journal, 11*(4), 17-27.

Stewart, G. L., & Brown, K. G. (2009). *Human resource management*. Hoboken: Wiley.

Stone, E. F., & Hollenbeck, J. R. (1984). Some issues associated with the use of moderated regression. *Organizational Behavior and Human Performance, 34*(2), 195-213.

Summers, T. P., & DeNisi, A. S. (1990). In search of Adams' other: Reexamination of referents used in the evaluation of pay. *Human Relations, 43*(6), 497-311.

Szilagyi, A. D., Sims, H. P., & Keller, R. T. (1976). Role dynamics, locus of control, and employee attitudes and behavior. *Academy of Management Journal, 19*(2), 259-276.

Tan, H.-T., & Lipe, M. G. (1997). Outcome effects: The impact of decision process and outcome controllability. *Journal of Behavioral Decision Making, 10*(4), 315-325.

Tan, S.-L., & Moghaddam, F. M. (1999). Positioning in intergroup relations. In R. Harré & L. Van Langenhove (Eds.), *Positioning theory* (pp. 178-194). Oxford: Blackwell.

Tannenbaum, A. S. (1968). *Control in organizations*. New York: McGraw-Hill.

Tashakkori, A., & Teddlie, C. (1998). *Mixed methodology*. Thousand Oaks: Sage Publications.

Taylor, F. W. (1911). *Scientific management*. Westport: Greenwood Press.

Taylor, M. S., Fisher, C. D., & Ilgen, D. R. (1984). Individuals' reactions to performance feedback in organizations: A control theory perspective. In K. M. Rowland & G. R. Ferris (Eds.), *Research in personnel and human resources management* (Vol. 2, pp. 81-124). Greenwich: JAI Press.

Teas, R. K., Wacker, J. G., & Hughes, R. E. (1979). A path analysis of causes and consequences of salespeople's perceptions of role clarity. *Journal of Marketing Research, 16*(3), 355-369.

Tetlock, P. E. (1985). Accountability: The neglected social context of judgment and choice. In L. L. Cummings & B. M. Staw (Eds.), *Research in organizational behavior* (Vol. 7, pp. 297–332). Greenwich: JAI Press.

Tetlock, P. E. (1992). The impact of accountability on judgement and choice: Toward a social contingency model. In M. P. Zanna (Ed.), *Advances in experimental social psychology* (Vol. 25, pp. 331-377). New York: Academic Press.

Thakur, M., Burton, G. E., & Srivastava, B. N. (1997). *International management: Concepts and cases*. New Delhi: McGraw-Hill.

Thibaut, J. W., & Walker, L. (1975). *Procedural justice: A psychological analysis*. Hillsdale: Erlbaum.

Thompson, J. D. (1967). *Organizations in action*. New York et al.: McGraw-Hill.

Thoms, P., Dose, J. J., & Scott, K. S. (2002). Relationships between accountability, job satisfaction, and trust. *Human Resource Development Quarterly, 13*(3), 307-323.

Tiessen, P., & Waterhouse, J. H. (1983). Towards a descriptive theory of management accounting. *Accounting, Organizations and Society, 8*(2-3), 251-267.

Tinker, A. M., Merino, B. D., & Neimark, M. D. (1982). The normative origins of positive theories: Ideology and accounting thought. *Accounting, Organizations and Society, 7*(2), 167-200.

Tjosvold, D. (1986). The dynamics of interdependence in organizations. *Human Relations, 39*(6), 517-740.

Toms, S. (2005). Financial control, managerial control and accountability: Evidence from the British cotton industry, 1700-2000. *Accounting, Organizations and Society, 30*(7-8), 627-653.

Tosi, H. (1971). Organization stress as a moderator of the relationship between influence and role response. *Academy of Management Journal, 14*(1), 7-20.

Tourangeau, R., Rips, L. J., & Rasinski, K. A. (2000). *The psychology of survey response.* Cambridge: Cambridge University Press.

Tracy, L., & Johnson, T. W. (1981). What do the role conflict and role ambiguity scales measure? *Journal of Applied Psychology, 66*(4), 464-469.

Tubre, T. C., & Collins, J. M. (2000). Jackson and Schuler (1985) revisited: A meta-analysis of the relationships between role ambiguity, role conflict, and job performance. *Journal of Management, 26*(1), 155-169.

Turner, R. H. (1962). Role-taking: Process versus conformity. In A. M. Rose (Ed.), *Human behavior and social processes* (pp. 20-40). Boston: Houghton Mifflin.

Turner, R. H. (1979). Strategy for developing an integrated role theory. *Humboldt Journal of Social Relations, 7*(1), 123-139.

Tyler, T. R., & Bies, R. J. (1990). Beyond formal procedures: The interpersonal context of procedural justice. In J. S. Carroll (Ed.), *Applied social psychology and organizational settings* (pp. 77-98). Hillsdale: Erlbaum.

Ueno, S., & Wu, F. H. (1993). The comparative influence of culture on budget control practices in the United States and Japan. *International Journal of Accounting, 28*(1), 17-39.

Ugras, Y. J. (1994). Factors affecting allocation of noncontrollable costs for performance evaluation use: A survey. *Advances in Management Accounting 3*, 255-278.

Ullrich, M. J., & Tuttle, B. M. (2004). The effects of comprehensive information reporting systems and economic incentives on managers' time-planning decisions. *Behavioral Research in Accounting, 16*, 89-105.

Urwick, L. (1943). *The elements of administration.* New York et al.: Harper & Brothers.

Van de Ven, A. H., Delbecq, A. L., & Koenig, R. (1976). Determinants of coordination modes within organizations. *American Sociological Review, 41*(2), 322-338.

Van de Vijver, F., & Hambleton, R. K. (1996). Translating tests: Some practical guidelines. *European Psychologist, 1*(2), 89-99.

Van der Doef, M., & Maes, S. (1999). The job demand-control (-support) model and psychological well-being: A review of 20 years of empirical research. *Work and Stress, 13*(2), 87-114.

Van der Stede, W. A. (2000). The relationship between two consequences of budgetary controls: Budgetary slack creation and managerial short-term orientation. *Accounting, Organizations and Society, 25*(6), 609-622.

Van der Stede, W. A., Young, S. M., & Chen, X. (2006). Doing management accounting survey research. In C. S. Chapman, A. G. Hopwood & M. D. Shields (Eds.), *Handbook of management accounting research* (Vol. 1, pp. 445-478). Amsterdam et al.: Elsevier.

Van Dyne, L., Cummings, L. L., & McLean Parks, J. (1995). Extra-role behaviors: In pursuit of construct and definitional clarity. In L. L. Cummings & B. M. Staw (Eds.), *Research in organizational behavior* (Vol. 17, pp. 215-286). Greenwich: JAI Press.

Van Dyne, L., & LePine, J. A. (1998). Helping and voice extra-role behaviors: Evidence of construct and predictive validity. *Academy of Management Journal, 41*(1), 108-119.

Van Sell, M., Brief, A. P., & Schuler, R. S. (1981). Role conflict and role ambiguity: Integration of the literature and directions for future research. *Human Relations, 34*(1), 43-71.

Van Veen-Dirks, P. (in press). Different uses of performance measures: The evaluation versus reward of production managers. *Accounting, Organizations and Society.*

Vancil, R. F. (1979). *Decentralization: Managerial ambiguity by design.* Homewood: Dow Jones-Irwin.

Vandenbosch, B., & Huff, S. L. (1997). Searching and scanning: How executives obtain information from executive information systems. *MIS Quarterly, 21*(1), 81-107.

Vehkalahti, K. (2000). *Reliability of measurement scales.* Helsinki: Finnish Statistical Society.

Viator, R. E. (2001). The association of formal and informal public accounting mentoring with role stress and related job outcomes. *Accounting, Organizations and Society, 26*(1), 73-93.

Viswesvaran, C., Sanchez, J. I., & Fisher, J. (1999). The role of social support in the process of work stress: A meta-analysis. *Journal of Vocational Behavior, 54*(2), 314-334.

Von Emster, G. R., & Harrison, A. A. (1998). Role ambiguity, spheres of control, burnout, and work-related attitudes of teleservice professionals. *Journal of Social Behavior and Personality, 13*(2), 375-385.

Vroom, V. H. (1964). *Work and motivation.* New York: Wiley.

Vroom, V. H. (1970). Industrial social psychology. In G. Lindzey & E. Aronson (Eds.), *Handbook of social psychology* (2 ed., Vol. 5, pp. 196-268). Reading et al.: Addison-Wesley.

Wageman, R. (1995). Interdependence and group effectiveness. *Administrative Science Quarterly, 40*(1), 145-180.

Walker, O. C., Churchill, G. A., & Ford, N. M. (1977). Motivation and performance in industrial selling: Present knowledge and needed research. *Journal of Marketing Research, 14*(2), 156-168.

Waller, W. S., & Chow, C. W. (1985). The self-selection and effort effects of standard-based employment contracts: A framework and some empirical evidence. *The Accounting Review, 60*(3), 458-476.

Walsh, J. T., Taber, T. D., & Beehr, T. A. (1980). An integrated model of perceived job characteristics. *Organizational Behavior and Human Performance, 25*(2), 252-267.

Warr, P. (2005). Work, well-being, and mental health. In J. Barling, E. K. Kelloway & M. R. Frone (Eds.), *Handbook of work stress* (pp. 547-574). Thousand Oaks et al.: Sage Publications.

Warr, P. (2007). *Work, happiness, and unhappiness*. Mahwah: Erlbaum.

Warren, C. A. (2002). Qualitative interviewing. In J. F. Gubrium & J. A. Holstein (Eds.), *Handbook of interview research: Context and method* (pp. 83-102). Thousands Oaks et al.: Sage Publications.

Weber, J., & Schäffer, U. (2008). *Einführung in das Controlling* (12 ed.). Stuttgart: Schäffer-Poeschel.

Weber, M., Gerth, H. H., & Mills, C. W. (1946). *From Max Weber: Essays in sociology*. New York: Oxford University Press.

Weiner, B., Frieze, I., Kukla, A., Reed, L., Rest, S., & Rosenbaum, R. M. (1971). *Perceiving the causes of success and failure*. Morristown: General Learning Press.

Weiss, D. J., Dawis, R. V., England, G. W., & Lofquist, L. H. (1967). *Manual for the Minnesota satisfaction questionnaire*. Minneapolis: Industrial Relations Center, University of Minnesota.

West, S. G., Finch, J. F., & Curran, P. J. (1995). Structural equation models with nonnormal variables. In R. H. Hoyle (Ed.), *Structural equation modeling: Concepts, issues, and applications* (pp. 56-75). Thousands Oaks: Sage Publications.

Widener, S. K. (2006). Associations between strategic resource importance and performance measure use: The impact on firm performance. *Management Accounting Research, 17*(4), 433-457.

Wilcox, J. B., Howell, R. D., & Breivik, E. (2008). Questions about formative measurement. *Journal of Business Research, 61*(12), 1219-1228.

Wong, S.-S., DeSanctis, G., & Staudenmayer, N. (2007). The relationship between task interdependency and role stress: A revisit of the job demands-control model. *Journal of Management Studies, 44*(2), 284-303.

Woodworth, R. S. (1928). Dynamic psychology. In C. Murchison (Ed.), *Psychologies of 1925* (3 ed., pp. 111-127). Worcester: Clark University Press.

Wortman, C. B., & Brehm, J. W. (1975). Responses to uncontrollable outcomes: An integration of reactance theory and the learned helplessness model. In L. Berkowitz (Ed.), *Experimental social psychology* (Vol. 8, pp. 278-336). New York et al.: Academic Press.

Wrzesniewski, A., & Dutton, J. E. (2001). Crafting a job: Revisioning employees as active crafters of their work. *Academy of Management Review, 26*(2), 179-201.

Yakel, E. (2001). The social construction of accountability: Radiologists and their record-keeping practices. *Information Society, 17*(4), 233-245.

Yaping, G., Shenkar, O., & Yadong, L. (2001). Role conflict and ambiguity of CEOs in international joint ventures: A transaction cost perspective. *Journal of Applied Psychology, 86*(4), 764-773.

Yarnold, P., Mueser, K., & Lyons, J. (1988). Type A behavior, accountability, and work rate in small groups. *Journal of Research in Personality, 22*(3), 353-360.

Yim, A. T. (2001). Renegotiation and relative performance evaluation: Why an informative signal may be useless. *Review of Accounting Studies, 6*(1), 77-108.

Yin, R. K. (2003). *Case study research: Design and methods*. Thousand Oaks: Sage Publications.

Young, S. M. (1996). Survey research in management accounting: A critical assessment. In A. J. Richardson (Ed.), *Research methods in accounting: Issues and debates* (pp. 55-68). Vancouver: Canada Research Foundation.

Yousef, D. A. (2000). The interactive effects of role conflict and role ambiguity on job satisfaction and attitudes toward organizational change: A moderated multiple regression approach. *International Journal of Stress Management, 7*(4), 289-303.

Yukl, G., Chavez, C., & Seifert, C. F. (2005). Assessing the construct validity and utility of two new influence tactics. *Journal of Organizational Behavior, 26*(6), 705-725.

Zeitz, G. (1980). Hierarchical authority and decision-making in professional organizations. *Administration and Society, 12*(3), 277-300.

Zimmerman, J. L. (1979). The costs and benefits of cost allocations. *The Accounting Review, 54*(3), 504-521.

Zimmerman, J. L. (2001). Conjectures regarding empirical managerial accounting research. *Journal of Accounting and Economics, 32*(1-3), 411-427.

Zimmerman, J. L. (2009). *Accounting for decision making and control* (Vol. 6). Boston et al.: McGraw-Hill.

MIX
Papier aus verantwortungsvollen Quellen
Paper from responsible sources
FSC® C105338

If you have any concerns about our products,
you can contact us on
ProductSafety@springernature.com

In case Publisher is established outside the EU,
the EU authorized representative is:
Springer Nature Customer Service Center GmbH
Europaplatz 3, 69115 Heidelberg, Germany

Printed by Libri Plureos GmbH
in Hamburg, Germany